SELZNICK'S VISION

Texas Film Studies Series *Thomas Schatz, Editor*

Gone with the Wind and Hollywood Filmmaking

Selznick's Vision

Alan David Vertrees

 University of Texas Press Austin

Publication of this book was assisted by a generous contribution
from Dr. W. H. "Deacon" Crain.

Printed in the United States of America
First edition, 1997

♾ The paper used in this publication meets the minimum requirements
of American National Standard for Information Sciences—Permanence of
Paper for Printed Library Materials, ANSI Z39.48-1984.

Library of Congress Cataloging-in-Publication Data

Vertrees, Alan David, 1952–
Selznick's vision : Gone with the wind and
Hollywood filmmaking / Alan David Vertrees.
p. cm. — (Texas film studies series)
Includes bibliographical references and index.
ISBN 0-292-78729-4 (pbk. : alk. paper)
1. Gone with the wind (Motion picture)
2. Selznick, David O., 1902–1965.
I. Title. II. Series.

PN1997.G59V47 1997
791.43'72—DC21 96-53554

CONTENTS

Acknowledgments
vii

Foreword by Thomas Schatz
ix

ONE. "The Vision of One Man"
1

TWO. Sidney Howard and the Screenwriting of *Gone with the Wind*
21

THREE. William Cameron Menzies and the "Script in Sketch Form"
55

FOUR. Film Direction and Production Design of *Gone with the Wind*
116

FIVE. Executive Producers and Classical Hollywood Film Production
184

Notes
217

Bibliography
225

Index
233

ACKNOWLEDGMENTS

This book would not have been written, nor would it have been published, without the effort of Thomas Schatz. I am extremely grateful for his advocacy and friendship, his counsel and encouragement, and his sensitive and substantive editing of the developing manuscript in his role as film studies series editor of University of Texas Press. I also wish to thank several others at the press, including director Joanna Hitchcock, manuscript editor Lois Rankin, copyeditor Mandy Woods, designer Jean Lee Cole, marketing manager Margaret MacDonald, direct-mail manager Nancy Bryan, editorial fellow Jim Burr, and sponsoring editors Ali Hossaini, Frankie Westbrook, and Betsy Williams.

I am grateful, too, for the privilege of studying in the Graduate School of Arts and Sciences at Columbia University and of inaugurating research for this book under its aegis. I would like to acknowledge with gratitude Annette Insdorf, chairperson of the film division of the School of the Arts, and Andrew Sarris, who graciously sponsored my doctoral dissertation. I am indebted to John Belton, who was my academic advisor and was of special support to me during the final defense. I also wish to thank Richard Koszarski, who accepted my original thesis proposal for publication in *Film History* in 1989; I am honored that he and Charles Musser served as additional members of my doctoral defense committee. Janet Staiger graciously volunteered to read drafts of several chapters of my dissertation, and I am extremely grateful for her assistance and encouragement.

I wish to thank Thomas Staley, director of the Harry Ransom Humanities Research Center at the University of Texas at Austin, for permission to conduct research in the Selznick collection and to reproduce selected images and documents in this book. Charles Bell and Roy Flukinger and their curatorial and clerical assistants accommodated my work over a period of twelve years, and Steve Wilson provided invaluable service at the end. Ray Daum donated his time on occasion, and Sue Beauman Murphy shared technical information. I am beholden particularly to John Chalmers, who, as librarian from 1980 to 1990, facilitated my access to this archive during its cataloging. I also wish to thank Richard R. Brettell, Linda Dalrymple Henderson, and Donald G. Davis, Jr., for introducing me to the HRHRC collections and for serving as models of scholarship during my earlier graduate work at the University of Texas at Austin in art history and library science.

The following individuals and institutions also should be acknowledged for assistance in my research and for permission to quote or reproduce documents in their collections: Anne Caiger, Lilace Hatayama, and David Zeidberg, Department of Special Collections, University Research Library, University of California, Los Angeles; Leith Adams, Ned Comstock, and Anne Schlosser, Doheny Memorial Library, University of Southern California; Sam Gill, Margaret Herrick Library, Academy of Motion Picture Arts and Sciences; Ronald Haver, Los Angeles County Art Museum; Cathy Manolis, Turner Entertainment; Debra Cohen, Time Inc.; Katherine Bang, UPI/Bettmann Archives; Donald Crafton, Wisconsin Center for Theater and Film Research, University of Wisconsin at Madison; Donald Albrecht, American Museum of the Moving Image; Mary Corliss and Ron Magliozzi, Museum of Modern Art; Howard Mandelbaum, Photofest; and Paul Spehr, Motion Picture Division, Library of Congress.

Most importantly, I wish to dedicate this book to my family. My parents, Martha and Ralph Vertrees, my grandparents, Ina May and Kelly Edgar McAdams and Eloise and Charles David Vertrees, Sr., and my parents-in-law, Gayle and John Charles Stetson, cojoined to ensure welfare and livelihood. I cannot thank them enough. To my wife, Susan Stetson, and to our sons, Alexander and Peter, I especially affirm my profound love.

Lake Forest, Illinois, 1996

FOREWORD

by Thomas Schatz

As the field of cinema studies reaches a certain maturity, we in it continue to be confounded, indeed threatened, by an obstinate question: What are we to do with *Gone with the Wind*? The most popular and commercially successful film of all time, embraced by popular historians and journalistic critics while generally reviled by "serious" scholars and cinephiles, *Gone with the Wind* stands as both a monument to classical Hollywood and a monumental anomaly. It is, for students and scholars of cinema, our proverbial 800-pound gorilla—an oversized nuisance that simply won't go away, too big to be ignored and an obvious menace to our carefully constructed habitat.

Central to the problem of what to do with *Gone with the Wind* is the nagging issue of authorship. Any effort to deal with the creation of the film faces two key challenges. The first of these involves sorting out and assessing the contributions of the film's many creators—the plethora of screenwriters and large team of designers, the numerous directors and top stars, the cinematographers and editors, and, inevitably, the executive producer, David O. Selznick. The other challenge involves the veritable mythology which has arisen over the past half-century about the film's genesis. The story of the making of *Gone with the Wind* has evolved into a narrative as vast, complex, and dramatic as the film itself, fueled by a publishing subindustry which has both expanded and exploited that mythology.

The two processes of mythmaking and filmmaking have been oddly, intimately related since the moment in 1936 when David Selznick purchased the screen rights to Margaret Mitchell's novel, just before its publication. The novel was an immediate, explosive hit, capturing the public imagination and quickly becoming the biggest best-seller in publishing history. Selznick, meanwhile, began work on the adaptation, which was to be by far the most ambitious and costly motion picture ever produced, and also the most widely publicized. Selznick's *Gone with the Wind* was literally "years in the making"—roughly three, all told—and during that time, Selznick not only oversaw production but also began to fashion the myth of its genesis. As Mitchell's novel took the nation and much of the world by storm, Selznick fueled interest in the film with a relentless promotional blitz.

The signing of Clark Gable as Rhett Butler and the two-year "search for Scarlett," for instance, were themselves brilliant media events and publicity stunts, as was the dramatic "burning of Atlanta" which kicked off actual production. The fire was filmed on the RKO back lot using every Technicolor camera then in existence, with sets from *King Kong* (the walls of the native village which kept Kong at bay) standing in for the flame-engulfed Atlanta. Although principal photography of the film was scheduled to start only a few weeks later, Selznick was in fact still searching for Scarlett. It was during the fire that Selznick's brother Myron, a leading Hollywood talent agent, introduced him to Vivien Leigh with the words, "Here's your Scarlett" (see Ronald Haver, *David O. Selznick's Hollywood,* pp. 254–258).

Stories like these, some apocryphal or mere fabrications and others quite accurate, surrounded *Gone with the Wind* and steadily coalesced into the meta-narrative of its making. Weaving fact and fiction, history and hype, this meta-narrative has come to comprise one of the central myths about the production of twentieth-century American culture.

The key figure in this myth is, of course, David O. Selznick, whose status therein has been curiously paradoxical. Despite his own role in originating much of the myth, and despite his efforts to present himself as epic-heroic creator of *Gone with the Wind*, Selznick is generally viewed as only incidental to its authorship—and more as an antagonist or impediment to its creation, in fact, than as a crucial shaping force. The governing perception of Selznick's role as producer, finally, is one of a necessary evil; at best, he is viewed as a well-meaning but troublesome meddler who managed to produce a masterpiece almost in spite of himself, and at worst he is reviled as a shameless self-promoter and vulgar philistine whom the top talent necessarily learned to ignore.

This negative view of Selznick's role in the genesis of *Gone with the Wind* has been tempered somewhat in recent years as a result of two principal factors. One is the increasing availability of actual production records related to the film—most notably, in this case, the archival materials in the David O. Selznick Collection in the Harry Ransom Center at the University of Texas. The other factor, a direct consequence of the now-available production records, has been the reassessment by film historians of the collaborative process of Hollywood filmmaking and of the producer's role within that process—particularly in the case of "creative producers" such as Selznick, Irving Thalberg, Darryl Zanuck, and Walter Wanger.

Selznick's stock has risen steadily due to the more accurate and favorable image conveyed in several such studies—namely, Ronald Haver's *David O. Selznick's Hollywood*, Leonard Leff's *Selznick and Hitchcock*, and my own case study of Selznick in *The Genius of the System*. But despite that general reassessment, we are only beginning to understand and appreciate Selznick's role in the making of *Gone with the Wind*. Despite the wealth of production-related material in the Selznick Collection—and, paradoxically, due in part to the sheer volume of that material—many crucial aspects of the making of *Gone with the Wind*, and not only those involving Selznick's role, have yet to be systematically examined and analyzed.

Now comes Alan Vertrees, film scholar and art historian, to assess David O. Selznick's role in the making of *Gone with the Wind* and, on another level altogether, to tackle the unique issues it raises about film authorship in classical Hollywood. As is clear enough in the book's title, Vertrees considers Selznick to have been not only central but absolutely essential to the film's creation, the end result being a product of his personal "vision." Vertrees supports this view with a carefully constructed argument based on actual production records and also on the film itself, the ultimate realization of Selznick's vision.

Alan Vertrees' original and provocative approach brings a new perspective not only to the making of *Gone with the Wind* but to classical Hollywood filmmaking in general. His approach, in essence, is to examine both preproduction and production, focusing primarily on the complex interplay between script development and production design and on the effective merging of the two in actual shooting (and thus in the finished product). Vertrees also focuses throughout on Selznick's role in supervising and coordinating the overall process. In so doing, he radically revises the view of Selznick as a self-centered autocrat capable of creating endless memoranda but little else, and who only impeded the film's creation. On the contrary, argues Vertrees, Selznick was clearly the chief architect and prime mover in the film's creation. He meticulously supports that view with evidence from every phase of the process, from the film's conception through its actual production.

Selznick developed the script with one eye on Mitchell's novel (and on the public's response to it) and the other on his visualization of the finished film. Indeed, the preliminary design of the film—not only as story but also as spectacle and as cinematic achievement—was in many ways as important as the script itself. Selznick saw *Gone with the Wind* not only as an adaptation of an enormously popular novel, but also as a display of the full potential of cinematic art. The film succeeded on both counts, which is itself a remarkable achievement. *Gone with the Wind* represents one of those rare instances in cinema when a best-selling novel and literary phenomenon is transposed to film and proves to be as captivating, successful, and enduring as the original novel, if not more so.

Thus, as well as clarifying Selznick's role, this book untangles and analyzes, at long last, two crucial aspects of the making of *Gone with the Wind*—namely, the scripting of the film and the production design. Alan Vertrees traces the two-year development of the script through countless revisions by nearly a score of writers—including Selznick, who served as collaborator and editor of a screenplay which is both faithful to the novel and yet a distinctive, singular work. At the same time, and particularly as the film approached actual production, Selznick carefully coordinated the writing and design of the film. In fact, as the script went through its final drafts after principal photography was already under way, the visual design of the film often dictated the development of the script.

While Vertrees clearly demonstrates that Selznick oversaw and coordinated this process, he is equally persuasive in his arguments on behalf of William Cameron Menzies. The dean of Hollywood production designers—indeed, the term "production designer" was coined by Selznick specifically for Menzies' work on this film—Menzies played a key creative role in "visualizing" the narrative during scripting and preproduction, laying out each scene visually in terms of camera placement and cutting continuity as well as set design. This enabled Selznick to control both the directing and the editing of the film before it was actually shot, which explains how so many directors (including such top filmmakers as Victor Fleming, George Cukor, and Sam Wood, as well as Selznick and Menzies) could work on the film without compromising its stylistic coherence and narrative integrity.

Nowhere are Selznick's control and Menzies' artistry more evident than in the fire scene, a narrative episode which was fairly incidental in the novel but which became the visual and dramatic centerpiece of the film. Vertrees' detailed case study of the fire scene is in many ways the centerpiece of this book as well, providing as it does an in-depth examination of the complex collaboration involved in creating *Gone with the Wind*, and of the varied contributions of its producer, directors, writers, designers, and others. The decision to expand the fire scene was, of course, made by Selznick, who closely supervised its elaboration and eventual production. But as Vertrees demonstrates, Menzies' drawings, sketches, and other visual renderings provided a storyboard for the spectacular sequence, providing a visual blueprint which was even more important than the shooting script.

In *Selznick's Vision: "Gone with the Wind" and Hollywood Filmmaking*, Alan Vertrees has made a lasting contribution not only to our understanding of the film's genesis, but to our general grasp of Hollywood filmmaking. Vertrees demystifies the process of the film's creation, untangles the complexities of its collaboration, and clarifies the role of David O. Selznick as its ultimate auteur. Indeed, like *Gone with the Wind* itself, Selznick emerges in this study as both utterly unique and profoundly symptomatic of Hollywood filmmaking circa 1939. Thus, Alan Vertrees provides an answer not only to the confounding problem of what to do with *Gone with the Wind*, but also to the question of what to do with David O. Selznick.

Equally significant, finally, is Vertrees' argument that William Cameron Menzies' contribution to *Gone with the Wind* has been grossly undervalued and largely misunderstood—as has the role of the production designer generally. Bringing an art historian's view to the auteurist debate, Vertrees contends that we simply must factor art direction and production design into the complex equation of motion picture authorship. As with his arguments on behalf of Selznick, here, too, he proves not only provocative but most convincing.

ONE

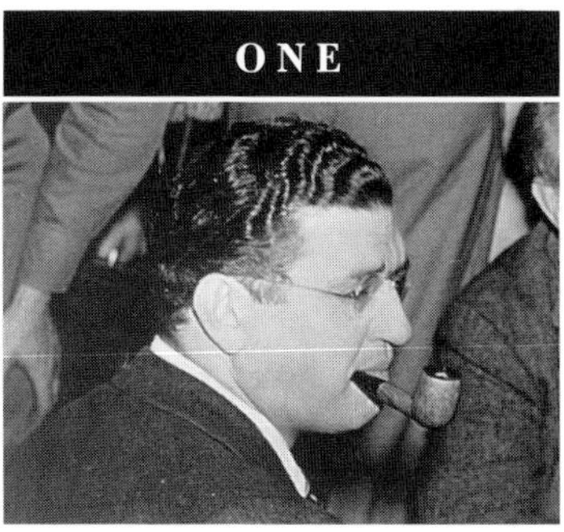

"The Vision of One Man"

The most successful motion picture of the classical Hollywood period is *Gone with the Wind.* For almost a quarter of a century after its release in the final month of 1939, this film surpassed every record established at the box office and at award ceremonies of the Academy of Motion Picture Arts and Sciences. Its virtual sweep of the 1939 Academy Awards which were presented in February 1940—only weeks after this picture premiered—appears all the more impressive in view of the strength of the major competitors—*Dark Victory*, *Goodbye, Mr. Chips*, *Mr. Smith Goes to Washington*, *Ninotchka*, *Stagecoach*, *The Wizard of Oz*, and *Wuthering Heights*—which were released earlier during this annus mirabilis of American filmmaking.

In addition to its producer David O. Selznick receiving the Irving G. Thalberg Memorial Award for "consistently high quality of motion picture production," *Gone with the Wind* won Oscars for best picture, best actress (Vivien Leigh for her portrayal of Scarlett O'Hara; see Figure 1), best supporting actress (Hattie McDaniel for "Mammy"), best screenplay (Sidney Howard), best direction (Victor Fleming), best interior decoration (art director Lyle Wheeler), best color cinematography (director of photography Ernest Haller and Technicolor associates Ray Rennahan and Wilfred Cline), and best film editing (Hal Kern and associate James Newcom). A special award also was presented to production designer William Cameron Menzies for "outstanding achievement in the use of color for the enhancement of

FIG. 1. Vivien Leigh listens to producer David O. Selznick between poses for photographers at the Cocoanut Grove in Los Angeles, February 29, 1940, after receiving an Academy Award for her portrayal of Scarlett O'Hara in *Gone with the Wind*. Unless noted otherwise, all reproductions are courtesy of Photography and Film Collections, Harry Ransom Humanities Research Center, University of Texas at Austin.

dramatic mood." Until very recently, in terms of theatrical box office performance (in figures adjusted for inflation), Selznick's adaptation of Margaret Mitchell's "story of the Old South" remained incontestably the greatest draw in the history of the cinema.[1]

Although this film's success may be attributed to a remarkable confluence of individual and contextual elements—not the least of which are a star-studded cast and a phenomenally best-selling novel from which the movie was adapted—David O. Selznick himself was a most significant influence, supervising every major aspect of the picture's making, from scriptwriting and production to editing and marketing. Paradoxically, the extent of this producer's involvement in the creation of what is regarded widely as the most "Hollywood" of movies was both exemplary and exceptional with regard to the conventions of the film industry. What appears to be indisputable is that *Gone with the Wind* is Selznick's magnum opus and that it epitomizes classical Hollywood cinema.

While praise as the "greatest motion picture ever made" has been questioned by critics for some time and although classical Hollywood produced a number of excellent motion pictures, few—if any—have offered an aura equal to that generated by *Gone with the Wind*. Two decades after Selznick undertook to produce this picture, Bosley Crowther, senior film critic for the *New York Times*, observed that "of all the motion pictures produced since the screen began, [*Gone with the Wind* was] the one that has reached the most people and may fairly be judged the most popular."[2] Ten years later, in 1967, Crowther was even more enthusiastic in his appraisal of this work's stature in his book *The Great Films: Fifty Golden Years of Motion Pictures*, in which he claimed:

> Of all the American motion pictures entitled to be designated great on the basis of *all* their qualifications, including the extent of the excitement they have caused, *[Gone with the Wind]* towers above all the rest. . . . Never before or since its making has so much attention been fixed upon the urgency and the responsibility of bringing a film into being. Never has the public's interest been so attracted in the preparation stage, and never has a national volition been so generously fulfilled and satisfied. . . . There have been more ambitious, more expensive and longer historical-spectacle films made in the years since this one. And there have been a few that have had more critical *réclame*. But there has never been one more effective than *Gone with the Wind*. There may never be.[3]

When polled in 1977 to select the "greatest American film of all time," 35,000 members of the American Film Institute awarded this honor to *Gone with the Wind* (*Citizen Kane* [1941] and *Casablanca* [1943] were elected to second and third place, respectively).[4] Selznick's epic picture had been broadcast for the first time on national network television the previous year and had received unchallenged ratings, earning it the additional distinction of being the "most popular film ever shown on U.S. television," according to a movie-related Guinness record book.[5] In 1979, it was considered the "only film in history which could be profitably revived for forty years."[6] Half a century after its premiere and on the occasion of the release of a newly restored Technicolor print in 1989, noted newspaper and television critic Roger Ebert observed that *Gone with the Wind* remained "one of the greatest of all Hollywood productions."[7] The film also has been lauded variously as the "quintessential Hollywood studio system product," the "Sistine chapel among movies," and the "single most beloved entertainment ever produced."[8] As a motion picture, television, and videographic presentation, it has been described—albeit wryly—as the "eternal flame of popular culture" in *Time*, whose reviewer speculated that "it is a safe bet that somewhere in the world, day and night, Clark Gable's Rhett Butler and Vivien Leigh's Scarlett O'Hara flicker across a screen."[9]

Another measure of the film's ongoing popular fascination is the secondary market that developed over the last two decades with the publication of a large number of histories of the picture's production. Many of these books' titles incorporated such prefixes and phrases as the following: *The Filming of . . .*, *The Making of . . .*, *The Art of . . .*, *The Ultimate Pictorial Treasury of . . .*, as well as *The Official . . . Companion*, *The Complete Reference*, *The Complete . . . Sourcebook*, and *The Complete . . . Trivia Book*. In some cases, the film title's mere initials, *GWTW*, served for effective exploitation. However appealing these volumes may be to the film's many fans, few have served the study of film history beyond publishing production stills (i.e., photographs of players receiving direction and/or of technicians operating on the shooting sets); many repackaged previously published information and anecdotes involving the film's stars and have perpetuated a received knowledge of the production itself. In 1989, in a review of several of these books on the fiftieth anniversary of the film's premiere, David Finkle, a contributor to the *New York Times Book Review*, pragmatically identified the primary value of these "redundant tributes" for their public. "Whether the contents of the books are 100 percent authentic may be beside the point," Finkle admitted, "for it's apparent that to the bona fide fan [these] books are not, first and foremost, books . . . they are collectibles."[10]

In the majority of these volumes, the making of the film adaptation is related in a manner that imitates the epic dimensions of Mitchell's novel. Framed by the legends of the book's history and of the film's premiere in Atlanta, the story line begins with Selznick's acquisition of the screen rights in the face of much skepticism expressed by other Hollywood studio chiefs and continues with anecdotes about the pursuit of an actress to portray Scarlett, for which a highly publicized national talent search was undertaken, together with auditions of numerous starlets. The deal with MGM for the loan of Clark Gable and Selznick's difficulties with screenwriters and directors also serve to complicate the plot. Scarce attention is given generally to the creative and interpretative aspects of screenwriting, production design, cinematography, directing, and editing. Instead, only the same few technical details are recounted at any length—for example, a common subject is the filming of the celebrated mobile aerial view of Scarlett's crossing of the Atlanta railyard, which is crowded with prostrated, wounded Confederate soldiers (a shot which—one reads—exhausted the resources of Central Casting and required use of great numbers of dummies and construction of a concrete drive so that a mechanical crane, from which the camera was suspended, would roll smoothly backward during the filming).

Another characteristic of the majority of these publications is their dismissal of Selznick. Invariably, these treatments rely on negative testimony and hearsay to affirm the producer's egotism and the degree of chaos engendered by his domination of others on and off the sets. Arguments are informed almost exclusively by the opinions of a selected number of Selznick's surviving subordinates without either modification of these claims in view of practices characteristic of other studios' producers or their verification by closer examination of the specific filmmaking acts in question (for example, there is no analysis of the development of a particular scene in order to determine its progress or degradation after executive influence). Production documents (including correspondence, script drafts, call sheets, production logs, and continuity and set designs) are analyzed rarely to a satisfactory degree but, rather, are presented in the manner of mute reliquaries. To date, the making of the most popular film in history has been presented by commentators—with few exceptions—as the creation of a "natural" screen entertainment which achieved its incomparable degree of success in great part *despite* the industry of the man most responsible for its realization. The result has been that, notwithstanding the many books published on the filming of *Gone with the Wind*, neither the producer nor the production itself have been understood adequately or accurately.

Although Margaret Mitchell persistently declined to participate in her novel's adaptation, the reputation of her best-selling book is credited by implication in many of these accounts for the film's enormously favorable reception. The picture's success is attributed also to the exploitation of its stars and of its early Technicolor format and to the post-Depression, pre-World War II period of its American premiere. In contrast, Selznick is characterized as a meddler and tinkerer. The reader of many of these histories is informed that Selznick suffered from indecision and as a result, hired and fired directors, cameramen, and screenwriters throughout the film's lengthy period of production. At the same time, the producer's insistence upon his adaptation's fidelity to the novel is portrayed as having posed a serious limitation to the more creative contributions of his collaborators.

In contrast with Margaret Mitchell, who willed that the manuscript and all drafts of her novel were to be destroyed following her death (in 1949), Selznick preserved approximately half a million documents pertaining to this film's production.[11] His personal archives, comprising over three million items covering in detail most of the motion pictures that he produced during the course of his career, were acquired by the University of Texas at Austin in 1980 for the Harry Ransom Humanities Research Center. Ironically, many scholars may be biased against *Gone with the Wind* as an appropriate subject for academic inquiry because of the exploitative, commercial nature of most of the popular books published on this film's making and the bold aesthetic claims that have attended the picture's release.

This negative attitude has been fostered also in part by the ascendancy and persistence of auteurism, a trend in American film criticism introduced by Andrew Sarris in 1962. Accordingly, the director has been privileged over other participants in the filmmaking enterprise to the extent that film authorship is bestowed repeatedly upon a technician whose primary influence on classical studio productions was the direction of actors. The fact that scenes in *Gone with the Wind* were directed by at least four individuals compromised its artistic integrity in many critics' minds. More recently, the orientation of Marxist psychoanalytic semiology, which succeeded auteurism as the dominant theoretical scheme in film studies, eschewed attributions of authorship and traditional hermeneutics altogether as valid pursuits and addressed issues involving reception and ideology rather than those of production. The analyses of documents from the adaptation of *Gone with the Wind* that are offered in this book challenge the prejudices of the above-mentioned conventional points of view and raise significant questions concerning the creation of motion pictures.

Consider, for example, the making of the "fire" sequence—the most spectacular episode in the film, in which Scarlett O'Hara and Rhett Butler escape the burning of Atlanta on the eve of its invasion. Most commentaries have noted that this sequence's production required the destruction of great numbers of preexisting sets on the studio lot (made over to simulate street scenes in Atlanta) and that it inaugurated the picture's filming on the evening of December 10, 1938, at which time Selznick also was introduced to Vivien Leigh by his brother, the agent Myron Selznick. Unacknowledged is the fact that the fire episode in Mitchell's novel was severely abbreviated in Sidney Howard's initial scripts because the screenwriter doubted the value of this scene to the film presentation.

In contrast, Selznick recognized its potential for spectacle and enlisted production designer William Cameron Menzies and several screenwriters—including Ben Hecht—to embellish on what Mitchell had written. The producer also considered filming much of its action in a pioneer widescreen format, although ultimately this idea was rejected. For the most part, the picture's initial director, George Cukor, observed the pyrotechnical drama from the sidelines that evening as the staging of several pairs of doubles was directed by Menzies, following specific continuity designs, before seven Technicolor cameras—the total number available for lease by studios at the time. Close-ups of Leigh and Gable were filmed the following year under the direction of Cukor's successor, Victor Fleming, and the sequence itself was revised many times under Selznick's supervision. The result was identified by a Gallup poll as the film's most memorable scene.[12]

In view of the abundance of documentation concerning the many changes made to the fire sequence and to other scenes in *Gone with the Wind*, the contributions of the principal creative technicians—the directors, the screenwriters, the production designer, the art director, the special-effects director, the cinematographers, and the editors—may be examined now vis-à-vis those of the "executive producer" (a title which purportedly was coined a few years earlier by Selznick himself). In this book, successive versions of the screenplay by different authors, dramatic continuity designs and "storyboard" sketches credited to the first production designer in film history, and the producer's correspondence and memoranda are analyzed in this concerted manner, emending the history of this film's making, establishing the critical importance of Selznick's central role, and disclosing both chaotic and creative aspects of his collaboration with his staff. The value of the documents in the Selznick archives to an understanding of how *Gone with the Wind* and other classical Hollywood films were produced argues for the publication of another book on this film.

David O. Selznick and "Prestige Unit" Film Production

Selznick firmly believed that producers should dictate and monitor every aspect of the filmmaking enterprise and not delegate responsibility for the supervision of production details to middle managers, or associate producers, on whom the major studios' central managers had relied routinely during the early part of the classical Hollywood era. Irving Thalberg (production chief of MGM from 1923 to 1933) and Darryl F. Zanuck (production chief of Warner Bros. from 1929 to 1933 and of 20th Century-Fox from 1935 to 1956) were notable central producers. In contrast, Selznick championed the use of "unit" production, which allowed individual producers to devote full attention to a limited number of film projects and to perfect their own work.

Although renowned principally as the "producer of *Gone with the Wind*," Selznick already had risen dramatically as a motion picture producer at Paramount between 1927 and 1931, at RKO from 1931 to 1933, and at MGM from 1933 to 1935 before going independent with Selznick International Pictures (SIP), from 1936 to 1940, and David O. Selznick Productions, from 1940 to 1949.[13] At Paramount, Selznick served as the executive assistant to Ben Schulberg, the managing director of production, and was responsible for reorganizing the story department and dictating script development policies during the studio's transition from silent to sound film production. During the final year of his tenure (1931), forty of the sixty-five films that Paramount produced were supervised personally by Selznick, who, never idle or immodest, professed to Schulberg that at MGM "the equivalent of my work is handled by no less than six high-salaried executives."[14] Schulberg's son, Budd, who befriended Selznick and who parodied

Hollywood in the novel *What Makes Sammy Run?*, recalled in his autobiography that, contrary to the "major studio 'factory' system . . . with 'supervisors' standing in for the studio chief but never completely responsible for the finished product, [Selznick] advocated a personal approach, with supervisors becoming full-fledged producers heading their own independent units"—a new mode of film production which was viewed as a "system of creative decontrol."[15]

Nevertheless, at the age of 29, Selznick himself assumed the duties of a central manager when he was hired as production chief of RKO, a major film studio formed in 1928 by David Sarnoff, president of RCA, and Boston financier Joseph Kennedy. Whereas Irving Thalberg waived the right to acknowledgment of his influence as production chief in the credits of MGM releases, Selznick publicized his own authority as RKO pictures' "executive producer." Although his responsibilities as vice president in charge of production were administrative, Selznick closely monitored and influenced the development of *A Bill of Divorcement* and *What Price Hollywood?*, both of which were directed by George Cukor in 1932; in fact, the basic story line of the latter film derived from his own original idea. Selznick resigned from RKO when the financial office and ownership in New York refused to grant him the freedom that Thalberg enjoyed from Nicholas Schenck, president of Loew's (the Manhattan-based theater chain which owned the MGM film studio in Southern California), and instead expected the deference that Ben Schulberg had given Paramount. Discontented with this arrangement, Selznick demanded the "final word in story purchase and assignment, as well as in all production matters."

Ironically, Thalberg's poor health between 1932 and 1933 and the desire of Schenck and Louis B. Mayer to reestablish control over their own studio made Selznick's employment as a "prestige unit" producer extremely appealing to MGM. Although the quip "the son-in-law also rises" was circulated for a time (Selznick had married Mayer's younger daughter, Irene, in 1930), the company benefited immensely from his productions. His first film, *Dinner at Eight* (1933), was an auspicious beginning and was directed by George Cukor (who was hired from RKO by MGM following completion of *Little Women*, much of which Selznick himself had planned before his own departure). Over the next two years, this producer also supervised three literary adaptations—*David Copperfield* (directed by Cukor), *A Tale of Two Cities* (featuring Ronald Colman), and *Anna Karenina* (played by Greta Garbo)—as well as three Clark Gable vehicles—*Night Flight*, *Dancing Lady* (with Joan Crawford), and *Manhattan Melodrama* (with William Powell and Myrna Loy).

High financing from John Hay ("Jock") Whitney and his family (who also had invested heavily in Technicolor), the availability for rental of the RKO-Pathé studio (which was located in the proximity of MGM facilities in Culver City), and a distribution contract with United Artists afforded Selznick the means of forming his own production company. In addition to making *Gone with the Wind* (distributed by MGM, which bore half of the initial budget and allowed the services of Clark Gable), SIP produced such classic films between 1936 and 1940 as *Rebecca* (1940; directed by Alfred Hitchcock and starring Laurence Olivier and Joan Fontaine), *A Star is Born* (1937; the first of several remakes of *What Price Hollywood?*), *The Prisoner of Zenda* (1937; featuring Ronald Colman and Douglas Fairbanks, Jr.), *Nothing Sacred* (1937; starring Carole Lombard and Fredric March), *Made for Each Other* (1939; with Carole Lombard and James Stewart), and *Intermezzo* (1939; which introduced Ingrid Bergman to American audiences).

Gone with the Wind and *Rebecca* won back-to-back Academy Awards for best picture of 1939 and 1940, respectively, and established Selznick as Hollywood's most successful film producer at the zenith of the industry's classical period. Although the major studios distributed as many as one feature per week each, none of these companies were rewarded with figures comparable to those that SIP earned from its smaller number of releases. Ironically, this independent studio was too small for its profits to have been amortized or defrayed in the manner of the majors, and thus it was liquidated for tax purposes in August 1940. In addition, Selznick's intense participation in his films' making had aged him considerably.

Although he quickly formed another production company which created a number of popular films, including three starring his second wife, Jennifer Jones—*Since You Went Away* (1944), *Duel in the Sun* (1947), and *Portrait of Jennie* (1949)—as well as *Spellbound* (1945), which was directed by Hitchcock, Selznick's attempts to achieve the phenomenal level of success that had been attained between 1939 and 1940 proved to be in vain. The critical consensus to date is represented by Douglas Gomery's report in *Movie History: A Survey* that, "after *Gone with the Wind*, Selznick then squandered his career by spending the rest of his life unsuccessfully trying to make a film to best it."[16] More harshly, it was proclaimed by Ezra Goodman in *The Fifty-Year Decline and Fall of Hollywood*, published in 1961, that by this same date, Selznick himself was "'gone with the wind' as far as Hollywood is concerned."[17] (The producer died of heart failure four years later in 1965.)

Much less professed is the fact that during the latter half of his career, Selznick had shifted his principal activity from producing independent films to "packaging" film projects—that is, acquiring literary properties which he sold at a profit to major studios for both production and distribution. Selznick continued to develop the filmscripts, to contract directors, and to cast the principal roles. Two examples of this form of enterprise are *Jane Eyre* (starring Joan Fontaine and Orson Welles) and *Notorious* (starring Ingrid Bergman and Cary Grant and directed by Alfred Hitchcock), which were produced by 20th Century-Fox and RKO in 1944 and 1946, respectively. Although his exploitation of "packaging" was an inspired career move and provided the industry with a model for practice, his influence on a project waned after a studio acquired a property, and the responsibility for production was assumed by others who often were less qualified and who were wary of the "overproduced" reputation of Selznick's own films.

In particular, the producer resented 20th Century-Fox's reluctance to invest in its 1962 adaptation of F. Scott Fitzgerald's *Tender is the Night* along the dimensions that he had envisioned and their characterization of his aspirations as extravagant and as *ars gratia artis*. "I have never gone after 'honors instead of dollars,'" he remonstrated in his letter of December 8, 1961, to studio president Spyros Skouras. "But I have understood the relationship between the two." Selznick continued with an assessment of his reputation as a film producer and a résumé of his professional philosophy:

> No pictures in the history of the industry ever received, picture for picture, as many honors as my own; no pictures in the history of the industry, picture for picture, have ever achieved comparable grosses or comparable profits. . . . I have seen studio

> administration after administration go under, because of the failure to realize that honors in the picture business are not only a satisfaction to the recipients, and proper rewards for work well done, but (a) worth millions in gross; (b) an incentive to better work; (c) invaluable to a studio's morale, and to its *commercial*—that is, "dollars," not "honors"—results on an over-all basis.

In another letter to Skouras on January 16, 1962, Selznick admitted the limitations of "packaging" and defended the contributions of creative producers.

> You continue to believe that if you hire a good director, and get a good title and put down a couple of casting names on paper, the picture is made. You fail to realize, apparently, that . . . great producers have not achieved their reputations in this fashion; that picture after picture is a failure *despite* these elements, because they have not been *produced* (whether by producer/director or by producer) with the skill and the experience and the showmanship to know what pays off, dramatically and commercially.

Summing up his own beliefs, Selznick argued that "great films, successful films, are made in their every detail according to the vision of one man, and through supporting that one man, not in buying part of what he has done."

Criticism of Selznick's Influence on Filmmaking as Producer

Ironically, Selznick's profession of a single "vision" was expressed in the same year as the publication of Andrew Sarris's "Notes on the Auteur Theory in 1962" in *Film Culture*.[18] Although this producer's opinion paralleled Sarris's critical approach with respect to the issue of an individual personality's domination of a filmmaking enterprise, "auteur theory" designated the director as the legitimate "author" of a film text. Since Andrew Sarris's application of auteurist policy in *The American Cinema: Directors and Directions, 1929–1968*, a film's success has been determined to a significant degree by the director's mastery of the production system and influence on the shooting set. "The auteur theory derives its rationale from the fact that the cinema could not be a completely personal art under even the best conditions," Sarris admitted. "The auteur theory values the personality of a director precisely because of the barriers to its expression," he explained. "It is as if a few brave spirits had managed to overcome the gravitational pull of the mass of movies."[19]

Sarris recognized that *Gone with the Wind* presented a "notable exception to the notion of directorial authorship" because of Selznick's employment of at least four directors on this production, and the producer was slighted by the critic for "incessant interference with a project that was always too big to be controlled by a single directorial style."[20] This attitude has continued to influence the film's critical reception. For example, although it is conceded in this producer's entry in *A Biographical Dictionary of Film* that *Gone with the Wind* resounds with the power of "vast entrepreneurial aplomb," the author David Thomson posited that the film is, "not surprisingly, void of creative personality"; he declared also that while "*Gone with the Wind* is film history, . . . *Rebecca* is a masterpiece without qualification," presumably because of Hitchcock's direction.[21]

Sarris was not the first critic to devalue Selznick's role. In a 1944 edition of *Time*, James Agee described Margaret Mitchell's novel as "perhaps the greatest entertainment natural in screen history" and added that the "duck that hatched a swan was lucky compared to . . . Selznick [who] hatched *Gone with the Wind* and has been trying to hatch another ever since."[22] Still prejudice against this producer burgeoned from auteurism's influence. Citing the many directors and writers employed on *Gone with the Wind*, Leslie Fiedler described the film in *The Inadvertent Epic: From "Uncle Tom's Cabin" to "Roots"* as a "patchwork job with no controlling intelligence behind it."[23] The most vitriolic invective came from Richard Schickel, who declaimed:

> Selznick, whose devotion to literacy was largely self-proclaimed (in Hollywood in those days anyone who could read without straining was like the one-eyed man in the blind kingdom) and belied by a career-long devotion to talky kitsch . . . busied himself with his insufferable memos, fretting over such trivia as sets, costumes, and make-up and guaranteeing that men of independence would not stay long at his side. The result was a film entirely worthy of its source—glossy, sentimental, chuckle-headed—not one that would transcend, as have so many that have been pulled from literature's bottom drawers, the original work.[24]

"No movie role has been so idolized, denigrated, or misrepresented as that of the producer," acknowledged Michael Webb in his catalog of an exhibition organized in 1986 by the Smithsonian Institution and entitled, *Hollywood: Legend and Reality*. Noting the fictional Monroe Stahr in F. Scott Fitzgerald's novel *The Last Tycoon* (reputedly inspired by Thalberg) and Sammy Glick in Schulberg's *What Makes Sammy Run?*, Webb admitted that "a favorite image is the cigar-chomping philistine, fondling flesh and spouting figures, fawned upon by acolytes as he takes a meeting beside a pool in Beverly Hills."[25] The casting of Selznick among this ilk is found in at least two historical surveys—namely, Philip French's *The Movie Moguls* and Norman Zierold's *The Moguls*. "Contempt for these men comes easily, and the terms to describe them—mogul, cinemogul, tycoon, czar and the rest—have a certain sneer about them, conjuring up as they do an unfavorable image of a cigar-chewing, language fracturing, power-mad, philistine ignoramus," wrote French, who added that "this image unfortunately is not entirely without foundation in fact."[26]

In contrast, Bob Thomas's biography of Selznick in 1970 echoed Bosley Crowther's assessment that accompanied the producer's obituary in the *New York Times* and stated that Selznick's principal contribution to film-making was the promotion and embodiment of the role of the "creative producer." Proclaiming that "nearly all of the Hollywood films were the product of the big-studio factory-like system" and "had the look of manufactured entertainment," Thomas lauded Selznick for having believed that "a motion picture was like a painting that had to be painted and signed by a single artist." More specifically, this biographer postulated that Selznick was convinced that the artist must necessarily be the producer and he felt that he had proved his theory with *Gone with the Wind*."[27]

Thomas's accounts of Selznick's film productions were supplemented two years later by Rudy Behlmer, who published a representative sampling of the extensive professional memoranda in Selznick's archives under the title *Memo from David O. Selznick*. Acknowledging that "the story of the creation of each of Selznick's films could fill its own book," Behlmer chose *Gone with the Wind* to serve as the principal "in-depth example" of this producer's oeuvre.[28] The inordinate extent of Selznick's personal supervision of most of the motion pictures that he produced is represented satisfactorily by the documents that are reprinted in the 550-page *Memo*, and that span his career. Most importantly, the selection demonstrates that Selznick's memo writing was crucial to his modus operandi as a creative producer. All the same, it was a source of chronic irritation to his directors—among whom (in addition to George Cukor, Victor Fleming, William Cameron Menzies, and Sam Wood on *Gone with the Wind* and on other films) were William Dieterle, Howard Hawks, John Huston, Alfred Hitchcock, King Vidor, and William Wellman—and as such formed the basis of much of the general disdain for this producer by auteurists.

David Thomson professed in his 1992 biography, *Showman*, that the documents reproduced in *Memo* comprised only a "tiny selection" of the extensive memoranda preserved among the "three million items, 57,000 pounds of paper, [and] some 6,000 Hollinger boxes" that form Selznick's total archival collection. According to Thomson, Behlmer's sample "emphasized the trait of decisiveness . . . whereas the full weight of the memos reveals a less certain and more beleagured man, compelled sometimes to take decisions." While acknowledging that "no one who worked for [Selznick] ever doubted that he had all the power on a project," Thomson posited that the producer's authority "never helped him make up his mind" and that his work should be evaluated as the "weary, frustrated product of indecision, confusion, luck, and accident."[29]

Pace Thomson, it should be recognized that Selznick relished multiple choices and that he eagerly sought menus of options when making decisions. To characterize this producer as "indecisive" is to deny the definite record of his achievements. The medium of the memo was one that Selznick radically exploited in order to petition superiors, to query subordinates, and to prescribe details, thereby advancing his own career. "I honestly don't remember in all the time I was working at MGM—or for that matter . . . [at] most other studios (except Paramount)—seeing a single memo written from one executive to another when these executives were in offices anywhere near [each other]," admitted Selznick, whose own prolixity with memoranda was described in 1942 in an article for the *Saturday Evening Post* wryly entitled "The Great Dictater."[30]

In 1958 *Life* magazine published a sample of the ten thousand memos purportedly generated by Selznick during his 1957 adaptation of Ernest Hemingway's 1929 novel *A Farewell to Arms*—the last motion picture which he personally produced and one which followed a hiatus from full-scale filmmaking of almost ten years. It was noted in this publication that "[Selznick's] memos have been famous in Hollywood for their content, range of interest and staggering volume. Those on *Farewell*, from 30 pages to a single sentence in length, give a revealing and fascinating look at both a movie and the perfectionist who, absorbed in every detail, made it."[31] Ironically, this article proved to be poor publicity for both the picture and its producer. "I take credit for my pictures when they are good, so I must take the blame when they are disappointing," Selznick himself acknowledged afterward, adding that *A Farewell to Arms* was "not one of the jobs of which I am most proud."[32]

Tension between producer and director reached a climax during this film's making when the director, John Huston, resigned following receipt of a typed, single-spaced, sixteen-page letter from Selznick on March 19, 1957 (a portion of which appeared in *Life*). In his letter, Selznick argued that Huston was not "entitled to the privileges of an artist with an investment" because of the director's salary. The producer admitted that he himself "would be up against an even more serious situation than when Cukor left *Gone with the Wind*" if Huston left the project. "But I can only be true to myself—and this is my show—and you yourself have repeatedly stated that it is my show," he reiterated. "I can only say what I said to Cukor: 'If this picture is going to fail, it must fail on *my* mistakes, not yours.' " Huston dismissed *A Farewell to Arms* in his autobiography as a "debacle."[33]

The opinion that Selznick's memo writing was a counterproductive practice (which Huston may have perceived rightly on *A Farewell to Arms*) has biased many accounts of this producer's contributions to *Gone with the Wind*. This erroneous view of his supervision of the earlier production may account for the sardonic tenor that characterizes the commentaries of Gavin Lambert's *GWTW*, Roland Flamini's *Scarlett, Rhett, and a Cast of Thousands*, and William Pratt's *Scarlett Fever*. For example, Lambert observed that Selznick "found time to rewrite practically all the scenes himself," adding that "of course, he regarded the film of *Gone with the Wind* as entirely his own conception, and perhaps it seemed logical to him that he could personally solve every problem." Selznick's posture during this time was "like God creating the world," although the producer was described also as "besieged, drugged, chain-smoking, [and] sleepless."[34] Despite their belittlement of Selznick, these books were marketed plainly to the film's fans. "Every now and again an editor or writer in one of these texts will murmur something about scholarship and history and the study of film, but the heart isn't in it," observed Michael Wood in his criticism in the *New York Review of Books* of several film books, including Lambert's *GWTW*. "Good old soupy nostalgia is what these books are about."[35]

In contrast, *David O. Selznick's Hollywood*, by Ronald Haver, late film curator of the Los Angeles County Museum of Art, reads seriously and accurately. Haver's educated use of documents in the producer's archives was supplemented by analysis of materials from additional sources. Of comparable value is the work of Richard Harwell, late curator of the Hargrett Rare Book and Manuscript Library of the University of Georgia at Athens. Harwell edited an anthology of essays entitled *"Gone with the Wind" as Book and Film*, and provided the preface for an unauthoritative, composite version of various states of Sidney Howard's filmscript published as *GWTW: The Screenplay*. To a degree, his attitude toward Selznick and the preparation of the film's script was biased by the opinions of the subjects of two other compilations which he also edited—namely, Margaret Mitchell (*Margaret Mitchell's "Gone with the Wind" Letters*) and Susan Myrick (*White Columns in Hollywood*). Upon Mitchell's recommendation, Selznick had hired Myrick as a technical advisor on the Southern dialect and had retained her in this capacity in the hope of enlisting the novelist's collaboration in the film enterprise. Indicative of a wry attitude toward the novel's adaptation, Myrick related to Mitchell on January 11, 1939, that "producers and what they do with scripts is like a chef making soup." She elaborated:

> The chef gets an idea from a soup he ate. He spends days making a stock that is just right. He tastes, adds seasonings, tastes again, adds again. Perfect. Then he does more things to it until he has the finest soup in the universe. Whereupon, he calls in the other chefs and they all stand around and pee in it! And this, the treasonable ones of us seem to agree is what happened about *GWTW*.[36]

Much Selznick-bashing and exploitation of this film's celebrity has continued under the guise of documentation and research. Herb Bridges' collection of multilingual editions of the novel, production and publicity photographs, and memorabilia is represented by three separate publications, yet the contents of the commentaries offered in these books are derived more from previously published material than from analysis of the materials reproduced therein. This same criticism may be made of the preface written by Bridges and Terryl C. Boodman to a problematic version of the filmscript entitled *"Gone with the Wind": The Screenplay*.[37] With respect to the quality of research exhibited in these publications—including the deluxe *The Art of "Gone with the Wind": The Making of a Legend* by Judy Cameron and Paul J. Christman and the exploitative *The Complete "Gone with the Wind" Trivia Book* by Pauline Bartel—it was observed in the *New York Times Book Review*'s already-cited critique of the "*Gone with the Wind* industry" that such accounts "don't seem to be turning up new ground so much as plowing one another's fields."[38]

The culmination of this trend is found in the 1988 documentary video *"Gone with the Wind": The Making of a Legend*, written by David Thomson and produced by Turner Entertainment, a subsidiary of Time Warner, which presently owns the motion picture. "Real history is often accidental and muddled," the narrator, Christopher Plummer, announces at the beginning of this video. "The truth is that *Gone with the Wind* came out of chaos and confusion, blind faith, and great good luck." The authority of this declamation emanates not only from the actor's impressive vocal apparatus but also from a covert anti-industrial source—that of auteurism—for the purpose of portraying Selznick as a false creator. "Finally, in his cutting room, Selznick was supreme," the viewer is informed in one of many instances of mockery. "Here, with no writers or directors to annoy or confuse him, he could vacillate to his heart's content." Thus the cutting of a 20,000-foot picture from half a million feet in less than half a year is deemed a "demented process" rather than a Herculean labor. Although the presentation acknowledges this film's unique, universal appeal, as well as Selznick's dominant role in its production, the potshots are many and obvious.

Authority in Classical Hollywood Film Production

The producer, directors, and writers of *Gone with the Wind* are factors of a filmmaking equation which exhausts simplistic notions of film authorship. Selznick's insistence upon a faithful adaptation of a best-selling novel, which was undertaken via a series of filmscripts by numerous authors and which was realized with the assistance of several directors, should be examined also in the context of the conventions and vicissitudes exhibited by other productions of the major studios. For example, one should inquire how many writers were employed normally on the adaptation of a literary work for a major film production, what variations of this norm existed, and what specific responsibilities defined the roles of the producer and director.

In the case of *Gone with the Wind*, the development of the narrative from book through numerous intermediary filmscript versions by various authors—including F. Scott Fitzgerald, Oliver H. P. Garrett, Ben Hecht, and Sidney Howard (the last being the only one credited)—has never been explored satisfactorily, nor has the relationship been analyzed between composition and continuity of this film's shots and visualization of imagery via the "storyboarding" attributed to production designer William Cameron Menzies. Closer examination of the integral progress of this film's screenplay and production design substantially enriches an understanding of the production of a motion picture which was directed by no fewer than four individuals yet is credited to the vision and supervision of its producer. Contextual analysis of scripts, storyboards, and other production documents also demonstrates that industrial routines and prerogatives of executive management are critical factors for consideration in cinema studies.

Principal authority for a film's creation has been assumed by individuals employed in different roles throughout the development of the motion-picture industry. In *The Classical Hollywood Cinema*, Janet Staiger chronicled the six management systems that have characterized American film production at different times in its chronology—namely, structures organized around the cameraman (prior to 1907), around the director (from 1907), around the director-unit (after 1909), around the central producer (after 1914), around the producer-unit (from the early 1930s), and around the package-unit (from the early 1940s and dominant by the 1950s). Staiger observed that although each successive system differed from the one that preceded it, each retained something of the predecessor's organization and suggested that the "tendency to attempt to attribute particular stylistic innovations to a single worker (producer, director, writer) may have reinforced the hierachical system." Staiger further argued that the introduction of unit production and of packaging—both pioneered by Selznick—promoted the "ideological attitude toward authorship . . . of assuming that one individual ought to control almost all aspects of the filming so that that individual's personal vision can be created." In opposition to the tenet of individual authorship, Staiger proposed that

> what was valuable in the Hollywood mode of production was its combination of the expertise of multiple crafts. Groups of specialists, although in divided labor, made films which just seem difficult to conceive having been created by workers in other work arrangements."[39]

In other words, Hollywood filmmaking resembled neither the intensive labor of a solitary artist nor the assembly-line procedures of a Ford manufacturing plant (except for release-print manufacturing). However, until recently, studio documents remained inaccessible to academic researchers—a condition which permitted growth of auteuristic criticism and semiological analysis. "The fact is that the history of the American film industry is extremely difficult to write, because many of the basic materials that would be needed are simply not available," wrote Edward Buscombe in 1975, in *Screen*. "The result is that when Hollywood has been written about its industrial dimension has been ignored."[40]

The Classical Hollywood Cinema, which appeared in 1985 and on which Staiger collaborated with David Bordwell and Kristin Thompson, derived from research of production documents, trade publications, and a statistically random film selection and attempted to synthesize analysis and history in a contextual manner—or, in the scholars' own words, to "historicize textual analysis and connect the history of film style to the history of the motion picture industry." Specifically, these three authors analyzed classical Hollywood film production as a "distinct mode of film practice with its own cinematic style and industrial conditions of existence." They propose that "the Hollywood mode of film practice constitutes an integral system, including persons and groups but also rules, films, machinery, documents, institutions, work processes, and theoretical concepts."[41] Because of its scope and integrity of research and analysis, *The Classical Hollywood Cinema* represents a watershed of American film studies.

A similar attitude is exhibited by Thomas Schatz in *The Genius of the System.* "The quality and artistry of all these films were the product not simply of individual expression, but of a melding of institutional forces," Schatz acknowledged. "In each case the 'style' of a writer, director, star—or even a cinematographer, art director, or costume designer—fused with the studio's production operations and management structure, its resources and talent pool, its narrative traditions and market strategy." However, the author asserted that "studio filmmaking was less a process of collaboration than of negotiation and struggle—occasionally approaching armed conflict" and proposed that "the chief architects of a studio's style were its executives," whom he described as the "most misunderstood and undervalued figures in American film history."[42]

Schatz's comparison of the professional roles of Selznick and Hitchcock and of their respective contributions to the films which they undertook—together and separately—serves to dramatize much of the industrial process of filmmaking. He also observed that, in contrast to the operations of the five major motion-picture companies (MGM, Paramount, RKO, 20th Century-Fox, and Warner Bros.) which dominated the market in which the three "minor" companies (Columbia, United Artists, and Universal) also competed, Selznick's productions were indeed "another story altogether." While the large studios pursued efficiency and productivity, Selznick and other major independents—such as Sam Goldwyn and Walt Disney—undertook only a few "high-cost, high-yield" films annually. "These filmmakers were in a class by themselves, turning out prestige pictures that often tested the economic constraints and the creative limits of the system, or challenged its usual division of labor and hierarchy of authority," wrote Schatz, who proposed a symbiotic relationship between independent and major studio production. "The independents needed the system for its resources and its theaters, while the system needed them to cultivate the 'high end' of the market and to keep the first-run theaters stocked with quality product—an obvious benefit to the majors since they took a sizable exhibitor's fee on these releases."[43]

Leonard J. Leff, in *Hitchcock and Selznick,* also observed that the number of annual releases by each of the major studios (i.e., approximately one feature per week from each in the latter half of the 1930s) "militated against a chief executive interesting himself in each film." Leff acknowledged that, contrary to the managerial routines of the major companies, Selznick "influenced everything that he touched, and he touched almost everything, from the acquisition of the literary property to screenplay development, cast selection, pre-production, production, post-production, distribution, exhibition, rerelease, and, near the end of his life, the recutting for television." With reference to the traditional southern colonial facade of Selznick's Culver City studio (which formerly belonged to director-producer Thomas Ince, who developed the "continuity script" in 1912 as a instrument of executive control), the author remarked, cleverly that "this plantation owner knew cotton from seed to the shirt." However, while he argued that the "dynamics of the relationship served both men," and that "Hitchcock did not succeed despite Selznick any more than Selznick succeeded because of Hitchcock," with respect to Selznick's production of three films which Hitchcock directed, Leff sided with auteurism when he professed that, in his opinion, "history subsequently proved that Selznick needed Hitchcock more than Hitchcock needed Selznick."[44]

As a critical practice, auteurism discredited the record of producers' influence on classical Hollywood filmmaking. Sarris's primary tenet—that the director's preeminence is a principal condition of a superior motion picture—was promoted to a popular audience in 1971 by Frank Capra in his autobiography, *The Name above the Title.* "I knew of no great book or play, no classic painting or sculpture, no lasting monument to art in any form, that was ever created by a committee—with the possible exception of the Gothic cathedrals," he professed. "In art, it is 'one man, one painting—one statue—one book—one film.' "[45]

After two decades of advancement in scholarship, this claim appears distended with respect to films of the classical Hollywood era. In his 1992 biography of this director, Joseph McBride professed that Capra "enjoyed the adulation of young, antiestablishment idealists, who helped him re-create his reputation" without adequate acknowledgment of producer Harry Cohn (who ruled Columbia Pictures as owner and president and for whose studio Capra was the most important "house director"), of cinematographer Joseph Walker (who filmed all of Capra's classic movies at Columbia and *It's a Wonderful Life* [1946]), or of screenwriter Robert Riskin (who wrote most of Capra's best works, including *It Happened One Night* [1934], *Mr. Deeds Goes to Town*

[1936], and *Meet John Doe* [1941]). McBride wrote, "A probably apocryphal story has Riskin, angered in the late thirties by all the talk about 'The Capra Touch,' marching into Capra's office, dropping 120 pages of blank paper on the director's desk, and demanding, 'Here! Give that "The Capra Touch"!'" He propounded that "what Capra called his 'formula' did not emerge until he began working with Riskin material in the early 1930s," and that "once the formula had been established, Capra was content to repeat it, with minor embellishment, for the rest of his career, eventually to diminishing effect."[46]

While identified as the "maker of *Gone with the Wind*" in his subsequent pictures' publicity, Selznick never failed to acknowledge the value of others' creative assistance. "The production of *Gone with the Wind* represents the complete devotion to their respective jobs, and the coordinated efforts, of a hundred artists, technicians, and department heads," he avowed in the program prepared for this film's premiere. Recognizing that "filmmaking in the era of the studio system is typically described as a collaborative process," Tino Balio argued in *Grand Design* that "it might be more accurate to say that filmmaking was a group effort involving a strict division of labor with a producer at the helm."[47] Joan Didion questioned references to Hollywood movie-making as a "collaborative medium" earlier and in stronger terms. "A finished picture defies all attempts to analyze what makes it work or not work: the responsibility for its every frame is clouded not only in the accidents and compromises of production but in the clauses of its financing," she wrote in the 1970s. "To read David O. Selznick's instruction to his directors, writers, actors and department heads in *Memo from David O. Selznick* is to come very close to the spirit of actually making a picture, a spirit not of collaboration but of armed conflict in which one antagonist has a contract assuring him nuclear capability."[48]

Although Selznick's authority in the making of what remains arguably the world's most successful film is not contested, what is allowed rarely is the proposition that this producer's influence was beneficial. Drawing from materials preserved in Selznick's archives, the following chapter offers an inventory and analysis of Sidney Howard's successive versions of the screenplay and demonstrates that Selznick's monitoring of its progress and interaction in its development were critical to the success of *Gone with the Wind*—contrary to most commentaries, which relate that the scriptwriting was unmanageable and that Selznick's interference was counterproductive. Previously undiscovered in the archives, the manuscript of Howard's initial draft, dated February 1937, is compared with this screenwriter's preliminary notes of December 1936, and with subsequent filmscript revisions of April, August, and November 1937. The mistaken notion that the original scenario was almost twice its actual length—and as such would have corresponded to a running time on the screen of six hours—has plagued the majority of the histories of this film's production. This fallacious claim is not as trivial as it may appear, because it supports the erroneous thesis that both Howard and Selznick were overwhelmed by the magnitude of Mitchell's text and that they were unable to abridge the narrative in any organized fashion. On the contrary, the threat of excessive duration was posed less by the filmscript's length than it was by predictions of Cukor's pacing of the performances.

In the manner of many Hollywood film productions, the screenwriting of *Gone with the Wind* continued through the period of its filming. In fact, filmmaking activities were not restricted by the conventional stages of Hollywood film production—namely, preproduction (or preparation), production (or filming), and post-production (or editing); for example, scenes featuring Vivien Leigh and portions of scenes requiring the use of doubles were retaken at the producer's command during the editing of the film. Nevertheless, in spite of most commentators' characterization of this film's production as a purely chaotic venture, script development may be represented reasonably by three groups of documents, all of which are available for comparison in the Selznick collection at the University of Texas at Austin. These documents consist of: Howard's early drafts; revisions made by Selznick and Oliver Garrett as late as January 1939; and a revised shooting script (after George Cukor was replaced as director by Victor Fleming), the pages of which date through the final day of "principal photography" and are the work of a number of contributors, including Selznick and Ben Hecht. Also preserved are three successive states of the cutting continuity which document stages of the film's editing.

In his memoranda Selznick offered two reasons for delegating to the production designer, William Cameron Menzies, the "complete" delineation of the filmscript in the form of continuity designs and storyboard drawings; according to Selznick, he did so (1) to reduce set construction by implementation of special-effects cinematography; and (2) to "pre-cut" the film prior to its shooting, in order to minimize expenses anticipated because of the picture's size and use of Technicolor (a process which required multiple negatives). With respect to the latter purpose, a comparison in chapter 3 of extant continuity drawings and various states of the scenario of the celebrated fire sequence discloses that while a significant portion of the artwork does correspond to a specific script version, the linkage of shots that comprises this episode was revised subsequently with little influence from these production designs.

The legend that the various directors and technicians faithfully followed a "complete script in sketch form" is confuted also in chapter 4. Although most of the continuity designs for *Gone with the Wind* correspond to descriptions of shots specified in various versions of the filmscript, application of these drawings to the production remained subject to their acceptance by the producer, directors, and screenwriters. Ultimately, Menzies' unprecedented assignment to "storyboard" the entire film remained a tentative program which Selznick exploited—much as he did the filmscript's development—for the purpose of controlling the picture and its directors. In spite of the plethora of documentation of others' creative contributions that was preserved by the producer, all technical and artistic interpretations of narrative and imagery were subject to Selznick's executive authority. The studio remained his atelier, and the producer used his decision-making prowess to exercise his mastery of the collective filmmaking enterprise on and off the shooting sets.

In summary, this book's purpose is threefold. Analyses of materials preserved from the making of *Gone with the Wind*—namely, scripts, artwork, and production documents—correct the record of the novel's adaptation that has been offered in previous commentaries. In view of this emended history, Selznick's contributions are reappraised also, and the role played by this executive is acknowledged as having been a major creative force in the film's production. Finally, the complexity of the producer's collaboration with the many principal technical personnel employed on this project (i.e., the screenwriters, directors, cinematographers, as well as the art director and production designer) is examined in order to ameliorate an understanding of the conflict, chaos, and creativity involved not only in this particular effort but in classical Hollywood film production generally.

In contrast to Selznick's view of filmmaking as the "vision of one man," cinema had been described by the art historian Erwin Panofsky as a collaborative or collective enterprise during the period of this producer's greatest triumphs. In his essay "Style and Medium in the Motion Pictures," which was written in 1934 and revised in 1947, Panofsky provided the metaphor of cathedral building to which Capra referred much later. Panofsky proposed:

> It might be said that a film, called into being by a cooperative effort in which all contributions have the same degree of permanence, is the nearest modern equivalent of a medieval cathedral; the role of the producer corresponding, more or less, to that of the bishop or archbishop; that of the director to that of the architect in chief; that of the scenario writers to that of the scholastic advisers establishing the iconographical program; and that of the actors, cameramen, cutters, sound men, make-up men and the diverse technicians to that of those whose work provided the physical entity of the finished product, from the sculptors, glass painters, bronze casters, carpenters and skilled masons down to the quarry men and woodsmen. And if you speak to any one of these collaborators he will tell you, with perfect *bona fides*, that his is really the most important job—which is quite true to the extent that it is indispensable.[49]

However, the fact that the directors played a limited role when Selznick delegated responsibilities to them during a film's production also may call to mind the technical nature of the duties assumed by the generally anonymous architect or architects and other craftsmen attending the abbot Suger, who, in the twelfth century, supervised the construction of the cathedral of St.-Denis, a monumental undertaking on which Panofsky himself devoted specific study and writing elsewhere. The popular historian Will Durant provided a concise account of this extraordinary cleric's influence on the building of this earliest masterpiece of Gothic architecture:

> In 1133 [Suger] brought together artists and artisans "from all lands" to raise and adorn a new home for France's patron St. Denis, and to house the tombs of the kings of France; he persuaded King Louis VII and the court to contribute the necessary funds. . . . We picture him rising early to superintend the construction, from the felling of the trees that he chose for timbers to the installation of the stained glass whose subjects he had selected and whose inscriptions he had composed.[50]

A comparison of Selznick's approach to filmmaking with Suger's manner of introducing the Gothic style to western art is not meant to overlook differences between these two figures—their religious backgrounds differed enormously, as did their daily routines (there are accounts that the film producer habitually slept late into the morning, having worked long hours during the night); nor is any equation suggested, in terms of their value to our culture, between Selznick's memoranda and the abbot's *Liber de Rebus in Administratione Sua Gestis*—or, for that matter, between *Gone with the Wind* and St.-Denis, or between Selznick and Suger. (However, if one were to liken films to monuments, very few motion pictures come as quickly to mind as *Gone with the Wind.*) The point is that Selznick was a remarkable man within his own sphere of activity and that he utilized numerous artists and technicians in the creation of at least one work of epic dimension. The comparison is meant to suggest that his method is worthy of scholarly inquiry and serious discussion.

TWO

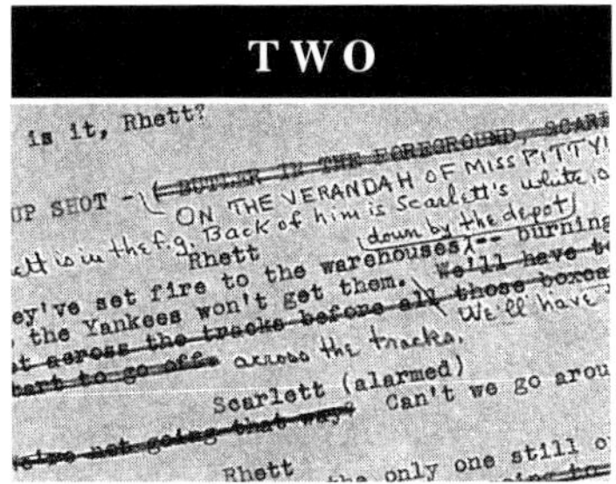

Sidney Howard and the Screenwriting of *Gone with the Wind*

A commonplace in film history asserts that motion pictures are only as good as the scripts upon which they are based. In fact, this truism is informed by a fundamental relationship that developed between the scenario and the screen. Preparation of a detailed filmscript had become a pre-production requirement of the American film industry as early as 1914 in order for its studios to ensure both quality of product and efficiency of operation. According to Janet Staiger in *The Classical Hollywood Cinema*, the "continuity script," in which each shot of a picture was prescribed and enumerated in advance of filming, served as the "blueprint from which all other work was organized."[1] She also proposed that, concurrently with the development of this shooting script, the organization of the film industry evolved from a director-unit system of production to an arrangement controlled by a central manager or producer.

Although the director continued to exercise authority over the filming of a motion picture, he was accountable no longer for all aspects of production but instead served, in Staiger's words, as a sort of "technical expert" who specialized in directing talent and crew during shooting. Staiger explained: "The producer chose a director from that department just as he would select a writer or designer or cameraman to be combined with a story and cast. In shooting, the director topped the hierarchy of workers, but the producer took over coordinating production decisions."[2]

This hierarchical arrangement continued with the development of the producer-unit system, a mode of film production that was championed in the early 1930s by Selznick himself. Under the "unit" system, studio-employed producers personally supervised the making of a limited number of films, monitoring and influencing their development from conception to completion. The "blueprint" by which all production work was organized often became subject to the variable element that was described by Robert Sklar in *Movie-made America* as the "manipulative style of producer control." According to Sklar, "some producers had a genuine talent for conceiving effective or popular film stories and for marshaling the resources—the right writer, director and players—to realize their conception." He cited Irving Thalberg as the progenitor of this type of producer, and identified David O. Selznick and Darryl F. Zanuck as Thalberg's most noteworthy successors.

> The manipulation of writers therefore became as essential a part of the producers' power game as the manipulation of stars. They aimed at developing a script that belonged more to them than to any of the writers who worked on it. Often a similar assignment was given to more than one writer; writers were asked to rewrite the work of others; different writers were assigned separate segments of the same script. When the shooting script was ready, the only steady hand that guided it along the way was more likely than not the producer's: he was the "author" whose conception the director was to put into visual images, and he retained authority to revise the director's work, whether by ordering changes after seeing the daily rushes, or by taking control of the final cutting and assembling of the picture.[3]

In the 1920s and the early 1930s, Thalberg, Selznick, and Zanuck served as production chiefs of MGM, RKO, and Warner Bros., respectively, and as such wielded enormous power as central producers over their studio's output. Subsequent positions as "prestige unit" producers at MGM between 1933 and 1935 allowed Thalberg and Selznick the time to exert even greater control over the motion pictures that were developed and realized under their supervisory authority. By the time he established Selznick International Pictures (SIP) in 1935 and arranged for distribution through United Artists as an independent production company, Selznick had grown to believe that greater rewards could be achieved by undertaking fewer, albeit grander, productions per annum. "There are two kinds of merchandise that can be made profitably in this business: either the very cheap pictures or the very expensive pictures," Selznick declared, stating his own preference for producing the latter kind. Of equal importance to his own vision of filmmaking was his belief that "in the making of good pictures [it was] essential for a producer to collaborate on every inch of the script, to be available for every conference, and to go over all details of production."[4]

Selznick's reputation for monitoring very closely the progress of screenwriters employed on the films that he produced and of editing their work personally was established early in his career. According to legend, the director William Wellman approached Selznick's table at the Academy Awards banquet of 1938 and offered the producer the Oscar statuette presented to Wellman himself for his part in the creation of the scenario of *A Star is Born*, with the remark, "Here, you deserve this, you wrote more of it than I did." The invariable course of Selznick's interaction in the development of his films' scripts led to his receiving formal credit as screenwriter of *Since You Went Away* (1944), *Duel in the Sun* (1946), and *The Paradine Case* (1947).

Selznick's supervision of the screenwriting process in his adaptation of *Gone with the Wind* is examined in this chapter. Although many commentators have described this producer's interaction with the filmscript as counterproductive and unjustified, a review of the successive versions of the screenplay preserved in the Selznick archives reveals that Howard's initial drafts are disappointing with respect to exploitation of many of the dramatic and spectacular features of Margaret Mitchell's novel and that Selznick's insistence upon revision was a critical factor in the film's success. Too often, in his efforts to condense the story line to a standard length for theatrical exhibition, Howard resorted to employing conventions that were characteristic of literary adaptations developed more for the stage than for the cinema. Howard also was inclined to invent scenes and dialogue that deviated markedly from the original novel's narrative.

Although Selznick objected to the latter tendency, he valued his screenwriter's literary reputation (both Mitchell and Howard had been awarded the Pulitzer Prize, in the respective categories of fiction and drama). During the lengthy time in which problems associated with the film's casting were resolved, Selznick hoped that a satisfactory collaboration might be effected between producer and scenarist and that a faithful transcription of the book might be written. Howard objected to Selznick's editorial role in the filmscript's revision and to his demand for fidelity to the novel, and he temporarily withdrew from the project. In spite of the number of other writers employed during his absence, Howard remained the only one to be credited for the task of screenwriting. Skeptical that the film could replicate both the story and the celebrity of her novel, Mitchell herself refused to participate in the enterprise despite Selznick's entreaties and, until the motion picture was released and its success was assured, she privately disparaged his attempt to adapt her work.

Read the Book, Visualize the Movie: Adapting a Bestseller

Selznick acquired the screen rights to *Gone with the Wind* on July 30, 1936, one month after the novel's publication and after much encouragement by John Hay Whitney and Katharine ("Kay") Brown, SIP's chairman of the board of directors and New York story editor, respectively. By this time, copies of Margaret Mitchell's novel had begun to sell at a remarkable rate. "A first novel does well if it sells five thousand copies in a lifetime," observed Edwin Granberry, who praised the book in a review for the *New York Sun*. "*Gone with the Wind* has run up such unprecedented sales as fifty thousand copies in a single day, a half-million in less than one hundred days, more than a million copies in six months." He also noted that Allen Hervey's *Anthony Adverse*, which he described as "its nearest rival in the history of publishing" to that date, had sold less than 400,000 copies in its first year (1933).[5]

Two million copies of Mitchell's novel had been sold by the time the film adaptation was released and to date the total has surpassed twenty-eight million. The $50,000 that Selznick agreed to pay for the screen rights may appear to have been a modest figure in view both of this novel's spectacular commercial history and of the publisher's original asking price of $100,000, but most commentators have maintained that Selznick's offer was a relatively generous one. At the time, the highest price paid for the screen rights for a first novel had been the $40,000 paid by Warner Bros. for *Anthony Adverse* (released as a film in 1936). Selznick also paid $50,000 in 1938 for the screen rights to *Rebecca*, which was written by a previously published author (Daphne du Maurier) and which became the second best-selling book on the market. Moreover, it is less commonly known that Whitney and Selznick later offered Mitchell an additional $50,000 as a measure of goodwill and as an investment in maintaining the author's approval of their work.[6]

Determined to mount a spectacular Civil War epic, Selznick had entertained remaking *The Birth of a Nation* at the time of his formation of SIP (before the publication of *Gone with the Wind* was brought to his attention), but had dismissed this idea because of the racial controversy which had become inseparable from the reputation of Griffith's film.[7] Selznick's decision to undertake the adaptation of Mitchell's book undoubtedly was influenced by the fact that it was breaking records as a bestseller, as well as by the fact that it had been lauded in the *New York Times Book Review* as "one of the most remarkable first novels produced by an American writer" and as the "best Civil War novel that has yet been written"[8]—in spite of the film industry's superstition surrounding stories set in this period and its prejudice against using them. The otherwise perspicacious Irving Thalberg purportedly cautioned Louis B. Mayer against MGM's purchasing the rights to Mitchell's work. "Forget it, Louis," Thalberg reputedly declared, "no one ever made a dime on Civil War pictures."[9] "[SIP] was less than a year old when David asked me if I wanted to see a movie of a Civil War story. Of course I didn't. *He* didn't. No one did, not conceivably," Irene Mayer Selznick, Selznick's first wife, confessed in her autobiography, *A Private View*. "It was a first novel, carrying a stiff price and a terrible title," she argued. "All that and the Civil War besides."[10]

Selznick himself telegraphed words of caution to Katharine Brown on May 25, 1936, concerning acquisition of film rights to *Gone with the Wind*. "I feel . . . that its background is very strongly against it, as witness *So Red the Rose* [the popular romance by Stark Young, published in 1934] which also threatened to have tremendous sale and which in some particulars was in same category and which failed miserably as a picture." In particular, a sympathetic view of the plight of landowning Southern families during the time of the War Between the States and disapproval of the Union's emancipation of the slaves impaired the marketing of Paramount's 1935 adaptation of Young's novel. The *New York Times*'s reviewer of this film concluded: "It is difficult in this turbulent day to subscribe to the film's point of view or to share its rage against the uncouth legions of Mr. Lincoln as they dash about the lovely Southern landscape putting crazy notions in the heads of the plantation slaves. By presenting the alien forces which destroyed this civilization as cruel and vulgar intrusions instead of inevitable realities, *So Red the Rose* cheats itself of contemporary meaning."[11]

In contrast, it is apparent to anyone familiar with Margaret Mitchell's novel that *Gone with the Wind* is more than a "story of the Old South" (as the book itself was subtitled)—or, more accurately, is more than a story of the periods of the American Civil War and Reconstruction, which provide a historical backdrop for the melodrama presented by its characters. "This book is really magnificent," wrote Charles W. Everett, a professor of English and American literature at Columbia University who also served as a reader for Macmillan, which published the novel upon his recommendation. "Its human qualities would make it good against any background, and when they are shown on the stage of the Civil War and Reconstruction the effect is breathtaking." Everett specifically praised as an "admirable" choice the "device of using an unsympathetic character to arouse sympathetic emotions."[12] What most appeals to the novel's readership even today is the story of this same main protagonist, Scarlett O'Hara, who not only survives this cataclysmic time for Southerners but prospers through her wiles, drive, and courage. "If the novel has a theme, the theme is that of survival," Mitchell herself wrote shortly after the book's publication, revealing a contemporary, personal relevance for many of its readers. She continued:

> What makes some people able to come through catastrophes and others, apparently just as able, strong, and brave, go under? We've seen it in the present Depression. . . . Some people survive; others don't. What qualities are in those who fight their way through triumphantly that are lacking in those who go under? What was it that made some of our Southern people able to come through a War, a Reconstruction, and a complete wrecking of the social and economic system? I don't know. I only know that the survivors used to call that quality "gumption." So I wrote about the people who had gumption and the people who didn't.[13]

The fact that the lives of many of this novel's initial readers had been affected by the stock-market crash of October 1929 and by subsequent events during the years of the Depression undoubtedly accounts for much of the identification with Scarlett's straits. Equally important was the recent entry into the workforce of great numbers of women who were readers and members of film audiences. In fact, female interest was crucial to the success of both book and film. In his history of American filmmaking in the thirties, Tino Balio recognized that because the "era's most successful [motion picture] production was targeted at women and employed a women's perspective . . . *Gone with the Wind* . . . should be more accurately classified as a prestige 'woman's picture' "—a genre in which Selznick specialized as a film producer.[14]

The novel relates the career of Scarlett O'Hara, a wealthy Georgia planter's attractive and willful daughter, whose infatuation with their neighbor's son, Ashley Wilkes, is not abated by the young man's marriage to his cousin, Melanie Hamilton, nor by Scarlett's own series of sudden—albeit shrewd—marital alliances. To spite Ashley and to become a member of his bride's family, Scarlett accepts the brash proposal of Melanie's brother, Charles, who marries her after enlisting in the Confederate Army and who shortly afterward dies. Widowed with a newborn son, Scarlett moves to Charleston to join Melanie's household and to maintain contact with Ashley during his infrequent furloughs; there, Scarlett experiences most of the Civil War's destructive trajectory over the South, as it arcs through states of optimism and braggadocio, of inflation and deprivation, and of invasion and collapse. In Ashley's absence, she assists in the delivery of Melanie's baby hours before fleeing the city with them during its evacuation on the eve of the Yankee onslaught; returning to Tara, she finds the plantation plundered by the invading army, her mother dead, and her father mad from grief. Combating starvation, as well as fending off marauders and tax collectors in her new role as the family's matriarch, Scarlett elicits a proposal from, and marries, her sister's fiancé, Frank Kennedy, to prevent foreclosure on Tara and, as a storeowner's wife, to benefit from the postwar boom in business and building in Atlanta.

Left with another child, Scarlett survives her second husband's premature demise and marries Rhett Butler, one of the richest men of the "New South," who amassed his wealth during the war as a speculator and blockade runner and afterward is rumored to have augmented this fortune with the bullion from the Confederate Treasury placed in his own care. Scarlett and Rhett have been acquainted with one another since early on in the narrative, when he introduced himself to her at a party in the Wilkes's plantation home after revealing that he inadvertently overheard her passionately pleading with Ashley to abandon his engagement with Melanie in favor of a romantic relationship with herself. ("Sir, you are no gentleman!" she reprimands Butler for having eavesdropped, to which he "airily" replies, "And, you, Miss, are no lady.")[15] Their sparring during his pursuit of her affection is in fact the true course of the novel. Rhett also assists Scarlett in one or two emergencies; for example, her evacuation from Atlanta with Melanie and the children during the war is expedited by his escort. Sadly, their marriage does not survive their own child's accidental death. The book concludes with Rhett departing their home in Atlanta, having requested a divorce after hearing news of Melanie's death. Tragically, Scarlett becomes aware of the profundity of her husband's love—now lost—only minutes before their separation and cannot prevent his exit. Still she refuses to accept defeat, deferring concern to the next day, when she plans to return to Tara for recuperation; she ultimately concludes, "Tomorrow is another day"—a truism that was also the book's original title.

Preliminary Screen Treatment and Differences of Opinion on Adaptation

Selznick's correspondence with Brown indicates as early as September 25, 1936, his interest in Ben Hecht and Sidney Howard as candidates for screenwriter of *Gone with the Wind*. Both writers were appealing to the producer for not being tied contractually to another studio, and were considered—in Selznick's words—to have been "rare in that you don't have to cook up every situation for them and write half of the dialogue." Hecht had achieved fame on Broadway as co-author with Charles MacArthur of *The Front Page* (1928) and *Twentieth Century* (1932) and had received an Academy Award for his screenplay of *Underworld* (1927), as well as an Oscar nomination for his filmscript of *Viva Villa!* (1934), which Selznick produced for MGM. He was described by Richard Corliss in *Talking Pictures* not only as the definitive Hollywood screenwriter but as a "personification of Hollywood itself."[16]

However, Hecht's oeuvre may not have appeared sufficiently representative of *belles-lettres* to promote the adaptation of *Gone with the Wind*. Instead, Selznick secured Howard for this job, and expressed his pleasure at having done so to Brown on October 8, 1936, although he regretted that the writer would not undertake the work in California but preferred to write the initial draft on his farm in the Berkshires in Massachusetts. "I have never had much success leaving a writer alone to do a script without almost daily collaboration with myself and usually the director," the producer admitted.

Howard was certainly an attractive candidate, and his theatrical and literary prestige specifically appealed to Selznick. Highly respected by the press as the adaptor of Sinclair Lewis's novel *Dodsworth* for the stage in 1934, and as the author of the 1925 drama *They Knew What They Wanted*, for which he was awarded a Pulitzer Prize, Howard had been lauded in *Time* magazine as "one of the half dozen ablest playwrights in the U.S." and as a "better theatrical craftsman" than Eugene O'Neill.[17] Moreover, his screen adaptations for Samuel Goldwyn were highly successful. *Arrowsmith* (1931)—one of Goldwyn's most critically acclaimed films of the 1930s—had been proposed as a project to the producer by Howard himself, who subsequently adapted Lewis's Nobel Prize-winning novel and received an Academy Award nomination after the film's release—as did the motion picture itself, in the best picture category.

Lewis, too, had been pleased by the cinematic presentation of *Arrowsmith* and had proposed that Howard undertake the dramatic adaptation of *Dodsworth*, which the playwright produced on Broadway and afterward sold to Goldwyn for film production. Howard's collaboration with the novelist involved numerous conferences in New York and on Lewis's farm in Vermont, during which fourteen "master scenes" evolved from a complete rewriting of the original work. Howard's term for the procedure was "dramatizing by equivalent"; it was a procedure that Lewis greatly admired, and was described by both writers separately in prefaces to the play's text, published in 1934.

Theoretically, Howard's method of adaptation entailed invention of scenes that were not presented in the book but which manifested ideas that were suggested in the original text. He himself confessed that the "filmed novel bears no more relationship to the real thing than any other variety of illustration." He also wrote:

> The truth of the matter is that no dramatization can do justice to any but a pretty completely inadequate novel. The road to happiness in dramatization begins, I am certain, with a lean novel, a novel deficient in both characters and incident, a novel which has attracted no readers to speak of.

He concluded his "Postscript on Dramatization" with the announcement that he would attempt no more adaptations in the future. "Works of art are best left in the form their creators selected for them," he explained and aphorized that "old books lose something when art shoppes cut their innards out to make cigarette boxes of them."[18]

Ironically, according to a biographer, Hollywood provided Howard (who, in a diatribe published in 1932 in the *New Republic*, parodied it also as the "Golgonda of the entertainment racket") with the "crowning accomplishment to his career" via his tenure on Selznick's production of *Gone with the Wind*.[19] The East Coast elements of classical American film production were distinguished from the Hollywood community not only in terms of studio ownership—the financial offices of the major film companies being located in Manhattan—but also by the superior, literary pose of many of the screenwriters, some of whose dramatic works had been produced on Broadway. Howard was among the most notable of these writers; although honored by an Academy Award for his script of *Gone with the Wind*, he persistently deprecated the work in his correspondence.

Howard's cynicism may have been aggravated by the indifference exhibited by the novel's author toward the task of adaptation. Margaret Mitchell had been resistant to leave her home in Atlanta in order to participate in the editing of her manuscript in New York and adamantly refused to journey to Hollywood after selling the screen rights to Selznick. "Of course, I would love to help out in any way I can but I have no ideas at all about changes and could be of no help whatsoever in such a matter," the novelist responded on October 16, 1936 to Brown's entreaty that she agree to assist members of the company in making "changes of continuity" in her work. "Besides, if news got out that I was in even the slightest way responsible for any deviations from the book, then my life wouldn't be worth living," the author also explained. "You see . . . each and every reader feels that he has part ownership in it and they are determined that nothing shall be changed."[20]

Mitchell was pleased to learn that Selznick had hired Howard for the task of adapting her novel for the screen, and she expressed knowledge of and admiration for the playwright's work in a letter to the producer on October 19, 1936. Nevertheless, she refused to cooperate in any part of her novel's dramatization.[21] Her reaction surprised Howard, who had written to her for assistance the following month when Selznick's publicity chief, Russell Birdwell, began to arrange a visit to Atlanta by Katharine Brown, George Cukor (who had been contracted as director), and set designer Hobe Erwin (with whom Cukor had worked on *Little Women*) for the purpose of scouting locations for filming and for generating publicity and eliciting goodwill from the region. Birdwell also had hoped to suggest to the public the novelist's participation in the film enterprise by her association with this group.

"You know you have given me more story than I can compress into the two hours a picture is, at the outside, permitted," Howard remarked in his letter of November 18, 1936 to Mitchell. "Some things will have to go because nothing is less adequate than a picture which tries to cover too much ground and so covers none of it properly." He asked Mitchell to examine his drafts and explained that this was the procedure followed successfully with Sinclair Lewis. "When I sold the book to Selznick Company, I made it very plain that I should have nothing whatsoever to do with the picture," she responded by letter on November 21. "I know just as much about Sanskrit as I do about writing for movies." The novelist also felt that she lacked the necessary time—not surprisingly, given that even the fan letters in her daily mail were answered without secretarial assistance (see Figure 2). Most of all,

FIG. 2. Margaret Mitchell, author of *Gone with the Wind*, reading written and wired congratulations of friends, in her home in Atlanta, Georgia, following the announcement in May, 1937, that her novel had won the Pulitzer Prize. (Reproduced with permission of UPI/Bettmann Archives.)

she was discouraged by the fear of being held accountable for the film's abridgment of her narrative.[22]

Howard explained in his reply on November 25 that the purpose of his earlier letter "was chiefly to assure you—in so far as it is in my power to assure you—that you would have all possible measure of approval or criticism of your picture before it reaches the irrevocable stage of celluloid." "I know you must have thought my abrupt letter the height of discourtesy," the novelist responded on December 1. "The truth of the matter is, as I wrote you before, that I haven't the time to work on the picture; I haven't the inclination; I haven't the experience—and moreover, I do not want to let myself in for a lot of grief." On December 5 Mitchell also informed Birdwell more bluntly, "I'll be very glad to meet Mr. Howard, for whom I have a vast admiration, but I will not read a line of the script."[23]

The task of adaptation remained entirely Selznick's responsibility. Bob Thomas wrote in his biography of the producer that, immediately after purchasing the rights to the property during the summer of 1936 and while on vacation in Hawaii with his wife, Selznick brought along his own copy of Mitchell's novel and "made elaborate notes in the margins, indicating what scenes and characters might be cut and what should be retained." Thomas also wrote that this same copy was loaned to Howard.[24] Both Howard and Selznick's initial impressions of the novel's story line may have been influenced, too, by the fifty-page synopsis prepared by Franclien Macconnell, a story-department employee. While Macconnell also summarized each of the book's chapters as a separate undertaking, her retelling of the general narrative provided not simply a denser reduction but was the first attempt to abridge the novel in a faithful manner but with a cinematic orientation.

Dividing her summary of the book into four sections, Macconnell opened the story not at Tara but with the bombardment of Fort Sumter by the Confederates; the first section concluded at the point in the story toward the end of the war when Rhett Butler leaves Scarlett O'Hara on the road to Tara, having escorted her safely from a besieged and burning Atlanta. The ensuing events at Tara open the second section, which concludes when Scarlett fashions a new dress from her late mother's parlor curtains and prepares to return to Atlanta in order to present Rhett with her offer of concubinage in order to raise money for the tax due on Tara. Beginning with Rhett's rejection of this offer, Macconnell's penultimate section concludes with his earnest proposal of marriage to Scarlett following the death of her second husband, Frank Kennedy, who himself had provided the money that was needed for the tax payment. Her final section summarized the remainder of the novel.

Notwithstanding the diligence of her rendition, Macconnell did not recognize that the five original divisions of Mitchell's novel signaled distinct stages in the story line—namely, Scarlett's departure for Atlanta to live with Ashley Wilkes's in-laws in order to continue her quest for his affection; the news of Ashley's imprisonment in the North; Ashley's return to Tara and to the arms of his wife, Melanie; Scarlett's marriage to Rhett Butler; and, finally, Melanie's death and Rhett's departure. In contrast to the conclusions of these five parts of the novel, in which triangular tension is maintained between Scarlett and Ashley and Rhett, those of Macconnell's four sections suggest that her synopsis exploited a simpler conflict between Scarlett and Rhett. In Mitchell's novel, Ashley Wilkes is allowed to motivate the conclusions of the first three parts, after which Rhett attempts to command Scarlett and the story line; Macconnell, on the other hand, relegated Ashley's part to a supporting role by her structural reorganization of the narrative.

The five parts of Mitchell's novel also bear a structural resemblance to classical tragedy. Scarlett is presented as an attractive, albeit flawed, protagonist who, in spite of enormous historical and environmental pressure, is responsible for her own misfortune by forsaking the love of Rhett Butler until it is too late, suffering instead from an extended infatuation with Ashley Wilkes, who is married to another. The novel's divisions recall the five acts prescribed for tragic drama by Horace in *Ars poetica*, and which were elaborated in pyramidal form, as a series of stages and crises, by Gustav Freytag in *Die Technik des Dramas*, published originally in 1863.

Specifically—and with respect to the pyramidal structure formulated in Freytag's treatise, which is claimed to have influenced the education of several previous generations of American playwrights—the novel's first part, which is set at Tara and at Twelve Oaks, serves to introduce the characters and their situations. The first crisis—Scarlett's discovery that she has lost Ashley to Melanie in marriage—initiates the rising movement which continues into the second part, in which Scarlett infiltrates the Hamiltons' home in Atlanta as Melanie's bereaved sister-in-law, following Ashley's departure to war. This action precedes a climax (*Hohenpunkt*, in Freytag's terminology), in which Scarlett assists in the delivery of the Wilkes's child and afterward, with Rhett's assistance, evacuates the besieged city, retreating in the company of Melanie and their children to Tara, which has been desolated by the war and where she is informed of her mother's death. This second crisis, or tragic moment, introduces the falling movement of the fourth part (*Umfehr*, translated as a "return"), in which Scarlett attempts to reconstruct her life and to preserve both Tara and Ashley's affection in Atlanta. The novel concludes with a catastrophe, in which Scarlett loses her love of Ashley in disillusionment, as well as the love of her own husband, who departs after Melanie's death.[25]

It is uncertain whether Howard—a professional dramatist educated at Berkeley and at Harvard—had recognized the novel's compatibility with this conventional tragic scheme and the unity of action which results from such comparison; his various treatments of its dramatization, between 1936 and 1937, into seven, ten, zero, eight, and eleven sequences, respectively, betray a different, episodic view of the narrative. While admitting to Selznick that "for screen purposes it is, I think, well to think of the book as Scarlett's story and of Scarlett herself as a character whose actions are consistently motivated by what she conceives to be the tragedy of an unrealized love," Howard began his fifty-page "Preliminary Notes on a Screen Treatment of *Gone with the Wind*" of December 14, 1936, with the pronouncement that "our chief difficulty will come from the lack of organization of the material of the second half of the novel—that is to say, the entire extent of the book after Scarlett's return to Tara from the siege of Atlanta."

The screenwriter also noted that "Part Five of the novel tells us how, as Rhett Butler's wife, Scarlett finally pays the piper for the very strength which has pulled her through. Unfortunately for our purposes, this accomplishment requires nearly two hundred pages of disjointed incident covering some five years." Perceiving that "there can be no doubt that the screen is at this point crying out for a swift final sequence" and that "there is at least two of everything in this book," Howard compressed over half of the novel's narrative into the final two of the seven sequences of his "Preliminary Notes." In contrast with the economy of this radical abridgment, his second sequence is devoted almost exclusively to the hospital bazaar and to Rhett's chivalrous return of the wedding ring that Melanie had donated selflessly to the Confederate cause.

Howard himself professed to having retained far too much story material "even in this considerably reduced treatment," yet, sensibly, did not question allotting adequate space early in the script for the exposition of the principal characters at Tara and at Twelve Oaks. "I should regret omitting the charming passage between Mammy and Scarlett," he declared, "as Scarlett dresses for the barbecue and Mammy forces her to eat so that she will not display an unladylike appetite." With respect to the important, recurring dream that haunts Scarlett through the latter half of the book, Howard confessed to Selznick without misgiving that he was "not fond of dream scenes on the screen" and had "not found any practicable way to include it" in his treatment.

In his letter to Howard of January 6, 1937, Selznick himself discouraged the screenwriter from attempting to preserve every element of the novel in the adaptation, yet stressed that any part chosen for inclusion must remain faithful to the original book. "I recognize, perhaps even more than you, the problem of length," the producer cautioned, disclosing that he was prepared for a treatment that might result in a film with a screening time of two and a half hours. "But even getting down to that length is going to be tough," he admitted. "We must prepare to make drastic cuts, and these cuts, I think, must include some of the characters because my feeling, based on experience adapting well-known and well-loved books, is that it is much better to chop out whole sequences than it is to make small deletions in individual scenes or sequences."

Contrary to the case of his earlier adaptation for MGM of *David Copperfield* (1935), which he cited, Selznick observed that both the recentness of the publication of Mitchell's novel and the existence of a contemporary audience "simply passionate about the details of the book"—which the novelist herself had recognized in her refusal to participate in the film enterprise—dictated "very strongly indeed" against alteration of the narrative. "These minor changes may give us slight improvements," Selznick conceded, "but there will be five or ten million readers on our heads for them; where, for the most part, they will recognize the obvious necessity of making drastic cuts."

With respect to Selznick's adaptations of two Dickens novels (*David Copperfield* and *A Tale of Two Cities*) for MGM in 1935, a remarkably high degree of fidelity to the original texts had been exhibited already, particularly when compared with other notable film adaptations of novels that had been released during this same period. Still, in terms of the books' sheer length, *Gone with the Wind* exceeded *David Copperfield*, the longer of the two Dickens novels, by twenty percent.[26] With respect to a motion picture's fidelity to an original literary source, in his 1949 doctoral dissertation for the University of Chicago Lester Asheim observed a seventeen- and an eighteen-percent deviation from the novels in the cases of Selznick's adaptations of, respectively, *David Copperfield* and *A Tale of Two Cities*; in comparison, *Wuthering Heights* (Goldwyn/United Artists, 1939) and *Les Misérables* (20th Century-Fox, 1935) deviated by thirty and forty-four percent, respectively.[27]

Selznick had not been opposed always to exploiting an adaptor's license by tampering more extensively with a literary source, as is indicated by his production of Tolstoy's *Anna Karenina* (1935) with Greta Garbo, to which Asheim assigned a deviational score of thirty-six percent.[28] However, it should be noted in contrast that Philip Dunne, who prepared the filmscripts for 20th Century-Fox of, among other titles, *The Count of Monte Cristo* (1934), *The Last of the Mohicans* (1936), and *How Green Was My Valley* (1941), estimated—with some exaggeration—that, in adapting less canonized literary material for the screen, it was this studio's practice to "discard something like 90 percent of what the [original] author wrote."[29]

Ethan Mordden surmised in *The Hollywood Studios* that "Selznick plumed himself on fidelity to text, not because so many readers demanded that their favorite novel be so honored—what lobby could Dickens claim?—but because Selznick believed that The Novelist is Right."[30] On the contrary, the producer believed that a novel's success was determined by the response of its readership and not simply by the efforts of its author—a conviction which he expressed to Howard in his comments of January 6, 1937, which address the latter's "Preliminary Notes." Selznick cautioned:

> I have learned to avoid trying to improve on success. One never knows what chemicals have gone to make something that has appealed to millions of people, and how much the balance would be offset by making changes that we in our innocence, or even in our ability, consider wrong.
>
> I am embarrassed to say this to you who have been so outstandingly successful in your adaptations, but I find myself a producer charged with re-creating the best-beloved book of our time, and I don't think any of us have tackled anything that is really comparable in the love that people have for it.

Nevertheless, Selznick suggested without hesitation the elimination from the filmscript of the character of Will Benteen, who marries Suellen O'Hara in the latter half of the novel and manages Tara in Scarlett's absence, in spite of Benteen's articulation of a major theme of Mitchell's novel in his homily over Gerald O'Hara's grave. Asheim noted that the characters and scenes that were chosen for dramatization in film adaptations exhibited a direct relationship to the principal romance depicted in the particular stories.[31] The central heterosexual romance's relevance to deployment of secondary narrative action was recognized also by David Bordwell in *The Classical Hollywood Cinema*.[32]

In agreement with this prevalent Hollywood attitude, Selznick proclaimed that Will Benteen "plays no part of importance in the story of Scarlett or in the story of Scarlett and Rhett; and I think that in weighing what characters go and what characters stay, those who do not play a vital part in the lives of our two leads or in their story, are those which must go first." The producer was more generous in his concern over the fate of the ex-convict Archie, who serves in the novel to escort Scarlett and other ladies in their carriages in Atlanta under Melanie's sponsorship during the unsettling period of Reconstruction. This character's peculiar humor may have reminded him of the comical driver Barkis in *David Copperfield* who was included as a minor character in the 1935 film. "I, too, would like to keep Archie," Selznick admitted to Howard, "although I frankly doubt we are going to have the room." He added that "this is the sort of character that certainly we should fight to keep, but before we get through I am afraid that we are going to have to make many sacrifices of this kind." Accordingly, Archie does not appear in any of Howard's filmscripts.

In his comments to Howard of January 6, 1937, Selznick also expressed concern over the element of slavery in the story, although what worried him more than depicting enforced servitude was acknowledging characters' racism. "I personally feel quite strongly that we should cut out the [Ku Klux] Klan entirely," he wrote Howard, adding that "there is nothing in the story that necessarily needs the Klan." With respect to the vigilantism against the predominantly black inhabitants of Shantytown following the assault upon Scarlett by two of its vagrants, Selznick cautioned against identification with the KKK—contrary to what was written in the novel. "The revenge for the attempted attack can very easily be identified with what it is without their being members of the Klan," he rationalized. "A group of men can go out to 'get' the perpetrators of an attempted rape without having long white sheets over them and without having their membership in a society as a motive."

Problems with Howard's Initial Screenplay and Its First Revision

"It is obvious that some radical amputation of book material will be obligatory," Howard conceded to Selznick in his letter of February 12, 1937 which accompanied the draft of a 250-page filmscript. The screenwriter admitted indecision "on what to cut out or on how to cut it out." Because Howard felt that the "book itself is so unwieldy," revision was advised only of material already selected for inclusion in this first script. "What you are getting is *Gone with the Wind* reduced from a thousand to 250 pages," he explained and estimated that "weeding" of its abridged dialogue and of "dead wood" would eliminate another fifty pages; "then you and I use the axe and I sew up the wound," added Howard, who explained that his original draft of *Arrowsmith* was equal in length to the filmscript of *Gone with the Wind* initially submitted to Selznick and that much revision of the former work had followed in the company of the novelist.

The common misconception that Howard's initial filmscript was 400 pages in length and corresponded to a running time on the screen of six hours has plagued many of the publications documenting the production of this film. The earliest appearances of this claim are in Thomas's biography of Selznick ("Howard's labors brought forth a mountainous script that would have required five and a half hours to unreel on the screen"), in Lambert's *GWTW* ("[Howard's original filmscript] was over four hundred pages long, almost six hours' running time on the screen"), and in Flamini's *Scarlett, Rhett, and a Cast of Thousands* ("Howard produced a first draft from the 1037-page novel. Despite massive cutting, it was a tome of 400 pages which would have run on the screen for over six hours."). This error continued to inform subsequently published works, such as the monograph by Bridges and Boodman, and Bartel's *The Complete "Gone with the Wind" Trivia Book*. Despite having access to the Selznick collection in his research for his book *Showman*, Thomson himself could not resist the influence of this legend, claiming that "by mid-February [1937] David had the script: 400 pages of it, enough for six and a half hours." He added, "Of course, that was too much, even making the book as two movies."[33]

This misconception is hardly trivial because the claim of a 400-page filmscript supports the erroneous thesis that both Howard and Selznick were overwhelmed by the magnitude of Mitchell's text and that they were unable to shorten the narrative in any organized fashion. In fact, the threat of excessive duration was posed less by the length of Howard's adaptation than it was by Cukor's predicted pacing of the acting. This film's editor, Hal Kern, estimated that the screenplay submitted to him by Selznick in 1938—which conformed to the version completed by Howard at the end of the previous year—would require about 26,000 feet of film or approximately four hours and twenty minutes (Kern's figure exceeds the length of the revised, released film by as much as forty minutes). "MGM's estimate was 29,000 feet [approximately half an hour longer than Kern's estimate and over an hour longer than the completed film], and David asked me why theirs was so different from ours," Kern reported. "I had to tell him that they were timing at what they knew to be Cukor's tempo, which was invariably slower than most."[34]

Howard's attitude in his undertaking of this picture's scenario was consistent with that expressed in his essay on screenwriting in *We Make the Movies*, an anthology of articles written by leading figures of the American film industry in 1937 concerning their own professional roles. "The screenwriter's task is really a job of adaptation hack writing, cut to the dimensions of the director's demands," and "the process by which the screen adaptor goes to work is in itself designed to cancel out inspiration," Howard himself lamented in its pages.[35] Nevertheless, unlike the more elite sources of many of his previous adaptations, Mitchell's novel tested this literate professional's tolerance. According to his "Preliminary Notes," what irritated Howard most about *Gone with the Wind* was a fault which he attributed to the novelist: "Scarlett bores me stiff after she marries Rhett," he remarked. "She turns into Fran Dodsworth, that is to say, a greedy woman whose only activity is being stupid about the sympathetic characters."

Howard's initial draft of 368 shots followed the story line of the principal characters with minor alteration. In general, the dialogue was not reproduced verbatim but was either paraphrased or invented to serve several original scenes. An example of a paraphrase is Ashley's remark to Scarlett in the library at Twelve Oaks, which in the filmscript reads, "Marriage isn't for people as different as you and I," and which reflects two statements made by him in the original scene in the novel—specifically, "Love isn't enough to make a successful marriage when two people are as different as we are"; and, "Can't I make you see that a marriage can't go on in any sort of peace unless the two people are alike?" An example of the invention of dialogue occurs in the scene that was fabricated involving the characters of Rhett Butler and Belle Watling, who were to be pictured together in public, seated in the prostitute's wagon and observing Scarlett's first arrival in Atlanta; asked by Belle whether he recognized the newcomer, Rhett was to reply simply that they had "never met officially," after which Belle was to rejoin, "Then I don't have to worry on her account."

Generally, most scenes were exploited neither for their spectacle nor for their dramatic potential. Instead, Howard abbreviated many of the conventions of the stage in the interest of condensing the novel's narrative to an acceptably short film length. "It does not matter how excellent a picture may be," he professed in *We Make the Movies*, "it is, in my opinion, too long if it runs beyond an hour and a half."[36] Thus, one of the results was that much of the novel's climactic episode of Scarlett's escape from an evacuated and burning Atlanta on the eve of its invasion was not chosen by Howard for dramatization.

Missing also from Howard's first filmscript is the scene of Ashley's returning to Melanie's arms after the war, before the eyes of Scarlett, who, in the novel, is restrained by Will Benteen from interrupting their embrace; this reunion was omitted entirely from the original screenplay, Howard electing instead to have Scarlett merely recount the news of Ashley's return during the writing of a letter to Aunt Pitty, in which the end of the war also is mentioned. Similarly, the scene in the novel in which Melanie unwittingly aids Scarlett's adulterous scheme by pleading with Ashley to accept the offer of partnership in Atlanta and not to move his family to New York was removed and replaced by Scarlett's informing Frank Kennedy that she has telegraphed the proposal to Ashley at Tara; "We'll make out, Ashley and I—you see if we don't!" she announces, indifferent to her husband's feelings.

While his low personal opinion of the novel inhibited exploitation of much dramatic material, Howard stooped to invent several scenes of vulgar melodrama. For example, Rhett proposes to Scarlett immediately after informing her of her second husband's death; thus, Howard robbed her of the delightfully selfish admission at a more appropriate moment later in the novel that she will agree to marry Butler in good part because of his money. In another scene, Rhett is allowed to overhear a tête-à-tête between Scarlett and Ashley, during which criticism of her husband's conduct is audible; afterward, the inveterate eavesdropper privately suffers an emotional breakdown, yet steels himself sufficiently during the following scene in which Scarlett refuses him conjugal rights. Although the miscarriage of the Butlers' second child is omitted, Rhett's sexual assault on Scarlett and her grateful summons to him from her pillow the following morning ("Rhett! Rhett, darling! Wake up, Rhett! It's your bride calling!" she cries in Howard's version) is followed by Butler's unrepentant confession of his having left their bed to enter that of Belle for more wanton purposes. This declaration precedes the accidental death of their daughter, "Bonnie," suggesting that the child's demise was justified eminently by her parents' conduct.

One of Howard's other inventions was that Scarlett does not sell her half of the milling business to Ashley, as she does in the novel, goaded by Rhett; instead, she offers it to Wilkes as a gift in observance of his birthday. After her departure from Ashley's office following her presentation of the gift and an embrace that is criminally interpreted by his spinster sister, India, Scarlett is shown cowering in her bedchamber, while India is seen condemning Butler's wife as an adultress before others in Atlanta; both shots are prescribed for melodramatic alternation. It is worth noting also that with the omission by Howard of Johnnie Gallegher, the manager of Scarlett's second sawmill, Ashley's business acumen is never questioned, whereas in the novel he is portrayed as one who can barely break even, while his less scrupulous rival prospers.

Scarlett appears more susceptible to stereotypical feminine weakness in Howard's first screenplay, in which she faints upon learning from her father of her mother's death. Gerald himself does not appear to die from drinking and riding, as he does in the novel—possibly as a solution to the omission of Will Benteen from the script, so that Benteen's homily and his concomitant apology for O'Hara's irrational behavior were no longer necessary; instead, Howard allowed the paterfamilias simply to fade away from the script after suffering a brief delirium at the dinner table. Charles Hamilton also was granted a dignified demise. In the filmscript, a series of dissolves was designed to lead from the wedding ceremonies of Scarlett and Charles and Melanie and Ashley to tearful farewells at the train station and to Charles's expiring in Ashley's arms from a fatal battle wound; shots were to follow of Scarlett unhappily being fitted for a black widow's habit and finding herself to be the mother of an unwanted son. In the novel, Charles less heroically succumbs to pneumonia following a case of the measles contracted in a camp far from the enemy lines.

Scarlett's dramatic oath is made in the novel after she returns to Twelve Oaks and views the sad remains of its destruction by the Yankees; in the filmscript, however, it is delivered at Tara. Howard also chose to employ it as part of this character's reaction to her shooting a marauder and appropriating his wallet and horse. After defiantly proclaiming lines which ultimately are heard immediately before the film's intermission—and which to most viewers epitomize Scarlett's spirit ("As God is my witness, the Yankees aren't going to lick me! I'm going to live through this and when it's all over I'm never going to be hungry again! No, nor any of my folks! As God is my witness!")—and while dragging the corpse of the vanquished trespasser out the door, she adds with comic irony in Howard's first draft, "And he [*sic*] certainly has His own way of providing." Less dramatically, in the filmscript Rhett does not conclude his marriage with Scarlett with the remark, "My dear, I don't give a damn," as he does at the end of the novel; instead, undoubtedly in fear of the censorious Production Code Administration (PCA), Howard has him confessing, "I wish I cared. But I don't."

Kitsch and high camp were part and parcel

of Howard's earliest conception of the filmscript. Given his association with the *New Republic* as a contributor, the screenwriter was aware of its criticism of Mitchell's novel (literary editor Malcolm Cowley complained in the September 15, 1936 issue that "*Gone with the Wind* is an encyclopedia of the plantation legend . . . false in part and silly in part and vicious in its general effect on southern life today"), and likely shared many of these negative opinions.[37] This bias may be apparent in his choice to employ the most hackneyed imagery in settings. Although Howard allowed that Tara should be constructed "only partly in the Neo-Grecque [i.e., neo-classical] style, for it has been added to haphazard," he recommended giving the mansion "all the charm required to satisfy the old plantation legend." More grandly, Twelve Oaks was to be "monumentally placed on a hill top," and Howard suggested that the structure should be "monumental according to the stateliest classic architectural manner," contrary to the more ordinary and historically acceptable form envisioned by Margaret Mitchell. An establishing shot of slavery at Tara was described as follows: "All the elements of homeward bound labor are united, singing, in the avenue of cedars which approaches the house"; and of the music itself to be selected for this scene, Howard recommended a bromide of "either some traditional negro melody or the Stephen Foster song, 'My Old Kentucky Home.' "

"My single object is to put the book roughly into picture form, sequence by sequence and scene by scene, including in it as many picture ideas as may occur to me, but making no particular effort towards a finished script," Howard admitted in *We Make the Movies*. "I proceed therefore on the theory that the sooner the first draft is on paper the sooner the real work will begin." He also advised that "it is not well to put too much of one's heart into this first draft."[38] Script pages were reduced to 197 numbered sheets in the revision of April 12, 1937, although these were supplemented by enough inserts on yellow-tinted paper to increase the total to 290 pages. While these optional scenes were not believed by Howard to be "absolutely essential to the screening of the picture," they were considered to be desirable if the film was to be presented in two parts—a possibility that Selznick had begun to consider.

Howard himself admitted that "the script as written treats the portion of the story which follows the return to Tara too briefly to carry conviction." At this time, the screenwriter invented a new context for Gerald O'Hara's death, placing his fatal fall from the saddle during the angry pursuit of Jonas Wilkerson and a tax collector who threaten to foreclose on Tara. Will Benteen was returned to the filmscript in the appended pages in order that an abridged version of the graveside homily—and the book's theme—might be presented.

"I feel that my sticking so closely to the Scarlett-Rhett story has robbed the book of a lot of historical size," Howard lamented specifically. Nevertheless, a most unusual invention that contributed to this revision was a montage of comical vignettes in which this couple's honeymoon travels were extended to include Rome, Venice, and Paris. Fabricated for these were such comments from Scarlett as—spoken in a carriage outside the Vatican—"I know I was brought up to be religious, Rhett, but I don't find churches as much fun as I used to." In a box at the Paris Opera, she exclaims, "Fiddle-dee-dee! If I don't like the music why shouldn't I talk? And if you really want me to love you you'll take me back to Atlanta and give me a chance to show all the old folks."

Howard wrote to Mitchell on June 5, 1937,

"I had planned—during the period when I was fool enough to believe that my work on your book would have been finished when my contract said—to drop in on you with all that behind both of us." Apparently, the screenwriter had been satisfied with his part to this date. "As you know, none of those connected with the picture has yet got down to brass tacks," he continued, and informed her that he was returning to the studio that July for revisions in order to complete the script to Selznick's satisfaction, and also that he would be collaborating with both producer and director at this time.[39]

Friendly correspondence had developed between novelist and screenwriter, and both enjoyed swapping skeptical remarks on the subject of Selznick's desire to adapt the book as faithfully as possible. Without doubt, Howard was impressed favorably by Mitchell's having been awarded the Pulitzer Prize for fiction in May 1937, and Mitchell may have been surprised equally to see Howard's photograph on the cover of *Time* magazine the following month (see Figure 3). "He is one of the most effectively organized workmen now making a living in the entertainment business," the magazine reported, "[and] his incisive mind likes to condense rambling yarns like *Dodsworth* . . . and *Gone with the Wind*." His working schedule in Hollywood that spring (during the period of the filmscript's first revision) was described as "characteristically methodical" by the article, which, most flatteringly, concluded that, "if Nobel Prizeman Eugene O'Neill . . . is posterity's playwright, if Maxwell Anderson is a poet's playwright, Sidney Howard is a playwright's playwright [because] common sense and order govern his muse."[40]

"I know so little about the movies that I thought the script was already finished," the novelist confessed in a letter to the screenwriter on June 9, 1937. Mitchell was referring to the manuscript that had lain visibly on George Cukor's desk during his visit to Atlanta that April, and which she herself reputedly had avoided asking to examine. Nevertheless, she appeared to be hungry for news of the film project. "Picture scripts are written and later rewritten in collaboration with the director who has, after all, to make the picture," Howard responded on June 14. "The script of *Gone with the Wind* is written but not yet re-written."[41]

This advanced stage of "pre-production" to which Howard was referring began shortly afterward, when Cukor was enlisted for filmscript revision. (Cukor had visited Howard briefly at the writer's farm in the Berkshires but, according to biographer Patrick McGilligan, had neither read nor remembered to bring a copy of the novel for discussion.)[42] "Cukor, Howard, and I have been spending practically every day—starting sometime between nine and ten and running sometime between twelve-thirty and one-thirty—on the script of the picture," Selznick wrote on July 29, 1937. "This will persist for some weeks, as will the hours in the afternoon that Cukor spends with Howard on the details of the script." At the same time, Selznick began to consider creation of the role of "production designer" and assignment of William Cameron Menzies to this new position; as originally envisioned, Menzies' duties were to include his complete "storyboarding" of the screenplay and supervision of the film's art direction, special effects, and color cinematography.

FIG. 3. Sidney Howard on cover of *Time*, June 7, 1937.
(Reproduced with permission by Time, Inc.)

Criticism from the Production Code Administration and More Revision

The significant changes in Howard's second filmscript revision, dated August 24, 1937, and composed of 460 shots on 239 numbered pages, involve action during the film's second half. The Butlers' honeymoon was returned to the States in this version, and scenes of the couple's nuptials in New Orleans, of their return to Atlanta and to the building of an ostentatious Victorian mansion, and of their failure to integrate themselves into traditional southern society (several members of which are represented reacting with "disdain" during the housewarming party) were to be presented in quick succession as a series of shots directed by Slavko Vorkapich (Hollywood's leading specialist of this form of montage sequence). Tastefully, Howard no longer hurried Rhett into proposing matrimony to Scarlett in the same scene in which he informs her of her second husband's sudden death. Sadly, Gerald O'Hara's burial does not include the graveside homily by Will Benteen because of the latter character's removal from the filmscript.

Instead of Benteen, it is Mammy who serves to restrain Scarlett from interfering with Melanie and Ashley's embraces during their reunion after the war, telling her, with an approximation of Benteen's words, "He's her husban', ain' he?" When Ashley visits privately with Scarlett afterward, he also delivers the tax bill due on Tara which was received from "our friend Wilkerson" and on which were to be written legibly "Third Notice" and "$300," for presentation in separate inserts or close shots. Scarlett brazenly returns to Tara to write the check for the tax payment in the presence of her sister, Suellen, to whom Frank Kennedy originally had been affianced, and afterward offers Ashley a partnership in the sawmill enterprise in Atlanta. Less complexly, Rhett was no longer involved in Scarlett's acquisition of the latter property and so was not betrayed by her offer of partnership to Wilkes, which was contrary to the conditions of Butler's instrumental loan to her for its purchase in the novel.

The description of Rhett's angry rape of his wife following India's accusation of Scarlett's infidelity with Ashley is unusually suggestive for motion pictures of this period and was written likely on Selznick's request; he may have hoped that his ultimately agreeing to omit these planted scenes from the shooting script might increase his bargaining power with the censors and allow the retention of less objectionable but more important adult material. (In contrast with the scene in the following passage, it should be remembered that more understatement was employed for this part of the film as it was shot and released, in which Rhett is shown to mount the grand staircase while lifting his struggling wife in his arms and promising, "This is one night you're not turning me out.") The screenplay includes the following directions:

> The night lamp is burning on the table as Rhett enters with Scarlett. He drops her on the bed. She shrinks from him in terror. He looks at her for a moment and then, dropping on his knees beside the bed, reaches towards her and drags her to him. She fights him off with what strength she has left but can put up no defense against his power. His lips meet hers and she lies in his arms helpless. Fade out.

A far more graphically rendered scene is that of Melanie in labor. "I think it's coming now," cries Scarlett amid many flies and much perspiration, and a series of shots which soon follows is described in the screenplay as: "Melanie's knees draw up in agony . . . Scarlett's face is distorted with horror . . . Prissy's hands place scissors in Scarlett's hands . . . [and] Melanie has fainted." In the novel, Mitchell herself summarized Scarlett's perception of the episode as a "nightmare of screaming pain and ignorant midwifery" which included Prissy's misplacing the scissors, spilling the basin of water on the bed, and dropping the newborn baby.

On January 12, 1938, Franclien Macconnell offered a number of suggestions to Selznick on Howard's revision of August 24, including the advice to emphasize the animosity of the sibling rivalry between Scarlett and Suellen in order to assuage audience outrage over the fact that the former steals the latter's beau in a marriage of convenience during the second half of the story. More importantly, she recommended not omitting reference to the dream that haunts Scarlett through the course of the second half of the novel, because it provides a rare instance of Rhett's exhibiting tenderness toward his wife, when he wakens and comforts her after one of its occurrences; furthermore, Macconnell added, "in the end Scarlett realizes the meaning of it"—that is, that "it is not Ashley, but Rhett and the safe haven of his arms that she has been seeking." On the lighter side, concerning the scene in the library at Twelve Oaks when Rhett exposes his supine eavesdropping after Scarlett has hurled and broken porcelain in angry reaction to Ashley's rejection of her declaration of love, Macconnell expressed regret over the "omission of Rhett's line, spoken from the depths of the sofa, 'This is too much.' . . ." (Rhett's response was rewritten much later.)

"Some spirit of madness moved Selznick to load the kit and kaboodle on a private car and bring them East to work with me here," Howard wrote Mitchell on October 7, 1937, while rehearsing his play, *The Ghost of Yankee Doodle Dandy*.[43] Selznick had invited Howard and Cukor to join him in a discussion with Joseph Breen, director of the PCA, concerning candidacy of scenes in the script for revision and censorship. Afterward, on October 14, Selznick received a seven-page letter from Breen listing objections to portions of the script of August 24, "all of which . . . may . . . easily be changed in order to bring the basic story into conformity with the Production Code." In particular, Breen demanded:

> There ought to be at no time *any suggestion of rape*—or the struggles suggestive of rape; Rhett should *not* be so definitively characterized as an immoral, or adulterous, man; the long scenes of childbirth should be toned down *considerably*; Scarlett should *not* offer her body to Rhett in the scene in prison; and the character of Belle should *not* definitively suggest a prostitute. [Breen's emphasis]

The association known as Motion Picture Producers and Distributors of America (of which SIP was a member) required that a film's release be prohibited without issuance of a certificate of approval signed by Breen and bearing the seal of his office (which was sponsored by the film industry itself as a form of self-regulation). For twenty years following inauguration of Breen's directorship in 1933, deference to the Production Code was enforced, although the judgments of its office might be influenced by arbitration. An appeal from Selznick to Will Hays, president of the PCA (aka the "Hay's office"), and payment of a

$5,000 fine for violation of a Code provision were necessary in order to license the release of *Gone with the Wind* with the "damn" intact in Rhett's concluding utterance.

Concerning the filmscript of October 1937, Breen reminded Selznick of the "*very great importance*" of the deletion of "such action and dialogue which *throws emphasis upon the pain and suffering of childbirth*"; specifically, Breen demanded, "there should be no *moaning* or loud *crying*," and recommended that "these scenes of childbirth be cut to *an absolute minimum* in order merely to suggest Melanie's suffering." On Scarlett's proposition of prostitution to Rhett in order to raise the tax money due on Tara, Breen cautioned, "It might be that you could have her put forth the blunt suggestion to Rhett, 'Will you marry me?' "; he insisted that "*this is very important.*" During the scene in which Rhett confronts Scarlett following her appearance at Melanie's party amid rumors of an adulterous affair with Ashley, "there should be no suggestion here that Rhett is about to rape Scarlett." Apparently, Cukor had offered the censor assurances that the actor portraying Rhett would merely "take [the actress portraying Scarlett] in his arms, kiss her, and then gently start with her toward the bedroom." Nonetheless, the Code director reiterated, "It is our thought that you should *not* go so far as to throw her on the bed."

Breen also advised that neither Rhett, Ashley, nor Dr. Meade be presented as "*offensively drunk*" in the scenes in which they comically pretend to be inebriated in order to delude a Yankee captain into believing that rather than having participated, as Scarlett's avengers, in the raid on Shantytown following her assault by two of its vagrants, they were partying instead in Belle's house of prostitution. Furthermore, he suggested "the elimination of the word 'establishment' from Rhett's speech [i.e., 'Much as I regret to say it . . . we've all been together at an establishment conducted by a friend of mine and the captain's. A Mrs. Belle Watling . . .'], and the substitution, possibly, of 'refreshment parlor,' making the line read, 'We've all been together at a refreshment parlor.' In this same speech, we ask that you delete the expression, 'there were ladies . . .' " Breen also asked that the phrase "as God is my witness" be removed from Scarlett's oath and the filmscript—very likely because Howard's use of the marauder's violent death as background violated more than one of the Biblical Commandments.

Howard's final filmscript revision of 1937, dated November 27 and composed of 315 shots on 231 numbered pages, addressed many of these objections and reflects some of the suggested changes. Scarlett's defiant oath was eliminated altogether. Instead, after she has killed the Yankee scavenger and acquired his wallet and horse as spoils of war, "the triumph dies out of Scarlett's face as she backs through the door, the body dragging after her"; before a fade out, she simply remarks, "I reckon I must have changed since I came home." Another effect of Breen's objections was the alteration of the brief scene of Charles Hamilton's honeymoon with Scarlett (credited to William Cameron Menzies in the previous filmscript), in which the groom approaches the matrimonial bed in his dressing gown as Scarlett shakes in fear and protest under the sheets. In the November revision, Scarlett stares in "almost comic bewilderment" at Charles, who smiles "pathetically" at her and at his marching orders, which were to be arranged visibly on the bedside table for the camera's view and audience's amusement.

Reference to the Vorkapich montage of Scarlett's elopement with Rhett disappeared in this fourth filmscript and instead her in-laws in Atlanta were to be informed of the marriage by telegram, after which Mammy exclaims that "Miss Scarlett ain' nuthin' but a mule in horse harness. . . ." Decently, Ashley no longer complains to Scarlett privately of Rhett's behavior in the Butlers' new home. When Rhett visits the prostitute Belle Watling—who is described radiantly in the November revision as the "eternal Magdalene with a heart of gold"—he is reminded properly by her that there is still Bonnie's future of which to think; the insertion of Belle's observation that "the child's worth more than the mother" was calculated to appeal to the Catholic "Legion of Decency," which influenced the formation and enforcement of the Production Code. Afterward, Rhett is motivated to lecture Scarlett on their need to cultivate greater respectability for the children's sake. Not surprisingly, the passionate scene preceding the off-screen rape of Scarlett by Rhett was removed from the filmscript.

All shots of childbirth were deleted also. Still, inspired by a scene in the novel, the filmscript has Dr. Meade advising Scarlett to give Rhett another baby quickly in order to check her husband's dissipation following Bonnie's death; Howard also enlists Melanie to help coax Butler on this mission and to announce that she herself is pregnant with another child. An additional scene was invented in which Scarlett, wearing a nightdress, waits for Rhett to pass her open bedroom door on his drunken path to his private quarters; although she confesses her procreative intention upon his appearance, he remains too demoralized by Bonnie's death to comply and retreats to his bed, while Scarlett sobs alone in hers.

Influenced by Macconnell's comments on the previous script, in the November revision Howard introduced Scarlett's dream within the context of this character's conversation with Rhett when she awakens to his comforting arms after having suffered from the dream during their honeymoon. Selznick also asked Macconnell for comments on this revision. Her response addressed two important issues, one concerning the question of who was to manage Tara after Gerald O'Hara's death—in Scarlett and Ashley's absence and in lieu of Will Benteen, who had been removed from the script—and the other concerning proper identification of Jonas Wilkerson when this character arrives to announce his plan of acquiring Tara when taxes are not paid by the O'Haras.

With respect to the latter scene, Macconnell believed that Wilkerson should be identified as the vengeful former overseer of Tara, which he is in the novel, and not simply as an anonymous Yankee carpetbagger, as he appears in the earlier filmscripts. "Since his connection with Emmie Slattery [the daughter of the O'Haras' 'poor white trash' neighbors who had been responsible for spreading an infection to Scarlett's ministering mother with fatal results] has already been established in the script, there would be no harm in introducing the woman herself at that point, for her flashy smartness would offer a significant contrast to Scarlett's shabby, poverty-stricken attire," Macconnell suggested, and she advised that this comparison might illustrate "by implication" changes wrought by the Union's program of Reconstruction. "Gerald could enter [the] scene just in time to hear Wilkerson's threats and Scarlett's final outburst," she explained. "The intimation that he might lose Tara penetrates his bewildered brain and the scene logically paves the way for his death, as in the script."

Howard had written to Mitchell the day before completing the November 27 revision that Selznick, upon departing New York, had asked that the screenwriter return to California early the following year for further work on the filmscript. Sardonically, Howard confessed to the novelist that he was looking forward to this trip, "not only because I should hate like the devil to turn the job over to some other writer but because I am interested to see how much money a picture producer is willing to spend to pay men for not being allowed to earn their pay." Howard continually objected to Selznick's editorial role. Frustration also grew from the producer's insistence that fidelity to the novel be observed ("It's not a movie script," Howard complained elsewhere, "it's a transcription from the book"), although the author of the phrase "dramatizing by equivalent" refused to desist from invention in each of his submitted drafts.[44]

"Sidney and I have a terrific job on our hands," Selznick admitted to Cukor on February 25, 1938. "I am weighing every word and every line most carefully, and Sidney's ideas are, as usual, excellent." Nevertheless, the producer remained adamant on the necessity of the screenplay's faithfulness to the original narrative, and wrote:

> I am also double-checking against the book once more and substituting valuable lines wherever I can for ordinary lines in the script. We are also double-checking against our story department's notes on things that they missed from the book [i.e., Macconnell's comments]; on [Wilbur] Kurtz' notes [as the production's historical advisor, and one whom Mitchell had recommended]; on production notes; on Hal Kern's cutting suggestions [as film editor]; on research notes from a society that complains about inaccuracies; and on Hay's office notes.

It may be of questionable value to ask whether Selznick's attention to these details was obsessional or commendable for one in the position of an independent Hollywood motion-picture producer at this time, yet certainly it may be said that his insistence upon fidelity was extraordinary. "The ideal script, as far as I am concerned would be one that did not contain a single word of original dialogue, and that was 100 percent Margaret Mitchell, however much we juxtaposed it," he informed Macconnell on December 5, 1938, only five days before the fire sequence was filmed on the studio's lot. Because of Howard's temporary refusal to continue on this project, Selznick had begun to work with other writers. Having completed the screenplay of *Made for Each Other* (1939), Jo Swerling accompanied the producer on a trip to Bermuda in order to assist with revising the screenplay of *Gone with the Wind*. Dissatisfied, Selznick sought Oliver H. P. Garrett upon returning to the States and facing the beginning of the film's production phase, although his collaboration with this screenwriter would prove to be disappointing also. F. Scott Fitzgerald himself was loaned to Selznick in early January of the following year for three weeks' work remaining on his contract as a screenwriter with MGM. Recognizing that the "author of *The Great Gatsby* and *Tender is the Night* was required to use only dialogue that came from Margaret Mitchell's novel," biographer Matthew Bruccoli observed correctly that the most frequent comments recorded in this screenwriter's copy of the filmscript are "cut" and "book restored."[45]

"As start day drew nearer, the quantity of writers multiplied, and it was all the newcomer could do to digest the masses of material accumulated in the previous two years," David Thomson observed in reference to the many files of revised filmscript pages by different screenwriters that are preserved in Selznick's collection. "The panic was building and with it the desperate confidence that [Selznick] could do more and more."[46] Undoubtedly, fidelity allowed for this self-assurance. "Naturally, and unfortunately, and with great beatings of breasts and letting of blood, we have had to make a great many cuts of scenes which we all love, but this is forced on us by the limitation of the length of any motion picture," Selznick conceded to Mitchell on January 24, 1939—two days before the filming of scenes with principal players commenced. "In what remains, however, we have been as faithful as possible; and even when we have had to make transpositions and alterations we have usually been able to find lines out of the book." On January 25 he advised the chairman of his board of directors, "Jack" Whitney:

> Don't get panicky at the seemingly small amount of final revised script. There are great big gobs that will be transferred from either the Howard script or the Howard-Garrett script, and it is so clearly in my mind that I can tell you the picture from beginning to end, almost shot for shot.

Script Revision Continues Throughout the Film Production

Selznick knew that he could afford repeated investment in the script's revision because of the delay encountered in scheduling this film's production dates because of difficulties posed by casting. On October 1, 1938 he wrote Ed Sullivan, for publication in the latter's column in the *New York Daily News*,

> You have been in Hollywood enough to realize that players under contract to a studio cannot be secured by another studio just for the asking, even for such a project as *Gone with the Wind.* The public's choice clearly was Clark Gable for Rhett Butler. . . . But you must have a rough idea as to how willing MGM would be to give up Gable for a picture to be released by another company—and bear in mind that my company was under an exclusive contract with United Artists. Accordingly, the only way I could get him was to distribute the picture through MGM, and this meant I had to wait until my contract with United Artists had expired. . . . Therefore, *Gone with the Wind,* with Clark Gable as Rhett Butler, couldn't under any circumstances have been made one day sooner.

The result of his contract with United Artists was that Selznick undertook the making of nine other feature-length motion pictures during the production of this one epic film. Specifically, between the purchase of the screen rights to *Gone with the Wind* in 1936 and its release as a completed film in the final month of 1939, Selznick personally produced *The Garden of Allah* (1936), *A Star Is Born* (1937), *The Prisoner of Zenda* (1937), *Nothing*

Sacred (1937), *The Adventures of Tom Sawyer* (1938), *The Young in Heart* (1938), *Made for Each Other* (1939), *Intermezzo* (1939), and *Rebecca* (begun in 1939 but released in 1940), all of which were distributed by United Artists according to the terms of a contract which also provided for the release of *Little Lord Fauntleroy* in April 1936. Selznick's inability to cast an actress in the role of Scarlett until he was permitted to film *Gone with the Wind* inspired an extraordinary talent search which effectively maintained heightened publicity for the motion picture during its lengthy period of preparation.

Selznick did not wait for a final shooting script of *Gone with the Wind* before preparing its budget. Various indices produced from the novel by the SIP story department served as "blueprints" for planning as much as did Howard's revisions of the continuity script. In *David O. Selznick's Hollywood,* Ronald Haver recounted that, late in 1936,

> Barbara Keon, Selznick's script secretary, Lydia Schiller, and several of the other women in the office began breaking the novel down, indexing every major event and action, cross-indexing this for time periods, seasonal changes, the historical background, and then making separate indexes for characterizations, dialogue topics, character relationships, clothing, descriptions of interior and exterior sets, so that even before there was an official script, there were ten detailed reference scripts that could be used as guides in the extensive pre-production work that was obviously going to be necessary.

From these breakdowns and from budgets prepared by Jack Cosgrove (for special effects), Raymond Klune (for production management), Walter Plunkett (for costumes), and Lyle Wheeler (for sets), the figure that emerged was two and a half million dollars—or, as Haver observed, the "entire year's production budget for Selznick International."[47]

This same figure was cited in negotiations with MGM, which, on August 24, 1938, presented Selznick with its promise of the loan of Clark Gable for use in *Gone with the Wind* and of its underwriting as much as half of the estimated budget in exchange for the film's worldwide distribution rights and half of its gross revenue. Several months earlier, MGM had offered to buy the production outright for $900,000 with the understanding that Selznick would be retained as producer. Selznick also considered co-producing the film with Warner Bros., which had offered the services of three of its leading stars—Errol Flynn (for $100,000 less than Gable's salary), Bette Davis, and Olivia de Havilland—and an investment up to $2.1 million, together with a lower distribution fee. Executive autonomy, financial reward, star appeal, and studio values were primary factors in Selznick's decision to co-produce with MGM. Still, the filmmaking ran over budget before completion, and in order for the production to maintain its independence from the distributor, a loan was necessary of one and a quarter million dollars, which required a personal guarantee of repayment by John Hay Whitney and which was arranged through Attilio Giannini (who was a member of the SIP board of directors and represented both United Artists and the Bank of America).

Although Mitchell's correspondence with Howard abated with the latter's absence from the film project, her friendship with Susan Myrick (whom she had recommended to Selznick as a technical advisor and dialogue coach) continued to provide the novelist with "inside" information. "Your letter had a laugh in every line," Mitchell wrote Myrick characteristically on February 10, 1939. "I must admit some of my laughter was on the wry side—especially when you described Twelve Oaks," the novelist explained, ignorant of Howard's complicity in its design. "I had feared, of course, that it would end up looking like Grand Central Station, and your description confirms my worst apprehensions."[48]

Stories of the difficulty experienced by Selznick in reducing Mitchell's narrative to a practicable shooting script remained a favorite topic of discussion for both correspondents. "Sue, it does sound incredible that the script is not finished," Mitchell gibed. "I have an idea (and correct me if I'm wrong) that they are using Sidney Howard's script for the first part of the movie—and it followed (so I am told by Mr. Howard) the book closely."[49] Because the novelist had refused to look at the screenplay, she was unaware of problems in earlier versions. "Well, dearie, you got another thought [coming]," wrote Myrick on February 14 in a similar manner of jest. Declaring that the "Howard script is beautiful" and was "just the book in spirit, every inch," Myrick related that

> David [Selznick], himself, thinks HE is writing the script and tells poor Bobby Keon ["script girl"] and Stinko Garrett what to write. And they do the best they can with it, in their limited way . . . [The resulting] opus does follow the book in a fashion but it does such queer things.[50]

Oliver Garrett had developed a reputation as a collaborator and adaptor and was an old acquaintance of Selznick's, having participated as a member of the producer's wedding party in 1930. He had collaborated with Dudley Nichols on *The Hurricane* for producer Samuel Goldwyn and director John Ford in 1937 and had received co-credit with Joseph L. Mankiewicz as screenwriter of the Gable vehicle, *Manhattan Melodrama*, which Selznick produced for MGM in 1934. His approach to literary adaptation is characterized by his work with J. Grubb Alexander on *Moby Dick* (1930), with Benjamin Glazer on *A Farewell to Arms* (1932), and with Maurine Watkins on *The Story of Temple Drake* (1933; based upon William Faulkner's novel, *Sanctuary*)—films which demonstrate eccentric deference to cinematic norms and extensive alteration of literary sources. The original manuscripts of the two principal shooting scripts of *Gone with the Wind*, dated January 16, 1939, and February 27, 1939, credit both Sidney Howard and Oliver Garrett on the title pages.

Myrick also informed Mitchell on February 14 of the following scene:

> So George [Cukor] just told David he would not work any longer if the script was not better and he wanted the Howard script back. David told George he was a director, not an author, and he (David) was the producer and the judge of what is a good script (or words to that effect) and George said he was a director and a damn good one and he would not let his name go out over a lousy picture and if they didn't go back to the Howard script (he was willing to have them cut it down shorter) he, George, was through."[51]

Cukor's departure was announced to the press the same day. Haver acknowledged disputes over the film's script and "concept" as major reasons for this rift ("Selznick and Menzies had decided on a florid theatrical look and feel for the picture, while Cukor was minutely detailing his characters, an approach that Selznick felt did not catch 'the big feel, the scope and breadth of the production,' " he wrote) but also proposed Gable's displeasure with Cukor as a contributory factor.[52] In his biography of the director, Patrick McGilligan also posited Gable's homophobia as a primary reason (Cukor having been a homosexual who may have been privy to some bisexual activity in Gable's past).[53] "I'm going to beg you not to go into that bullshit about, 'What happened on *Gone with the Wind*?' " Cukor himself pleaded of an interviewer. "It's as though I asked you, 'What happened [in grade school] when your teacher sent you home? You peed your pants and you were sent home—now tell me the truth of it.' "[54]

Mitchell admitted amusement over the production's problems. "I hate to say 'I told you so' but there is no one but you to whom I can say it," she wrote Myrick on February 28, explaining:

> Before I signed the contract I told Katharine Brown and the other Selznickers assembled in the room they were making a great mistake, for the picture could not be made from that book. They all laughed. . . . They said it was a natural. . . . I said yes indeed and thank you, but I knew how that book was written. It had taken me ten years to weave it as tight as a silk pocket handkerchief. If one thread were broken or pulled, an ugly ravel would show clear through to the other side of the material. Yet they would have to cut for a script, and when they began cutting they would discover they had technical problems they had never dreamed about. . . . Now they have run into exactly the problem I foresaw. And may God have mercy on their souls.[55]

Selznick had written to Mitchell with another entreaty for assistance on January 24, shortly after principal filming had begun. "If you sympathize with our plight," he begged of her at the conclusion of his request, "I hope that if you still feel that you want to steer clear of the script you will at least understand and forgive my cry of distress." Mitchell again refused. "Have they got a script yet?" she queried Wilbur Kurtz on March 11. "As you can gather, I do get a great deal of fun out of this affair, and my greatest sense of enjoyment comes from a sense of thanksgiving that I have nothing to do with it and am not in Hollywood."[56]

In two of the books that Richard Harwell edited, the following seventeen writers and "tinkerers" (in alphabetical order) were credited with contributing to the assembly of the filmscript: John Balderston, F. Scott Fitzgerald, Michael Foster, Oliver Garrett, Ben Hecht, Sidney Howard, Barbara Keon, Wilbur Kurtz, Val Lewton, Charles MacArthur, John Lee Mahin, Edwin Justus Mayer, Winston Miller, Selznick himself, Donald Ogden Stewart, Jo Swerling, and John Van Druten.[57] Although it had become a common practice in Hollywood to exploit the talents of numerous individuals during the writing of a screenplay, the fact remains that this list of contributors is very lengthy—indeed, it is padded. Even without Bradbury Foote (a writer hired by MGM to prepare a script of *Gone with the Wind* with a "happy ending"), unassigned and uncreditable persons—namely, Keon, Kurtz, Lewton (Selznick's West Coast story editor), and Mac-

Arthur—account for almost a quarter of the names cited, and over half—namely, Balderston, Fitzgerald, Foote, Foster, Mahin, Mayer, Miller, Stewart, Swerling, and Van Druten—did not sustain more than tentative association with the preparation of the screenplay. Of the three screenwriters remaining (i.e., Garrett, Hecht, and Howard), Howard had unquestionably the longest tenure.

"In those days, the major studios operated on the principle that the more writers on a script, the better it was going to be. . . . It was not uncommon to have three, four, even six writers on a screenplay," observed I. A. L. Diamond, who began his career as a screenwriter in the 1940s and who later collaborated with Billy Wilder on several film productions, including *Some Like It Hot* (1959) and *The Apartment* (1960).[58] Donald Ogden Stewart, who contributed to the screenplays of *Dinner at Eight* and *The Prisoner of Zenda*, concurred that "producers had a theory that the more writers they had to work on scripts, the better the scripts would be."[59] An exceptional project for MGM, *The Wizard of Oz* (which completed its production ahead of *Gone with the Wind* in 1939 and was directed by Victor Fleming and at least three others) also reputedly employed the talents of ten to fourteen writers in the preparation of its script. (Fleming, who was Clark Gable's favorite director, was contracted for work on *Gone with the Wind* following Cukor's departure.)[60] John Lee Mahin, who worked on both pictures and has been described as Gable's favorite writer, claimed that screenwriters were treated as "factory boys" at MGM, which at one time maintained over one hundred writers under contract for purposes including collaboration and revision.[61]

Being ignorant of Hollywood's peccadillos, Mitchell confessed to Myrick on April 17, 1939 that the latter's letter of April 9, "which announced that Sidney Howard was back on the script, kept us [i.e., the novelist and her husband, John Marsh] laughing all day" and that "every time we thought of the history of the script and the full circle which has been made we laughed again." She added, "I would not be at all surprised to learn that the script of the sixteen other writers had been junked and Mr. Howard's original script put into production."[62] (Mitchell's count derived from Myrick, who, in her letter of April 9, had confessed, "I haven't the faintest idea how many folks that makes in all who have done the script. I lost count after the first ten and all I know is Howard is somewhere around the sixteenth, though he may be the twentieth." Harwell later claimed that Myrick "counted better than she thought.")[63] Although neither provide a figure for the number of screenwriters employed on the project, accounts of the script situation two months earlier by John Lee Mahin and Ben Hecht when they worked separately and consecutively as writers on the film project follow this same story line. "I said, 'For God's sake, let's go back to Margaret Mitchell's book and Sidney Howard's wonderful script,' " Mahin professed. "Sidney did the first script and then they'd brought in some people and they fooled around with it."[64] In his autobiography, *A Child of the Century*, Hecht offered a similar opinion—namely, that Howard's work was superior to the revisions undertaken prior to his own engagement. The stage of filmscript revision that had been endured by Hecht himself, sequestered as he had been for a week in his own apartment with Selznick and Fleming, was recounted more with humor than with credibility. According to him, the trio worked eighteen-to-twenty-hour shifts each day and subsisted on a diet of bananas and salted peanuts. Hecht also admitted that he had not read the novel and was confused by Selznick's attempts to relate its story. "I argued that surely in two years of preparation someone must have wrangled a workable plot out of Miss Mitchell's Ouidalike flight into the Civil War," he wrote, in mocking reference to *Gone with the Wind* and Marie Louise de la Ramée, the prolific Victorian-era English romance novelist who used the nom de plume Ouida. "After an hour of searching," Hecht continued, "a lone copy of Howard's work was run down in an old safe."[65]

Harwell objected that Hecht's account of the film's screenwriting is "so full of demonstrable untruths and exaggerations (as is the rest of that autobiography) that it should be heavily discounted." Specifically, this scholar observed that Hecht wrote fallaciously "of the difficulty of finding a copy of Howard's script discarded three years before, of toasting the 'dead craftsman' (seven months before Howard's untimely death in August 1939), etc., etc."[66] Selznick and Fleming reputedly collapsed at the end of the week, concluding the collaboration. "The wear and tear on me was less," Hecht claimed, "for I had been able to lie on the couch and half doze while the two darted about acting . . . David specializing in the parts of Scarlet [*sic*] and her drunken father and Vic playing Rhett Butler."[67]

Although Selznick had desired no further involvement with Howard following the latter's refusal to return to the project as requested in October 1938, the screenwriter was again on the payroll for five hundred dollars a day the following April. Material from this period includes another original honeymoon scene of the Butlers in Europe—now in Vienna. The setting of Bonnie's nightmare also changed from Atlanta to London. Because father and daughter are presented alone and far from their home in the States, the object of Butler's reprimands is no longer Scarlett—who is chastised by him in the novel for her lack of compassion—but an anonymous English nurse. This unhappy excursion is the only scene in the film to be played before a European backdrop.

A more significant contribution to the screenplay during this same period was the revision of the final scene of the film, which previously had concluded simply with Scarlett, abandoned on the threshold. The new version reads thus:

> From the last shot of Scarlett,
> Dissolve to:
> Ext. Tara—Day
>
> Scarlett standing in front of Tara, where she stood with her father at the beginning of the picture, and with Rhett at the end of the honeymoon. She is looking out over the land, and there may be singing, the ghosts of the negro voices of the old days. Over the singing, she hears three voices clearly: her father's, Ashley's, and Rhett's.
>
> *Gerald's voice*
> Land's the only thing in the world that lasts.
> *Ashley's voice*
> Something you love even better than me . . . Tara.
> *Rhett's voice*
> You get your strength from the red earth of Tara.
>
> She fills her lungs, and her head comes up, and she is able to face whatever the rest of her life may hold for her.

Selznick's influence may be perceived in the affirmative quality of this scene, which was developed further following Howard's final departure from the project. Consistent with the novel, the new ending transforms the story line from a tragedy, concluded by Scarlett's defense mechanism of "thinking about it tomorrow" because "tomorrow is another day," to a narrative with a sentimental plot, at the end of which one experiences awe or admiration for the protagonist rather than Aristotelian pity and fear. The effect is more an apotheosis than a catharsis. One is reminded also—even by the career of this fictional character—that Selznick's greatest gift, according to William Cameron Menzies, was an "ability to make people transcend themselves."[68]

The power of Selznick's influence also attracted criticism. In his biography of Mitchell, *Southern Daughter*, Darden Asbury Pyron argued that although Selznick sought fidelity to the novel and achieved it "to a remarkable degree," the adaptation is representative more of Hollywood than of the story. "Vivien Leigh was just too beautiful, and she played the role with too much intelligence," Pyron complained. "If Scarlett is courageous and indomitable, she is also coarse, vulgar, violent, mean-spirited, vengeful, and uncultured." He also observed that, with exception of the black parts, the film eliminated most characters of lower-class origins. "The net effect of Selznick's omissions confirms the themes he chose to celebrate—nostalgia for the innocent, lost world of the plantation South."[69]

Selznick has been faulted, too, for his picture's stereotypical treatment of Afro-Americans and its inadequate exposition of racial issues. "The film's most controversial aspect remains its portrayal of race relations," concluded Catherine Clinton in her review of this film in *Past Imperfect: History According to the Movies*. "*Gone with the Wind* may be the first plantation film to feature Afro-American characters who *don't* spontaneously burst into song, but the picture still reflects historian U. B. Phillip's 'plantation school' view of the Afro-American experience which portrayed happy-go-lucky 'darkies' loyal to benevolent masters."[70] In *Toms, Coons, Mulattoes, Mammies, and Bucks: An Interpretive History of Blacks in American Film*, Donald Bogle offered a fair assessment of this film's position. "The problem with Civil War spectacles has never been that they presented Negroes as slaves—for how else could they be depicted?—but that the films have humiliated and debased them far beyond the calling of the script," he observed and noted that "the really beautiful aspect of [*Gone with the Wind*] was not what was omitted but what was ultimately accomplished by the black actors who transformed their slaves into complex human beings."[71]

A special concern of other commentators remains the issue of Selznick's extensive involvement in the film's production. Negative comparisons of Selznick's role have been made with parts played by other producers in script development. Donald Ogden Stewart described Selznick as a "terribly overbearing person" who always insisted that the producer was "*right*, and you weren't supposed to argue with him"; in contrast, Stewart remarked, "Irving Thalberg never did that. Irving would try to help you, encourage you: 'No, this isn't it, try it again.' But David was a much more overriding sort of personality."[72]

Contradicting this testimony regarding Thalberg, however, are numerous instances of his ability to "bear down" during his active involvement in the story conferences for *Grand Hotel* (1932), which were described by Thomas Schatz. Transcripts of sessions between the producer, associate Paul Bern, and writer-director Edmund Goulding during the preparation of what was described as "perhaps the consummate expression of the MGM style during Thalberg's regime" document that "at some point in virtually every conference Thalberg would launch into detailed analysis, often running on for minutes at a time, laying out the entire story line or untangling some particular script problem." Thalberg asserted once over Goulding's objections, "Over my dead body you'll cut that scene," and Schatz observed that the "discussions became more direct and practical, the negotiations less congenial, and the general atmosphere more intense" the closer these sessions approached the film's production date.[73]

In a monograph on Goldwyn, Richard Griffith related how Sidney Howard had categorized motion-picture producers into two kinds: "the kind who clears a space in which his writers and directors can do their work, and the kind who tries to write the story himself on both the script and the directorial level."[74] Very likely, for Griffith these two categories referred, respectively, to Goldwyn and to Selznick. "For myself," Howard himself wrote in the essay for *We Make the Movies*, "I prefer the type which undertakes to produce, more or less, the picture the director and screenwriter have given him." Of the other type of executive, "of which there are too many examples," the screenwriter described a "producer who is neither director nor writer and would like to be both." Howard concluded that "his determination to get his picture script written and rewritten until it coincides exactly with his own conception is more than likely to choke out the last germs of spontaneity and life," and noted that the inability of this type of producer to value another's view "frequently leads him to engage a whole series of writers, both in collaboration and in sequence."[75]

It is important to note that the above remarks were published in 1937 following the course of the "Goldwyn touch" on adapting *Dodsworth* and thus date from very early in the planning stages of *Gone with the Wind*, when Howard served as the sole adaptor of Mitchell's novel. Goldwyn's contributions to the screenwriting of *Dodsworth* are worth recounting in detail in view both of Howard's subsequent experience with Selznick and of the legend which developed that Howard's original treatment of Mitchell's novel was superior to much of the filmscript's later revision by others, among whom Selznick has been cast as the principal bungler by most commentators.

Acting for Lewis, Howard originally offered Goldwyn the option on *Dodsworth* for a mere $20,000, which the producer declined. Afterward, Howard purchased the rights himself, but adapted the work first as a play, which opened to rave notices at New York's Schubert Theater in 1934, whereupon Goldwyn purchased the rights from the playwright for $160,000. "This way I buy a successful play, something already in dramatic form," the producer purportedly told Howard. "With this, I have more assurance of success and it's worth the extra money I pay."[76] A variation of this claim is cited by A. Scott Berg in *Goldwyn: A Biography* in a manner more characteristic of Goldwyn's own *parole*: "This way, I buy a successful play. Before it was just a novel."[77]

More ironic still is the story that Goldwyn remained unsatisfied with the property, which he believed should focus not on Dodsworth's retirement and marital difficulties in Europe but on work in the automobile industry, and thus Edward Chodorov was paid $50,000 to write a different screenplay. Chodorov eventually submitted a script that was not very different from the original; "Mr. Goldwyn," he himself tried to explain, "this isn't a story about automobiles." Not satisfied, the producer hired five other writers, who labored over the project another two years. "The expenditure was enormous," Chodorov recalled. "There must have been eight different drafts before [Goldwyn] realized that I was right, that you couldn't tamper with Sidney's play construction."[78] The film follows the original version for the most part, and Howard is credited as the screenwriter.

In his biography of the producer, Lawrence J. Epstein argued:

> In being dissatisfied with the Chodorov draft, Goldwyn was merely exercising his artistic conscience. As Goldwyn saw it though, the two years and the substantial sums of money paid out to five different rewrite men had not been wasted. To be dissatisfied and not to try seemed worse to him than the two years of additional effort which, as their result, justified the original effort as being the best possible adaptation of the original Lewis work.[79]

Howard's negative opinion of this process is surmised easily, and one may suspect also that the screenwriter later believed that Selznick exhibited tendencies similar to those of Goldwyn. Nevertheless, in view of the uneven success of Howard's initial screenplays of *Gone with the Wind*, a more reasonable conclusion than his is that Selznick was justified in reserving the right to "exercise" his own "artistic conscience" by demanding further revisions.

In summary, commentary on script development for *Gone with the Wind* has been surveyed in this chapter and, by comparing the novel, the initial screenplay, and numerous revisions, the record of a significant part of this film's making has been emended. In the process, Selznick's influence on the adaptation process is revealed to have been a major constructive force, and a more accurate account has been offered of the complexity of the collaboration involved in screenwriting.

Contrary to opinions expressed by this film's only credited screenwriter, it is apparent after an examination of his successive drafts that the novel had not been adapted adequately by Sidney Howard in the filmscript's earliest versions. Selznick was aware of defects in these scripts but valued Howard's literary cachet; by commissioning him repeatedly for further revisions, the producer hoped that this screenwriter might be influenced to create what was expected. This endeavor was compromised fundamentally because Selznick espoused fidelity to the original novel, whereas Howard sought to invent "equivalent" narrative and dialogue, whether appropriate or not. Other writers were enlisted when Howard temporarily withdrew from the project.

Overall, Selznick's "manipulative style" as producer assured that the drama and spectacle of Mitchell's novel were realized as much as possible. Toward this end, Selznick saw that the undertaking of the picture's shot compositions and continuity design by William Cameron Menzies followed closely upon the script's development. Without a doubt, the magnitude of this film's success is as much a testament to the producer's role in its making as it is to the authority of those elements that contributed to the novel's acclaim.

THREE

William Cameron Menzies and the "Script in Sketch Form"

The title *production designer* was invented by David O. Selznick in order to distinguish the contributions of William Cameron Menzies to *Gone with the Wind* from those of art director Lyle Wheeler. Very early in the planning stages, Menzies was charged with the complete "storyboarding" of the screenplay—an assignment that was without precedent for a major Hollywood film production at the time. In his introduction to *By Design*, a collection of interviews with motion picture production designers, Vincent LoBrutto encapsulates current opinions of Menzies' influence on film design and on *Gone with the Wind* thus:

> Menzies' contribution helped to expand the function of the art designer beyond the creation of sets and scenery to responsibility for the entire visualization of a motion picture. [Menzies'] detailed work incorporated color and style, structured each scene, and encompassed framing, composition and camera movement for each shot in the film.[1]

There is little doubt of Menzies' influence on the filming of *Gone with the Wind* with respect to his command of color and lighting, which is documented. The similarity between palettes employed in the preliminary artwork and the use of Technicolor in the picture is apparent also. Still, surviving drawings rarely jibe with corresponding shots and sequences. Because of script revision, storyboarding of *Gone with the Wind* remained a tentative exercise. The actual use of the majority of the drawings that have survived from this film's making (many of which feature architectural and/or spectacular backgrounds) was not as continuity designs but rather as preparatory work for set construction and for the use of miniatures and of special-effects cinematography. Moreover, because both the art director and the director of photography were subordinate to the production designer with respect to decisions concerning color, sets, and lighting, Selznick's supervision of Menzies' role ensured that the producer maintained control over the "look" of this picture.

Over two hundred watercolor and gouache drawings of various dimensions from this film's production are preserved in the Selznick collection in Austin. A great portion of this artwork delineates the continuity of a single episode—namely, the fire sequence—in which, with Rhett's help, Scarlett evacuates Atlanta the night before the Yankee invasion and narrowly escapes looters and incineration. The filming of this sequence formally inaugurated the production and required the staging of a great pyrotechnical spectacle. According to a Gallup poll of members of original audiences in North America, the fire sequence was identified at the time as the most memorable episode in the film.

These dramatic storyboard sketches are examined in this chapter in the light of other surviving production documents and are compared with the film and with prescriptions for shot compositions and continuity in the screenplay's successive versions. As in the previous chapter, use of this analysis is threefold: to correct the history of this film's making offered in previously published commentaries; to establish the critical importance of Selznick's role as producer; and to disclose both chaotic and creative aspects of his collaboration with the film technicians.

William Cameron Menzies and "Cinema Design"

The following description of recent filmmaking practice and of the production designer's contribution is provided in Elliot Stein's revision of Leon Barsacq's history of film design, *Caligari's Cabinet and Other Grand Illusions*:

> The production designer functions as a coordinator of the film's disparate components well before shooting starts. With all minor problems solved on paper, the director has more time to devote to the actors, and delays in shooting can be reduced by twenty-five percent. This presupposes that the producer, scriptwriter, director, production designer, and director of photography work together for at least a few weeks after the initial work on the scenario. . . . Starting from a series of drawings called continuity sketches . . . the production designer conceives the sets and the illustrators render the shooting script sequence by sequence.

It also was noted in this book that "American directors are now accustomed to this system of using an illustrated shooting script that they follow faithfully during shooting." Moreover, Menzies' work on *Gone with the Wind* was recognized as the "first official thoroughgoing job of production design, [which] . . . exceeded the usual scope of a studio art director."[2]

In the course of examining art direction and production design in their survey of these disciplines in *Film Comment*, Mary Corliss and Carlos Clarens professed that "every major art director acknowledges a debt to Menzies," whom they described as the "ubiquitous artist, dominating the world of art direction in Hollywood through the thirties and early forties." These authors also indicated that, "from Menzies on, the production designer had a hand in the dynamics of filmmaking."[3] According to Ted Haworth, an Academy Award winner who was introduced to Alfred Hitchcock by Menzies himself and who worked as art director on *Strangers on a Train* (1951), Menzies's honorary inclusion was considered by the membership of the art directors' union to be requisite to the development of their profession. "Menzies was not in the Society of Motion Picture Art Directors, and after *Gone with the Wind*, [this group] realized what an advantage it would be if they could get him to join," Haworth stated. "The minute that Bill joined, all of the art directors suddenly became production designers."[4] Boris Leven, who assisted Menzies early in his own career and later served as production designer of *Giant* (1956), *West Side Story* (1961), and *The Sound of Music* (1965), epitomized his mentor's influence on the definition of this new role when he stated that "the production designer's greatest contribution to the film is his creation of visual continuity, balance, and dramatic emphasis," and that "the rapport between the director and the production designer is the major factor on which the success of their efforts depends."[5]

Before Menzies was employed on *Gone with the Wind*, this Yale alumnus had distinguished himself as art director of Douglas Fairbanks's *Thief of Baghdad* (1924) and as the director of Alexander Korda's production of H. G. Wells's *Things to Come* (1936). Menzies' contributions to these films represent two stages of his development as a filmmaking artist—first, as a set decorator and art director in the 1920s, and then, beginning in the 1930s, as a film designer and director. In particular, they demonstrate an evolution from background design and set construction to responsibility for determining compositions, content, and continuity of shots. Both creative periods were recognized formally by the Academy of Motion Picture Arts and Sciences. As art director of *The Dove* (1927) and *Tempest* (1928), Menzies was the recipient in 1929 of the first Oscar awarded for best interior decoration, and he was rewarded also with a special award for the dramatic use of color in *Gone with the Wind* in 1940, when Lyle Wheeler was honored by an Academy Award for this film's sets.

Menzies' interest in the composition of film continuity as an art director was expressed as early as 1929 in a lecture entitled "Pictorial Beauty in the Photoplay," delivered at the University of Southern California. In it, he stated:

> As an art director, I am interested in the photoplay as a series of pictures—as a series of fixed and moving patterns—as a fluid composition, which is the product of the creative workers who collaborate in production. As soon as the writer commences work on the scenario, the composition of the picture begins. When the art director receives the finished scenario, he begins to transpose the written words into a series of mental pictures. As he reads, he visualizes as nearly as possible each change of scene, collecting in his mind the opportunities for interesting compositions.[6]

The working relationship that would allow development in the American film industry of the role that Menzies envisioned and that was inaugurated on *Gone with the Wind* under the title *production designer* was prescribed one year later by Paul Rotha in an essay in *Close Up*. "The incorporation of draftsmanship is of the greatest importance for the clarity and perfection of representing visual images in the shooting manuscript," Rotha declared. "I believe that not only should the scenario be written but [that it] should also be drawn."[7] The procedure to which filmmakers in Germany may have referred already as *Regiesitzungen*[8] is described by Rotha thus:

> I put forward the argument that three or four persons should have the organization of the shooting plan in their control. The scenarist, the director, the art director and the cameraman. Their work would proceed as follows: the selection of the theme by the scenarist or director and its treatment in narrative form. Then, the preparation of the shooting script during which the art director shall contribute diagrams and plans, with his special knowledge of sets and their construction for emphasis of content by distortion and illusion. Of these the cameraman shall suggest the movements and setups of his instrument, in accordance with the layout of the sets. Meanwhile, the art director shall, in conjunction with the director and scenarist, scatter the text (which is being composed) with small drawings of individual shots, showing proposed schemes of lighting, arrangement and contrast of masses, etc. The film manuscript will thus be the collective work of the four most prominent film technicians. Both pictorially and textually, *the scenario will indicate the exact course of events* in the studio, on exteriors and in the cutting room.[9]

Menzies' discourse on the making of motion pictures (in the "pictorial beauty" lecture and also in his essay on cinema design, published the same year in *Theatre Arts Monthly*) was limited to the part played by his own professional role (the cooperation of producer, director, cinematographer, and screenwriter was implicit in his discussion); nonetheless, his espousal of the same collaborative spirit and aptitude for drawing shot compositions in the interest of predetermining camera views and découpage (the successive shots comprising a scene's presentation) exemplifies the contributions of the art director in Rotha's scheme.[10] In fact, Menzies' use of storyboarding for the planning of a motion picture and the praise that he received for it in *Creative Art* in 1929 antedate Rotha's description of this same method.[11]

According to a profile by Ezra Goodman of the production designer published in *American Cinematographer* in 1945, the first use of Menzies' continuity sketches in the planning of a motion picture was during his engagement as art director of Samuel Goldwyn's production of *Bulldog Drummond* (1929), the screenplay for which was Sidney Howard's first adaptation of a popular work of literature. "For this picture [Menzies] established the technique of doing a complete layout of every camera setup," Goodman reported, and also noted that although between 1,200 and 1,400 drawings were produced for the average motion picture on which Menzies was employed, 2,500 were drawn for his grand design of *Gone with the Wind*. Goodman wrote:

> There is a sketch for every individual camera setup that will be seen in the finished film. Working from the script, he first draws numerous thumbnail sketches that indicate the lighting and pattern of a scene broken into its component elements. For key scenes he will do a big sketch in detail. If these could be skimmed rapidly before the eye they would add up to a sort of preview of the motion picture in question.

The article concluded, nonetheless, with admissions that "it was impossible to plan everything on paper" and that very often "alternate sketches will be produced to cope with conditions during shooting, and the final result will be a compilation of a number of ideas that are cemented on the set."[12]

Production Design and "Blueprinting" of *Gone with the Wind*

The idea that Menzies might undertake the visual design of *Gone with the Wind* was broached by Selznick to his general manager Henry Ginsberg in correspondence on July 29, 1937. Menzies had assisted Lyle Wheeler with a portion of the art direction of *The Adventures of Tom Sawyer* and had impressed the producer by his sketches for this film's "cave" sequence, as well as by his collaboration with special-effects director Jack Cosgrove. Selznick quickly recognized the value of Menzies' exploitation of Cosgrove's technical expertise in realizing dramatic shot designs, and told Ginsberg:

> I feel that some one man, and this man obviously Menzies, should be charged with the physical responsibilities of the creative side of the picture at this time. I am further hopeful that he will be able to do a broken-down sketch script of the entire production, which I am certain would prove of enormous value to Cukor, who would welcome this guidance and assistance more than any other director I know. If we carry out this sketch script idea fully we should be able to save an enormous fortune in shooting time alone, and just that much more if the picture should be in Technicolor.

Selznick envisioned Menzies' duties as being extensive, and stated:

> I should like to see him actively take charge of the physical preparation of *Gone with the Wind*, including advance work on the sets, handling and selection of location shots, process shots, etc.; layouts and effects, etc. for the mass action scenes; investigations and suggestions leading to the proper handling of the street sets without an inordinate expense; and a dozen other things leading to proper organization of the great and troublesome physical aspects of *Gone with the Wind*.

In fact, duties specified by Menzies' preliminary contract with SIP as early as June 5, 1937 included "supervisor of art department and special effects department and assistant to producer, with credit on the screen as 'assistant to producer.' "

In another letter to Ginsberg, dated August 12, Selznick again discussed Menzies' execution of a "complete cutting script with sketches from the first shot to the last on the entire job of *Gone with the Wind*." The producer confessed that this plan "may be the answer to what I have long sought for, which is a pre-cut picture and that with or without the help of Hal Kern, or some cutter specifically designated for the purpose, we might be able to cut a picture eighty percent on paper before we grind the cameras." The innovation in Selznick's conception of Menzies' role as designer of *Gone with the Wind* and of the undertaking of a "complete script in sketch form" was described also in the producer's letter to John Hay Whitney on September 1, 1937, in which he wrote:

> I hope to have *Gone with the Wind* prepared almost down to the last camera angle before we start shooting, because on this picture really thorough preparations will save hundreds of thousands of dollars. When [Menzies] gets the complete script, he can then do all the sets, sketches, and can start on what I want on this picture and what has only been done a few times in picture history (and these times mostly by Menzies)—a complete script in sketch form, showing the actual camera setups, lighting, etc. This is a mammoth job that Menzies will have to work on very closely with Cukor. In short, it is my plan to have the whole physical side of this picture . . . handled by one man who has little or nothing else to do—and that man, Menzies. Menzies may turn out to be one of the most valuable factors in properly producing this picture.

By December 15, 1937, Selznick admitted to being "completely sold" that Menzies was the man for this picture's design. "It would be my thought to have [Menzies] keep an eye on the art department, and particularly to be available for anything difficult [on other film projects]," the producer continued in his memorandum of this date to Ginsberg, "but I should prefer to have him free at least 90% of the time for *Gone with the Wind*." One month later, while Howard was concluding the final revision of his initial filmscript, Russell Birdwell drafted a press release announcing that Menzies had been delegated the job of "designing" the film—an assignment that the publicist described as the "most comprehensive task of its kind ever undertaken in motion pictures." According to the press release,

> Menzies . . . will place on paper, in watercolors, every scene in the screenplay, sequence by sequence—working in collaboration with Selznick, George Cukor who will direct the picture, and with Sidney Howard, on photographic conceptions of each scene. When this project is completed, the sketches will form an "art gallery preview" of the picture itself. The process might be called the "blueprinting" in advance of a motion picture. Chief value of the "designing," according to Menzies, is the saving of time and effort in actual production. Also, it is pointed out, the sketches afford a visual story plan, augmenting the typewritten descriptions of the script.

Shortly afterward, in a letter dictated to Cukor on February 25, 1938, Selznick proclaimed that he himself was "more enthusiastic than ever about the script" and would be "calling Menzies in to conferences practically each day so that by the time we finish the script, we will have almost all the physical production mapped out, as well." Selznick's employment of Menzies for the purpose of controlling Cukor's direction is suggested also in the producer's correspondence with his production designer later that same year on November 20. Selznick informed Menzies:

> It is my hope on *Gone with the Wind* that before we go into each sequence we will have a meeting at which you and Hal Kern and myself will lay out in detail the exact camera angles to be used in the sequence. Hopefully you will have ready for each of these meetings your ideas and Hal's, in sketch form, on the camera angles and the lighting, with any alternate ideas that may occur to either of you, the selection and decision by myself. After we have finally decided on these angles we will then meet with George to see if he has any different ideas.

In his biography of Cukor, Patrick McGilligan noted this director's deference to the suggestions of art directors. "It was they who would orchestrate the visual design, freeing Cukor to deal with the actors," claimed McGilligan. "Just as it became part of Cukor's mystique—though it was not so unusual among directors—that he rarely looked through a lens, so it was that the art director, with Cukor's blessing, often laid out the camera setups."[13] Cukor's interest was performance more than visual composition; his dependence on art directors for shot composition extended their duty as set designers and was said to have begun with Hobe Erwin on *Little Women* (the planning of which Selznick supervised as production chief of RKO before departing for MGM in 1933). Remarks by Gene Allen, an art director who collaborated later with Cukor for a period of at least eighteen years, support this generalization. "Before sets were even thought of, Cukor would have books of research done on every aspect of life in the time in question," Allen noted, and added that afterward the director "would leave the visualization with me . . . only checking it and offering occasional suggestions."[14]

Nevertheless, Cukor objected to use of the word *designing* in the publicity material promoting Menzies' role in the making of *Gone with the Wind* and instead suggested use of the term *drafting*, according to correspondence from Birdwell to Selznick on February 11, 1938. Authority was plainly an issue. "I do not think the word *drafting* is fair to Menzies," Selznick responded on February 14—one year to the day before Cukor departed from the production in great part in protest over insufficient authority on the shooting set. "This term in motion picture language means simply a draftsman working under an art director," the producer explained. "Menzies' task is a monumental one, and I am anxious that he receive a fair credit."

Cukor may have been annoyed also by the superiority of Menzies' role as production designer to Wheeler's as art director, as well as to Hobe Erwin's as the film's initial interior decorator. Erwin himself had agreed to act as a consultant during the production's preparatory phase without compensation (but with the guarantee of five thousand dollars for ten weeks' work once filming began) and had visited Atlanta with Cukor (who accepted four thousand dollars a week throughout the lengthy period of his employment on this picture) for purposes of research and publicity. Erwin ultimately relinquished this option and recommended Joseph Platt, a consultant for *House and Garden*, as his own replacement.

In much the same way in which supervising art directors functioned at other studios, Menzies delegated the responsibility of set construction and a great part of its design to the unit art director (Wheeler, in the case of *Gone with the Wind*), yet monitored the work of the art department and acted as liaison to Selznick, presenting items to the producer personally for discussion and approval. This working arrangement and division of labor between production designer and art director persists in the American film industry today, and those in both positions are represented now by the same union—the Society of Motion Picture and Television Art Directors. (Separate guilds exist for set designers and model makers, painters, and illustrators and matte artists.) "The title *art director* until recently designated the person now referred to as the *production designer*," explains David Draigh in his reference book, *Behind the Screen*. "Likewise, the art director used to be called the *set designer*," adds Draigh, who further relates that it is the art director's responsibility to organize the art department into an "efficient unit for accomplishing the design work . . . envisioned by the production designer."[15]

Film Authority and Storyboarding of *Gone with the Wind*

In contrast to the disorder that, according to most commentaries, has characterized the preparation of the filmscript of *Gone with the Wind*, the reputed order and integrity of this film's visual design have been accorded positive, legendary status. For example, Gavin Lambert observed a uniformity of style in scenes in *Gone with the Wind*, in spite of Selznick's employment of four or more directors.[16] Roland Flamini, too, noticed "no perceptible difference" between scenes in this film despite the succession of directors and cinematographers (Ernest Haller replaced Lee Garmes after Fleming succeeded Cukor as film director); moreover, Menzies' sketches were credited for this consistency. "Every day, working from Menzies' rough originals, his staff of young artists . . . turned out dozens of detailed shot-by-shot illustrations, not just of major scenes, but also of continuity sequences," Flamini recounted, adding that these drawings were the "blueprints on which each setup was based." He also wrote that "every camera angle, close-up shot, or picture composition was drawn, with the relevant lines of dialogue as captions"[17] (see Figures 4–8).

Similarly, in their survey of motion-picture designers in *Film Comment*, Mary Corliss and Carlos Clarens concurred that, in spite of the many film and technical directors employed, "visually [*Gone with the Wind*] never falters because Menzies drew a thousand small, perfectly composed sketches for the camera to follow—every shot on paper, even to the light effect," and it was posited that "the various egos submitted to Menzies' vision."[18] Likewise, in *The Art of Hollywood*, John Hambley and Patrick Downing claimed, "It is no exaggeration to say that Menzies was more responsible for the finished film than anyone else."[19] These

FIG. 4. Production designer William Cameron Menzies speaks with Clark Gable and Vivien Leigh on the shooting set. Among other responsibilities, Menzies was entrusted by Selznick with the task of creating a "complete script in sketch form" for this motion picture early in its production.

FIG. 5. Menzies (left) and art director Lyle Wheeler surveying the construction of sets on the studio's back lot.

FIG. 6. Special-effects director Jack Cosgrove (left) worked closely with Menzies on process shot compositions.

FIG. 7. Art director Lyle Wheeler poses with a large watercolor set design illustrating Scarlett and Gerald O'Hara standing before their plantation house, Tara.

judgments have informed other film histories. Tino Balio, in *Grand Design*, reiterated that "working directly from the book—since a screenplay had yet to be written—Menzies created a 'complete script in sketch form,' showing actual camera setups, lighting, etc." He added that "the directors who worked on the film followed his storyboards slavishly."[20]

Estimates of the number of continuity drawings produced for this motion picture have been great. In his biography of Selznick, Thomas reported that while "pioneering the field of production design, [Menzies] drew three thousand sketches of scenes, including every camera angle," and that "his visualizations were carried out by Lyle Wheeler who amassed thousands of drawings, photographs, and descriptions of the southern locales which figured in the story."[21] Lambert concurred that "Cameron Menzies, with Macmillan Johnson, [*sic*] created 3,000 sketches covering all the major scenes in the film."[22] Although this figure is five hundred more than that cited in *American Cinematographer* in 1945, it was derived from an article on the film's production which appeared in the *New York Times Magazine* on December 10, 1939—five days before the premiere in Atlanta. According to this article,

> Howard's script [was] worked over by the production designer, William Cameron Menzies, and Lyle Wheeler, the art director. As the scenes began to shape up verbally, [Menzies and Wheeler] commenced their series of 3,000 sketches, almost after the Disney technique, indicating background, camera angles, close-ups and long shots. These—like everything else in and about the picture—had to be approved by Selznick.[23]

The producer's influence on the film's appearance and narrative continuity extended from development of the filmscript through designs drawn by the art department, all of which were justified financially. As special-effects work was capable of limiting the number and dimensions of sets required for a production, it was important for economical reasons that the film presentation was visualized adequately—shot by shot in many instances—prior to any construction being undertaken. Selznick's desire to control the adaptation and appearance of *Gone with the Wind* and to manage a budget merged with the duties of art direction and of production design in this basic relationship. That Menzies was chosen to undertake the film's design reflected this scheme. This production designer's predilection for delineating continuity also made him a perfect foil for Selznick's deployment against a director's authority on the shooting set—a strategy which the producer inaugurated successfully on *Gone with the Wind* with the filming of the fire sequence in December 1938, yet conceived earlier during implementation of special-effects work for the cave sequence in *The Adventures of Tom Sawyer*.

Selznick wrote Ginsberg on August 12, 1937:

> I am confident that [Menzies] is going to have more than earned his salary for the initial period on the "cave" sequence in *Tom Sawyer*, not merely through what promises to be a brilliant result, but through the splendid and efficient manner in which he has laid out the cutting and continuity of this sequence, which should result in a saving in shooting time that will more than offset the additional cost of the set itself. Wheeler's inexperience, as against Menzies' very wide experience, was never better demonstrated than by their respective presentations of the cave sequence.

FIG. 8. Selznick, director Victor Fleming, and cinematographer Ernest Haller (left to right) examine artwork on set prior to filming a scene, while chief electrician James Potevin observes in the background. "Selznick personally supervised each detail in the making of the film," reads the accompanying caption provided by the publicity department.

Afterward, on August 19, the producer also declared to his general manager that "there is everything to be gained and little if anything to be lost by Menzies' starting just as soon as he is available on plans for the physical production of *Gone with the Wind*, including sketches for that group of sets which we know positively will be in the picture, and some of which are very complicated." In another letter to Ginsberg on January 31, 1938, Selznick advised that special-effects director Jack Cosgrove would be "of enormous value . . . on starting to work with Menzies on *Gone with the Wind* figuring out just what sections of sets he can save and just what effects he can give us that otherwise might be either unobtainable or too costly."

Nevertheless, a hidden agenda lay behind Selznick's fiscal concerns when his use of the art department extended from set construction and special-effects work to predetermining camera setups for most of this film's shots. "For years I have been trying in vain to get pictures camera-cut to a far greater degree than has generally been done," he related to Menzies in a memorandum dated November 20, 1938. "I have always felt that the shooting of two or three hundred thousand feet of film to secure an eight or nine thousand finished picture is, on the face of it, absurd." Selznick's expressed desire for more economical use of film stock was hypocritical considering his own reputation for ordering rewrites and retakes on film projects, yet these pronouncements illustrate his anxiety over Cukor's style of direction and pacing of scenes.

The producer further informed his production designer in this same memo that:

> On *Gone with the Wind* a more thorough camera-cutting becomes not merely desirable, but actually almost essential, if we are to bring the picture in at a cost that is not fabulous. This is particularly true because we will find that Cukor will probably eat up a great deal of film—and I need not go into the expense of Technicolor film—through the number of his takes, although I have already spoken several times to George about the necessity of his doing more rehearsal where desirable and shooting less takes, to hold down costs, and I intend to watch this very carefully and to go into it with George again and again if necessary.

A more conservative figure of the continuity sketches drawn for this film production than had been cited previously was professed by Ronald Haver, who reproduced numerous examples by Menzies and staff artists Dorothea Holt and J. McMillan Johnson of the "1,500 production sketches made to guide the director and cinematographer in obtaining the proper look and feel of *Gone with the Wind*." These include a storyboard that illustrates the fire sequence and is attributed to Menzies (see Figure 9). Haver claimed that his figure derived from an accounting of art-department reports, although extant records are hardly complete.[24]

Inventory of production designs became problematic after the film's release. "We have literally thousands of drawings of sets and camera setups," the producer informed MGM publicity director Howard Dietz, who was offered a "selection of a hundred or more of these" on November 11, 1939. "My thought is that there is no reason why every single good shop window in Atlanta without exception could not have one of these drawings," he added. Selznick also dictated the following message, on June 4, 1940, to Katharine Brown:

> As for the great number [of drawings] remaining, I wish you would check once more to see whether [MGM] wouldn't like to borrow these for exploitation. . . . It seems to me this is the very best exploitation material in the world and that it is a pity not to make use of it. . . . I don't want to be just "yessed" on it or told to send them along and that maybe they'll be able to make use of them, because I would rather distribute them among all the people who worked so hard on the picture than do this; but on the other hand, the company is entitled to their benefit for exploitation use if there still is a benefit.

The likelihood that MGM's response was positive is implied by an office memo dated September 6 of the following year, which documents that employees were "having a bad time locating the millions [*sic*] of *GWTW* sketches . . . which Mr. Selznick is sure he told someone to keep carefully" and that "the explanation seems to be that they were sent back and forth to New York, to Atlanta and to Australia (from where we didn't actually expect them back) so often that lots got lost enroute." (Today, no drawings of this kind are to be found in the MGM archives in Los Angeles.)

The value of Menzies' role as production designer was upheld by Selznick himself after the film's production. "I am giving him an ex-

FIG. 9. Seven unsigned gouache and watercolor drawings, five of which are stapled to a 20 × 30-inch paperboard base and are surmounted by two drawn on the base itself, illustrate shot compositions for the fire sequence and are attributed commonly to William Cameron Menzies.

traordinary credit on the screen," the producer admitted on October 23, 1939, during its editing. "But his contribution to the picture is, in my opinion, one of the greatest of all the many people who worked on it." On January 22, 1940, he wrote Frank Capra (who was serving as president of the Screen Directors Guild) that "Bill Menzies spent perhaps a year of his life in laying out camera angles, lighting effects, and other directorial contributions to *Gone with the Wind*, a large number of which are in the picture just as he designed them a year before Victor Fleming came on the film." (In a memo to MGM general manager Eddie Mannix dated October 17, 1939, and which was not sent, Selznick admitted having asked Fleming's opinion regarding acknowledgment of the directorial contributions of others in the form of a separate "card" in the film's credits. "Vic obviously, and no doubt understandably, wasn't happy about the idea," Selznick related.)

Film historians have acknowledged the unprecedented and extensive character of Menzies' assignment, but none have investigated the actual influence of storyboarding on the film's composition and direction, the degree to which continuity designs were faithful to or deviated from the novel and screenplays, or the practical importance of these drawings to set construction, special effects, and filming with and without the presence of the principal director. These inquiries are requisites for the proper evaluation of the contributions made to *Gone with the Wind* by the production designer—and by the artwork for which this figure is credited.

Reconstructing the Fire Sequence's "Script in Sketch Form"

The largest series of continuity designs preserved in the Selznick collection consists of sixty-six unsigned and undated gouache and watercolor sketches, of various dimensions, representing the fire sequence. The style of the majority of these drawings suggests they are the work of Joseph McMillan ("Mac") Johnson. The possibility that most of this artwork was produced by an art-department draftsman is supported by comparing the figures in these sketches with numerous others in Johnson's signed drawing of townspeople awaiting casualty lists outside the *Atlanta Examiner* building (see Figures 10–11). (Johnson was employed by Selznick during the following decade as the production designer of *Duel in the Sun* [1946] and *The Paradine Case* [1947]; he also served as art director of *Portrait of Jennie* [1948], and received an Academy Award for its special effects.) If the artwork is indeed that of an assistant rather than that of Menzies himself, its accurate attribution may call into question whether the credit previously granted to the production designer in terms of these sketches' composition and narrative continuity is justified. However, an equally defensible response may be—to borrow art historian S. J. Freedberg's remark on paintings attributed to Raphael but executed by others (notably, Giulio Romano and Gianfrancesco Penni) in this artist's workshop—that the *capomaestro* "is, so to speak, behind these works if he is not in them."[25]

Regardless of the agency involved in their physical creation, the fact remains that imagery in these drawings differs in many obvious ways from the fire sequence as presented in the film—a discrepancy which challenges claims of film authorship that are based on continuity design. In order to appreciate this artwork's value to the film production and, more specifically, to determine the degree of its contribution to shot composition and découpage (or continuity of shots), a survey is required of successive forms of this sequence's narrative—from the original novel through shooting scripts and "cutting continuities" (or editing transcripts). After this episode's development is charted, the drawings may be compared with these various versions in order to determine degrees of correspondence. This procedure will ascertain the period in the production during which the sketches were executed and the conditions and limitations of their influence.[26]

The evolution of the fire sequence as dramatized in Selznick's adaptation of *Gone with the Wind* may be categorized effectively into ten principal forms, following the chronology of script development surveyed in the previous chapter and drawn from the numerous documents preserved in the producer's collection.

1. The archetype of this scene is provided by the passage in Margaret Mitchell's novel, which was published in June 1936.[27]

2. The screen rights were purchased by Selznick International one month later, and the 1,037-page book was synopsized several times that year by Franclien Macconnell, an employee in Selznick's story department, in order to assist the producer and his staff in the early planning stages of the film's production.

3. Sidney Howard's initial screenplays were preceded by his lengthy notes and suggestions, written in December 1936, and by Selznick's response to these the following month. The first filmscript was completed in February 1937, and three revisions of this initial work were undertaken by Howard in April, August, and November of this same year.

4. An alternate script was offered in November 1938 by Bradbury Foote, a writer under contract with MGM.

5. An elaborate version of the fire sequence was prepared separately by Menzies this same month.

6. This scenario was revised by Oliver Garrett in time for the extensive burning of the studio's backlot on December 10, 1938, which was intended by production manager Raymond Klune, by Menzies, and by Wheeler to clear the way for the construction of accurate sets required for subsequent filming and to simulate the burning of Atlanta for spectacular background shots necessary for the presentation of the fire sequence. By January 16 of the following year—six weeks after this fiery event inaugurated the picture's production—Howard's script had been revised by Garrett, and the latter's revision of Menzies' episode was incorporated without significant alteration.

7. There also exists a "final shooting script," dated January 24, 1939, and credited solely to Sidney Howard, although the date inscribed on this version is suspect for several reasons, including the fact that there are numerous changes in the fire sequence which are not documented elsewhere until later that year (in July).

8. Conventional accounts of the film's production relate that Cukor was replaced as director after two weeks of "principal photography" in 1939. Among the reasons given for this director's departure is a disagreement between Cukor and Selznick over the shooting script, although many of the same sources recount that Cukor's successor, Victor Fleming, also demanded a new screenplay. This revision was undertaken by Ben Hecht in February 1939.

9. More detailed shooting scripts were written specifically for the fire sequence in June 1939, and post-production notes and "cutting continuities" (or editing transcripts) were made between July and November.

10. The completed version is documented by Hal Kern's "final cutting and dialogue continuity script" which was transcribed from the film in December 1939—the month of the picture's premiere.

The episode which Mitchell invented for the novel relates in four to five pages how, on the eve of the Yankee invasion, Rhett Butler escorts Scarlett, her infant son Wade, and servant Prissy from Atlanta in a stolen wagon, together with Melanie Wilkes, prostrate in the back with her newborn. The fire is caused not by Union bombardment but by the Confederates' decision to explode their own munition trains in the railyard rather than risk their

FIG. 10. A 24 × 36-inch gouache and watercolor drawing on paperboard, depicting townspeople awaiting casualty lists outside the *Atlanta Examiner* office building, bears the signature of Joseph McMillan ("Mac") Johnson in the lower right-hand corner. Johnson was the studio art department employee who likely drew most or all of the drawings of the fire sequence preserved in the Selznick collection.

capture and use by the opposing force. Upon their departure from Aunt Pittypat's house on Peachtree Street, Rhett declares that they must hurry in order to pass the drunken mob on Decatur Street and the fire on Marietta Street; he also offers Scarlett his pistol, which she declines because she is armed already with one that had belonged to her dead husband. Their wagon pauses before retreating rebel troops, and Scarlett and Rhett observe a young, traumatized soldier who collapses and is carried by an older comrade. They next drive through a "tunnel of fire" created by buildings burning on both sides of the passage that delivers them through a maze-like series of side streets from the city and its fire.

Characterized by Mitchell initially as "decadent" and sardonic, Rhett is impressed by the display of the ragged troops and is silently contemptuous of Scarlett's compliment afterward that he was not as foolish as those who joined the lost cause. He departs her company in the following pages to return to volunteer in the Confederate army. "Ask Rhett Butler now if the cause means anything to him," remarked Macconnell in her synopsis of the novel dated August 26, 1936, and she noted on October 26, 1936, in more detailed "chapter breakdown" analyses, that the "pitiful sight" of the ragged Confederate army in retreat "stirs in Rhett all the patriotism he has tried to suppress."

In contrast, Scarlett's concern remains one of mastering her own fear in her endeavor to return to her parents and the family plantation,

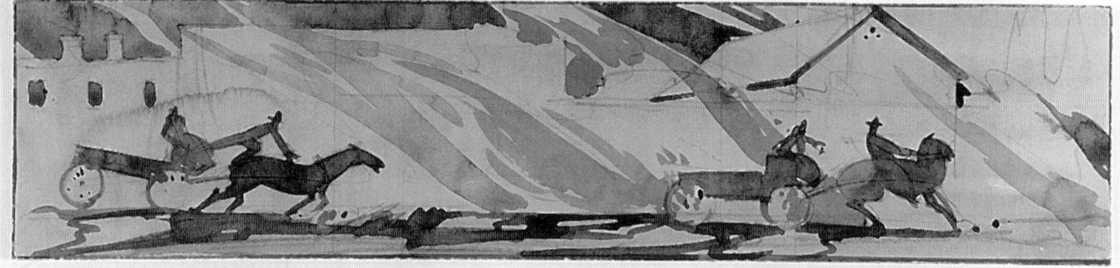

FIG. 11. The style of these panoramic sketches, similar to that of the majority of the drawings for the fire sequence in *Gone with the Wind,* suggests that they are Johnson's work.

Tara. She continues to show an ambivalence toward her guide. In the novel much of this episode is described in terms of its abstract impression on Scarlett, who, dependent upon her escort, is guided through the perils of the fire and of the night as though in a trance. "A glare brighter than a dozen suns dazzled her eyes, scorching heat seared their skins and the roaring, crackling and crashing beat upon their ears in painful waves," relates the text. "For an eternity, it seemed, they were in the midst of flaming torment and then abruptly they were in semidarkness again." Rhett's participation in this event is set forth as "automatic." His face is described as "set and absent, as though he had forgotten where he was."[28]

Howard's principal invention in his initial screen treatment of this episode was the placement in it of shots suggestive of looting. Slightly earlier in the novel, after hurrying into town to seek medical assistance for Melanie, who has entered labor, Scarlett is surprised to see women and children struggling to carry foodstuffs from the commissary, which was opened to the public at the last moment by the evacuating army.[29] Rhett's explanation of the legality of this group's conduct, which was planted by Howard in the course of the fire episode in his initial screenplay, was removed in its revision. The implication of civil unrest is heightened also in Howard's initial versions of the screenplay by the description of shots of the wagon forcing its way through the crowd and of Scarlett accepting a pistol from Rhett, along with his advice to shoot anyone who threatens their safety.

Preferring to develop dramatic characterizations rather than to exploit the spectacular potential of this episode with respect to looting and the fire, Howard allowed the wagon to proceed out of town without incident, pausing only for the line of soldiers and the young man whose weary collapse was transcribed verbatim from the novel in the script's early drafts. "I have always had a little trouble in believing Rhett's sudden decision to desert

Scarlett and enlist in the army," Howard confessed, adding, "to motivate this decision, however, we shall have to use either some of the shots Miss Mitchell has given us of the evacuating army or invent something new which befalls Rhett and Scarlett on their way out of the city"; however, he questioned the need for "the burning of the munitions and other army stores or any impression of noisy mobs at this point, though it is easy enough to include them if they seem of value."

In contrast—and from the outset—Selznick imagined this scene's presentation in terms of a spectacular display and considered utilizing a wide-screen device for more dramatic exploitation. In a letter to Katharine Brown dated December 20, 1937, the producer admitted to being "very hot" about the proposal of using the double camera and projector system developed by Fred Waller for wide-screen film presentation at the 1939–1940 New York World's Fair—"especially for the burning and evacuation of Atlanta, especially the ride of Rhett and Scarlett, so that the audience would have the sense that they were actually in the middle of the fire and in the middle of the evacuation." Although this scheme was abandoned ultimately, purportedly because of the extra expense and expected delay of the film's release in order to equip all theaters, numerous interoffice memos attest that the decision was delayed until late June 1939, by which time it was necessary to complete the principal photography. (In 1952, Waller successfully marketed a three-projector version of this wide-screen process as "Cinerama," for which he received a special Academy Award the following year.)

Menzies himself prepared a scenario of a spectacular fire sequence, which was mailed to Selznick on November 9, 1938, when film-script revision was in progress with Jo Swerling in Bermuda. In a separate letter of the same date, Menzies also informed the producer that Cukor had seen and approved a "detailed drawing continuity" of this episode:

> I am writing this letter in Ray Klune's presence who is rather anxious to have you realize the increased scope of this sequence over what the present script calls for. I have explained to him that it is now your desire and Mr. Cukor's to make an important spectacle of this sequence. . . . Do not misunderstand by this that we are trying to make a Chicago fire of six reels. . . . We are still aiming at a big pre-intermission spectacle shot . . . [and] it is essential that we get one terrific fire effect shot.

Menzies offered more than an "amplification" (his own term) of Howard's initial six-shot episode. This production designer's script devoted twenty-eight of its thirty-three organized shots to a "fire" sequence, eleven of which were invented to show Rhett leading the horse and wagon on foot through the fiery railyard, after which buildings in the background spectacularly collapse. Another of Menzies' inventions was the replacement of a previous scene, in which women and children are mistaken for looters, with shots of threatening "toughs," past whom the wagon rides. The last five shots concern Rhett's announcement to Scarlett of his intention to volunteer for the Confederate army and his departure after passionately forcing a kiss from her.

In contrast, this episode's concurrent treatment in the script by Bradbury Foote was described, in its one-line continuity form of November 23, 1938, simply as "montage scenes of destruction of Atlanta, over which is superimposed moving buckboard [*sic*]." Foote was responsible for writing a version of the filmscript with a happy ending, in which Scarlett throws herself into Rhett's arms as he departs Atlanta by train. Although Selznick derided Foote's ideas as "awful," this screenwriter's advice that Rhett should not offer his pistol to Scarlett until after he has announced his intention to depart for enlistment—noted on October 18, 1938, in his critique of Howard's third revision—was followed in subsequent versions of the screenplay.

Selznick announced his plans to discuss Menzies' scenario with Oliver Garrett on November 21, 1938 to his secretary Marcella Rabwin and requested that she advise the production designer to prepare "new sketches . . . for the fire sequence with particular emphasis on a constantly mounting violence in the shots and the fire getting greater and greater as they drive through the streets, climaxing in the panoramic effect on which we are working." By this date, Selznick himself had begun to question the economy of capturing the spectacle of this sequence by sacrificing his studio's exterior sets to fire. On the previous day, he had confided to Ginsberg in a memo that MGM had warned that burning the backlot would prove to be an unnecessary extravagance. Nevertheless, he wished to satisfy the "showmanship requirements of the picture," explaining to his general manager:

> I feel very strongly that people have a general idea that *Gone with the Wind* plays against a much bigger canvas than is actually the case and that they are going to be disappointed with the intimacy of the story and with its lack of spectacle unless we give them a smashing and sensational spectacle in the fire sequence and in the ride of Rhett and Scarlett through the burning town. I feel that it will be the equivalent of the Chariot Race in *Ben Hur* [1924] and that it is our one chance, particularly since we are in color, to give them a sensational stunt.

With exploitation of a panoramic device tentatively planned, the conventional découpage designed by Menzies for the railyard shots—comprising the most fiery portion of the episode—was replaced, in several revisions written by Garrett early the following month, with the description of a single shot setup bearing the term "Grandeur Screen," dictating use of a wide-screen cinematographical apparatus and extensive pyrotechnical staging.[30] In addition, Garrett's inventions entailed the looting of a bakery and saloon, the inclusion of a "Bacchanalian" scene "designed to give a Dante's Inferno effect," and an altercation with a group of "toughs" who attempt to steal the horse and wagon; sensibly, Rhett retains his pistol in order to defend himself and his passengers.

In his elaboration of the plight of these characters, Garrett mistakenly thought that the Yankees were bombarding the city at this moment, and thus had a cornice of a building blown away by an artillery shell, obstructing the wagon's passage by its fall. (Although shelling of Atlanta by Federal artillery is described in Mitchell's novel, such barrage does not contribute to her account of the escape.) Finally, in order not to dilute these scenes of spectacle and suspense with an element of pathos, the drama of the collapsing soldier was removed from this sequence and inserted in a following one outside the city, shortly before Rhett's departure. The latter's patriotic conversion was no longer to be a principal issue of the fire sequence (see Figures 12–19).

Orig from which copied Dec 5, 1938

Menzies-Garrett
December 2, 1938

"GONE WITH THE WIND"

FIRE SEQUENCE

1 EXT. PEACHTREE STREET IN FRONT OF MISS PITTY'S HOUSE -- MED. SHOT AT FRONT DOOR - NIGHT -

As Rhett Butler comes out the door with Melanie in his arms, Prissie, with the baby, is at his heels. Bringing up the rear are Scarlett and the frightened Wade Hampton. Butler glances off down Peachtree Street, stops short. The others group behind him.

Scarlett (from the rear)
What is it?

2 LONG SHOT FROM BUTLER'S POINT OF VIEW - PEACHTREE STREET AND THE CITY IN THE DISTANCE - (COSGROVE)

A glow of fire over the town is discernible in the distance.

Scarlett's Voice
What is it, Rhett?

3 GROUP SHOT - ~~(BUTLER IN THE FOREGROUND, SCARLETT IN BACKGROUND)~~ ON THE VERANDAH OF MISS PITTY'S HOUSE
Rhett is in the f.g. Back of him is Scarlett's white, anxious face.

Rhett
They've set fire to the warehouses (down by the depot) -- burning up the supplies -- so the Yankees won't get them. ~~We'll have to hurry -- get across the tracks before all those boxcars of ammunition start to go off.~~ We'll have to hurry to get across the tracks.

Scarlett (alarmed)
~~We're not going that way?~~ Can't we go around?

Rhett
The McDonough Road is the only one still open. The Yankees have cut all the rest. ~~If we're going to get there we'll have to go right through.~~
(sardonically)
Still want to go to Tara?

Scarlett
Yes -- yes -- hurry.

He goes down the steps out of scene. The others follow.

4 MEDIUM SHOT ACROSS WAGON TOWARD HOUSE

Rhett is already installing Melanie and the mattress in the back of the wagon. Prissy and the baby are followed by Scarlett and Wade Hampton. Rhett takes

ct

FIGS. 12–14. Shot numbers 1–12 of an emended copy of the December 2, 1938, fire-sequence scenario attributed to Menzies and Oliver H. P. Garrett, the penciled changes on which correspond to the revised script of December 5.

2

4 CONTINUED (2)

the baby from Prissy and places it beside Melanie and then hoists Wade Hampton into the wagon. Rhett ~~fixes the tailboard and~~ boosts Prissy into the wagon and fits the tailboard in place.

Rhett (to Scarlett)
You get up in front with me.

5 FULL SHOT OF PEACHTREE STREET - (HORSE IN FOREGROUND) - INCREASED FIRE EFFECT IN SKY (COSGROVE SPLIT SCREEN)

As Butler and Scarlett ~~come to~~ reach the head of the wagon, She is still carrying the lamp.

Rhett (mounting to the driver's seat)
Not much of a horse for ~~this kind of~~ a race but he's the best I could steal. All I ask is he doesn't fall ~~to pieces~~ apart before we get ~~across the tracks.~~ through the fire.

Scarlett sets the lamp down on the mounting block. He helps her mount to the seat beside him. He picks up the reins.

Scarlett
Wait! I forgot to lock the door.

Rhett laughs.

Scarlett
What are you laughing at?

Rhett
At you, locking the Yankees out.

He whacks the reins on the horse's back, turns the wagon around and starts off down the street. The wagon disappears into the deep shadows. In the foreground, the lamp, still burning, sheds its little circle of yellow light on the street.

6 PEACHTREE STREET - THE WAGON - PANNING SHOT

Toward Camera comes the horse at a lope,the wagon swaying behind as it bumps over the ruts. The horse, the wagon, and the people in it are only dim figures in the darkness under the trees along Peachtree Street. They are the only moving figures on the street. Camera PANS with the wagon as it passes,and reveals once again, at the far end of the street, the glow and smoke from the street above the rooftops and through the trees, at the center of town.

ct

FIG. 13

3

7 LONG SHOT - BY THE CHURCH - (TREE-SHADOWED PORTION OF PEACHTREE STREET IN THE BACKGROUND)

The wagon appears out of the darkness, moving into the relatively open space in front of the church. It makes a half-turn, heading into the business section of Peachtree Street.

8 TWO SHOT - RHETT AND SCARLETT ON THE WAGON - (TRANSPARENCY)

As they continue to drive along, their faces are lit up for the first time by the glow from the fire.

9 LONG SHOT - BUSINESS SECTION OF PEACHTREE STREET - (FROM THEIR ANGLE)- (COSGROVE)

At the far end of the street flames are seen for the first time.

CUT BACK TO:

10 TWO SHOT - RHETT AND SCARLETT ON THE WAGON - (TRANSPARENCY)

Their faces are high-lighted by the flames as they continue to approach them. Scarlett seems to shrink closer to Rhett.

~~Scarlett~~

~~Do we have to go through it -- right through the fire?~~

~~Rhett (smiling)~~

~~They're just warehouses. Wait 'til it reaches the ammunition.~~

11 FULL SHOT - BUSINESS SECTION PEACHTREE STREET - ~~REVERSE ANGLE FROM PREVIOUS SHOT~~ APPROACHING WAGON IN B.G.

An intersecting street is between CAMERA and ~~Camera is now shooting toward~~ the approaching wagon. ~~across an intersecting street.~~ In the f.g., down the intersecting street, ~~as the wagon~~ comes ~~closer, appears~~ a detachment of Confederate troops, ~~the last of those to evacuate the city. The wagon is forced to pull up for a moment to permit them to pass.~~ forcing Rhett to pull in the horse and wait for them to pass.

12 TWO SHOT - RHETT AND SCARLETT ON THE WAGON - (TRANSPARENCY)

They are watching the troops pass.

Scarlett (impatiently)

~~Why don't they hurry?~~

Oh, dear. Why can't they hurry?

~~Rhett~~

~~Don't be so impatient. With them goes the last of law and order. Now the Decatur Street roughs will stand the town on its head.~~

Rhett
(smiles grimly)
I wouldn't be too impatient. With them goes the last semblance of law and order. Now the Decatur Street roughs will stand the town on its head.

ct

FIG. 14

Already Shot 288 ~~7~~ 117 ~~8~~

TREE-SHADOWED PORTION OF PEACHTREE STREET - CHURCH IN F.G.- LONG SHOT -

showing the wagon coming out of the darkness of the sheltering trees into the relatively open space in front of the church. The wagon makes a half-turn, heading into the business section of Peachtree Street.

Already Shot 289 ~~8~~

TWO SHOT - (TRANSPARENCY) - RHETT AND SCARLETT ON THE WAGON -

as the light of the fire at the far end of Peachtree Street is reflected on their faces for the first time. At this point, between their two figures and behind them, appears Prissy's black face, utterly terror-stricken, the light reflected on her as well.

Already Shot 290

BUSINESS SECTION OF PEACHTREE STREET - LONG SHOT FROM THEIR VIEWPOINT - CAMERA HOLDING HORSE'S HEAD IN F.G. (COSGROVE SPLIT SCREEN)

Flames are visible at the far end of the street for the first time. Beyond the burning building an explosion shoots flames and sparks high in the air.

CUT BACK TO:

Already Shot 291 ~~10~~

TWO SHOT - (TRANSPARENCY)-SAME ANGLE AS #8 - RHETT AND SCARLETT ON THE WAGON

Prissy ducks out of view. Scarlett shrinks closer to Rhett, clinging to his arm.

Already Shot ~~11~~ 292

BUSINESS SECTION OF PEACHTREE STREET - LONG SHOT SHOOTING AWAY FROM FIRE ACROSS INTERSECTING STREET TOWARD APPROACHING WAGON IN B.G.

As the wagon approaches the intersection, it is forced to halt by a detachment of weary, slipshod, Confederate troops who appear in f.g., crossing Peachtree Street and heading down the intersecting thoroughfare.

Already Shot 293 ~~12~~

TWO SHOT - (TRANSPARENCY) - RHETT AND SCARLETT ON WAGON

Impatiently, they watch the troops pass.

Scarlett
Oh dear! Why can't they hurry?

Rhett (smiles grimly)
With them goes the last semblance of law and order. Now the Decatur Street roughs will stand the town on its head.

ct

FIG. 15. Shot numbers 7–12 of the December 7, 1938 fire-sequence script were changed by pencil to numbers 288–293 for inclusion in Garrett's filmscript of January 16, 1939.

4

13 SAME ANGLE AS #11 -

as the last of the Confederates in f.g. straggle off down the intersecting street. Rhett slashes at the horse with the reins. The wagon lurches forward, going past Camera down Peachtree Street. For a moment, ~~we~~ Hold on ~~the~~ empty ~~portion of~~ Peachtree Street, SHOOTING ~~still shooting~~ towards the church. ~~a series of~~ The sound of more explosions and bright flashes ~~follow~~ of light follow.

14 BUSINESS SECTION OF PEACHTREE STREET - VERY LONG SHOT STILL SHOOTING AWAY FROM FIRE TOWARD APPROACHING WAGON

The street is completely empty except for the distant wagon. The reflection of the flames (which are behind the Camera) against the buildings should give a weird, frightening effect. For a protracted moment the wagon clatters down the street toward Camera as if through an abandoned city. The only sound at the moment is the clop-clop of the horse. Suddenly ~~the relative silence is broken by the~~ there is a crash of breaking glass.

15 BAKERY SHOP WINDOW - CAMERA INSIDE

One pane of glass has already been broken. Outside the window, a Decatur Street tough flings a huge missile, smashing the rest of the window so that it seems to splinter directly past the Camera. Through the gaping hole we get a glimpse of the horse and wagon passing in the b.g. An instant later, three or four other toughs join the one who threw the missile outside the window. They start grabbing bread from inside the shop window. Interspersed with this action ~~comes~~ the sound of ~~a series of~~ more explosions accompanied by bright flashes of light.

16 CORNICE OF A BUILDING

The light of the fire is reflected on the building. The whine of projectiles going through the air is heard, followed by a sharp explosion. ~~and the corner of~~ A Part of the ~~building~~ cornice blows off.

17 PEACHTREE STREET - HORSE AND WAGON APPROACHING CAMERA

As the falling masonry crashes to the street in f.g. between horse and Camera. Rhett pulls up the horse sharply which rears in panic.

18 PEACHTREE STREET - CAMERA SHOOTING FROM NARROW, DARK ALLEY

Beyond the entrance of the alley, the horse and wagon may be seen, their passage blocked by the debris. Past the Camera ~~and~~ out of the alley run a number of hooligans.

ct

FIGS. 16–19. Shot numbers 13–35 of the revised fire-sequence script of December 7, 1938, by Menzies and Garrett.

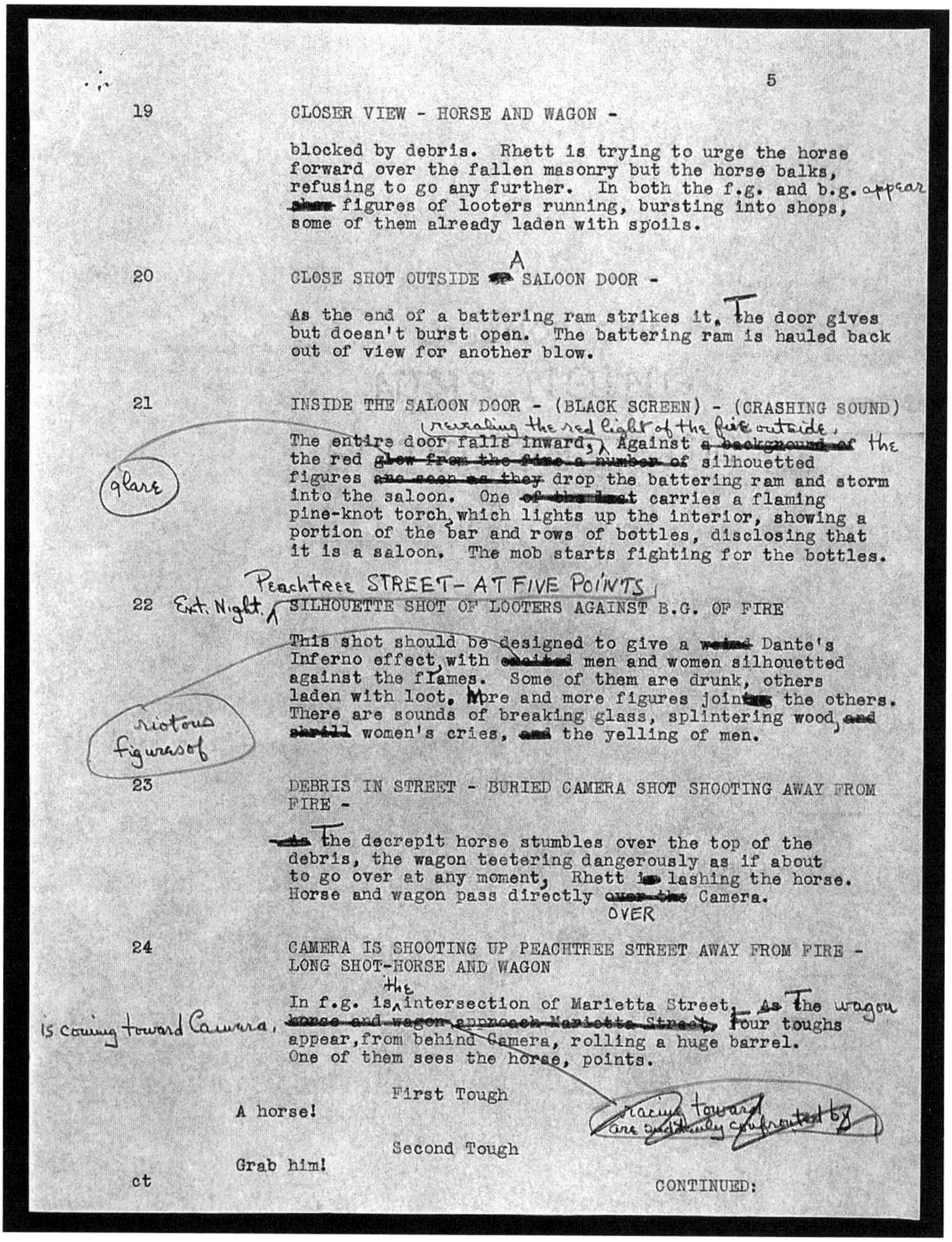

5

19 CLOSER VIEW - HORSE AND WAGON -

blocked by debris. Rhett is trying to urge the horse forward over the fallen masonry but the horse balks, refusing to go any further. In both the f.g. and b.g. ~~show~~ appear figures of looters running, bursting into shops, some of them already laden with spoils.

20 CLOSE SHOT OUTSIDE ~~OF~~ A SALOON DOOR -

As the end of a battering ram strikes it. The door gives but doesn't burst open. The battering ram is hauled back out of view for another blow.

21 INSIDE THE SALOON DOOR - (BLACK SCREEN) - (CRASHING SOUND)

The entire door falls inward, (revealing the red light of the fire outside). Against ~~a background of~~ the the red ~~glow from the fire a number of~~ glare silhouetted figures ~~are seen as they~~ drop the battering ram and storm into the saloon. One ~~of the first~~ carries a flaming pine-knot torch, which lights up the interior, showing a portion of the bar and rows of bottles, disclosing that it is a saloon. The mob starts fighting for the bottles.

22 Ext. Night. Peachtree STREET - AT FIVE POINTS - SILHOUETTE SHOT OF LOOTERS AGAINST B.G. OF FIRE

This shot should be designed to give a ~~weird~~ Dante's Inferno effect, with ~~excited~~ riotous figures of men and women silhouetted against the flames. Some of them are drunk, others laden with loot. More and more figures join ~~ing~~ the others. There are sounds of breaking glass, splintering wood, ~~and shrill~~ women's cries, ~~and~~ the yelling of men.

23 DEBRIS IN STREET - BURIED CAMERA SHOT SHOOTING AWAY FROM FIRE -

~~As~~ The decrepit horse stumbles over the top of the debris, the wagon teetering dangerously as if about to go over at any moment, Rhett ~~is~~ lashing the horse. Horse and wagon pass directly ~~over the~~ OVER Camera.

24 CAMERA IS SHOOTING UP PEACHTREE STREET AWAY FROM FIRE - LONG SHOT-HORSE AND WAGON

In f.g. is the intersection of Marietta Street. ~~As~~ The wagon is coming toward Camera, ~~horse and wagon approach Marietta Street,~~ four toughs appear, from behind Camera, rolling a huge barrel. One of them sees the horse, points. (racing toward — are suddenly confronted by)

First Tough

A horse!

Second Tough

Grab him!

ct CONTINUED:

FIG. 17

6

24 CONTINUED (2)

Third Tough (to Fourth, indicating barrel)
Watch it. We'll take care of him.

The Fourth Tough stays with the barrel. The others start forward.

25 High Angle - FOLLOW SHOT OF WAGON - (CAMERA TRUCKING) - SHOOTING ACROSS SCARLETT AND RHETT'S BACKS

The fire at the end of the street is no longer in view because this is a high, sharply angled shot. The toughs run into scene obviously intending to stop the wagon.

First Tough (yelling)
Give us that horse!

Rhett jerks savagely on the reins, the wagon swerves away, into Marietta Street, going out of scene Camera Right. Camera halts. The Toughs run up ~~here~~ into:

MED. CLOSE SHOT of THE THREE TOUGHS,

so we can clearly distinguish their faces looking off in consternation after the wagon. The first Tough, obviously, the leader, gestures in the direction from which they came.

First Tough
Down the alley. ~~We can~~ Cut ~~them~~ 'em off.

They run out the way from which they came.

~~27~~ 26 PORTION OF MARIETTA STREET ~~[illegible]~~ in immediate f.g.

SHOOT ACROSS a pile of debris which blocks the street. In the b.g. is the dark opening of ~~the~~ alley. The wagon enters scene, toward CAMERA, ~~approaching the alley and~~ swerves ~~sharply~~ abruptly into ~~the~~ the alley, on

~~28~~ 27 ALLEY - LONG SHOT

Down the alley, toward Camera, come the horse and wagon rocking crazily. CAMERA PANS to the other alley leading off Peachtree Street and converging with the first. The toughs appear, running down this alley. CAMERA PULLS BACK showing how the two alleys converge. The Toughs reach the intersection point first and spread across the alley, blocking the way. Rhett stands up and lashes at the horse, ~~riding~~ to ride the toughs down.

~~29~~ 28 LOW ANGLE SHOT ~~OF TOUGHS~~ - Rear View of Toughs

ct ~~as~~ They leap at the horse, One is knocked down. The wagon drives over him. The others jump aside. Horse and wagon go out of scene PAST CAMERA

FIG. 18

7

~~30~~ 29 REAR VIEW OF WAGON - SHOOTING DOWN ALLEY TOWARD FLAMES IN B.G.

The wagon bounces about from side to side dangerously, as it races down alley away from Camera. A burning building is at the far end of the alley.

~~31~~ 30 CLOSE SHOT - MELANIE -

lying face up on the mattress, one limp arm about the bundled baby. They are being roughly tossed about. Melanie is biting her lip to keep from crying out.

~~32~~ 31 HORSE AND WAGON IN A BRIGHT GLARE OF FLAMES

The horse abruptly stops without being pulled in and rears back. Scarlett cries out.

~~33~~ 32 TWO SHOT - (TRANSPARENCY) - RHETT AND SCARLETT

~~For the first time~~ She is clinging to him desperately. Even he looks alarmed. Behind them Prissy's frightened face appears from the back of the wagon. She screams.

~~Prissy~~

~~Lawdy!~~

~~Screams~~

~~34~~ 33 BURNING BUILDING AND BOXCAR - FROM THEIR ANGLE

Only a few feet beyond the boxcar is a flaming building. Sparks, embers, and bits of burning wood are showering the boxcar. Carry ~~of~~ over this SOUND of Prissy's scream.

~~35~~ 34 GROUP ~~TWO~~ SHOT - (TRANSPARENCY) - RHETT, ~~AND~~ SCARLETT AND PRISSY

~~Prissy~~ Prissy is still screaming.

~~Scarlett turns and pushes Prissy down out of sight.~~

Scarlett (to Prissy)

Shut up.

(She thrusts her down out of sight.)

Rhett (to Scarlett; gravely)

Those boxcars'll be blowing up in a minute. They're loaded with shells. We'll have to go around another way.

~~36~~ 35 HORSE AND WAGON - ~~BY~~ BOXCAR AND BURNING BLDG. IN VIEW

Rhett lashes at the animal, pulling him around to make a half-turn away from the burning building and the boxcar and across the open freight yards. The panic-stricken horse finally starts forward. The wagon goes out of view Camera Left.

ct

FIG. 19

Scarlett's character also was affected by the excision of her infant son, Wade Hampton Hamilton, from Garrett's final revision of the filmscript in January of the following year. Since the child was the only apparent proof of the consummation of Scarlett's marriage to Charles Hamilton the week of his fatal enlistment, with his removal, the young widow appears still to have been claimed by no man. This deletion was certainly a response to economy. "We must prepare to make drastic cuts and these cuts, I think, include some of the characters," Selznick had written Howard two years earlier. (Nevertheless, the producer objected at that time to Howard's suggestion to omit little Wade.)

To reiterate, the fire sequence itself—portions of which were shot throughout the picture's making, with or without the use of principal players—was the first episode (other than those performed as screen tests) to be filmed, although it antedated the official opening of the production—or "principal photography"—by a little more than one month. "December 10, 1938, was a grand night, with enough Technicolor flames on view to melt facts into romance," observed David Thomson, cynically referring in part to Selznick's legendary introduction to Vivien Leigh on this occasion. "Three captains and thirty firemen were present in case the Shermanizing got out of hand," he also noted, adding that, because no public warning was issued, great numbers of alarmed citizens jammed emergency telephone lines, believing that MGM was imperiled by the flames.[31] It has been reported elsewhere that enough film was shot to have printed a conventional motion picture of this vintage and that portions of sets from *King Kong* (1933) and Cecil B. DeMille's *King of Kings* (1927) were burned in order to clear the backlot for the extensive set construction required for principal photography. Lambert allegorized this dramatic moment by remarking archly that "there was something Napoleonic in the image of the thirty-seven-year-old producer elevated on his platform, surrounded by a court, waiting to give the order that would set the world on fire," adding that, because of Myron Selznick's late arrival, "the order was delayed—like almost everything else connected with the picture"[32] (see Figures 20–21).

Because the filming involved doubles and was intended to produce spectacular backgrounds for ornamentation of shots that were filmed much later with the principal players, Menzies served as director while Cukor merely observed. Clarence W. D. Slifer, who assisted Jack Cosgrove, summarized the techniques employed in the making of several of these composite shots in 1982 in an article in *American Cinematographer*. In his account, Slifer also credited the implementation of these methods to the creative collaboration of a number of technicians and to production manager Raymond Klune. "We had quite a few production managers since Selznick International started, but only Ray Klune grasped the idea that you needed more than script to make pictures of the quality that Selznick wanted," Slifer wrote. "You needed an efficient organization and equipment to do the job"[33] (see Figure 22).

Haver also acknowledged Klune's contributions to the success of this evening's filming—from the positioning of cameras to his employment of special-effects technician Lee Zavits specifically for the design of a network of water and gas lines by which the fire's intensity was controlled—and cited much of the production manager's own account.

FIG. 20. Filming of the fire sequence on the back lot the night of December 10, 1938, utilized doubles of principal players.

FIG. 21. Photographed in conference with Selznick (second from right) and film director George Cukor (right), Menzies (left) was charged with directing the initial filming of the fire sequence.

FIG. 22. Production manager Ray Klune with studio artwork.

> We planned the whole thing sort of as a football rehearsal. We built a miniature.... We rehearsed for ten days, every move, every camera position—we decided during these rehearsals that instead of changing lenses on the cameras, which was a brute of a job on those Technicolor things, we'd move the cameras instead. We'd move the camera from position one to position five—different lenses on each camera because we wanted to get a medium shot, a long shot, and a close shot from almost every position. So we had all the camera positions indicated on the model, and the camera crews.[34]

Haver recounted that Klune reassured Selznick several times when the producer questioned the feasibility of this undertaking. Once the sets were ablaze, the photography itself lasted seventy-five minutes. In order to assure filming of all required views, the event was scheduled on a date when every available Technicolor camera could be leased. Slifer related how the fiery collapse which contributed as background to the sequence's spectacular final shot was recorded, miraculously, only seconds before the film negative was depleted in the camera which he himself was operating.[35]

The "shooting script" of this episode that developed subsequently in the production is represented by the original cut-and-stapled draft of the filmscript bearing the date February 27, 1939. This is the so-called rainbow filmscript, the epithet deriving from the fact that, while its creation began that same month, during a legendary week of all-nighters in which Selznick and Fleming labored closely with Ben Hecht, revised scenes on variously colored pages were inserted into stenciled copies throughout the period of filming. Although Hecht reputedly suggested discarding the Garrett version and revising the original Howard filmscript, the fire sequence itself varies little from the previous month's scenario.

One departure from that scenario is a grotesquerie in the form of seven shots that was invented to heighten the effect of debauchery and bestiality in the looting scenes. Revised script pages describe shots of a "hooligan with a woman's hat on his head, his arms full of billowing dresses," of others making off with a demijohn of liquor and with their arms around laughing women, and of five looters who pass the wagon carrying "dressed carcasses of hogs on their shoulders, the heads of the swine swaying up over their own craniums, giving a weird effect of half-human, half-animal figures, the white cadavers pale against their flanks." In addition, the window to be broken was altered from that of a bakery to one of a music shop, shifting motivation from hunger and panic to illegal, violent revelry.

None of these changes appears in the final film, although production logs and call sheets dating from April and May 1939 indicate that much was shot as written (see Figures 23–29). The broken window reverted to that of a bakery in an emended script dated March 23, 1939. Shots of the exploded cornice and of the debris and delay of the wagon were deleted from the purported "final shooting script" of January 24, 1939. Indicative of its suspect date, this version also provides an advanced shot breakdown of scenes of the altercation with the hooligans and of the wagon crossing the burning railyard without reference to the "Grandeur Screen." Shot breakdown or découpage was developed to such an extent in this filmscript and in the series of continuity scripts written for this sequence much later in June that several multiple-shot combinations were created in forms that were retained in the film as released.

More specifically, copies of the "Continuity for Fire Sequence," dated June 16, 1939, which belonged formerly to Klune and to Barbara Keon, the production's scenario assistant or continuity clerk (aka "script girl"), also provide notes establishing dates of the filming of many of the sequence's shots. Close-ups of Leigh and Gable were filmed under Fleming's direction on this same date and on several other days that month, and reaction shots were taken of Olivia de Havilland (as Melanie) with Butterfly McQueen (as Prissy) in the back of the wagon as late as July 1.

Other production documents indicate that editor Hal Kern supervised the filming of a series of three miniature boxcar explosions on July 11 and that added shots were taken on October 2 and 7, respectively, of Gable's double's fists and feet pounding various "toughs" and of a horse, rearing before rear-projected flames that had been filmed the previous December. Various notes and two cut-and-stapled drafts of cutting continuities of the film as a whole were produced from late July through November and provide records of the creativity involved in the assembly process (see Figures 30–31). The "final cutting and dialogue continuity" was completed by Kern on December 9 and corresponds to the film that was viewed by the press in Los Angeles on December 12 and that premiered in Atlanta on December 15 (see Figures 32–35).

The sequence as presented begins, upon a dissolve, with the wagon traveling down Peachtree Street towards an inflamed section of Atlanta where, by an ellipsis, the party pauses before a line of ragged, retreating Confederate soldiers. Rhett does not speak sardonically of a "Glorious Cause in retreat" as he does in the novel at this point but instead corrects Scarlett's impatience over the delay with his observation that "with them goes the last semblance of law and order." (The latter line first appeared in the Menzies-Garrett script of December 2, 1938. Although it was not acted upon in subsequent versions, F. Scott Fitzgerald's only suggested change to the fire sequence—which is found among script pages dated January 21, 1939—was the deletion of the initial prepositional phrase in this particular sentence, so that the line reads thus, "There goes the last semblance of law and order.")

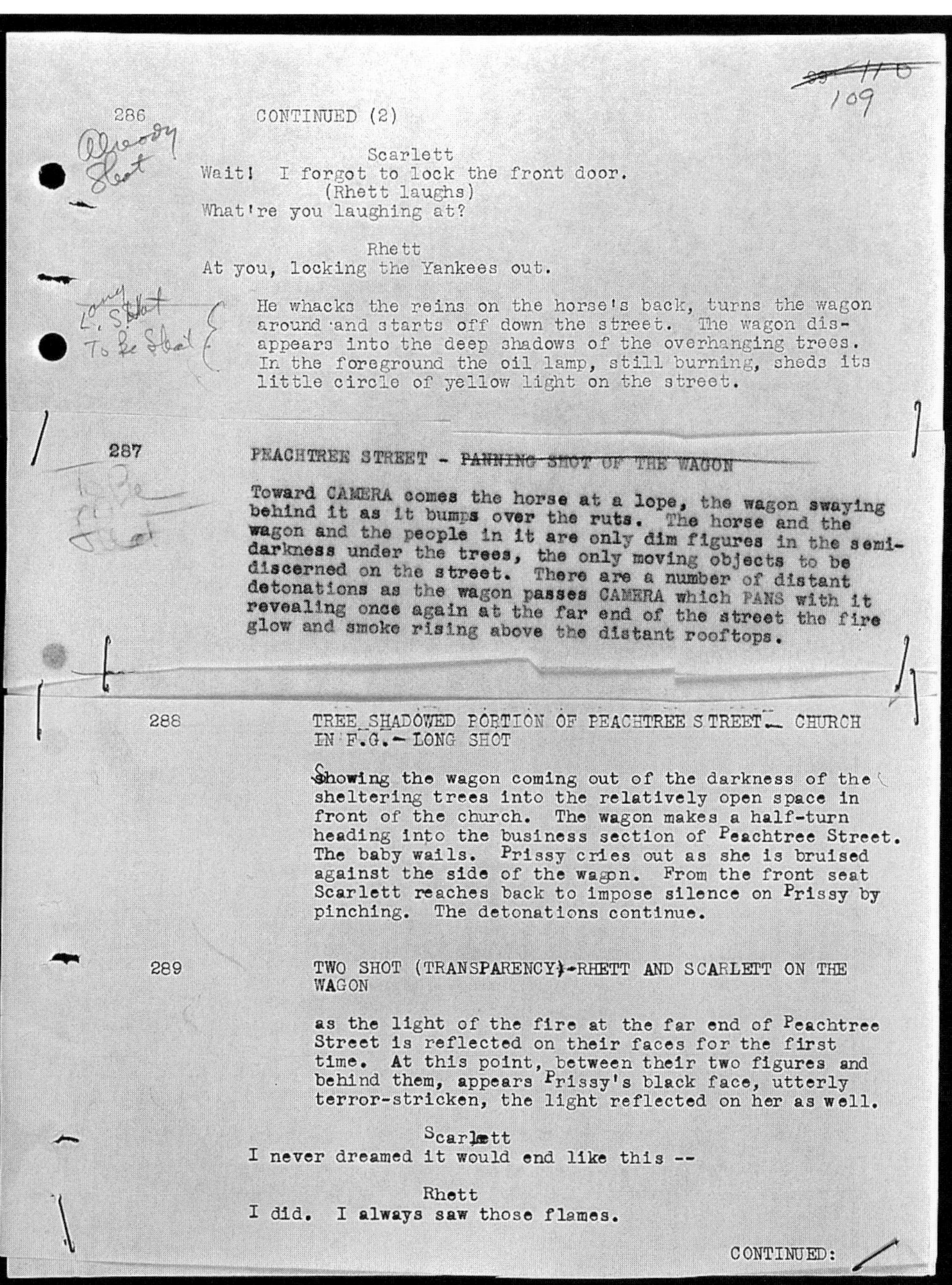

109

286 CONTINUED (2)

Scarlett
Wait! I forgot to lock the front door.
(Rhett laughs)
What're you laughing at?

Rhett
At you, locking the Yankees out.

He whacks the reins on the horse's back, turns the wagon around and starts off down the street. The wagon disappears into the deep shadows of the overhanging trees. In the foreground the oil lamp, still burning, sheds its little circle of yellow light on the street.

287 PEACHTREE STREET - ~~PANNING SHOT OF THE WAGON~~

Toward CAMERA comes the horse at a lope, the wagon swaying behind it as it bumps over the ruts. The horse and the wagon and the people in it are only dim figures in the semi-darkness under the trees, the only moving objects to be discerned on the street. There are a number of distant detonations as the wagon passes CAMERA which PANS with it revealing once again at the far end of the street the fire glow and smoke rising above the distant rooftops.

288 TREE SHADOWED PORTION OF PEACHTREE STREET - CHURCH IN F.G. - LONG SHOT

Showing the wagon coming out of the darkness of the sheltering trees into the relatively open space in front of the church. The wagon makes a half-turn heading into the business section of Peachtree Street. The baby wails. Prissy cries out as she is bruised against the side of the wagon. From the front seat Scarlett reaches back to impose silence on Prissy by pinching. The detonations continue.

289 TWO SHOT (TRANSPARENCY) - RHETT AND SCARLETT ON THE WAGON

as the light of the fire at the far end of Peachtree Street is reflected on their faces for the first time. At this point, between their two figures and behind them, appears Prissy's black face, utterly terror-stricken, the light reflected on her as well.

Scarlett
I never dreamed it would end like this --

Rhett
I did. I always saw those flames.

CONTINUED:

FIGS. 23–27. Pages of the original "rainbow" manuscript, detailing the fire sequence, dating from February 27, 1939, and showing much cutting-and-stapling in the script's composition.

289 CONTINUED (2) ~~16~~ ~~26~~ 11D

Scarlett
It's like the whole world was turned into a bonfire.

Rhett
It is. That's more than Atlanta burning.

290 BUSINESS SECTION OF PEACHTREE STREET - LONG SHOT FROM THEIR VIEWPOINT - CAMERA HOLDING HORSE'S HEAD IN F.G. (COSGROVE SPLIT SCREEN)

Flames are visible at the far end of the street for the first time. Beyond the burning building an explosion shoots flames and sparks high in the air.

291 TWO SHOT - (TRANSPARENCY) - ~~SAME ANGLE AS #8~~ - RHETT AND SCARLETT ON THE WAGON

Prissy ducks out of view. Scarlett shrinks closer to Rhett, clinging to his arm.

292 BUSINESS SECTION OF PEACHTREE STREET - LONG SHOT SHOOTING AWAY FROM FIRE ACROSS INTERSECTING STREET TOWARD APPROACHING WAGON IN B.G.

As the wagon approaches the intersection, it is forced to halt by a detachment of weary, slipshod, Confederate troops who appear in f.g., crossing Peachtree Street and heading down the intersecting thoroughfare. An officer counts "One - Two - Three - Four" in a pathetic effort to count the step and keep up the morale of his men.

293 TWO SHOT - (TRANSPARENCY) - RHETT AND SCARLETT ON WAGON

Impatiently, they watch the troops pass.

Scarlett
Oh dear! Why can't they hurry?

Rhett (smiles grimly)
With them goes the last semblance of law and order. Now the Decatur Street roughs will stand the town on its head.

294 SAME ANGLE AS SCENE 292

as the last of the Confederates in f.g. straggle off down the intersecting street. Rhett slashes at the horse with the reins. The wagon lurches forward, going past CAMERA down Peachtree Street. For a moment HOLD on empty Peachtree Street, SHOOTING toward the church. The sound of more explosions and bright flashes of light follow.

295 BUSINESS SECTION OF PEACHTREE STREET - VERY LONG SHOT STILL SHOOTING AWAY FROM FIRE TOWARD APPROACHING WAGON

The street is completely empty except for the distant wagon.

The reflection of the flames (which are behind the CAMERA) against the buildings should give a weird, frightening effect. For a protracted moment the wagon clatters down the street toward CAMERA as if through an abandoned city. The only sound at the moment is the clop-clop of the horse.

cont'd

FIG. 24

295 (2) Scarlett
Faster, Rhett, faster!

Rhett
He's making all the speed he can.

Scarlett
No, no! Faster!

Suddenly there is a crash of breaking glass.

296 ~~BAKERY~~ Music SHOP WINDOW - CAMERA INSIDE
Silhouetted in f.g. are one or two instruments of the period.

One pane of glass has already been broken. Outside the window, a Decatur Street tough flings a huge missile, smashing the rest of the window so that it seems to splinter directly past the CAMERA. Through the gapping hole we get a glimpse of the horse and wagon passing in the b.g. An instant later, three or four other toughs join the one who threw the missile outside the window. They start grabbing ~~bread~~ instruments from inside the shop window. Intersperse with this action the sound of more explosions accompanied by bright flashes of light.

297 CORNICE OF A BUILDING

The light of the fire is reflected on the building. The whine of projectiles going through the air is heard, followed by a sharp explosion. A part of the cornice blows off.

298 PEACHTREE STREET - HORSE AND WAGON APPROACHING CAMERA

- as the falling masonry crashes to the street in f.g. between horse and CAMERA. Rhett pulls up the horse sharply which rears in panic.

299 PEACHTREE STREET - CAMERA SHOOTING FROM NARROW, DARK ALLEY

Beyond the entrance of the alley, the horse and wagon may be seen, their passage blocked by the debris. Past the CAMERA, out of the alley, run a number of hooligans.

300 CLOSER VIEW - HORSE AND WAGON

- blocked by debris. Rhett is trying to urge the horse forward over the fallen masonry but the horse balks, refusing to go any further. In both the f.g. and b.g. appear figures of looters running, bursting into shops, some of them already laden with spoils. The whole lags on atmosphere of disorder and drunkenness - a city falling into chaos as it nears its death.

300A EXTERIOR - STREET

A hooligan with a woman's hat on his head, his arms full of billowing dresses, goes by in front of the wagon.

FIG. 25

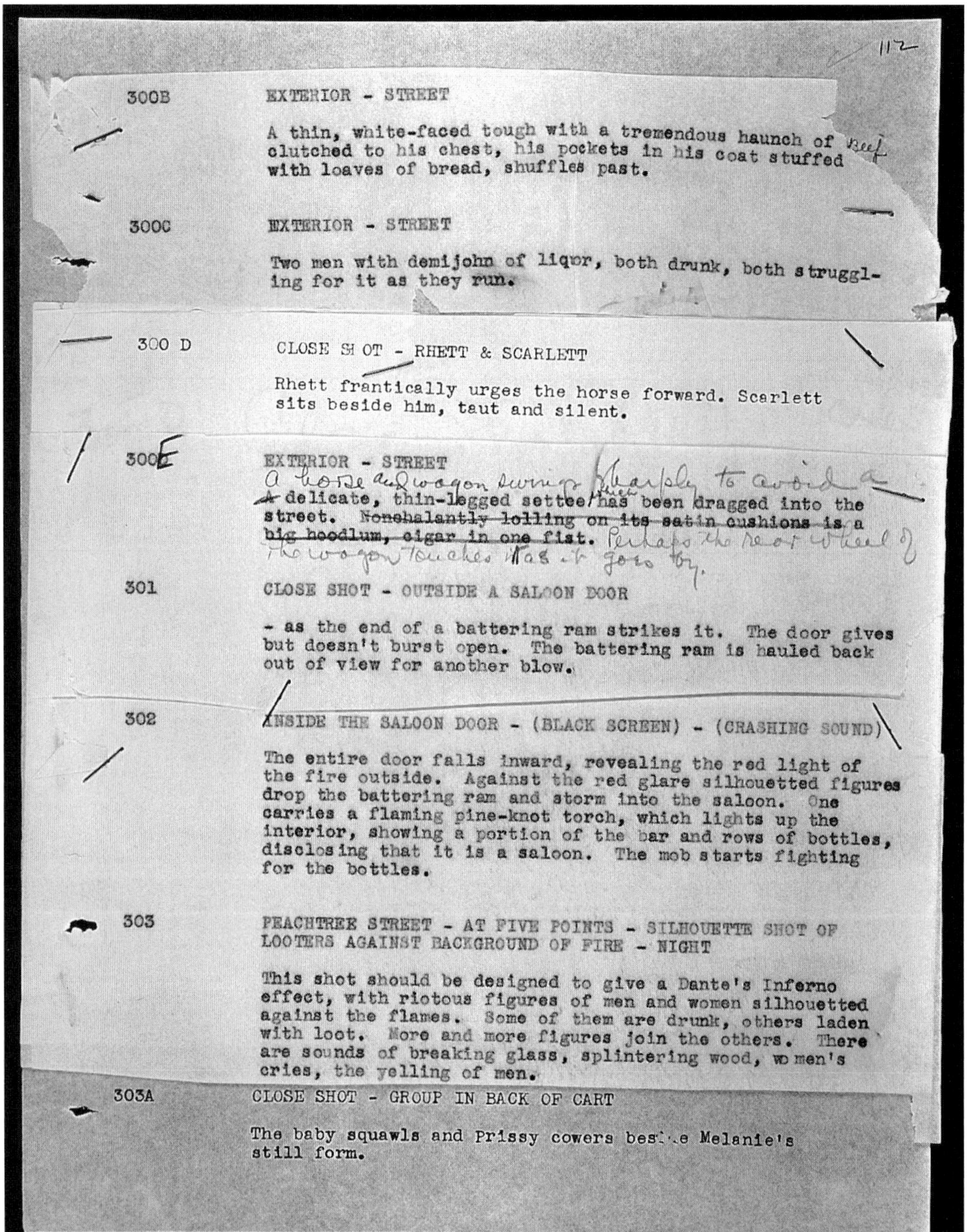

112

300B EXTERIOR - STREET

A thin, white-faced tough with a tremendous haunch of Beef clutched to his chest, his pockets in his coat stuffed with loaves of bread, shuffles past.

300C EXTERIOR - STREET

Two men with demijohn of liquor, both drunk, both struggling for it as they run.

300 D CLOSE SHOT - RHETT & SCARLETT

Rhett frantically urges the horse forward. Scarlett sits beside him, taut and silent.

300E EXTERIOR - STREET

A horse and wagon swings sharply to avoid a ~~A~~ delicate, thin-legged settee/ which has been dragged into the street. ~~Nonchalantly lolling on its satin cushions is a big hoodlum, cigar in one fist.~~ Perhaps the rear wheel of the wagon touches it as it goes by.

301 CLOSE SHOT - OUTSIDE A SALOON DOOR

- as the end of a battering ram strikes it. The door gives but doesn't burst open. The battering ram is hauled back out of view for another blow.

302 INSIDE THE SALOON DOOR - (BLACK SCREEN) - (CRASHING SOUND)

The entire door falls inward, revealing the red light of the fire outside. Against the red glare silhouetted figures drop the battering ram and storm into the saloon. One carries a flaming pine-knot torch, which lights up the interior, showing a portion of the bar and rows of bottles, disclosing that it is a saloon. The mob starts fighting for the bottles.

303 PEACHTREE STREET - AT FIVE POINTS - SILHOUETTE SHOT OF LOOTERS AGAINST BACKGROUND OF FIRE - NIGHT

This shot should be designed to give a Dante's Inferno effect, with riotous figures of men and women silhouetted against the flames. Some of them are drunk, others laden with loot. More and more figures join the others. There are sounds of breaking glass, splintering wood, women's cries, the yelling of men.

303A CLOSE SHOT - GROUP IN BACK OF CART

The baby squawls and Prissy cowers beside Melanie's still form.

FIG. 26

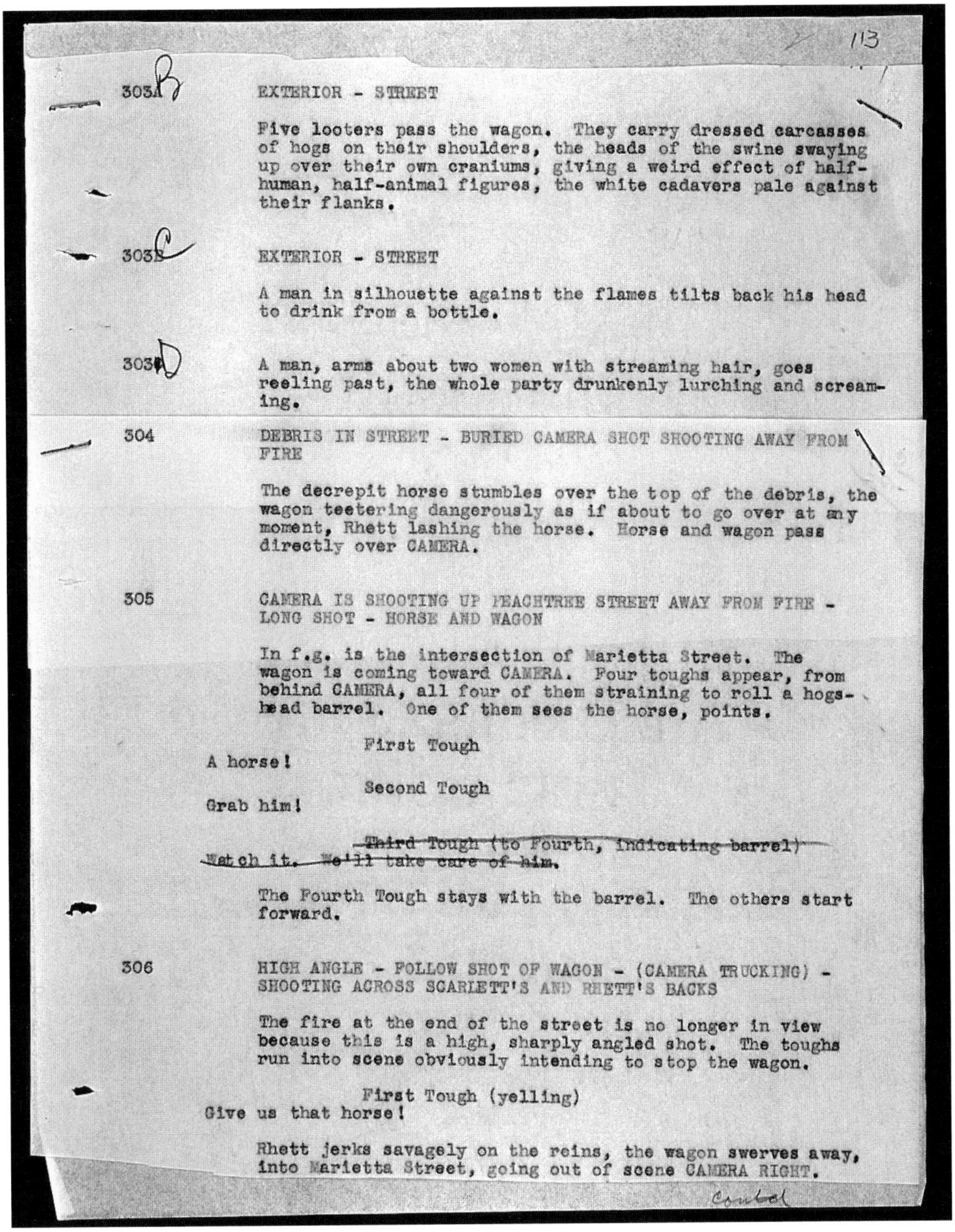

113

303B EXTERIOR - STREET

Five looters pass the wagon. They carry dressed carcasses of hogs on their shoulders, the heads of the swine swaying up over their own craniums, giving a weird effect of half-human, half-animal figures, the white cadavers pale against their flanks.

303C EXTERIOR - STREET

A man in silhouette against the flames tilts back his head to drink from a bottle.

303D A man, arms about two women with streaming hair, goes reeling past, the whole party drunkenly lurching and screaming.

304 DEBRIS IN STREET - BURIED CAMERA SHOT SHOOTING AWAY FROM FIRE

The decrepit horse stumbles over the top of the debris, the wagon teetering dangerously as if about to go over at any moment, Rhett lashing the horse. Horse and wagon pass directly over CAMERA.

305 CAMERA IS SHOOTING UP PEACHTREE STREET AWAY FROM FIRE - LONG SHOT - HORSE AND WAGON

In f.g. is the intersection of Marietta Street. The wagon is coming toward CAMERA. Four toughs appear, from behind CAMERA, all four of them straining to roll a hogshead barrel. One of them sees the horse, points.

First Tough

A horse!

Second Tough

Grab him!

~~Third Tough (to Fourth, indicating barrel)~~

~~Watch it. We'll take care of him.~~

The Fourth Tough stays with the barrel. The others start forward.

306 HIGH ANGLE - FOLLOW SHOT OF WAGON - (CAMERA TRUCKING) - SHOOTING ACROSS SCARLETT'S AND RHETT'S BACKS

The fire at the end of the street is no longer in view because this is a high, sharply angled shot. The toughs run into scene obviously intending to stop the wagon.

First Tough (yelling)

Give us that horse!

Rhett jerks savagely on the reins, the wagon swerves away, into Marietta Street, going out of scene CAMERA RIGHT.

Contd

FIG. 27

SELZNICK INTERNATIONAL PICTURES, INC.

CALL SHEET

2ND UNIT

DATE THURS., MAY 25, 1939

PICTURE "GONE WITH THE WIND" PROD. NO. 108M DIRECTOR WM. MENZIES

SET EXT. ATLANTA STREETS - ESCAPE SEQUENCE - NIGHT (WEATHER PERMITTING)

LOCATION 40 ACRES SET NO. 17M SCENES 300A-300B-300C-303 303B-303C-303D(Cont.)

NAME	TIME CALLED ON SET	TIME CALLED MAKE-UP	CHARACTER, DESC., WARDROBE
Yakima Canutt	9:00 AM	8:00 AM	Double for Rhett
Aileen Goodwin	9:00 AM	8:00 AM	" " Scarlett
18 Tough Men	8:00 PM	7:00 PM	Hoodlums
7 " Women	8:00 PM	7:00 PM	"
Camera Boom & Oper.	Will notify		PROP REQUIREMENTS
P.A. System	6:30 PM		
Cameras	7:00 PM		Escape wagon & horse
Spec. Effects	7:00 PM		Double horses
Cosgrove & Crew	7:30 PM		Dummies in wagon
First Aid Man	7:30 PM		Demijohns & bottles
			Bags & Bundles
3 Standby Cars	7:00 PM		Small trunk
			Liquor Kegs
Midnight Meals	11:30 PM		Women's clothes
			Haunch of beef
			Pig carcasses
			CONSTRUCTION REQUIREMENTS
			Breakaway window for Bakery
			Wild wall (brick) 12 ' x 12'
			Remove door & frame from store

ASSISTANT DIRECTOR HARVE FOSTER

FIG. 28. Second-unit call sheet scheduling filming of revised shots for the fire sequence under Menzies' direction.

Selznick International Pictures

DAILY PRODUCTION LOG

2dn UNIT

#108 — Prod. No. | "GONE WITH THE WIND" (108) — Picture | May 25, 1939 — Date

SET EXT. ATLANTA STREETS - Escape Seq.) NIGHT STAGE NO. 40 Acres

TIME	LEGEND
7.00 PM	Company call. 8.00 Shooting Call.
	Lining up Cosgrove Matte Shot
9.23	Rehearsal
9.29	SHOOTING SCENE 303 - Take 1 - PRINT
	Lining up new setup. While this setup at church was being lined up, the dolly-boom shot at other end of street was also being lined up.
10.04	SHOOTING SCENE 289A - Take 1 - NG Action
10.10	" 2 - PRINT
10.14	" 3 - inco. NG Action
10.16	" 4 - PRINT
	Lining up Stationary Plate
10.21	SHOOTING SCENE P-289A - Take 1 - PRINT
	Lining up Dolly-Boom shot - and rehearsing
12.05-1.05am	SUPPER
1.18	SHOOTING SCENE 300A - Take 1 - PRINT
1.23	" 2 - HOLD
1.31	" 3 - inco. NG Camera action
1.33	" 4 - NG Action
1.39	" 5 - inco. NG Action
1.40	" 6 - " " "
1.44	" 7 - PRINT
	Lining up Camera Truck shot in alley. 2nd camera stationary.
3.42	SHOOTING SCENE 308 (2nd camera: X308) Take 1 - inco. NG Action
3.48	" 2 - PRINT (B&W) on X camera
	(Note: XCamera did not turn on Take 1 and slated Take 2 as their Take 1 -- and is to be Printed in B&W)
3.54	Take 3 - NG Action
3.59	" 4 - " "
4.06	" 5 - PRINT
4.14	" 6 - PRINT
	Lining up - same setup as above - covering exit
4.26	SHOOTING SCENE 309 (X309)Take 1 - PRINT
	Lining up new setup -- 2 cameras
4.36	SHOOTING SCENE 309A (X309A) Take 1 - PRINT
	Lining up Plate
4.44	SHOOTING SCENE P-312 - Stationary Plate - Take 1 - PRINT (Above mis-slated. Should be "P-313")
	Lining up new setup
5.00	SHOOTING SCENE 316 - Take 1 - NG Action
5.05	" 2 - PRINT (Above mis-slated. Should be ### "312")
5.20	COMPANY DISMISSED.

FIG. 29. Production log documenting filming of shots for fire sequence under Menzies' second-unit direction.

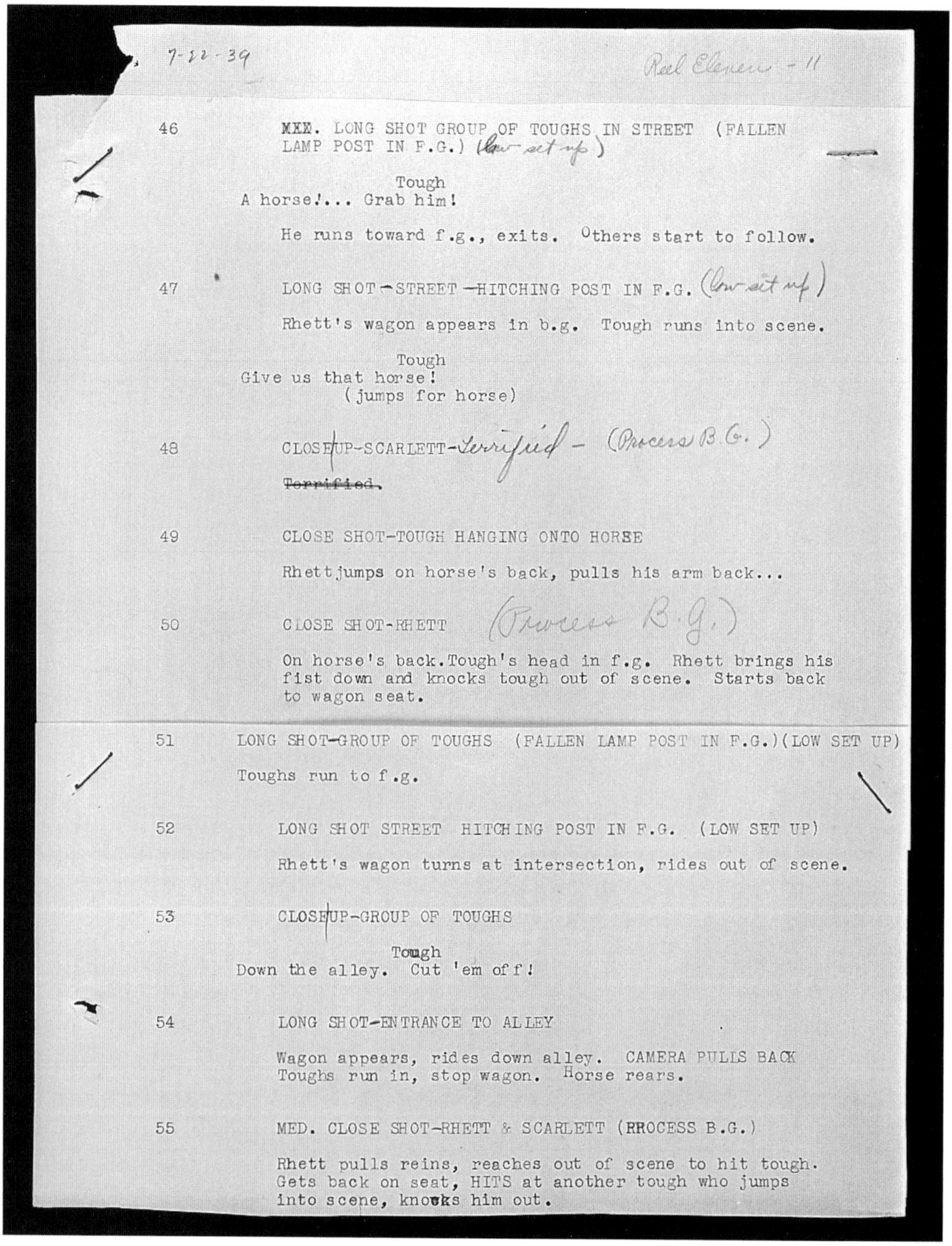

7-22-39 Reel Eleven - 11

46 XXX. LONG SHOT GROUP OF TOUGHS IN STREET (FALLEN LAMP POST IN F.G.) (low set up)

Tough
A horse!... Grab him!

He runs toward f.g., exits. Others start to follow.

47 LONG SHOT-STREET-HITCHING POST IN F.G. (low set up)

Rhett's wagon appears in b.g. Tough runs into scene.

Tough
Give us that horse!
(jumps for horse)

48 CLOSE UP-SCARLETT-Terrified - (Process B.G.)

~~Terrified.~~

49 CLOSE SHOT-TOUGH HANGING ONTO HORSE

Rhett jumps on horse's back, pulls his arm back...

50 CLOSE SHOT-RHETT (Process B.G.)

On horse's back. Tough's head in f.g. Rhett brings his fist down and knocks tough out of scene. Starts back to wagon seat.

51 LONG SHOT-GROUP OF TOUGHS (FALLEN LAMP POST IN F.G.)(LOW SET UP)

Toughs run to f.g.

52 LONG SHOT STREET HITCHING POST IN F.G. (LOW SET UP)

Rhett's wagon turns at intersection, rides out of scene.

53 CLOSE UP-GROUP OF TOUGHS

Tough
Down the alley. Cut 'em off!

54 LONG SHOT-ENTRANCE TO ALLEY

Wagon appears, rides down alley. CAMERA PULLS BACK Toughs run in, stop wagon. Horse rears.

55 MED. CLOSE SHOT-RHETT & SCARLETT (RROCESS B.G.)

Rhett pulls reins, reaches out of scene to hit tough. Gets back on seat, HITS at another tough who jumps into scene, knocks him out.

FIG. 30. This page from intermediate cutting continuity, dating from July 18–22, 1939, shows emendations to the fire sequence.

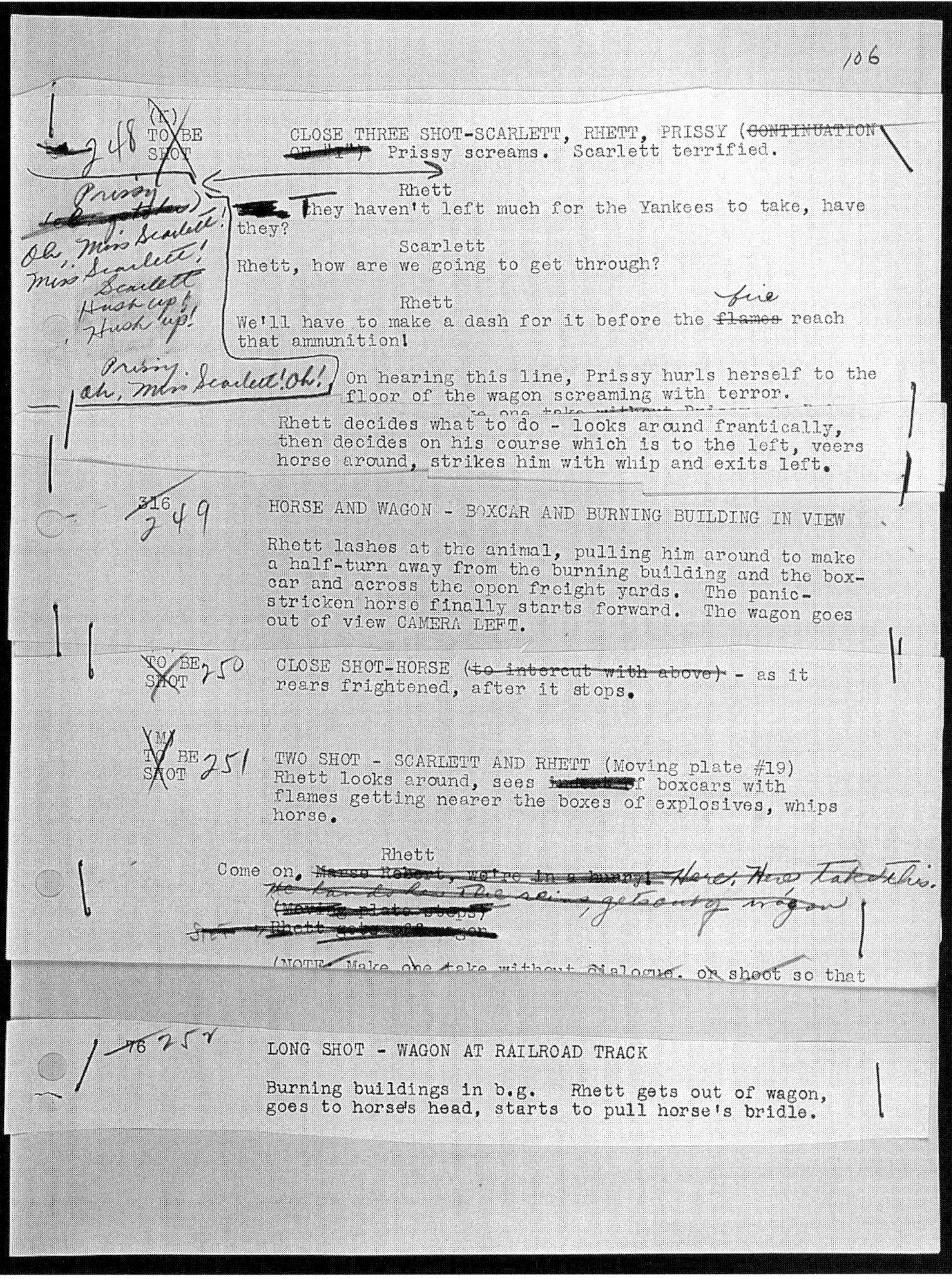

106

(I) ~~TO BE SHOT~~ 248 — CLOSE THREE SHOT-SCARLETT, RHETT, PRISSY (~~CONTINUATION OF "I"~~) Prissy screams. Scarlett terrified.

Prissy
Oh, Miss Scarlett! Miss Scarlett! Scarlett Hush up! Hush up!

Rhett
They haven't left much for the Yankees to take, have they?

Scarlett
Rhett, how are we going to get through?

Rhett
We'll have to make a dash for it before the ~~flames~~ fire reach that ammunition!

Prissy
Oh, Miss Scarlett! Oh!

On hearing this line, Prissy hurls herself to the floor of the wagon screaming with terror.

Rhett decides what to do - looks around frantically, then decides on his course which is to the left, veers horse around, strikes him with whip and exits left.

~~316~~ 249 — HORSE AND WAGON - BOXCAR AND BURNING BUILDING IN VIEW

Rhett lashes at the animal, pulling him around to make a half-turn away from the burning building and the box-car and across the open freight yards. The panic-stricken horse finally starts forward. The wagon goes out of view CAMERA LEFT.

~~TO BE SHOT~~ 250 — CLOSE SHOT-HORSE (~~to intercut with above~~) - as it rears frightened, after it stops.

(M) ~~TO BE SHOT~~ 251 — TWO SHOT - SCARLETT AND RHETT (Moving plate #19) Rhett looks around, sees ~~[illegible]~~ of boxcars with flames getting nearer the boxes of explosives, whips horse.

Rhett
Come on, ~~Marse Robert, we're in a hurry!~~ Here, Here take this.
~~(Moving plate stops)~~
~~Rhett gets off wagon~~

(NOTE: Make one take without dialogue, or shoot so that

~~76~~ 252 — LONG SHOT - WAGON AT RAILROAD TRACK

Burning buildings in b.g. Rhett gets out of wagon, goes to horse's head, starts to pull horse's bridle.

FIG. 31. Cutting-and-stapling of cutting continuity dating from November 1939 shows alteration of the fire sequence at this late date.

	NO	FEET	FRAMES	DESCRIPTION	REEL 5 PAGE 6
Cukor	28A	Continued		Rhett ...if we're going to get across the tracks. Scarlett You're not going that way! Rhett We have to. The McDonough Road's the only one the	
		476	2	Yankees haven't cut yet.	
	29A	480	4	C.U. Scarlett and Prissy. Scarlett puts lamp down.	
	30A			M.S. Baby as it is lifted in and put down beside	
		490	4	Melanie in wagon.	
	31A	13-9		M.S. Scarlett and Rhett on seat of wagon. Scarlett Oh, wait. I forgot to lock the front door. Well, what are you laughing at? Rhett At you, locking the Yankees out.	
					DISSOLVE TO:
Menzies	32A	11-4		L.S. Street. Rhett and his wagon load driving away	
		514	8	from CAMERA.	
Menzies	33A			L.S. Straggling army. Rhett and Scarlett enter left	
		525	13	b.g. in wagon, drive toward CAMERA and stop.	
Flem Menz plate	34A			M.L. Reverse shot Rhett and Scarlett watching the stragglers pass. Scarlett Oh, dear, I wish they'd hurry. Rhett I wouldn't be in such a hurry to see them go if I	
		534	0	were you, my dear.	
	35A			M.C.S. Rhett and Scarlett on seat of wagon. Rhett	
		538	0	With them goes the last semblance of law and order.	
Menzies	36A	541	3	L.S. Window as bench goes thru it.	
Menz plate Flem	37A			M.L.S. Rhett and Scarlett on seat of wagon. Rhett	
		543	10	The scavengers aren't wasting any time.	
Menzies	38A			L.S. of street - people running every which way.	
		551	4	Fire in b.g.	
	39A			M.L.S. Rhett and Scarlett shooting past horse's head. Rhett whips horse. Rhett	
		554	3	We've got to get out of here fast.	
	40A			L.S. Street full of hoodlums. One hoodlum spys Rhett's horse off scene and runs toward CAMERA.	
	REEL 5 PAGE 6				CONTINUED:

FIGS. 32–35. Hal Kern's "final dialogue and cutting continuity" of December 9, 1939, transcribes the completed film; penciled notes identify the director of each film shot.

	NO	FEET	FRAMES	DESCRIPTION
				REEL 5 PAGE 7
	40A continued			Tough
		558	11	There's a horse!
	41A			L.S. Street. Rhett and Scarlett in wagon in b.g.
		563	0	Tough enters from right and grabs at horse.
Flem	42A	565	1	C.U. Scarlett screaming.
Menzies	43A			M.S. Tough grabbing horse. Rhett jumps on horses'
		566	8	back swinging at tough.
Flem	44A	570	0	M.S. Rhett as he hits tough knocking him away.
Menz	45A	571	7	M.L.S. Group of toughs running toward CAMERA.
	46A			L.S. Rhett and Scarlett in wagon. Rhett beats the
		572	14	horse and the wagon starts out to left.
	47A			C.U. Toughs
				Tough
		575	8	Down the alley - cut them off.
	48A			L.S. Rhett and Scarlett in wagon coming toward CAMERA
				thru alley. The toughs enter from f.g., and surround
		582	13	the horse. Horse rears.
Flem	49A	585	3	M.S. Rhett and Scarlett. Rhett raises his whip.
	50A	587	6	C.U. Tough as Rhett hits him in the jaw.
	51A	589	15	M.S. Rhett fighting off toughs from every side.
	52A			M.S. Scarlett. A tough makes a grab for her and Rhett
		593	9	lashes out at him.
	53A	594	7	M.C.S. Rhett as he kicks at a tough.
Menzies	54A			C.U. Tough as Rhett's foot connects with his face.
				Another tough comes at Rhett. Rhett socks him.
				Tough
		598	2	Give me that horse.
Flem	55A			C.S. Scarlett; Prissy appears behind her.
				Prissy
		600	5	Miss Scarlett! Miss Scarlett!
Menz	56A			M.L.S. Wagon with Rhett swinging whip riding thru
		602	1	toughs.
Flem	57A	606	3	C.S. Melanie, baby and Prissy in back of wagon.
Menz & Cukor	58A			L.S. Reverse Shot - Rhett and Scarlett on seat of
		612	4	wagon driving away from CAMERA toward flames in b.g.

REEL 5 PAGE 7

FIG. 33

NO	FEET	FRAMES	DESCRIPTION — REEL 5 PAGE 8
59A	617	3	M.S. Rhett and Scarlett on seat of wagon - Prissy standing in b.g. coming toward CAMERA. Prissy Miss Scarlett!
60A	625	15	L.S. Burning warehouses. CAMERA PANS showing the extent of the fire. Rhett They haven't left much for the Yankees to take, have they?
61A	631	9	M.S. Rhett and Scarlett. He whips horse and they start out. Rhett We'll have to make a dash for it before the fire reaches that ammunition.
62A	636	8	M.S. Box cars with fire in b.g. Boxes in car reading EXPLOSIVES HIGHLY INFLAMMABLE.
63A	642	2	L.S. Shooting thru buildings. Rhett and Scarlett enter in wagon and drive thru, pulling over boxes.
64A	650	0	L.S. INFERNO. Fire falling around them. Rhett and Scarlett drive into scene. Horse stops.
65A	653	6	M.L.S. Horse as it rears.
66A	664	15	L.S. INFERNO. Rhett jumps from wagon and goes to horse's head. Rhett Come on!
67A	668	9	M.S. Boxes marked EXPLOSIVES in box car.
68A	671	7	C.U. Melanie, baby in her arms, and Prissy.
69A	673	12	C.S. Rhett at horse's head Rhett Throw me your shawl.
70A	675	7	M.C.S. Scarlett. She throws shawl.
71A	682	5	M.C.S. Rhett at horse's head. He catches shawl and wraps it around horse's head. Rhett Sorry, but you'll like it better if you don't see anything.
72A	688	7	L.S. INFERNO. Rhett takes horse by the head and leads him thru fire.
73A	691	12	C.U. Melanie in wagon. Baby by her side.

REEL 5 PAGE 8

FIG. 34

NO	FEET	FRAMES	DESCRIPTION
Cukor Menzies 74A			L.S. INFERNO. Rhett leading horse on the run thru
	709	2	the flames away from CAMERA. They exit left b.g.
Kern 75A	711	10	M.L.S. Box car, it is on fire. It explodes.
76A	713	7	M.L.S. another box car - it explodes.
77A	716	12	M.L.S. another box car - it explodes.
Cukor Menzies Cosgrove 78A	13		E.L.S. INFERNO. Horse and wagon in silhouette going from right to left. They almost get out and the building in background falls shooting fire everywhere. DISSOLVE TO:
Menzies 79A	17-4		L.S. Straggling soldiers coming toward CAMERA. Rhett and Scarlett can be seen in b.g. coming toward CAMERA.
	750	12	FINISH SECTION "A".

REEL 5 PAGE 9

REEL 5 PAGE 9 pb

FIG. 35

Immediately afterward, a shop window is broken, and pandemic looting ensues, forcing the wagon's occupants into a confrontation with a group of "toughs," who attempt to steal the horse and vehicle. Breaking free, Rhett directs the wagon down an adjacent alley, where their flight is checked by the same hoodlums who, after being knocked about again by Rhett, are left behind once more. The spreading fire and balky horse complicate the wagon's subsequent passage through the railyard. Leaping from his seat on the wagon and covering the animal's eyes with Scarlett's shawl, Rhett leads horse and wagon on foot, exiting to safety as the munition boxcars explode. The screen is filled with the flames of the collapsing warehouses, and the scene fades by another dissolve (see Figures 36–83).

The sequence no longer serves to stir Rhett to make a patriotic commitment, but instead confirms in Scarlett a cynical view of the world. Their desperate dispute with looters over possession of the stolen horse and wagon, their subsequent escape from the fire, and the symbolic self-destruction of the Confederacy all serve to sanction for protagonists and viewers such social-Darwinist attitudes as the "survival of the fittest" and the exploitation of opportunity. Much of the accompanying musical composition, which provides a menacing orchestral variation on the theme of Dan Emmett's "Dixie," underscores the adventure's undermining of jingoism and sentimental idealism by manipulation of fear. The wagon episode also serves as an effective vehicle for exhibiting Rhett's masculine prowess and for exploiting Gable's macho screen appeal. Although Selznick advised Howard, in a letter dated January 3, 1937, not to invent a sequence showing Rhett "doing his stuff" as a blockade runner, the producer reconsidered this advice two years later. Writing to his West Coast story editor, Val Lewton, on March 13, 1939, Selznick admitted that it was imperative to present "in action scenes" characters who "stand around during most of the picture doing so much talking," and that he sought an "excuse to do a good blockade running incident with Rhett Butler." Although these "action scenes" were never taken, Selznick's concern over their necessity undoubtedly influenced the rewriting of much of the fire sequence.

FIGS. 36–83. These 48 frame enlargements (reading left–right, top–bottom) represent the 47 shots comprising the fire sequence in *Gone with the Wind,* identified by corresponding shot numbers from Hal Kern's final dialogue and cutting continuity of December 9, 1939.

FIG. 36. Reel 5, shot number 32A. Director: Menzies. FIG. 37. Reel 5, shot number 33A. Director: Menzies. FIG. 38. Reel 5, shot number 34A. Director: Fleming; Menzies, background plate for process shot. FIG. 39. Reel 5, shot number 35A. Director: Fleming; Menzies responsible for background plate for process shot. FIG. 40. Reel 5, shot number 36A. Director: Menzies. FIG. 41. Reel 5, shot number 37A. Director: Fleming; Menzies responsible for background plate for process shot.

FIG. 42. Reel 5, shot number 38A. Director: Menzies. FIG. 43. Reel 5, shot number 39A. Director: Menzies. FIG. 44. Reel 5, shot number 40A. Director: Menzies. FIG. 45. Reel 5, shot number 41A. Director: Menzies. FIG. 46. Reel 5, shot number 42A. Director: Fleming. FIG. 47. Reel 5, shot number 43A. Director: Menzies.

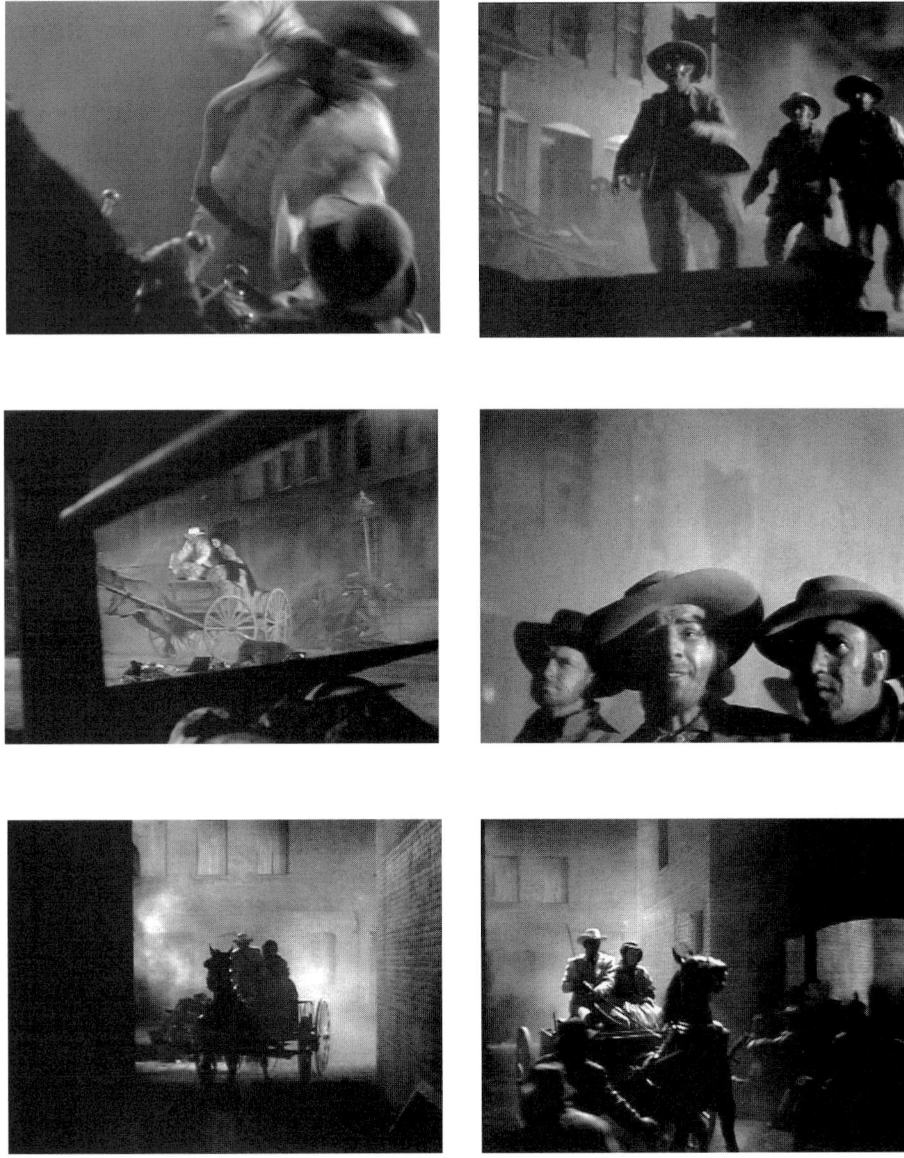

FIG. 48. Reel 5, shot number 44A. Director: Fleming. FIG. 49. Reel 5, shot number 45A. Director: Menzies. FIG. 50. Reel 5, shot number 46A. Director: Menzies. FIG. 51. Reel 5, shot number 47A. Director: Menzies. FIGS. 52–53. Reel 5, shot number 48A. Director: Menzies.

FIG. 54. Reel 5, shot number 49A. Director: Fleming. FIG. 55. Reel 5, shot number 50A. Director: Fleming. FIG. 56. Reel 5, shot number 51A. Director: Fleming. FIG. 57. Reel 5, shot number 52A. Director: Fleming. FIG. 58. Reel 5, shot number 53A. Director: Fleming. FIG. 59. Reel 5, shot number 54A. Director: Menzies.

FIG. 60. Reel 5, shot number 55A. Director: Fleming. FIG. 61. Reel 5, shot number 56A. Director: Menzies. FIG. 62. Reel 5, shot number 57A. Director: Fleming. FIG. 63. Reel 5, shot number 58A. Both Menzies and Cukor credited for direction. FIG. 64. Reel 5, shot number 59A. Director: Fleming; Menzies responsible for background plate for process shot. FIG. 65. Reel 5, shot number 60A. Both Menzies and Cukor credited for direction.

FIG. 66. Reel 5, shot number 61A. Director: Fleming; Menzies responsible for background plate for process shot. FIG. 67. Reel 5, shot number 62A. Director: Hal Kern. FIG. 68. Reel 5, shot number 63A. Both Menzies and Cukor credited for direction. FIG. 69. Reel 5, shot number 64A. Both Menzies and Cukor credited for direction. FIG. 70. Reel 5, shot number 65A. Both Hal Kern and assistant director Eric G. Stacey credited for direction. FIG. 71. Reel 5, shot number 66A. Both Menzies and Cukor credited for direction.

FIG. 72. Reel 5, shot number 67A. Director: Hal Kern. FIG. 73. Reel 5, shot number 68A. Director: Fleming. FIG. 74. Reel 5, shot number 69A. Director: Fleming; Menzies responsible for background plate for process shot. FIG. 75. Reel 5, shot number 70A. Director: Fleming; Menzies responsible for background plate for process shot. FIG. 76. Reel 5, shot number 71A. Director: Fleming; Menzies responsible for background plate for process shot. FIG. 77. Reel 5, shot number 72A. Both Menzies and Cukor credited for direction.

FIG. 78. Reel 5, shot number 73A. Director: Fleming. FIG. 79. Reel 5, shot number 74A. Both Menzies and Cukor credited for direction. FIG. 80. Reel 5, shot number 75A. Director: Hal Kern. FIG. 81. Reel 5, shot number 76A. Director: Hal Kern. FIG. 82. Reel 5, shot number 77A. Director: Hal Kern. FIG. 83. Reel 5, shot number 78A. Cukor, Menzies, and Cosgrove credited for direction of this final shot.

Corresponding Scripts and Sketches of the Fire Sequence

In *Hollywood Art: Art Direction in the Days of the Great Studios*, Beverly Heisner aptly remarked that "the most famous continuity sketches in film history are William Cameron Menzies' for *Gone with the Wind*." She also recognized that "their unprecedented completeness is widely credited with having shaped the picture's cohesiveness despite its numerous directors."[36] As discussed already in this chapter, the latter claim has been proffered by many authors—Flamini, Corliss and Clarens, Hambley and Downing, and even Balio. In 1994, in *Setting the Scene*, Robert S. Sennett joined these ranks and brusquely concurred that "Menzies' sketches provided visual stability," in contrast to "leadership [which] changed with the weather, . . . scripts [which] were written, torn up, rewritten, filmed, and refilmed, . . . [and a] scatterbrained shooting schedule and constant battle with and interference from the producer that the cast and crew had to tolerate."[37]

However, comparison of this picture's largest extant group of continuity drawings with successive versions of the fire sequence's scenario discloses evidence contradicting opinions such as these—that the film crews and directors routinely deferred to storyboards and that the production designer's work proceeded independently of the producer's dictations. In general, treatment of this episode in these sixty-six "storyboard" sketches corresponds to Selznick's recommendation of placing "particular emphasis on a constantly mounting violence in the shots" and on "the fire getting greater and greater as [the characters] drive through the streets, climaxing in the panoramic effect" which was prescribed in his memo of November 21, 1938. The confrontation with "toughs" is illustrated by twenty-four of these drawings, and another twenty-four address the business of the protagonists facing the fire; in contrast, retreating soldiers are subjects in only four of the drawings, and their portrayal is cursory. The remainder of the sketches consist of a limited variety of exterior views and reaction shots of Scarlett and Rhett in close-up. None of these drawings jibe with Howard's initial screenplays, and only a few correspond to specific imagery in the picture.

The length of this sequence of shots in the film is demarcated formally by a pair of dissolves. Following Rhett's laughter over Scarlett's intention to delay their departure by returning to Pittypat's front door and "locking the Yankees out," the episode begins with a special-effects shot of the wagon moving away on Peachtree Street toward an inflamed downtown Atlanta and concludes with the spectacular collapse of the warehouses in the railyard, over which was printed the wagon being led to safety by Rhett. Although Howard had placed the first dissolve in a position within the narrative consistent with a break (i.e., a typographical spacing) in Mitchell's twenty-third chapter, Menzies chose to begin his own scenario of the fire sequence with an establishing shot of the facade of Pittypat's house and of Rhett helping to load the wagon—a point of departure observed by Garrett in his revisions.[38] The drawings of this sequence in the Selznick collection adhere to the latter scheme.

A corresponding relationship between artwork and filmscript can be discerned when the

FIG. 84. Lyle Wheeler poses with storyboard of sketches corresponding to shot numbers 1 through 8 of the revised Menzies-Garrett fire-sequence scenario of December 7, 1938. (Note that placement of Prissy's figure between Scarlett and Rhett in final sketch on storyboard distinguishes December 7 script from earlier ones dated December 2 and 5.)

scenes depicted on the storyboard of twelve sketches held by Lyle Wheeler in a publicity photograph reproduced in the *New York Times Magazine* on December 10, 1938 are compared with descriptions provided of shot numbers 1–8 in the revision of the Menzies-Garrett "Fire Sequence" scenario, dated December 7, 1938[39] (see Figure 84; cf. Figures 12–15). Specifically, the presence of the figure of Prissy between Scarlett and Rhett in the final, bottom-right drawing on this storyboard (drawings are read from left to right, top to bottom) distinguishes the draft of the scenario dated December 7 from earlier versions by Garrett dated December 2 and 5, which feature only Scarlett and Rhett in shot number 8.

Likewise, those scenes depicted on a different storyboard of twelve drawings which is preserved in the Selznick collection and is marked with a prominent "2." in the upper-right corner of the original support board display a similarity to the actions described first in shot numbers 9 through 20 in this same scenario of December 7. Confirming this correspondence, penciled notations of the identical shot numbers were discovered on the reverse sides of these sketches when they were removed temporarily from the original support board for the purpose of conservation[40] (see Figure 85; cf. Figures 15–17). Inclusion of the exploded cornice in shot 16 (corresponding to the fourth drawing from the left on the middle row) distinguishes this scenario from earlier scripts by Garrett and Menzies.

This same scenario is represented by additional numbers of continuity drawings. Attention to the visible numbers penciled on the reverse of fourteen of the remaining fifty-four unmounted drawings in the Selznick collection and to the scenes depicted on the obverse identifies these sketches as illustrations of shot numbers 21 through 30 in the December 7 script (see Figure 86; cf. Figures 17–18). The fact that numbers on these drawings run from 21 to 30 and not from 302 to 311, as numbers of these same shots do in an emended copy of the December 7 script, dated December 27, 1938, also attests to the likelihood that the sketches were produced from the former script before the latter date. (Note also that description of action within some shots in the filmscript required the drawing of more than one sketch; the ratio of shots enumerated and sketches drawn is thus an uneven one.) In summary, a comparison of artwork and filmscripts has disclosed that this series of continuity drawings was drawn for the purpose of illustrating compositional requirements of shots enumerated in a specific filmscript dating only a few days before the filming of the fire on the backlot.

Approximately twenty other unmounted drawings in the collection correspond to shots described in Garrett's earliest revisions of Menzies' "Fire Sequence" scenario, dated December 2 and 5, 1938. Half of these sketches illustrate the same opening shots that were redrawn with alteration for the storyboard produced to illustrate the December 7 script and are pictured in the photograph of Lyle Wheeler in the *New York Times Magazine*. Most of the remaining drawings in this group apply to corresponding shot descriptions provided in all script versions produced by Garrett. Specifically, the "Bacchanalian" scene with its "Dante's Inferno" effect and the concatenation of the close-up of Melanie sheltering her baby, the reverse shot of the wagon fleeing from the looters yet hurrying toward the flames, and the "two-shot" of Scarlett and Rhett, reacting with alarm to a point-of-view shot of the fiery railyard, are represented by storyboard illustrations which are recognizable in the released form of the filmed sequence.

A few of the drawings which correspond to opening shots of the December 2 and 5 fire sequence scripts may have been prepared earlier for the November 8 scenario that was written by Menzies himself. These include the establishing shot of Pittypat's doorstep and view of the wagon's departure with emphasis on the lamp carried by Scarlett, abandoned yet burning by the gate in the foreground; however, these same shots are found in Garrett's scripts of early December. Only a single pair of sketches in the Selznick collection definitely represents obstruction of the wagon's path by the line of retreating Confederate troops in a manner unique to Menzies' November 8 script (see Figure 87).

A comparison of the preserved artwork with Menzies' own scenario of November 8 discloses that extant storyboard illustrations represent little more than one fifth of the shots; few of these are recognizable in the released film. In contrast, most of the Menzies-Garrett revisions of the following month are represented, if evidence of the storyboards pictured with Lyle Wheeler in the publicity photograph is taken into consideration; nevertheless, only a quarter of the shots described in these scenarios are accounted for in the film presenta-

FIG. 85. Original 20 × 30-inch storyboard of twelve mounted watercolor sketches corresponds to imagery described in shot numbers 9 through 20 of the revised Menzies-Garrett fire sequence scenario of December 7, 1938.

tion. The percentage of script-to-screen shot correspondences (i.e., the percentage of descriptions in particular script versions matching shots that actually contributed to the film sequence as released) is doubled by further shooting scripts written through June 1939; cutting continuities dating from July and November boost this percentage to, respectively, eighty-five and ninety-five.

(The equation for determining the percentage of script-to-screen shot correspondences is simply the division of the specific number of corresponding shots in a particular intermediate script version by 47—i.e., by the exact number of shots in the fire sequence constructed by Selznick and Hal Kern for the film's release. The purpose of this exercise is to chart the episode's development by indicating what percentages of shots were influential in the sequence's ultimate composition in each of the successive filmscripts.)

In other words, although a "complete script in sketch form" of the fire sequence was produced in early December 1938, it cannot be said even of this most spectacular episode in *Gone with the Wind* that the film was "pre-cut," which had been Selznick's expressed intention. Construction of this sequence was altered by subsequent production scripts and continuities, and the ordering of as many as half of the shots changed dramatically during the post-production period, when shots were taken still and inserted.

To reiterate, elaboration of the brief scene in Mitchell's novel began when Selznick recognized its spectacular potential and the importance of his company's meeting the "showmanship requirements of the picture." Whereas

FIG. 86. Reconstructed storyboard arrangement of eleven original, loose watercolor drawings corresponds to shot numbers 21 through 27 in the revised Menzies-Garrett fire sequence scenario of December 7, 1938.

Howard saw nothing of interest in the episode itself and devoted little space initially to its dramatization, Menzies took the initiative of preparing his own scenario of the sequence and introduced two obstacles to the wagon's retreat—specifically, looters and the fire in the railyard—thereby lengthening the episode's duration and intensifying its dramatic value.

Selznick and Garrett revised this scenario several times before the filming on December 10. Shots described in the December 7 version which were drawn for storyboarding and remain in the sequence as released include that of the wagon halted by retreating troops, that of the smashing of the bakery window, that of Peachtree Street "designed to give a Dante's Inferno effect," that of the camera panning as the wagon's path through an alley converges with that taken by the "toughs" to "cut them off," that of a rear view of the wagon departing the alley in the direction of flames rising in the background, which is followed by a close-up of Melanie sheltering her newborn, and that of Prissy popping up in alarm behind Scarlett and Rhett on the wagon seat, her screams carrying over into their view of the burning railyard.

A series of additional continuities of this sequence was written before the filming of shots requiring principal actors was undertaken in the middle of June, for which storyboards were consulted still. "I think that just as soon as possible I should like to have a meeting with Menzies and Kern to discuss the exact continuity of the fire sequence and the old men and boys sequence," Selznick advised Klune earlier in a memo of June 2, "at which time we should run these two sequences on

FIG. 87. This pair of individual sketches represents obstruction of the wagon's path by retreating Confederate troops in a manner unique to Menzies' written script of the fire sequence and corresponds to shot numbers 123B and 124.

the Moviola and have available rough sketches showing exactly what is missing and where we are going to cut in the transparency shots with the principals and any other missing shots." The linkage of shots of retreating soldiers, of Rhett's observation of the departure of martial law, of the smashing of the shop window, of Rhett's delivery of the line, "The scavengers aren't wasting any time," and of the "Cosgrove 'Dante's Inferno' " (i.e., of the general looting scene on Peachtree Street at Five Points) was constructed as it appears in the released sequence, and much of the organization of shots depicting events in the railyard is in place. Principal photography was completed officially on June 27, when Gable departed from the production. On July 5, Menzies was loaned to Alexander Korda in England for the remake of *The Thief of Baghdad* (1940). The remaining half of this sequence's shots was reordered in the editing room, where Selznick and his "cutters" sequestered themselves in late 1939, working relentlessly toward a premiere deadline.

With respect to the claim of Menzies' design of this motion picture by way of its storyboarding, it has been demonstrated in this chapter that the influence of the continuity drawings on development of the fire sequence was both substantial and limited. Examination of earlier scripts was undertaken to facilitate an effective comparison with the sketches themselves which, if compared with the film alone, would yield far less apparent correspondence for comment. Although a significant number of sketches was discovered to correspond to an intermediate version of the filmscript, it was shown that this sequence's final form benefited from each of its stages of development.

In the case of the making of the fire sequence—arguably the most spectacular and memorable episode in this motion picture—the contributions of the successive screenplays, of the many writers and directors, and of the drawings credited to the first production designer in film history, who also served as a contributor to the filmscript, have been examined in this chapter in relationship to one another's influence and to the producer's executive authority. The analysis of this most famous example in classical American cinema of storyboarding of a film sequence also demonstrates the power exercised by a most prominent Hollywood producer through his unprecedented commission of a film designer, his ploy of playing this creative technician against the film director in order to generate greater options, and his revision of any portion of the script in order to assure his own control of the shape taken by the enterprise. In the next chapter, other examples of continuity drawings that a[illegible] served from the making of *Gone with the Win*[illegible] are examined in order to question the legend of the "complete script in sketch form" at greater length and to determine to what degree exploitation of Menzies' designs in the staging of the fire sequence was representative of this film's production.

FOUR

Film Direction and Production Design of *Gone with the Wind*

Production design developed as a specific industrial assignment within the commercial filmmaking process as a result of Selznick's pursuit of both artistry and economy in the creation of imagery for *Gone with the Wind*. Since Menzies' inauguration of this role, the production designer has been credited for much of a film's "look." According to Selznick's memoranda, the purpose of Menzies' storyboarding of the screenplay was twofold: to aid in the composition of shots (the production of which required special effects in a great many instances), and to assist in their continuity (by "pre-cutting" the picture before filming and by regulating use of color). In contrast with the art director's task, Menzies' duties were not restricted to interior design and set construction. His influence extended from the film's planning, through visualization of imagery for determining set requirements and special effects, into the filming itself, through his program for dramatic use of color cinematography and lighting and through the placement of actors within the picture frame, which challenged the director's authority on the shooting set. Nevertheless, delineation of continuity remained subject to script revision. Moreover, monitoring the design work, revising the script, and arbitrating conflicts between the production designer and film directors were part of Selznick's own role and, as such, facilitated the producer's control over the film's making.

In the previous chapter, analysis of storyboards drawn for the fire sequence in *Gone with the Wind* disclosed the contributions and limitations of the production designer's role in the making of a most important scene in this film. Without a doubt, working for Selznick tested Menzies' collaborative ability when the producer's revisions of the script and of scenes already filmed, together with his replacement of cameramen and directors, altered the continuity of shots and precluded use of many of the compositions designed for this picture prior to filming. The comparisons of sketches and passages from scripts of other sequences in this film which are offered in this chapter confirm the production designer's extraordinary influence on *Gone with the Wind* and his deference to the decisions of its producer.

Approximately two hundred watercolors from this film production, many of them continuity sketches, are preserved in the Selznick collection. These designs represent only a fraction of the total number of drawings purportedly produced. Following a production's completion, artwork was not esteemed to be of the same value to the company as scripts, which most studios preserved with intermediate drafts in the event of copyright litigation or the sale of remake rights. Art-department drawings were appropriated by individuals as souvenirs or were discarded. Because little artwork has survived from the classical Hollywood era, the drawings preserved from *Gone with the Wind* provide rare examples of this type of pre-production design. Even for this film, the fact that greater numbers of sketches were produced than have been preserved is attested to by images in publicity stills of Menzies and special-effects director Jack Cosgrove standing before stacks of these drawings and of Lyle Wheeler holding a fire-sequence storyboard next to which are countless shot compositions stashed in a set of drawers and now lost, as is much of this work (see Figures 6 and 84).

The artwork that survives from the film production of *Gone with the Wind* exists in various dimensions. Greater attention to architecture and to set design is exhibited in most of the larger drawings. In contrast, the smaller sketches address shot composition, color use, and continuity design and in many instances are mounted in groupings, in storyboard manner. Most of the latter sketches appear to have been drawn in reference to shot descriptions specified in various intermediate filmscripts.

Visualization of shot compositions, while credited for enabling the realization of a distinctive and consistent "look," limited the requirements of set construction when drawings served as designs for "process photography," or special-effects cinematography—such as rear projection, glass shots, and matte work. With the last technique, portions of a setting could be created entirely by painted elements or miniatures, which were combined with live action via multiple exposure of the motion picture film. In his book *The Technique of Special Effects Cinematography*, Raymond Fielding explains that while procedures for matte work are various, all derive from a fundamental process, which he summarizes:

> In conventional earlier practice, part of the image which was recorded by the camera was obscured during first exposure by a "matte"—an opaque card or plate inserted into the external matte box or the intermittent movement of a camera—so as to prevent the recording of certain portions of a set or scene. During a subsequent exposure, a "counter-matte," whose outlines conformed exactly to those of the matte, was similarly inserted, and a new scene was exposed and fitted into place with the rest of the already recorded image.[1]

FIG. 88. Unsigned watercolor drawing, 22 × 30 inches, depicting carrion on battlefield.

The purposes of using matte work in the composition of shots were aesthetic, narratological, economical, and industrial. Scenes were ornamented by the additional decorative elements, narrative presentation was enriched by more convincing delineation of settings, construction costs were reduced by the need to build only a fraction of the architecture, and a separate department was established in most studios for undertaking this specific work. Clarence W. D. Slifer, who was employed as Cosgrove's assistant at SIP and who rose to become director of special-effects photography at 20th Century-Fox, recalled that at least one hundred matte shots utilizing painted imagery contributed to the making of *Gone with the Wind*.

In an article published in *American Cinematographer* in 1983, Slifer divulged the procedures employed in producing many of these composite views; effects in the film ranged from the apparently mundane (for example, a train's arrival at the old Atlanta station) to the spectacular (such as the pull-back shot of Scarlett and her father overlooking Tara that appears at the film's beginning and that combined the silhouettes of doubles with separate matte paintings of the spreading oak in the foreground and of house and sky in the background).[2] Additional examples of matte work

FIG. 89. Drawing of dead on an abandoned battlefield, through which Scarlett drives a horse and wagon along the line of the horizon on the left side; 30 × 40 inches, signed by "Mac" Johnson.

and of other special-effects techniques exploited in *Gone with the Wind* are reproduced in Haver's books and in the video presentation written by David Thomson, *"Gone with the Wind": The Making of a Legend*.

Many examples of artwork in the Selznick collection are designs for portions of more complex assemblages or are archetypes of shots that were realized more elaborately through special-effects processes. Illustrative of the first case are several large polychrome drawings of carrion on battlefields. In contrast, intricate composite photography, according to Haver, allowed the creation of the battleground through which Scarlett drives her wagon on the return to Tara following the escape from Atlanta in the film. "This shot of the battlefield was a combination of five separate pieces of film," Haver claimed. "The wagon and its occupants were filmed separately; the curling black smoke was another piece; the foreground and left side of the frame, with the dead soldiers, was a Cosgrove painting; the overturned canvas wagon was a separate miniature; and the sky was another painting"[3] (see Figures 88–89). Typical of the second case is the sketch of Mammy, Prissy, and Pork arriving on foot at the doorstep of the Butler mansion; as demonstrated in the video *"Gone with the Wind": The Making of a Legend*, this shot's produc-

FIG. 90. Unsigned drawing of Mammy, Uncle Peter, and Prissy before Butler mansion in Atlanta; 16 × 22 inches.

tion required composite use of a matte painting of larger architectural scale and live action filmed at the entrance to Selznick's studio (see Figure 90).

An instance of artwork approximating the dramatic intensity of a composite shot is the rendering of Scarlett at the foot of the ravaged staircase at Twelve Oaks which is signed by Menzies' assistant, Joseph McMillan ("Mac") Johnson. This drawing was composed in a vertical format and corresponds to the description of a shot in the filmscript of February 27, 1939, which was altered between June 19 and 20 that year to read: "Int. Ruined stairway of Twelve Oaks (Miniature). Camera pans down the once beautiful stairway to Scarlett (double) entering in the ruined hall below, looking around her aghast." Although the direction of the camera tilt changed from down to up in the final process shot, which was directed by Menzies himself, the match of sketch and scene as shot and released is unaffected (see Figures 91–94).

The film presentation certainly benefited from these planned compositions. "Jack [Cosgrove] was a great man for spotting opportunities for matte shots," Slifer admitted.[4] That Selznick himself demanded as much from the

FIG. 91. This dramatic watercolor rendering of Scarlett at the foot of the ravaged grand staircase at Twelve Oaks is signed by "Mac" Johnson and corresponds to shot number 345 of the "rainbow" script of February 27, 1939, which was altered between June 19 and 20, 1939, for "process work"; 24 × 16 inches.

FIG. 92. Another drawing of Scarlett in the ruins of Twelve Oaks, signed by Dorothea Holt; 22 × 23 inches.

FIG. 93. Miniature of Twelve Oaks utilized for filming.

art and special-effects departments is indicated in his memo of June 20, 1939 to both Cosgrove and Menzies, with the request, "I should like one of you to get up for me a really good sketch showing exactly what we are going to get in the pull-back of Gerald and Scarlett and in the pull-back of Scarlett at the end of the picture." Slifer's description of the similar method used in the composition of both shots was noted earlier in this chapter. The latter shot is in fact the final one in the film and also recalls Scarlett's defiant pose during delivery of her pledge of "never going hungry again," which concludes the film presentation at the point of intermission and which benefited also from the producer's specific dictations to the production designer. "I think we ought to pan with Scarlett from the shot on the ground where her despair changes to determination, the camera following her as she raises herself to full height, and staying with her for the oath," Selznick advised Menzies in the same memorandum.

Such prescription was characteristic of the producer's use of the production designer. "We get so few opportunities to see Tara in the first part of the picture that I think we might plan a long night shot . . . with the carriage driving up and with perhaps some dogs barking . . . to precede the shot of Mammy in the interior of the house as the household comes to life on Ellen's return," Selznick dictated on March 20, 1939, concerning the creation of an establishing shot which contributed ultimately to the film's composition. "I wish Mr. Menzies would do a sketch of it and check it with Mr. Fleming and myself and I think it could be picked up by Mr. Menzies if Mr. Fleming has no objections," the producer added, politely acknowledging their respective roles. (Haver credited this shot's realization exclusively to the use of matte paintings and of miniatures.)[5]

The teamwork manifested by the many creative technicians employed in this film's making is acknowledged also in Slifer's article:

FIG. 94. Frame enlargements of shot filmed under Menzies' direction, described in cutting continuity of December 9, 1939 (Reel 5, page 15, shot number 38B) as follows: "E.L.S. [Extreme Long Shot] Scarlett near staircase, Prissy in wagon seen in b.g. Camera pans up to ruined second story."

> Bill Menzies . . . and Jack [Cosgrove] worked very closely together. All of Menzies' ideas were either sketched by him [*sic*] or by his sketch artists, Dorothea Holt Redman, J. McMillan Johnson, and Howard Richman. When one of his ideas was okayed by Mr. Selznick we would plan on the best way to put it on film. We also worked very closely with Lyle Wheeler in achieving his ideas for the sets. After we photographed a matte shot we would send an 11 × 14 enlargement of the matted scene to Lyle . . . [who] would have one of his men draw upon this print what he wanted in the completed shot. From this working sketch-photograph our matte artists would then paint the matte shot. We also worked very closely with film editors Hal Kern and James Newcom. Whenever possible Jack would run all the shots or tests with them and Mr. Selznick for whatever changes they might wish.[6]

In addition, MGM's cooperation and collaboration were enlisted for the production of a spectacular moment in the film's presentation which is credited to Menzies's design and is represented in the Selznick collection by an unsigned watercolor (see Figure 95). The brief shot of troops marching in parallel, diagonal lines through an abstract field of clouds, fire, and smoke appears at the beginning of the film's second half under the superimposed words, "And the wind swept through Georgia . . . Sherman!" According to Haver,

> as production neared completion, time was running short, and Cosgrove's work load was fierce, so Hal Kern took some unused battle footage, some fire effects, and some of Menzies's sketches over to the MGM special effects department, where Peter Ballbusch combined them all and came up with this stunningly effective collage, which invariably drew applause when the picture was given its first press and industry screenings."[7]

Like the analyses of production materials offered in the previous chapters, the examination of representative samples of continuity sketches and of set designs that continues in this section clarifies and corrects the record of the making of *Gone with the Wind*. Specifically, Menzies' role is evaluated not as an individual artist or "auteur," but rather in terms of the production designer's constructive influence as a principal collaborator. Selznick's interaction in this film's composition is represented also, and his exploitation of the filmmaking collective is illustrated by an examination of alterations made to the motion picture during the development of its screenplay, which spanned the entire period of production. As with the analysis in the previous chapter of the fire sequence's development, successive filmscripts are examined and compared with extant artwork, which, if contrasted only with the film presentation, would yield less correspondence for an appreciation and understanding.

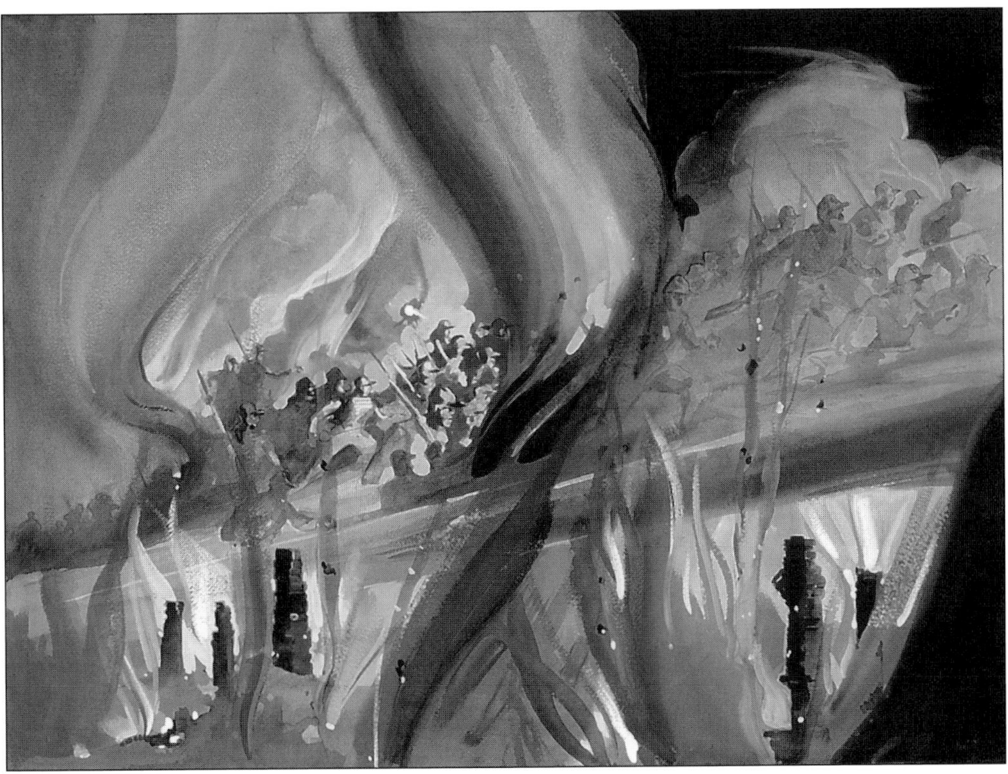

FIG. 95. Unsigned design for abstract shot of troops which opens second half of film presentation; 22 × 30 inches.

Analyses of More *Gone with the Wind* Continuity Drawings

The responsibilities of the production designer and of the art director are illustrated by the different purposes served by various examples of artwork drawn for *Gone with the Wind* and preserved in the Selznick collection. For example, shot composition and continuity design—tasks for which the role of production designer was established by Selznick—are the main purpose of the storyboard of four sketches of Scarlett and Ashley in the library at Twelve Oaks which appears to have been drawn by Menzies himself and which demonstrates classical reverse-angle two-shot découpage in its depiction of these two characters engaged in an intimate conversation (see Figure 96). In contrast, a single watercolor of a library setting, in which these same characters are depicted, was made by Dorothea Holt (who was one of the few women employed by a studio art department for work involving design and illustration).[8] The latter drawing's obvious proposal of the set's appearance—rather than of continuity design—identifies its use in art direction (see Figure 97).

A pair of drawings of the library set design bearing signatures of "Mac" Johnson more closely reflects what was constructed for the filming (see Figures 98–101). Holt and Johnson drew most of the set designs for *Gone with the Wind* which are preserved in the Selznick

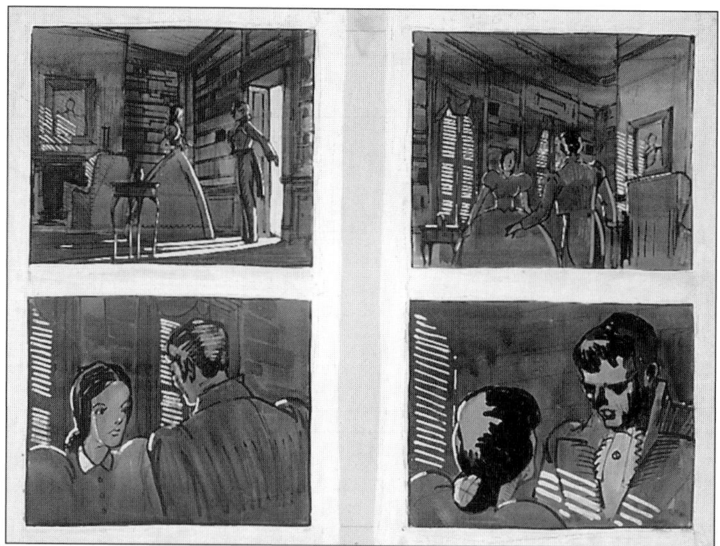

FIG. 96. Classical reverse-angle two-shot scene construction is illustrated by this unsigned storyboard of four watercolor drawings depicting Scarlett's confrontation of Ashley in the Twelve Oaks library; 20 × 30 inches.

FIG. 97. In contrast to Figure 96, set design was the purpose of this watercolor drawing by Dorothea Holt; 15 × 22 inches.

collection. Menzies and Wheeler were assisted by these same draftspersons and by others employed in the art department, and Menzies himself rendered many architectural drawings (see Figures 102–104).

As with the drawings of the fire sequence that were examined in detail in the previous chapter, the limited influence of other continuity designs preserved in the Selznick collection, which are equally representative of this film's production and which are examined in the course of the present section, reveals the misunderstandings that inform claims of film authorship via artwork. Menzies' task of determining color, compositions, and continuity prior to filming through storyboarding was one of the principal collaborative factors in the making of *Gone with the Wind* but was subject to modification for various reasons.

One impediment to their use was that the complexity of many of these production designs discouraged their acceptance by the producer and directors. Menzies' predilection for arranging actions of players in different focal planes within the same shot antedates the celebrated use of "depth of field" in *Citizen Kane*, but was considered too mannered for Selznick's presentation.[9] The production designer had, too, a penchant for exaggerated angles which, in many instances, appeared equally contrived and distracting to the producer and directors. While Menzies' primary interest appears to have been formal or compositional (in other words, "visual"), of paramount importance to Selznick, Cukor, and Fleming was dramatic presentation of the players' performances. The producer's routinely exercised option of revising the shooting script and of altering or removing shots or whole scenes also obviated use of many of Menzies' production designs in the filming.

FIGS. 98–99. Two drawings signed by "Mac" Johnson provide additional designs for the Twelve Oaks library which assisted construction of its set; 18 × 24 inches each.

FIGS. 100–101. The Twelve Oaks library set as constructed for filming.

These principal explanations as to why, in so many cases, scenes in the film correspond little or only vaguely to Menzies's artwork—that is, because of the complexity of the designs and filmscript revision—are demonstrated by the examples of the continuity sketches of three scenes in Sidney Howard's scripts of 1937. These drawings illustrate the opening dialogue between Scarlett O'Hara and the Tarleton brothers on the verandah of the plantation house at Tara, the arrival at Twelve Oaks of a messenger with news of war, and Scarlett's return to her home after the flight from Atlanta. Although most of the sketches are unsigned (which is characteristic of the majority of continuity designs in the Selznick collection), each is suggestive of Menzies' handwork. Specifically, his style is demonstrated by the general rendering of the figures, by the similarity of the palette to that employed in several of his signed drawings of Scarlett and Gerald O'Hara in this same collection, and by the peculiar angularity of his compositions—that is to say, by the use of extreme angles of points of view and of dramatically raking lines and shadows (see Figures 105–108).

Proposed shots for the film's opening, of Scarlett and the Tarleton brothers in conversation on the verandah of Tara and of two servants in attendance and eavesdropping, are illustrated by a storyboard of four drawings (see Figure 109). This scene corresponds to the novel's first half-dozen pages, in which these characters, their clothing, and the setting are described. "Scarlett O'Hara was not beautiful, but men seldom realized it when caught by her charm as the Tarleton twins were," the book begins. "Seated with Stuart and Brent Tarleton in the cool shade of the porch of Tara, her father's plantation, that bright April afternoon of 1861, she made a pretty picture." Conversation ranges from the twins' recent dismissal from the University of Georgia ("the

FIG. 102. Art-department design for Tara; 20 × 30 inches.

FIG. 103. Art-department design which emphasizes the "red earth of Tara" in its composition; 29 × 39 inches.

FIG. 104. Another exterior view of Tara; 28 × 33 inches.

fourth university that had thrown them out in two years"), the bombardment of Fort Sumter two days before ("If you say 'war' just once more, I'll go in the house and shut the door," threatens Scarlett), and Ashley Wilkes's engagement to Melanie Hamilton ("Scarlett's face did not change but her lips went white—like a person who has received a stunning blow without warning and who, in the first moments of shock, does not realize what has happened," reads the text, which continues, "Some time had passed before [the twins] realized that Scarlett was having very little to say"). After some lingering, the brothers depart, disappointed by not having been invited to stay for supper.[10]

This scene was abbreviated in the film presentation to save screen time. The top two sketches on Menzies' storyboard (i.e., those of an oblique view of the conversation on the verandah and of an interior shot within the mansion showing Mammy and Pork in attendance near an open window, through which Scarlett is depicted, seated between her two rising guests) correspond to shot numbers 2 and 3 of Howard's revised scripts of August 24 and November 27, 1937, which feature servants eavesdropping from a position within the house. However, the latter shot in these filmscripts prescribed that the camera follow Mammy's course from the parlor through an open French window to the verandah outside, where she is to chide Scarlett, after the gentlemen's departure, for not having demonstrated the courtesy of inviting them to stay for supper. Instead of this, a medium two-shot of Scarlett and Mammy on the porch was offered by Menzies in the lower-right illustration on

FIG. 105. This drawing of Gerald O'Hara and daughter Scarlett bears Menzies' initials in the top left-hand corner; 18 × 23 inches.

FIG. 106. Menzies' initials in the top right-hand corner of this drawing of Scarlett are covered partially by a label reading, "Set #16 EXT. Atlanta Street Hospital"; 15 × 20 inches.

FIG. 107. Unsigned view from upstairs window of plantation house is characteristic of the complexity of Menzies' designs and his penchant for extreme angles; 15 × 20 inches.

FIG. 108. This unsigned drawing of refugees against an expanse of sky is typical of Menzies' designs; 20 × 28 inches.

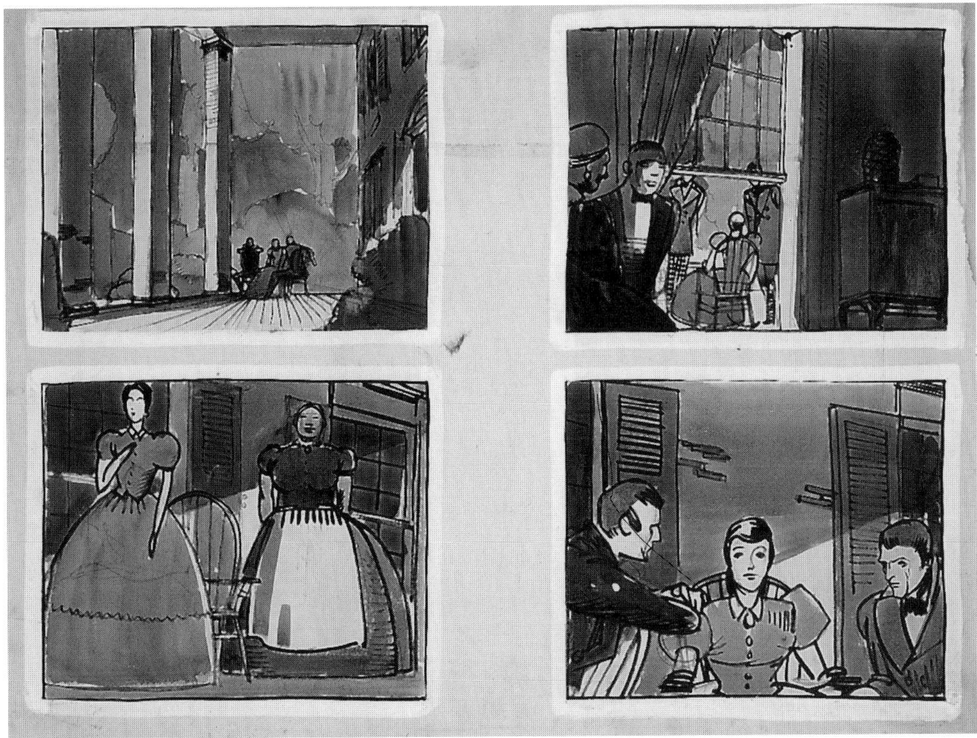

FIG. 109. A storyboard of four unsigned sketches illustrates the film's opening scenes at Tara; 20 × 30 inches.

this board, which, in fact, corresponds to an earlier shot description that is identified as number 8 in Howard's script of April 12; the corresponding shot in the February 12 film-script features Pork on the verandah also.

Depiction of a servant's eavesdropping was recommended to Howard by Selznick himself in notes on the undated draft of the first script's first sequence and is consistent with the novel.[11] Its use as a compositional device was omitted in Garrett's script of January 16, 1939, in which Scarlett abandons the men on the porch in a more aggressive display, angered by their news of Ashley's engagement to Melanie and by their repeated talk of war. Mammy was returned to the scene in its February 27 revision in order to scold Scarlett in front of the guests for not having invited them to supper, and her appearance is made through a window; however, this shot was filmed to appear at an upper-story level, and the servant only sticks her head out to complain. The remaining sketch displays a three-shot of Scarlett and the two brothers, and its breach of continuity with the other three drawings (read left to right, top to bottom) suggests that the purpose of these sketches was to demonstrate practicable compositions of shots described in Howard's scripts of August and November scripts of 1937 (which include identical descriptions of this scene), rather than strictly to illustrate the line of this scene's narrative or continuity. Although it may have been intended that the drawings were to be cut from the storyboard on which they were drawn for configuration in a different order (as was done with other sketches in the collection), the original arrangement has remained (see Figures 110–111).

"GONE WITH THE WIND"
Revised 2/23/39

FADE-IN: (Miniature)
LONG SHOT FORT SUMTER - with Confederate flag being raised.

DISSOLVE TO:

1. EXT. FRONT VERANDAH TARA. (LATE AFTERNOON APRIL, 1861)
GREAT CLOSEUP SCARLETT O'HARA.

Scarlett (disgusted)
~~Fort Sumter! War!~~ This war talk's spoiling all the fun at ~~all~~ every party this Spring!

War, war, war! Fiddle-dee-dee!

CAMERA STARTS TO PULL BACK, and we see that Scarlett in her billowing skirts, forms the apex of a traingle of which the sides are the Tarleton twins - handsome, long-legged, high-booted - lounging on either side of her with their mint juleps. The whole grouping is formal in composition, like a 'conversation piece', with the columned Colonial house a decorative period background.

Scarlett (continues)
Pa talks war morning, noon, and night -- and all the gentlemen that come here talk war 'til I could scream! If either of you boys says 'war' just once again, I'll walk in the house and slam the door!
(The twins look uncomfortable and embarrassed)
Besides, there isn't going to be any war.

Brent (indignantly)
Not going to be any war!

Stuart
Why, honey -- of course there's going to be a war!

Scarlett rises indignantly and starts toward the door. Brent and Stuart call to her, almost together, both rising.

Brent
Scarlett, honey, please. We're sorry.

Stuart
We'll talk about something else. I promise we will.

Scarlett sits down again. Relieved, they follow suit.

Stuart
We're eating barbecue with you over at Twelve Oaks tomorrow, don't forget.

Brent
And we want all your waltzes tomorrow night at the ball.
(nodding to his twin, then to himself, in succession)
First Stuart, then me, then Stuart again, and so on.

Stuart
Promise?

CONTINUED:

FIG. 110. First page of the original manuscript of the "rainbow" script dated February 23, 1939.

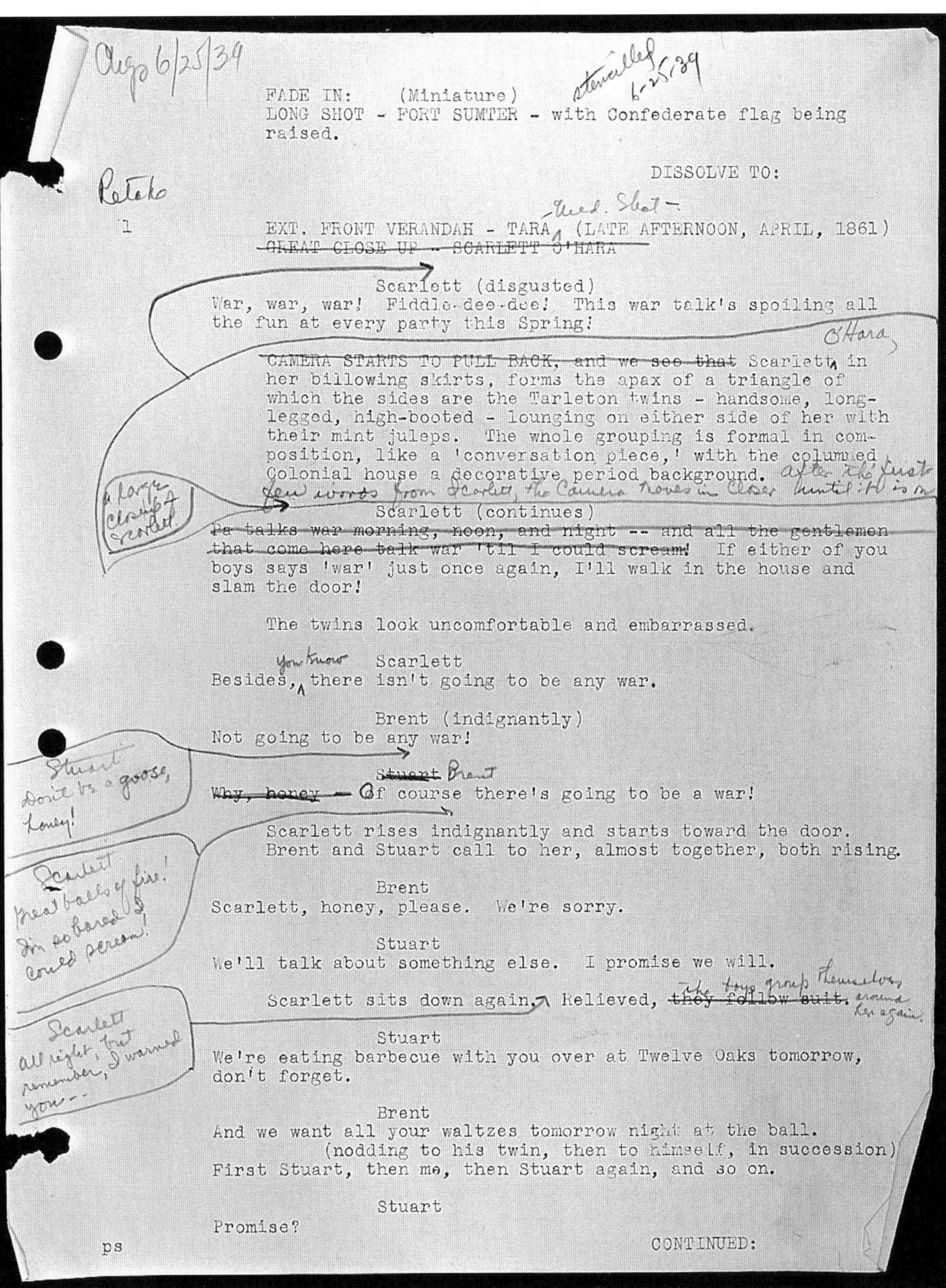

FADE IN: (Miniature)
LONG SHOT - FORT SUMTER - with Confederate flag being raised.

DISSOLVE TO:

1 EXT. FRONT VERANDAH - TARA (LATE AFTERNOON, APRIL, 1861)
~~GREAT CLOSE UP - SCARLETT O'HARA~~

Scarlett (disgusted)
War, war, war! Fiddle-dee-dee! This war talk's spoiling all the fun at every party this Spring!

~~CAMERA STARTS TO PULL BACK, and we see that~~ Scarlett, in her billowing skirts, forms the apax of a triangle of which the sides are the Tarleton twins - handsome, long-legged, high-booted - lounging on either side of her with their mint juleps. The whole grouping is formal in composition, like a 'conversation piece,' with the columned Colonial house a decorative period background.

Scarlett (continues)
~~Pa talks war morning, noon, and night -- and all the gentlemen that come here talk war 'til I could scream!~~ If either of you boys says 'war' just once again, I'll walk in the house and slam the door!

The twins look uncomfortable and embarrassed.

Scarlett
Besides, there isn't going to be any war.

Brent (indignantly)
Not going to be any war!

~~Stuart~~
~~Why, honey --~~ Of course there's going to be a war!

Scarlett rises indignantly and starts toward the door. Brent and Stuart call to her, almost together, both rising.

Brent
Scarlett, honey, please. We're sorry.

Stuart
We'll talk about something else. I promise we will.

Scarlett sits down again. Relieved, ~~they follow suit.~~

Stuart
We're eating barbecue with you over at Twelve Oaks tomorrow, don't forget.

Brent
And we want all your waltzes tomorrow night at the ball.
(nodding to his twin, then to himself, in succession)
First Stuart, then me, then Stuart again, and so on.

Stuart
Promise?

ps CONTINUED:

FIG. 111. Changes in the opening scene dated June 25, 1939.

The scene as released is far less complicated than that envisioned either by Howard or Menzies, but without doubt is effective in its exposition of Scarlett's character. No longer mediated by eavesdropping attendants positioned within the house, the scene focuses simply upon her conversation with the Tarleton brothers on the verandah outside, and its conclusion is flavored by Mammy's comically delivered criticism from an upper-story window when Scarlett defiantly departs on foot down the drive. This scene was the first of the production to be filmed with a principal player and was possibly also the last, requiring Vivien Leigh's return to the set late in the post-production period (see Figures 112–114). It had been retaken several times already under the direction of both Cukor and Fleming so that the actors' hairstyles could be altered and the actress's costume changed from the same green-sprigged dress worn at the Twelve Oaks barbecue to a white, ruffled one (Scarlett's dress remains green in Menzies' sketches, which is consistent with the novel). The scene as released was the final version filmed and was shot under Sam Wood's direction in Selznick's presence; although the camera's viewpoint of the verandah is similar to the storyboard's initial sketch, the placement of the cast was brought forward so that the players were framed—but not diminished in scale—by the architectural setting.

FIG. 112. The caption on back of this publicity photograph reads: "MAKING UP . . . Vivien Leigh, as Scarlett O'Hara, prepares for a take in *Gone with the Wind*, Selznick International Technicolor production starring Clark Gable, Miss Leigh, Leslie Howard and Olivia de Havilland, *directed by Victor Fleming*. Aiding Miss Leigh is Eddie Allen of the makeup department, while the Tarleton twins, played by *George Reeves* (r) and *Fred Crane* (l) look on. Measuring light in front of camera is Ernest Haller, head cameraman, while in foreground, left to right, are G. J. Cartensen, Paul Hill, and Arden Cripe, members of the technical crew."

"GONE WITH THE WIND" 1.
9/27/39

FOREWORD TITLE

DISSOLVE TO:

RETAKE QUITTING BELL AT TARA
- being rung.

DISSOLVE TO:

2nd UNIT "QUITTING TIME" SHOTS

DISSOLVE TO:

RETAKE EXTREME LONG SHOT EXT. FRONT OF TARA.
(COSGROVE. Possibly one already made?)
A little pickaninny chases a turkey across the lawn toward the verandah.

RETAKE LONG SHOT (POSSIBLY COSGROVE) EXT. FRONT OF TARA.
(SAME ANGLE ON TARA AS PRECEDING SHOT, BUT CLOSER)

The turkey runs past the camera -- the pickanniny after it.

In the background we see the Tarleton twins, Brent and Stuart, on the verandah steps with their backs to camera. One of them is standing, perhaps reaching for a mint julep glass from a nearby table.

RETAKE CLOSE THREE SHOT (SAME ANGLE AS LONG SHOT)

The Tarleton twin who is standing is blocking Scarlett from the camera.

Brent
What do we care if we were expelled from college, Scarlett? The war's going to start any day now, so we'd have left college anyhow.

Stuart
War! Whee! Isn't it exciting, Scarlett? Those fool Yankees actually want a war! We'll show 'em!

Scarlett's voice
Fiddle-dee-dee!

The twin who has been covering Scarlett moves casually and gradually aside as the CAMERA MOVES IN unobtrusively to reveal a LARGE CLOSEUP OF SCARLETT. She has been sitting on a chair on the verandah facing the boys.

Scarlett
War, war, war! This war talk's spoiling all the fun at every party this Spring! I get so bored I could scream!

She makes a motion to indicate in affected fashion just how annoyed she is by this boring subject.

FIG. 113. Revised script of the final retake of the opening scene.

FIG. 114. Frame enlargements from shots in the opening scene arranged in storyboard manner for comparison purposes.

The four drawings of the arrival of news of war at Twelve Oaks also exhibit the draftsmanship and angularity of composition characteristic of Menzies' handwork and correspond to Howard's scripts of August 24 and November 27, 1937 (see Figure 115). The palette is roughly similar to that used in the depiction of Scarlett and her suitors at Tara and, except for the fluting of the columns on the verandah at Twelve Oaks, much of the facade of the Wilkes's mansion is indistinguishable from the O'Hara residence drawn in the previously discussed sketches. Delineation of shot compositions in terms of continuity and of point of view, rather than the mere depiction of set decoration, was the principal purpose of these drawings. In the novel, Scarlett, from her position behind the large bay window on the grand staircase's landing inside the mansion, observes the arriving horseman, who announces his news to gentlemen who have congregated on the Wilkes's back lawn. After overhearing criticism of herself spoken by other ladies at the party, she attempts to leave Twelve Oaks, but is confronted on the verandah by Charles Hamilton, who excitedly relates the news and proposes marriage to her.[12] Howard merged the public announcement of the news and the private proposal of marriage into the same space by bringing the horseman and the gentlemen to the front lawn and by allowing the ladies to pour onto the verandah afterward, at which time Charles approaches Scarlett to propose.

Menzies' four sketches correspond to shot numbers 33, 34, and 35 in the scenarios of Au-

FIG. 115. Four unsigned drawings, 8 × 10 inches each, depicting the arrival of news of war at Twelve Oaks and corresponding to shot descriptions in Sidney Howard's filmscripts of August 24 and November 27, 1937.

gust and November 1937. Most particularly, the high-angled view of the men running from the verandah to the drive below reflects these scripts' description of the camera setup as being "from the girls' angle"—that is, from a front, upper-story window under the expansive porch roof which allows a view through the columns (a shot for which process photography might be prescribed). A similar composition is exhibited in the sketch that Menzies drew for D. W. Griffith's *Abraham Lincoln* (1930) and that, with other examples of this designer's artwork, was published in book form in Europe in 1931 and in the United States, by Dial Press, in 1938.[13] By delineating this short three-shot sequence in the form of four drawings, Menzies offered a slight revision of the scene as written; a second drawing of the activity described in shot number 33 provides a closer view of the messenger and represents either another, closer shot or the end of a fluid camera movement.

Howard's scheme was abandoned by Selznick and Garrett; this alteration is indicated as early as January 11, 1939, in a breakdown synopsis of their filmscript of January 16, which was then in progress. In the latter and in the film as released, frustrated by Ashley Wilkes and humiliated before Rhett Butler, Scarlett exits the library on the first floor and climbs the stairs against the tide of ladies who descend while the gentlemen depart to enlist. She is met by Charles on the landing, from where, through the grand window, she observes Ashley and Melanie Hamilton embracing outside while she herself receives a proposal of marriage. In

FIG. 116. This drawing bearing Menzies' initials in the top left-hand corner and depicting Scarlett's return to Tara following her escape from Atlanta corresponds to all versions of the script written by Sidney Howard in 1937; 15 × 20 inches.

spite of establishing/reestablishing shots combining interior and exterior activities via process photography (that is to say, Scarlett and Charles are shown twice before the window, which frames a view of the scurry of men departing for enlistment below), most of the action is presented in the form of separate shots which are linked effectively in terms of an eyeline match suggestive of Scarlett's point of view. In contrast with Menzies' briefer and more formal conception of the action as depicted in his sketchwork, the scene presented in the film is representative more of Scarlett's self-absorption and resentment of Ashley's engagement to another; these are signified by her ascent of the stairs against the flow of others in the mansion who follow the shouts of news of war outdoors and by her acceptance of a proposal of marriage before a window which frames both the recruitment and the romance on the lawn.

A definite correspondence with each of Howard's 1937 scenarios is apparent in Menzies' signed drawing of Scarlett confronting her father on the front steps of Tara upon returning from Atlanta during the war (see Figure 116). In the novel, on arriving at the plantation house, Scarlett abandons the wagon and its occupants on the drive to run toward the steps. "Then she saw a form, shadowy in the dimness, emerging from the blackness of the front verandah and standing at the top of the steps," reads the novel, in which Scarlett's joy is immediately curtailed by the gloominess of this scene. "The house was so dark and still and the figure did not move or call to her," the text continues. "What was wrong? What was wrong?" it repeatedly asks.[14]

All filmscript versions produced that year describe Scarlett's approach in the foreground from the bottom of the porch steps, while Gerald emerges as a broken figure on the verandah from the darkened doorway in the background. Accordingly, the angle depicted in the sketch is relatively low, and the steep rise of steps is exploited in order to heighten the drama of the moment. Scarlett is presented conventionally in her green formal dress which does not appear to have suffered distress, despite this character's assistance in Melanie's delivery and passage through fire and wilderness in an open wagon in the course of the script's preceding pages; thus, compositional features again appear to have been Menzies' principal concern and not authentic rendering of decorative elements. In fact, stock treatments of costumes and sets were employed consistently by the production designer in preparation of his continuity sketches. Nevertheless, the filmed scene differs from Menzies' sketch primarily because the action was altered by Garrett's scenario of January 16, 1939. In the film, Scarlett hurriedly mounts the steps of the front porch and raps upon the door, which is opened by Gerald, who stands face to face with his daughter in the darkened doorway.

Direction and Production Design: Menzies on the Shooting Set

In the filming of *Gone with the Wind*, problems posed by the script's revision affected use of artwork by the production designer himself. As indicated by the great number of sketches representative of the fire sequence (one third of the drawings in the Selznick collection illustrates this single episode), much of this artwork may have been drawn to serve as Menzies' own "director's notes," for, in addition to contributing to the picture as its designer, Menzies personally directed approximately fifteen percent of the scenes; in contrast, George Cukor directed only five percent of the film.[15] These statistics most assuredly reveal the directorial aspect in the producer's definition of Menzies' operational role. That the artwork was created for the purpose of assisting Menzies' own direction of the filming of a significant number of shots and scenes in this film is indicated also by Lyle Wheeler's statement to Corliss and Clarens that, while Menzies drew "excellent" sketches for *Gone with the Wind*, the production designer's "major function was second unit direction."[16]

"Second unit" crews were formed for the purpose of filming shots and scenes employing doubles and/or presenting picturesque background material for insertion in the dramatic narrative; generally, these did not require participation of principal cast members, who received instruction from Cukor, Fleming, or Wood. Certainly Selznick's delegation to Menzies of much of this work was consistent with the producer's admission to Raymond Klune on January 11, 1939 that "so much of the beauty of the picture is going to be dependent upon the second unit material." Nevertheless, Menzies' figure also remained an omnipresent one on the principal sets much of the time. A report in the *New York Times* published during

FIGS. 117–118. This drawing bearing Menzies' initials in the bottom left-hand corner depicts slaves in a cottonfield in a manner corresponding to an emended description of shot number 6 in the filmscript of January 16, 1939; 15 × 20 inches.

the period of filming described the production designer as "running all over the place, squinting through the camera" alongside the director of photography, and supervising the sets' lighting. In this article it was noted that the last of these tasks involved his "conjuring up a window frame to cast its shadow decoratively across a four-poster bed" and his "bloodthirstily commanding the men on the catwalks to 'kill that broad' "—in reference to a less nuanced form of set illumination.[17]

As demonstrated in the previous chapter's analysis of artwork produced for the fire sequence, Menzies' presence on the set or direction of a second unit did not ensure that filming followed his sketchwork. Nevertheless, he very likely participated in implementing many of the alterations made to his prior compositions during shooting. An example of this can be seen in the shot of slaves that is part of the "quittin' time" scene, which, during the introductory portion of the film as released, serves to connect Scarlett's departure from the Tarleton brothers and her father's arrival on horseback at Tara; in this scene, the line of field hands halting behind their plows in a field at sunset differs from Menzies' sketch of a line of slaves that is drawn in perspective recession and in which all hands are depicted hoeing a field while a gentleman—presumably Gerald O'Hara—passes on horseback in the background.

Menzies' drawing does not correspond to shot descriptions in any of Howard's filmscripts, in which slaves and their equestrian master occupied separate film frames for pre-

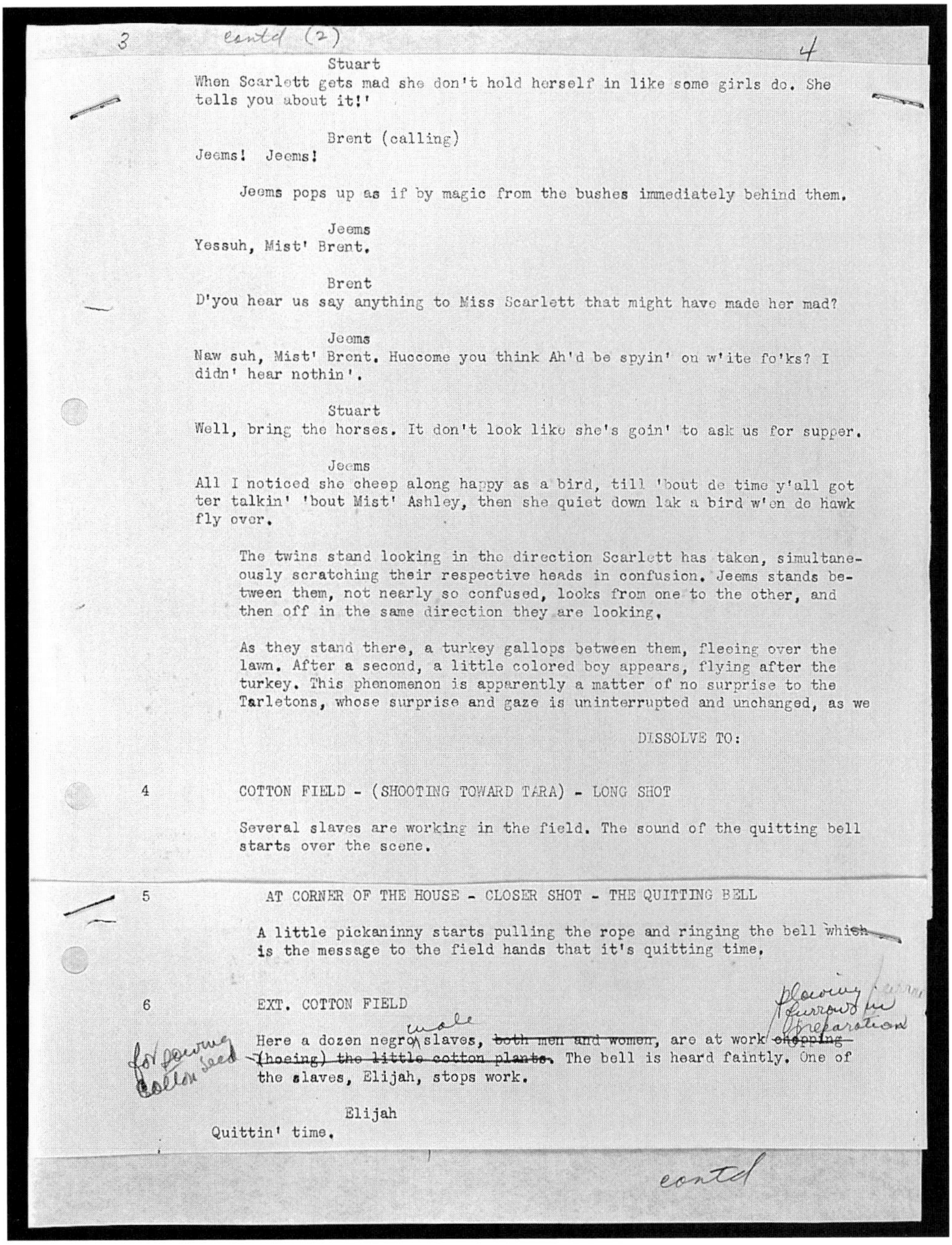

3 contd (2) 4

Stuart
When Scarlett gets mad she don't hold herself in like some girls do. She tells you about it!'

Brent (calling)
Jeems! Jeems!

Jeems pops up as if by magic from the bushes immediately behind them.

Jeems
Yessuh, Mist' Brent.

Brent
D'you hear us say anything to Miss Scarlett that might have made her mad?

Jeems
Naw suh, Mist' Brent. Huccome you think Ah'd be spyin' on w'ite fo'ks? I didn' hear nothin'.

Stuart
Well, bring the horses. It don't look like she's goin' to ask us for supper.

Jeems
All I noticed she cheep along happy as a bird, till 'bout de time y'all got ter talkin' 'bout Mist' Ashley, then she quiet down lak a bird w'en de hawk fly over.

The twins stand looking in the direction Scarlett has taken, simultaneously scratching their respective heads in confusion. Jeems stands between them, not nearly so confused, looks from one to the other, and then off in the same direction they are looking.

As they stand there, a turkey gallops between them, fleeing over the lawn. After a second, a little colored boy appears, flying after the turkey. This phenomenon is apparently a matter of no surprise to the Tarletons, whose surprise and gaze is uninterrupted and unchanged, as we

DISSOLVE TO:

4 COTTON FIELD - (SHOOTING TOWARD TARA) - LONG SHOT

Several slaves are working in the field. The sound of the quitting bell starts over the scene.

5 AT CORNER OF THE HOUSE - CLOSER SHOT - THE QUITTING BELL

A little pickaninny starts pulling the rope and ringing the bell ~~which~~ is the message to the field hands that it's quitting time.

6 EXT. COTTON FIELD

Here a dozen negro male slaves, ~~both men and women~~, are at work ~~chopping (hoeing) the little cotton plants~~ plowing furrows for preparation for sowing cotton seed. The bell is heard faintly. One of the slaves, Elijah, stops work.

Elijah
Quittin' time.

contd

FIG. 118

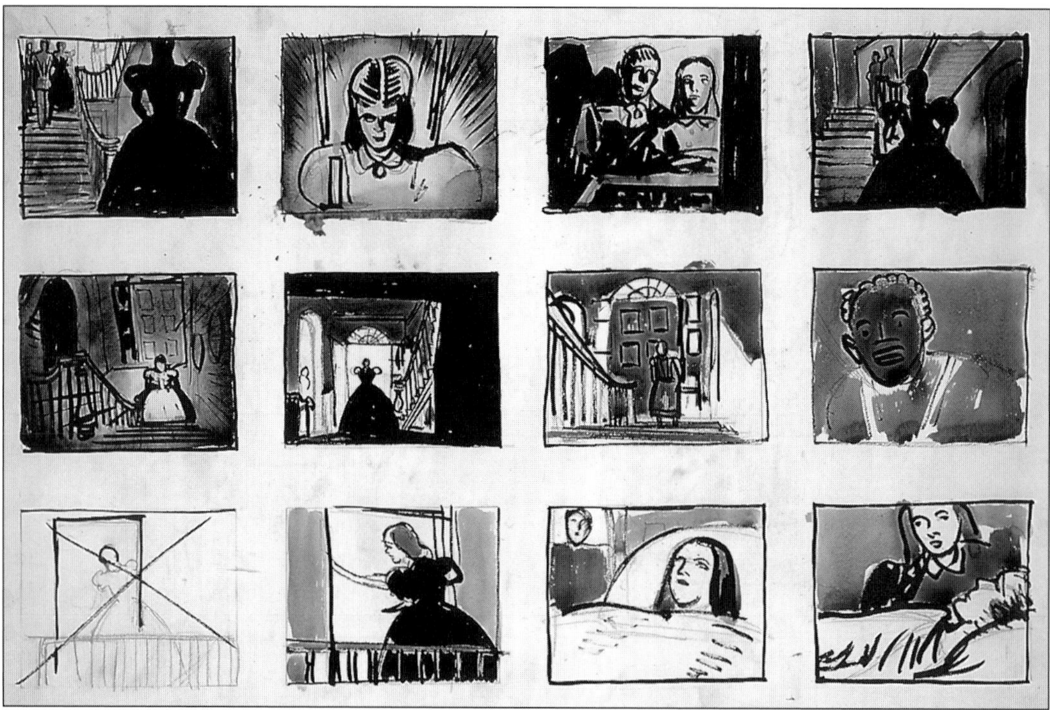

FIGS. 119–120. These two unsigned storyboards are attributed to Menzies and illustrate this production designer's creative contribution to continuity design; 20 × 30 inches each.

sentation of this scene; instead, it matches the shot description that was emended in pencil in the original manuscript of Garrett's scenario of January 16, 1939, so that "negro male slaves . . . at work plowing furrows," who were filmed under Menzies' second unit direction, supplanted the earlier image of "men and women . . . chopping (hoeing) the little cotton plants" as was drawn (see Figures 117–118). Because the news of war is announced at the Wilkes's barbecue on the day following the activity depicted in this shot, and because Lincoln's declaration of war occurred in April 1861, Georgia's agricultural calendar dictated the change from harvesting (actually done by hand, not by hoe) to planting.[18]

Two unsigned storyboards bearing evidence of Menzies' handwork, on which were drawn two different scenes that utilize the staircase in Aunt Pittypat's house in Atlanta as settings, illustrate the production designer's creative contributions to the principal filming, his dependence on the director's acceptance of the artwork's designs, and the producer's election to revise the filmscript (see Figures 119–120). The first five sketches on the first board depict the scene in which Scarlett and Melanie and Ashley bid each other good night before the latter two withdraw to their bedchamber the evening of the Christmas furlough. In the novel, the servant Uncle Peter lights the way up the stairs, while Scarlett, Pittypat, Melanie, and Ashley quietly follow with eyes lowered to the carpet. "Until that moment when they stood in the upstairs hall, Ashley had been hers, only hers, even if she had not a private word with him that whole afternoon," relates the text from Scarlett's

FIG. 120

point of view, as Wilkes retires to his room with his wife. "But now . . . the door closed behind them, leaving Scarlett open mouthed and suddenly desolate."[19]

In Howard's screenplays of February and April 1937, Uncle Peter no longer serves as a participant in this scene, nor does Scarlett ascend with Melanie and Ashley to the upstairs bedrooms, but instead witnesses their flight from the foot of the staircase. "From her angle [i.e., Scarlett's], as the music swells, we see Ashley and Melanie round the curve of the stair above, disappear through the door of Melanie's room and close it behind them," read both filmscripts. "Then the camera returns again to Scarlett . . . alone at the foot of the stair . . . [and] unmindful of anything but her tragedy," while Aunt Pittypat's voice is overheard bidding her dinner guests a good night on the ground floor. Pittypat and her guests were removed from this scene in Howard's revisions of August and November 1937, although Uncle Peter returned as a silent participant. "Music. Scarlett stands in the parlor arch looking up the stair," read these scripts. "From her angle, the camera behind her, Ashley and Melanie can be seen just turning the corner of the stair above, Uncle Peter lighting their way with the silver candelabra. Fade out."

Garrett's revision of Howard's screenplay, dated January 16, 1939, prescribed the form of slow disclosure for this scene, beginning with a close-up of Scarlett "as she turns her head slowly, her eyes following the upward movement of someone out of scene" while "tears gather in her eyes" and the "camera moves back to reveal [her] standing with a candle in her hand at foot of stairs looking up." The next shot is described thus: "Stairs—Scarlett in f.g. [foreground] Mounting the second floor are Melanie and Ashley, arm in arm. Uncle Peter is lighting the way for them, holding aloft a fine silver candelabra." At the top of the stairs, Melanie and Ashley wish Scarlett a good night and exit the frame. Following is another close-up of Scarlett with a single candle in her hand, "still gazing upward after them" and looking "utterly wretched"; "the sound of the upstairs bedroom door's being closed is heard [over]," after which she murmurs, "Oh, Ashley!" before a fade.

The original manuscript of the "rainbow" shooting script, dating from February 27, 1939, offers two different versions, the earlier having been filmed under Cukor's direction during his final day on the production (February 14) and the latter having been revised for Fleming's direction, when additional dialogue between Melanie and Ashley was inserted. Specifically, parts of previous shot descriptions were excised in pencil but remain *sous rature* for comparison with the alterations (see Figures 121–126). Ignoring all elisions and emendations, the first version reads thus:

> 180 (Already shot)—Int. Aunt Pitty's Hallway (Low Camera Setup Shooting Upstairs with Scarlett's Back in F.G.) Night. Melanie and Ashley mounting to the second floor, arm in arm. Uncle Peter is lighting the way for them, holding aloft a fine silver candelabra.
>
> 181 (Already shot)—Close Shot Scarlett. At the foot of the stairs—a candle in her hand—looking up at Melanie and Ashley—despair in her eyes.
>
> 182 (Already shot)—Close Two Shot Melanie and Ashley. As they reach the top of the stairs they pause [and bid Scarlett good night].
>
> 183 Closeup Scarlett. Still gazing upward after Melanie and Ashley. She is utterly wretched. . . . The light effect on Scarlett's face changes as light from Uncle Peter's candle vanishes, but her face remains lit by the candle she herself is holding.

The revised form of this scene is as follows:

> R-180—Int. Aunt Pitty's Hallway—Melanie and Ashley mounting to the second floor, arm in arm. Uncle Peter is lighting the way for them, holding aloft a fine silver candelabra. . . . [Ashley thanks Melanie for her Christmas present.] As they reach the top of the stairs they pause.
>
> R-181 To be Shot—Long Shot (from their angle) shooting diagonally across the stairs. Scarlett standing in the doorway to the living room, her hand on the drape, watching Ashley and Melanie off scene. The scene is lighted by a candle on a table beside Scarlett and by Uncle Peter's candle o.s. [off-screen].
>
> R-182 To be Shot—Two Shot Ashley and Melanie—looking back at Scarlett [and bidding her good night].
>
> R-183 Closeup Scarlett. Still gazing upward after Melanie and Ashley . . . wretched . . . her face remains lit by the wan light of the candle beside her.

CALL SHEET

DATE TUESDAY, Feb. 14, 1939

PICTURE "GONE WITH THE WIND" - Prod. #108 DIRECTOR GEORGE CUKOR

SET Int. Aunt Pitty's - Lower Floor WINTER, 1863

LOCATION Stage #4 - Set #15 Scs. 180 to 194

NAME	TIME CALLED ON SET	TIME CALLED MAKE-UP	CHARACTER, DESC., WARDROBE
Vivien Leigh	8:45 AM	7:30 AM	Scarlett #8A
Olivia de Havilland	8:45 AM	7:30 AM	Melanie #4A
Leslie Howard	8:45 AM	7:30 AM	Ashley #3
Part of Uncle Peter	8:45 AM	8:00 AM	Uncle Peter #1
Stand-ins	8:15 AM	8:00 AM	--
			PROPERTY DEPT.
			Aunt Pitty's Carriage and horse - WILL NOTIFY
CAMERAS	8:15 AM		
SOUND (Ready)	9:15 AM		
SPECIAL EFFECTS (Rain & Mist)	WILL NOTIFY		

ADVANCE SHOOTING SCHEDULE
ON REVERSE SIDE OF CALL SHEET

ASSISTANT DIRECTOR ERIC STACEY

FIG. 121. Call sheet scheduling Cukor's direction of principal players on February 14, 1939.

Selznick International Pictures

DAILY PRODUCTION LOG

108 — Prod. No. | "GONE WITH THE WIND" — Picture | Feb. 14, 1939 — Date

SET INT. LOWER HALL - and Living room (Aunt Pittypat's) STAGE NO. 4

TIME	LEGEND
8:45 AM	COMPANY CALL
	Lining up trick life effect - with stand-ins.
9:30	Rehearsing with Miss Leigh and Mr. Howard, and Miss De Haviland.
9:45	Rehearsing -(Lining up) with stand-ins. (Miss Leigh notto be in scene.)
10:10	Rehearsing with principals and making corrections for camera. (candles,etc)
10:20	SHOOTING SCENE 180 take 1. Complete. NG.
10:22	" " 2 NG. action.
10:24	" " 3 OK Print. (Tech)
10:25	" " 4 Incomplete.
10:27	" " 5 "
10:30	" " 6 OK Print. (B&W)
10:32	SHOOTING STILLS.
	Lining up next scene. (Trick light effect with Scarlett.)
11:40	Rehearsing with Scarlett. (checking light effect)
11:55	SHOOTING SCENE 181 take 1. Incomplete
11:58	" " 2 Complete. NG
12:01 PM	" " 3 OK Print. B & W
12:05	" " 4 OK Print. (Tech)
12:06	Rehearsing next scene to pick set-up.
12:18	LUNCH Back at 1:20.
1:20	Lining up reverse shot (Rain effect - outside front door)
2:15	Rehearsing with Scarlett. (Then making necessary corrections in for camera)
2:40	Rehearsing scene with Scarlett and Uncle Peter.
	Working on line-up with standins - (Jerry Wright discussing changes with G.C.)
3:05	Rehearsing scene with Scarlett and Uncle Peter.
3:15	SHOOTING SCENE 184 take 1. Incomplete
3:24	" " 2 NG action.
3:25	" " 3 Incomplete -(Rehearsing Uncle Peter.)
3:32	" " 4 Incomplete. NG Dialogue " "
3:34	" " 5 NG. action
3:35	" " 6 Complete. (Missed his marks. NG camera)
3:45	" " 7 OK Print. (B & W)
3:47	" " 8 Incomplete. NG dialogue.
3:50	" " 9 Incomplete. "
3:53	" " 10 Complete. HOLD
3:55	" " 11 OK Print. (Tech)
3:58	RECORDING WILD TRACK. for scene 184.
	Lining up new scene.
4:40	Rehearsing action with Scarlett.
4:50	SHOOTING SCENE 184 A take 1. Fair.
4:52	" " 2. NG. action.
4:54	" " 3. Print. B & W
4:56	" " 4. OK Print. (Tech) (2 takes in 1.)
	Recording Wild track - for scene 184 A.
	Lining up new scene. with Stand-ins.
6:10	Rehearsing scene with principals.
6:18	SHOOTING SCENE 186 take 1. Incomplete.
6:20	" " 2. Complete. Fair. (Wrong exit)
6:27 - 6:32 - 6:35	Takes 3, 4 and 5. (Print. 4 B&W) Print 5. (Tech)
6:38	Company finished shooting. DISMISSED.

FIG. 122. Production log of filming on February 14, 1939.

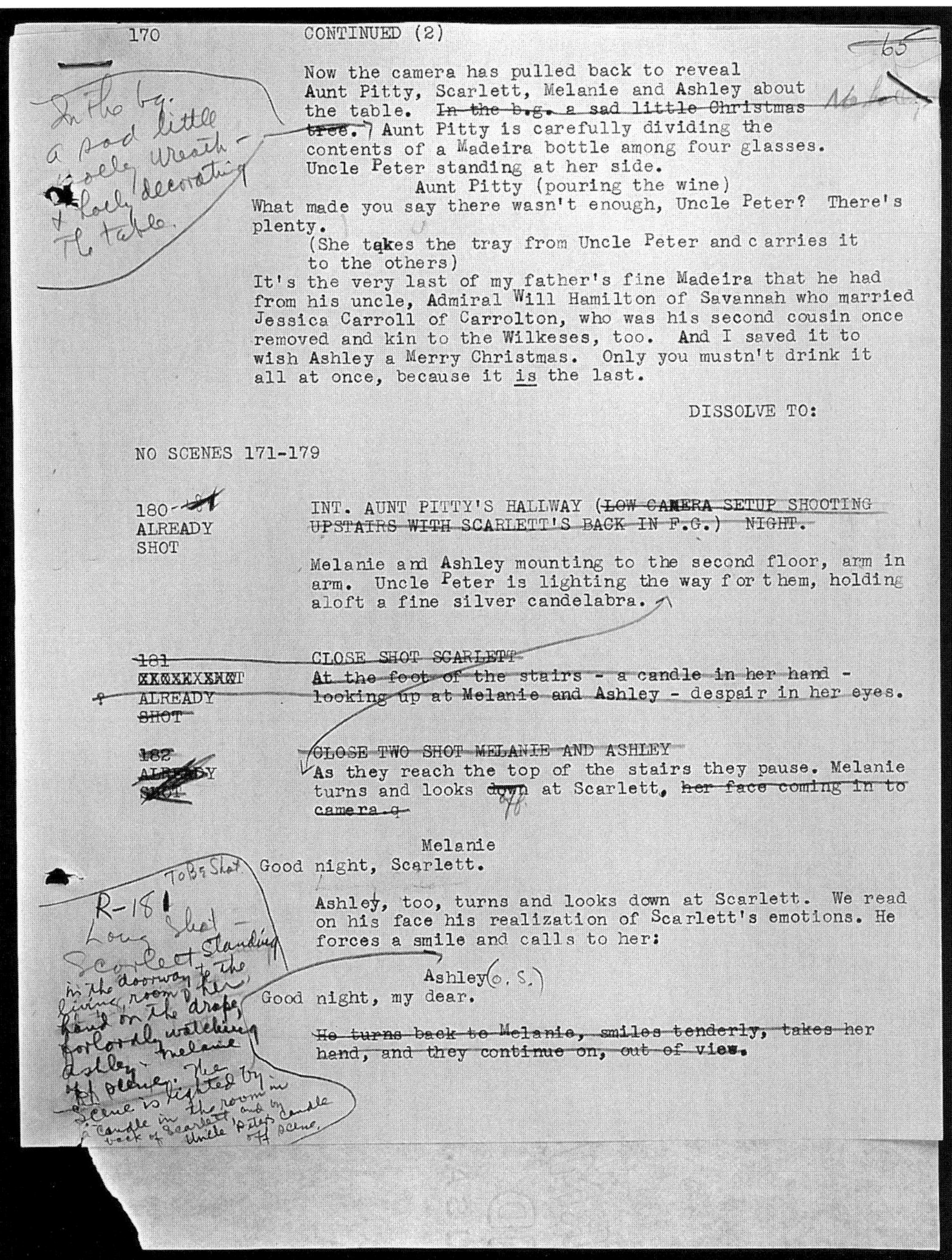

170 CONTINUED (2)

Now the camera has pulled back to reveal Aunt Pitty, Scarlett, Melanie and Ashley about the table. ~~In the b.g. a sad little Christmas tree.~~ Aunt Pitty is carefully dividing the contents of a Madeira bottle among four glasses. Uncle Peter standing at her side.

In the b.g. a sad little holly wreath – & holly decorating the table.

AUNT PITTY (pouring the wine)

What made you say there wasn't enough, Uncle Peter? There's plenty.

(She takes the tray from Uncle Peter and carries it to the others)

It's the very last of my father's fine Madeira that he had from his uncle, Admiral Will Hamilton of Savannah who married Jessica Carroll of Carrolton, who was his second cousin once removed and kin to the Wilkeses, too. And I saved it to wish Ashley a Merry Christmas. Only you mustn't drink it all at once, because it is the last.

DISSOLVE TO:

NO SCENES 171-179

180 ~~181~~ ALREADY SHOT

INT. AUNT PITTY'S HALLWAY ~~(LOW CAMERA SETUP SHOOTING UPSTAIRS WITH SCARLETT'S BACK IN F.G.)~~ NIGHT.

Melanie and Ashley mounting to the second floor, arm in arm. Uncle Peter is lighting the way for them, holding aloft a fine silver candelabra.

~~181 ALREADY SHOT~~

~~CLOSE SHOT SCARLETT~~
~~At the foot of the stairs – a candle in her hand – looking up at Melanie and Ashley – despair in her eyes.~~

~~182 ALREADY SHOT~~

~~CLOSE TWO SHOT MELANIE AND ASHLEY~~
As they reach the top of the stairs they pause. Melanie turns and looks ~~down~~ at Scarlett, ~~her face coming in to camera.~~

MELANIE

Good night, Scarlett.

Ashley, too, turns and looks down at Scarlett. We read on his face his realization of Scarlett's emotions. He forces a smile and calls to her:

ASHLEY (o.s.)

Good night, my dear.

~~He turns back to Melanie, smiles tenderly, takes her hand, and they continue on, out of view.~~

To Be Shot
R-181
Long Shot – Scarlett standing in the doorway to the living room, her hand on the drape, forlornly watching Melanie & Ashley. The off scene is lighted by candle in the room and by candle in back of Scarlett and by Uncle Peter's candle off scene.

FIGS. 123–124. Original "rainbow" script of February 27, 1939, offers two versions of the scene on Aunt Pittypat's staircase. This first version is a description of what was "already shot" under Cukor's direction, corresponding to much of Menzies' storyboarding.

R.182 66

TO BE SHOT

CLOSEUP SCARLETT

Still gazing upward after Melanie and Ashley. She is utterly wretched. She tries to mumble an answering goodnight, but fails.

The light effect on Scarlett's face changes as ~~the~~ light from Uncle Peter's candle ~~being held by Ashley goes out of view,~~ vanishes, but her face remains lit by the candle ~~she herself is holding.~~ beside her.

to scene 183. ~~FADE OUT.~~ Dissolve To:

R-184

FADE IN:
INT. HALL AUNT PITTY'S - TWILIGHT - MIST

Uncle Peter is coming down the stairs carrying Ashley's blanket roll. Scarlett enters the scene hastily as he reaches the bottom step.

Scarlett
Is it time yet, Uncle Peter? Is it time for Mr. Ashley to leave?

Uncle Peter
Pretty quick now, Miss Scarlett.

Scarlett
Miss Melanie isn't going to the depot with him? She hasn't changed her mind?

Uncle Peter
No, ma'am, she's layin' down. She's so upset Mist' Wilkes tole her she cain't even come down stairs.

He exits out the front door with Ashley's blanket roll. Scarlett turns distracted and desperately unhappy, and walks a few steps away from the bottom of the stairs.

Then she hears Ashley's footsteps on the stairs and turns back hastily.

R-185

Med. SHOT ASHLEY - coming down the stairs.

He is miserable at the farewell scene he has just been through with Melanie. He stops as he sees Scarlett.

R-185A

CLOSEUP ASHLEY

His face reveals his nervousness as he sees Scarlett waiting for him. He wishes he did not have to face what is going to be a difficult scene, in view of the last time they were alone together at Twelve Oaks.

CLOSE SHOT SCARLETT (from Ashley's angle)

She runs toward the bottom of the stairs, looking eagerly up.

Scarlett
Ashley!

R-186

TWO SHOT
As Ashley reaches the lower steps, Scarlett runs up two steps to meet him, speaking as she runs:

Scarlett
Ashley, let me go to the depot with you?

FIG. 124

Now the CAMERA has pulled back to reveal Aunt Pitty, Scarlett, Melanie, and Ashley about the table. In the b.g. a sad little holly wreath and holly decorating the table. Aunt Pitty is carefully dividing the contents of a Madeira bottle among four glasses. Uncle Peter stands at her side.

Aunt Pitty (pouring the wine)
What made you say there wasn't enough, Uncle Peter? There's plenty.
(she takes the tray from Uncle Peter and carries it to the others)
It's the very last of my father's fine Madeira that he had from his uncle, Admiral Will Hamilton of Savannah who married Jessica Carroll of Carrolton, who was his second cousin once removed and kin to the Wilkeses, too. And I saved it to wish Ashley a Merry Christmas. Only you mustn't drink it all at once, because it <u>is</u> the last.

DISSOLVE TO:

NO SCENES 171-179

R-180
To be
shot

INT. AUNT PITTY'S HALLWAY
Melanie and Ashley ~~xxxxing~~ climbing the stairs to the second floor, arm in arm. Uncle Peter is lighting the way for them, holding aloft a fine silver candelabra. Ashley is walking with studied casualness, glancing down at Melanie's finger-tips on his sleeve; she is walking with downcast eyes.

Ashley (tenderly, but at the same time giving the impression that he's saying it as a safe sort of thing to fit into his ~~xxxxxx~~casual air -- just as if they had walked upstairs together like this every evening for all these months.)
But I meant it, my dear. It <u>was</u> a lovely Christmas gift -- really. Only generals have tunics like this nowadays.

Melanie (still not looking at him)
I'm ... so happy you like it, dear.

Ashley
(strokes the tunic and continues a little too brightly, so that he sounds slightly affected:)
But where <u>did</u> you get the cloth?

Melanie (hesitating)
Well, dear, I -- it was sent me by a Charleston lady. I nursed her son in the hospital, Ashley -- before he died -- and --
(She looks at him imploringly at her own reminder of the danger to her beloved)
Oh, you will take care of it, won't you? You won't let it get -- torn? Promise me!

Ashley
You mustn't worry -
(lightly)
I'll bring it back to you without any holes in it.
(tenderly)
I promise.

They have reached the top of the stairs. Melanie turns.

FIGS. 125–126. Second version of scene on Aunt Pittypat's staircase in original "rainbow" script of February 27, 1939: a revision for retaking.

3-23-39 65a

R-181 To be shot — LONG SHOT (from their angle) shooting diagonally across the stairs.

Scarlett standing in the doorway to the living room, her hand on the drape, watching Ashley and Melanie off scene. The scene is lighted by a candle on a table beside Scarlett and by Uncle Peter's candle o.s.

R-182 To be shot — TWO SHOT ASHLEY AND MELANIE -looking back at Scarlett.

On Ashley's face we read his realization of Scarlett's emotions. His eyes flicker a little and he glances

CONTINUED:

quickly again at his wife's hand on his new sleeve. But immediately he forces a smile and xtxxtxxtx calls to Scarlett.

Ashley (abrupt and crisp)
Goodnight, my dear.

Melanie tenderly throws a kiss to Scarlett.

Melanie
Goodnight, Scarlett darling.

R-183 — CLOSEUP SCARLETT.

Still gazing upward after Melanie and Ashley. She opens her lips to mumble a wretched goodnight to them, but fails, and closes her lips again with a long breath. Standing there completely motionless for a moment, she hears their footsteps going into their bedroom, a slight embarrassed cough from Ashley and then the sound of the door closing softly but decisively. At that, her fingers, holding the drape, clench into a fist for an instant, and then slowly and hopelessly relax and slip down the drape. The light effect on Scarlett's face has been changing for the past moment or two as Uncle Peter's candle vanishes, but her face remains lit by the wan light of the candle beside her.

DISSOLVE TO:

FIG. 126

The first three of Menzies' five sketches of this scene were influenced by shot descriptions in Garrett's January 16 filmscript but were reorganized into an arrangement that corresponds to the excised descriptions of the three shots, numbers 180–182, marked "already shot" in the original filmscript manuscript of February 27. The fourth sketch is an inventive continuation of the setup depicted in the first sketch, which also illustrates the concluding shot of Howard's final version, but in which the monumentality of Scarlett's silhouetted back (that is, its large size relative to other images within the frame) is diminished as her figure moves from the foreground in the first sketch to the foot of the staircase in the penultimate one. In the final sketch, the graphic diminution of Scarlett's figure continues with a high-angle shot of her small, solitary form, viewed from the upper story, which dramatically emphasizes her exclusion and powerlessness to possess Ashley. This concluding setup is also the same as that prescribed for the final portion of the establishing shot in Garrett's January 16 filmscript. Nevertheless, the earlier transcription of the four shots in the February 27 manuscript (shot numbers 180–183) indicates that the scene did not end as depicted in the final two sketches, but instead returned to a close-up of Scarlett.

To reiterate, various descriptions of shots comprising this sequence that are found in both Howard's and Garrett's filmscripts were borrowed and reorganized for presentation on this storyboard, much of which corresponds to descriptions of camera setups indicated as having been "already shot" under Cukor's direction in the original manuscript of the February 27 "rainbow" script. In other words, the only description of shots in a filmscript that correspond to this sketchwork is to be found in the record of what already had been filmed—as opposed to the prescription of what should be filmed, which was provided in the previous version of the shooting script by Garrett, but which was altered during this scene's initial filming under Cukor's direction.

Menzies' drawings reveal the production designer's distinctive contributions to shot composition and continuity, as well as the liberties taken with the various scripts in Cukor's filming of this scene during this director's final day on the production. In particular, Menzies is shown to have exploited the high and low angles of the two different perspectives of Scarlett observing Melanie and Ashley ascending the steps which resulted from camera positions being prescribed for both floors. The script was revised when sentimental dialogue between Melanie and Ashley was added. Camera setups employed in the filming of this scene under Fleming's direction provided viewpoints primarily from the upper floor (documented in a portion of the final cutting continuity, reproduced below). The scene in the film as released owed little debt to Menzies' compositions but conforms to a generic MGM style which informed much of Cukor's, Fleming's, and Selznick's work and which, as Mary Corliss observed, eschewed "Expressionist volume" and "distorted perspectives"[20] (see Figure 127).

> Section "B," Reel 3, 36B—Uncle Peter holding lighted candelabra. Ashley, with Melanie on his arm, comes out to him. Camera moves with them as they climb the stairs. They turn their backs to camera and look over railing to Scarlett o.s.
> [cf. R-180, above]

FIG. 127. Frame enlargements from shots in the staircase scene arranged for comparison with Menzies' storyboard.

37B—Long Shot—shooting down—Scarlett looking up at Melanie and Ashley O.S. [cf. R-181, above; see also 40B, below]

38B—M.S. [Medium Shot] Ashley and Melanie. Melanie blows Scarlett a kiss and they exit. [cf. R-182, above]

39B—C.U. [Close-up] Scarlett. [cf. R-183, above]

40B—L.S. shooting down on Scarlett. Shadow crosses her face.

Portions of another scene at Pittypat's house, directed by Cukor and included in the released film, and in which Melanie confesses to Scarlett that she has entered an early stage of labor, are illustrated by the remaining drawings on these two storyboards. A specific correspondence with the same February 27 filmscript, which also refers to this scene as "already shot," is indicated below a few of the sketches themselves in the form of penciled lines of dialogue, the ordee of which is unique to the original manuscript of this shooting script. However, the extreme angularity of the points of view and the arrangement of characters at different distances from the frame in many of these sketches—both features being hallmarks of Menzies' own compositional style—were replaced in the filmed version by

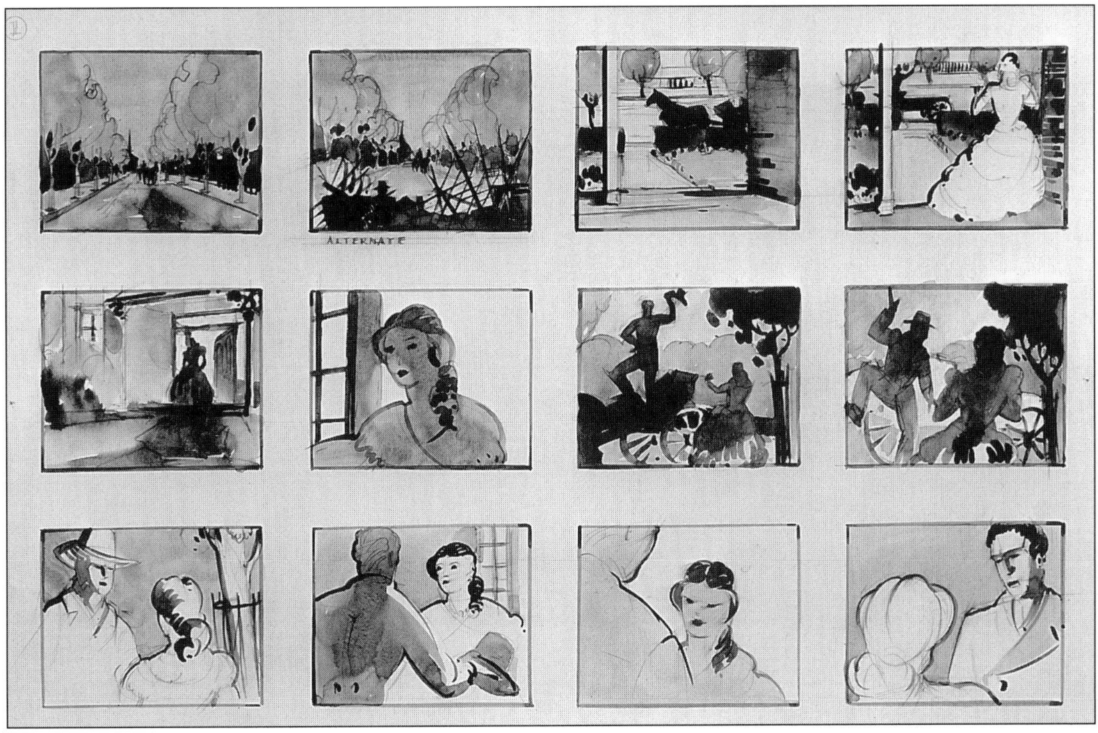

FIG. 128. An unsigned storyboard; 20 × 30 inches.

simpler two-shots of characters conversing face to face and in profile.

Dialogue between Scarlett and Prissy on the staircase landing outside Melanie's bedroom door, which was delineated by Menzies but was filmed differently under Cukor's direction, illustrates this change. The result is that in this scene in the film, these characters interact in a democratic, classically balanced space (that is, the players are given an equal part of the picture plane when facing one another), which presents the antithesis of the more baroque arrangements in the continuity sketches showing figures arranged along diagonal lines, one form dominating the other. A definite influence on this film's style of presentation, Selznick expressed his preference for the former approach in a memo to Menzies on November 20, 1938—one month before the filming of the fire sequence in 1938—describing Cukor as an "ideal director with whom to put in practice a more comprehensive camera-cutting in that George is very cooperative about holding down the number of angles and places less foolish emphasis on unnecessary camera angles than do most directors."

In general, straightforward presentation of actors' performances remained of greater value to the producer and to the directors than provocative visual compositions which interrupted delivery of lines or diminished figures. For example, for the scene preceding the fire sequence—in which Rhett arrives with the stolen horse and wagon and, against his better

FIGS. 129–130. The assault on Scarlett outside Shantytown is depicted in a series of eight unsigned drawings on heavy paperboard, $8^1/_4$–$9^1/_2 \times 10^1/_4$–$11^3/_4$ inches, marked A–H, respectively, on the reverse sides. Fig. 129 reproduces sketches A–D.

judgment, agrees to escort Scarlett and her charges to Tara—Cukor's choice to dolly the camera from a position outside Pittypat's porch to one before the front-door frame was made in disregard of the complex découpage of alternating over-the-shoulder and reverse-angle two-shots of Scarlett and Rhett that was presented in the storyboard drawn for this sequence. Instead, the scene in the film presents the characters face to face and in profile; by dollying the camera toward the actors, the performance was interrupted minimally during filming—a decision which suited Cukor's style of direction and was in accord with Selznick's respect of direct storytelling (see Figure 128).

The production designer's deference to the film director's authority to alter camera setups that had been prescribed by continuity sketches prior to filming and to Selznick's option to revise any part of the shooting script at any moment during the production in order to align a scene's presentation with the producer's vision also explains why Menzies' eight-drawing composition of the episode of Scarlett's assault near Shantytown differs from the episode in the released film (see Figures 129–130). In the novel, the scene is set at dusk upon Scarlett's return in the buggy she drove earlier, and without escort, to the sawmill outside Atlanta. The text relates that "the sun had completely gone when she reached the bend in the road above Shantytown and the woods

FIG. 130. An SIP art-department photograph of sketches E–H documents their storyboard arrangement. The originals are preserved also in the Selznick collection.

about her were dark." Soon afterward, Scarlett is assaulted by two tramps but is saved from rape and possible death by the sudden, aggressive intervention of Big Sam, a former slave of the O'Hara family who was freed by the war but was left destitute.[21]

Although Howard preserved the time of day in his dramatization of this episode, the assault was to be visible from the Shantytown campfires in the foreground, where Big Sam is alerted. (In contrast, in the novel, Scarlett discovers Big Sam in Shantytown on her way to the mill and arranges for him to meet her on the road upon her return.) Garrett's script separates the activities of the struggle and of Big Sam's reaction to Scarlett's cries of distress into two distinctly scenographical spaces which are juxtaposed by cross-cutting. The portion of this continuity in Shantytown is ignored in Menzies' sketches, which illustrate only the setups required for the ambush itself and emphasize Scarlett's isolation on a lonely road in a dark wood set at a frighteningly high elevation. Characteristic of the designer's proclivity for melodramatic points of view, both high and low angles were employed.

Misleadingly, it appears that the "axis of action" was intended to have been crossed at the moment of ambush. A fundamental premise of classical Hollywood continuity editing is that in order to maintain consistency of direction within multiple shots comprising

FIG. 131. Four more unsigned sketches of assault were drawn directly on the surface of the paperboard base, and are identified by the label, "Set #44 Ext. Shantytown"; 20 × 30 inches.

scenes, the viewpoint should be from a position on the same side of the 180-degree axis of action created by the camera setup for the previous shot. Indeed, in Menzies' series of sketches, the "axis of action" is crossed at this unsettling moment; however, the axis would not appear to have been crossed on the screen when shots taken separately on the Shantytown set, of Big Sam departing in the direction of Scarlett's cries, were inserted into the sequence.

The ordering of these eight sketches is indicated on their reverse sides by respective notation of the letters A through H. The similarity of the compositions of the first two sketches and the lateral shift of their respective viewpoints suggests a correspondence to the pan shot prescribed for this sequence in Garrett's filmscript of January 16, 1939. The placement of the buggy in the foreground of two of the final sketches also suggests a relationship to this same script. Revision of the February 27 script on June 10 altered the setting by the addition of a bridge. Four continuity sketches of this revised episode, drawn out of sequential order on a storyboard, are preserved in the Selznick collection and are suggestive of the handwork of art-department employee Frank Bowers, who also made a drawing of the campfire scene in Shantytown (see Figure 131). These drawings were created likely for the purpose of assisting second-unit production of shots requiring employment of Vivien Leigh's double and also for the making of background plates for use in shots filmed later of the principal player performing before rear-projected imagery.

The storyboard of Scarlett's ambush on the bridge ultimately contributed very little either to this sequence's formation or to the camera setups employed, despite the correspondence of the bottom-right sketch to the description of one of the shots in the revised February 27 script. (The fact that the bottom portion of a bridge appears as a compositional part of this sketch but that the script does not identify this architectural backdrop as part of the setting until the following shot's description very likely indicates that these sketches were drawn after the writing of this episode's revision.) Another aspect of the February 27 filmscript is that Sam's viewpoint is taken when Scarlett escapes—an alteration which meant that only the back of Leigh's double needed to be filmed in showing Scarlett's flight on the wagon in its departure from the camera's position. This point of view is the exact opposite (that is, the reverse-angle) of the shots of the concluding part of the episode which Menzies had sketched. Ultimately, more complicated process photography was employed, and the second-unit work was directed by B. Reeves ("Breezy") Eason, who had coordinated much of the spectacular chariot-race and land-rush sequences in *Ben-Hur* (1925) and *Cimarron* (1931), respectively. Although medium shots were taken, under Fleming's direction, of Leigh on the carriage seat, none of the dramatically angular effects exhibited in Menzies' sketches for this sequence were attempted.

Because of artwork's general adherence to descriptions of shots provided in the screenplays, in the case of *Gone with the Wind* there are very few instances in which evidence of an artist's inventiveness with the narrative is presented by a continuity sketch. Menzies' collaboration with Cukor in the construction of a sequence, which transcended prescriptions specified by the shooting script and which is documented by the production designer's storyboard of Scarlett observing Melanie and Ashley mounting the steps to their bedroom on Christmas Eve, has been examined already at some length. A sketch on a different storyboard serves to illustrate one other rare instance when an artist may have deviated from filmscript material and influenced the development of a scene.

No exact match exists between shots in any of the numerous extant filmscripts and the unsigned storyboard that displays evidence of the handwork of "Mac" Johnson and begins with a sketch of Scarlett grasping a horse by its bridle under a bridge over which mounted troops pass during her trek from Atlanta to Tara (see Figure 132). This dramatic moment under a bridge is not recounted in the novel, although Scarlett is described as pulling her wagon off the road and into the adjacent overgrowth during the course of the night in order to avoid detection by passing cavalry and mounted artillery. The latter scene is dramatized variously by Howard in his different versions of the screenplay. In his early drafts, Scarlett proceeds on her journey after hiding next to the road, avoids detection by soldiers at a nearby campfire, and, the following day while collecting apples at the abandoned Mallory estate, is horrified by the sight of the corpse of a sharpshooter. Because of Breen's objections, Howard removed the corpse from the filmscript in its November 1937 revision.

Nevertheless, in Garrett's subsequent version of the screenplay, a sniper's corpse is described as hanging luridly from a tree limb, under which Scarlett, unaware, parks her

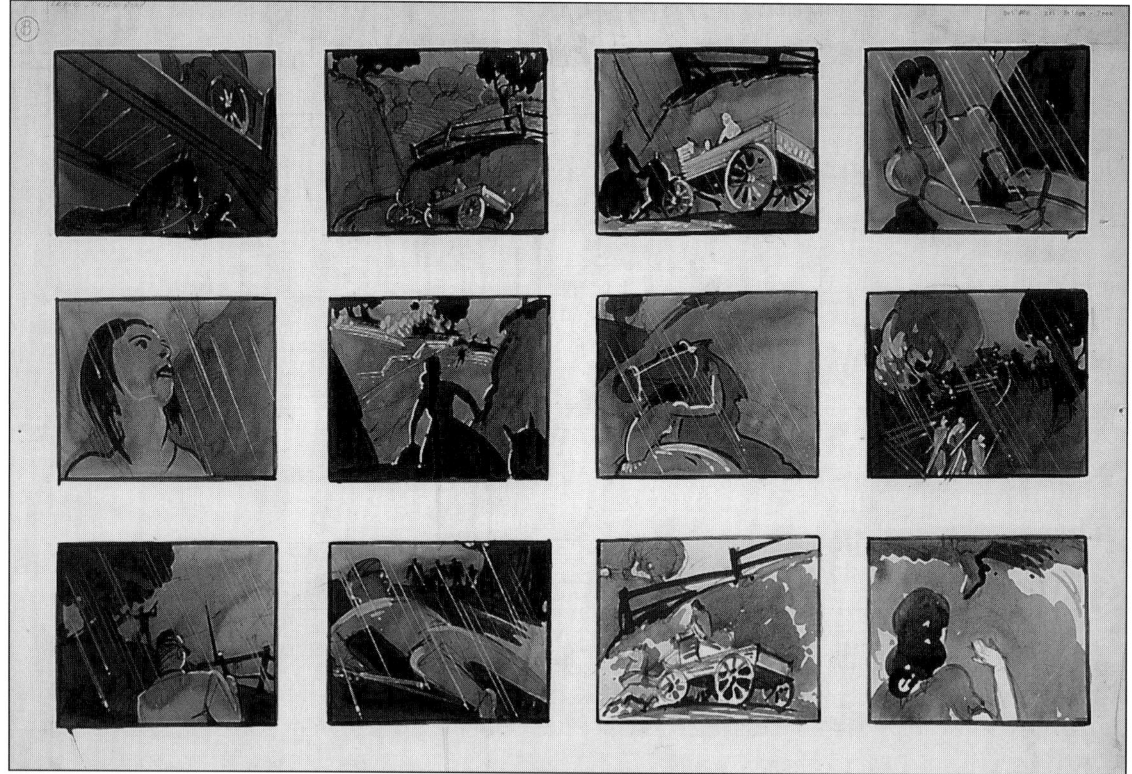

FIG. 132. Twelve unsigned watercolor sketches executed directly on the surface of the heavy paperboard base and identified by the label, "Set #26—Ext. Bridge—Trek"; 20 × 30 inches.

wagon during the night, and is horrified by its sight when she awakens the following morning. The same scenario also prescribes that the wagon and its occupants hide under a bridge. In the storyboard, the minimal use of a bridge, the depiction of Scarlett's witnessing a distant battle in the rain, and her discovery the following morning of what may have been intended in delineation as a leg of the suspended corpse, at the site where her horse collapsed the previous night, suggests that these sketches were drawn after Howard's early screenplays were completed but before Garrett's revision was written. It is plausible that the first sketch in this storyboard may have influenced the filmscript's development by its introduction to the narrative of the use of a bridge.

Four various shots of Scarlett and her wagon under a bridge are described in a revision dated June 20 of the shooting script of February 27, 1939. While this revision is similar to the sketch of Scarlett under a bridge on Johnson's storyboard and to a more elaborate drawing of the same subject by Menzies, there is no mention of rain; instead, only dust from the cavalry passing above is described as falling on those hiding below. However, the intense precipitation depicted in most of the remaining sketches on the storyboard likely influenced the use of a downpour in the five shots devoted to this scene in its screen presentation, the design of which is presented in other drawings by Menzies, Johnson, and Jack Martin Smith (see Figures 133–137). Smith was

FIG. 133. An unsigned drawing of Scarlett hiding with horse and wagon under a bridge while cavalry and artillery cross; 15 × 19 inches.

loaned as an artist to SIP for three months by MGM, where he worked on *The Wizard of Oz*; in 1961, he replaced Lyle Wheeler as supervising art director of 20th Century-Fox, and he received Academy Awards for work on *Cleopatra* (1963), *Who's Afraid of Virginia Woolf?* (1966), and *Hello, Dolly!* (1969).

Smith drew an alternate design, depicting Scarlett in a wagon at the bottom of a steep ravine near a river's edge, the surface of which reflects mounted troops passing above her. This design was inspired very likely by Johnson's drawing of Scarlett and wagon at the bottom of another ravine, above which a Yankee encampment is depicted, illustrating the near confrontation of refugees and troops which is described in Howard's filmscripts (see Figures 138–139). Although the vertical format of Johnson's drawing indicates a tilting of the camera (the specific prescription for which is not found in any description of this shot in any script version), the correspondence of its subject to a shot included in Howard's early scripts and the similarity of its content and style to Johnson's storyboard of Scarlett's trek reinforce the dating of the composition of both artworks to the period between the completion of Howard's and Garrett's filmscripts. This dateline also supports the argument that the use of a bridge in this scene originated with its appearance in a continuity sketch and that an artist thus contributed original narrative material to this film's presentation.

FIG. 134. An unsigned drawing of Scarlett hiding with horse and wagon under a bridge; 12 × 15 inches.

FIG. 135. This polychrome drawing of Scarlett and horse and wagon under a bridge is signed by Jack Martin Smith; 15 × 22 inches.

FIG. 136. Photograph of bridge scene drawn by Menzies.

Changes 10-4-39

"GONE WITH THE WIND"
Revised
10/3/39

pgs. 10-12

TREK

AS SHOT — DISSOLVE IN:

"REFLECTION" LONG SHOT wagon crossing countryside. EVENING.

DISSOLVE TO:

ADDED SCENE

XXXX
COSGROVE LONG SHOT-SKY.-DAWN.-RAIN.
A bolt of lightning flashes through the rain in the sky.

ADDED SCENE

EXT. AT BRIDGE AND SWAMP. (GREENISH RAIN EFFECT) — CLOSEUP-SCARLETT
The rain falling on her terrified face. We hear the rumble of horses' hooves and artillery wheels passing over the wooden bridge above her.

CAMERA (ON BOOM) PULLS BACK until we see that the wagon with Prissy, Melanie and the baby is in a swamp under a bridge. Scarlett stands at the horse's bridle, knee deep in the green slime of the swamp. The wagon is tilted at a precarious angle, having been pulled down a slippery embankment to comparative safety under the bridge., Prissy is cowering in the front seat.

In continuous movement, CAMERA NOW TILTS UPWARD until it includes the lower portion of artillery wheels passing overhead on the wooden bridge.

ADDED SCENE

CLOSEUP-PRISSY (for intercut)
Whimpering and nearly overcome with terror.

ADDED SCENE

CLOSE SHOT-MELANIE AND BABY (doll) - for intercut.

Melanie holds her hand over the baby's face to protect it from the rain which falls through the cracks in the floor of the bridge.

ADDED SCENE

LONGER ANGLE (continuation of above boom shot)
The last of the artillery passes over the bridge. Scarlett wipes her hand over her face in relief and starts tugging at the horse to start it out of the swamp.

DISSOLVE TO:

FIG. 137. Script of "added" scenes, September 28, 1939.

FIG. 138. Unsigned drawing; 26 × 17 inches.

Art Direction, Shot Composition, and Continuity Design

Accurate assessment and adequate recognition of the contributions of art directors and production designers have been problematic for many film historians and for the film industry itself. In their 1978 survey in *Film Comment*, Mary Corliss and Carlos Clarens characterized these film designers as the participants in filmmaking who were the "most distinguished and least acknowledged." They also related that "it was the department head who, until the mid-thirties, took credit for the work of anonymous unit art directors, sketch artists, and blueprint boys."[22] That same year, in *The Art of Hollywood*, John Hambley and Patrick Downing specifically criticized the lengthy period of Cedric Gibbon's direction of the MGM art department and the industry's neglect to reward original work contributed by his unit art directors. "Cedric Gibbon's contract ensured that his name appeared on every film produced by MGM between 1924 and 1956, and he received Academy awards for eleven of them," these authors acknowledged yet argued that "no evidence exists that he produced a single design for any of these eleven, let alone the 1,500 others that bear his name." In his foreword to their book, Orson Welles corroborated that at this time the "head of the art

FIG. 139. Drawing by Jack Martin Smith; 22 × 30 inches.

department was essentially a bureaucratic functionary [who] did little or none of the actual designing for which he took credit and received awards [and] no more designed a movie than Louis B. Mayer directed one."[23]

Hambley and Downing professed that Anton Grot and Menzies represented the "opposite end of the scale" and "came nearest to (and sometimes achieved) the total translation of their original ideas into finished motion pictures." They claimed that these two designers " 'wrote' films on their sketch pads and drawing boards long before the camera began turning" and that "[their] frame-by-frame drawings and continuity sketches [were] followed precisely shot by shot" during filmmaking and are "revelatory indicators of film authorship."[24] Two decades later, in *Sets in Motion*, Charles Affron and Mirella Jona Affron affirmed that advocacy of these designers by Hambley and Downing still "constitutes a strong claim for the art director as auteur."[25]

In *Hollywood Art*, Beverly Heisner has compared Menzies to Richard Day, who served as art director on films by John Ford and Erich von Stroheim, because the freelance status of both designers—which was unusual in the classical Hollywood period—made possible the "best that Hollywood art direction was ever to achieve." In contrast, Heisner described Grot as having risen within the ranks of Warner Bros. to become its "most formidable" art director and as having enjoyed the "security of a steady pay check" (although his salary of $450 per week was less than half the amount Menzies received during the same period for work on *Gone with the Wind*).[26]

On the basis of a passage in *One Reel a Week* by cinematographer Arthur Miller and silent-filmmaker Fred J. Balshofer, Heisner also credited Grot for pioneering use of continuity sketches as early as the 1920s. Menzies himself had served as Grot's assistant on Pathé film productions at Fort Lee, New Jersey, before both moved to Hollywood. According to Balshofer and Miller, Grot's earliest sketches "showed a full shot of each set [which,] . . . when constructed, duplicated his drawings in camera angle as well as showing sizes of objects in their proper relative proportions when photographed with a 40mm lens," and "Anton . . . taught Billy [Menzies] the trick of making drawings, using his dimension scale, which William Cameron Menzies used throughout his long and distinguished career as a production designer."[27]

In *An Evening's Entertainment*, Richard Koszarski interpreted Miller's account as evidence of Grot's authority on shot compositions via set designs but did not extend this art director's influence to composition of continuity per se. "Grot created charcoal illustrations of the sets that displayed the scale and perspective of various motion-picture lenses," explained Koszarski. "This technique enabled him to build only those segments of the set that would actually be used and resulted in substantial savings in construction costs."[28]

To many film commentators, development of storyboarding is linked more fundamentally to animation than to set and shot designs. Specifically, a routine established in the Disney studios has been credited as the precedent for continuity designs of *Gone with the Wind*. Haver observed that "the idea had come to Selznick when he heard Merian Cooper [SIP vice president, 1935–1937] relate what Walt Disney was doing on his feature-length cartoon, *Snow White and the Seven Dwarfs*" (released by RKO in 1937). He added that "Cooper had been impressed with Disney's 'storyboarding' technique and remembered having done the same thing with *King Kong* [as its producer in 1933 at RKO—during Selznick's tenure as production chief]."[29] In *The Disney Version*, Richard Schickel credited the invention of this technique to Webb Smith, a former newspaper cartoonist who was employed in Disney's story department:

> Smith had retained his habit of sketching out gag sequences instead of writing them down. These he generally spread all over the floor of his office, an unsightly and sometimes confusing business that he one day abandoned in favor of pinning his sketches on the walls. At first, it is said, Disney was furious at the notion: he claimed that the holes left by the pins would ruin the walls, which he had spent a good deal to redecorate. But the conflict between his rage for artistic order and his rage for tidy housekeeping was resolved when quantities of corkboard were ordered (they had the virtue of being portable, too), and Smith's idea quickly became an established—even ritualistic—part of the studio's planning procedure.[30]

Schickel concluded that this process was a "key innovation in the process of rationalizing the chaos of cartoon creation—a process that was one of Disney's principal preoccupations throughout the thirties."[31] Most importantly, this routine also facilitated the monitoring and control of a film project by the producer.

It should be noted that storyboarding was employed, too, on one of Selznick's live-action productions for MGM—namely, *Viva Villa!* (1934), much of which was filmed in Mexico. In the year of the film's release, the director of photography, James Wong Howe, described, in an article published in *American Cinematographer*, how he and art director Harry Oliver collaborated on sketching out much of the shooting script prior to filming:

> We studied the script together, and made hundreds of sketches of the way we visualized each scene. Frequently, we would make half-a-dozen different sketches of each scene, finally selecting the one which seemed most perfectly suited to the photographic and dramatic requirements of the scene, as we jointly conceived it. These sketches were incorporated in the final script of the picture: they served the dual purpose of simplifying both the production and pre-production problems, and of assuring better coordination between the director and director of photography.[32]

It is not known whether Howard Hawks agreed to these designs' use when he served as this film's initial director, nor is it known whether his successor, Jack Conway, referred to them after recasting required retaking of more than half of the picture. Rewriting of the script also took place by telegraph between Selznick in Los Angeles and Ben Hecht in the writer's home in Nyack, New York. (Both Hecht and *Viva Villa!* received Oscar nominations in 1935, in the categories of best original screenplay and best picture, respectively.)

It is likely that Howe was influenced not so much by film animation as he was by Sergei Eisenstein's use of sketches for the making of *Que viva Mexico!* (1931–1932), which was brutally cut by its American distributor for release in 1933 under the title *Thunder over Mexico*. Eisenstein himself had designed shots and sequences for his films in preliminary drawings as early as 1925, with *Battleship Potemkin*.[33] Anecdotes of other directors sketching their own ideas in advance of shooting have been circulated also. "Fritz Lang was another one who thought he could design a picture himself," recounted Boris Leven, who claimed that Lang "would sit and plot with different-colored pencils; he'd use a slide rule—every shot, every scene—until his page of notes was so cluttered you couldn't read it."[34] A former art director himself, Alfred Hitchcock professed to having illustrated copies of his film's scripts also (unfortunately, no examples are preserved among the numerous copies of screenplays in the director's own collection).[35]

A unique case has been preserved of a completely delineated filmscript of a live-action motion picture that was produced in Hollywood during the period preceding the making of *Gone with the Wind* and that is the work of Menzies. Although the artwork was redrawn for duplication by stenciling, the original manuscript of the screenplay of *Alice in Wonderland* (1933) offers a pencil sketch and typed description with dialogue and emendations of single shots on each of its 642 pages; this arrangement suggests that text and imagery were composed by Menzies in collaboration with art director Robert Odell.[36] Ultimately, the credit for screenwriting was shared by Menzies and Joseph L. Mankiewicz, who revised the scenario for filming. (Mankiewicz later received Academy Awards for the direction and screenplay of *All About Eve* in 1950.) Directed by Norman McLeod, Paramount's *Alice in Wonderland* has been described by various sources as a "disaster." Although a great number of this studio's leading players were enlisted for this production, many were either miscast (for example, the young Gary Cooper disguised as the bald White Knight) or are unrecognizable in costumes designed from the book's original illustrations by John Tenniel (for example, Cary Grant as the Mock Turtle).[37]

While advanced planning of compositions and continuity of shots for action or musical sequences was not uncommon during the classical Hollywood period, the complete storyboarding of a script prior to filming was unusual. Generally, principal authority was assumed by film directors only on the shooting set. Although Heisner praised Wilfred Buckland's designs for films by Famous Players-Lasky (an early form of Paramount Pictures) in the teens as a "milestone in the recognition of art direction as an integral part of movie making," she added that often "directors, in particular Cecil B. DeMille, objected to his 'interference.' "[38] Buckland had served as art director of David Belasco's Broadway stage productions and had achieved notoriety for the dramatic play of contrasts—or chiaroscuro—in his lighting of *The Cheat* in 1915.

Upon their arrival in Hollywood, both Grot and Menzies acted as Buckland's assistants on the design of Douglas Fairbanks's *Robin Hood* (1922). Afterward, while Buckland's stature plummeted, Grot himself was hired as one of seven "associated artists" to work under Menzies' supervision on Fairbanks's *Thief of Baghdad* (1924). Menzies' career as an art director was established by the fantastic sets that were constructed for this picture, and his reputation as both an independent film designer and a collaborative technical director was strengthened by subsequent work on films directed by Cecil B. DeMille, Howard Hawks, and Ernst Lubitsch for Paramount and produced by Samuel Goldwyn and D. W. Griffith through United Artists.

Grot's tenure at Warner Bros. eventually gave this designer the authority to endow many of its films with a "visual quality as identifiable as Cedric Gibbons' at MGM, but very much its opposite in execution and effect," according to Hambley and Downing.[39] During this period, Grot designed sixteen films for Michael Curtiz, including *Captain Blood* (1935) and *The Private Lives of Elizabeth and Essex* (1939); ten for William Dieterle, including *A Midsummer Night's Dream* (1936) and *Juarez* (1939); and eight for Mervyn LeRoy, including *Little Caesar* (1931) and *Anthony Adverse* (1936).

Producer Hal Wallis related that, for *A Midsummer Night's Dream*, even the internationally famous stage director Max Reinhardt "visualized everything in sketches drawn up for him by our art director, Anton Grot," and that "[William] Dieterle [who co-directed the picture with Reinhardt] set up cameras accordingly."[40] For the most part, however, only set designs are preserved in the Anton Grot collection at the University of California, Los Angeles, which represents this art director's contributions to almost fifty films with more than eight hundred drawings.[41] An example in the Grot collection of set designs that were drawn for a picture produced contemporaneously with *Gone with the Wind* and that appear problematically to represent continuity delineation is a series of eight individual graphite drawings with notational references to scenes on certain pages of an unspecified filmscript of *Juarez* (see Figures 140–146).

FIGS. 140–146. These seven annotated drawings, 5 × 7 inches each, in the Anton Grot Collection, correspond to scenes in an intermediate script of *Juarez* (Warner Bros., 1939) entitled "The Phantom Crown" and dated June 2, 1938. Reproduced with permission of Special Collections, University Research Library, University of California, Los Angeles.

P. 24
EXT. PUBLIC PLAZA
PEONS EXHORTED NOT TO VOTE
FOR MAXIMILIAN

P. 24
EXT. PUBLIC PLAZA
PEONS PROTEST FORCED VOTE

FIGS. 141–142

P. 24
EXT. PUBLIC PLAZA
PEONS PROTESTING FRENCH FORCED VOTE

P. 24
EXT. PUBLIC PLAZA
MEXICAN PEON EXHORTS CROWD NOT TO VOTE
FOR MAXIMILIAN

FIGS. 143–144

P. 24
EXT. RURAL HEMP FACTORY.
MALE WORKERS FORCED TO VOTE FOR
MAXIMILIAN

VIVA JUAREZ
P 25
EXT MEXICAN STREET.
PEONS USE LYE TO REMOVE WRITING
ON WALLS SUPPORTING JUAREZ.

FIGS. 145–146

Closer analysis of this artwork for *Juarez* discloses important distinctions in the designs prepared for Selznick by Menzies. As illustrated by Grot, this sequence begins with the martial enforcement of the polling of the bogus Mexican plebescite, by which the Austrian archduke Maximilian is tempted by Napoleon III of France into accepting the crown of Mexico, and continues with shots of plebeian protestation and military intervention. A script entitled "The Phantom Crown" (the name of the 1934 novel by Bertita Harding upon which the film was based) and dated June 2, 1938 provides a match with the descriptions and page numbers noted on these sketches but—similarly to the case of the many versions of the screenplay of *Gone with the Wind*—it was not the only treatment. The June 2 filmscript is an uncredited revision of the initial scenario completed in February by Wolfgang Reinhardt (the son of the stage director). Subsequent revisions are dated September 17, October 22, and October 29 (the last of which incorporated changes made as late as January 9, 1939) and are entitled *Juarez*, in great part in order to emphasize the casting of Paul Muni in the title role (Warner Bros. had benefited from the critical acclaim Muni had won for his portrayal of the title roles in *The Story of Louis Pasteur* and *The Life of Emile Zola* in 1936 and 1937, respectively).[42]

The sequence illustrated by Grot begins with a notice of the polling decree being posted and follows with a shot of soldiers knocking on the door of "a dobe [*sic*] hovel," through which the camera was to move as they enter to collect supporting votes from all male occupants, including an infant; only an exterior view is depicted in the sketch. The scene that follows is described in the filmscript as "an assembly of peons and poorer-class townsfolk listening to a speaker who is standing on a bench in a public plaza." The series of four sketches enriches the square architecturally and, by a succession of different points of view, may either define the orator and his audience or simply offer a choice of camera setups, but it does not illustrate the gathering's dispersal by cavalry. The final two shots—of soldiers forcing Mexicans, including an old man and a young girl, to immerse their hands in buckets of corrosive lye in the attempt to force them to remove slogans supporting Juárez from the city walls—are illustrated by a single sketch; again, it was the delineation of establishing shots that was undertaken rather than the depiction of the continuity of all shots. Scenes of the adobe hovel and of the conscription of Mexicans to wash walls with lye were removed from the September 17 script, and the description of the assembly of peons before a speaker appears as before. Nothing depicted in the sketches contributed to the revised continuity of shots.

Pairs of sketches were drawn of additional scenes in *Juarez*. An example of these is a board on which two unsigned monochrome sketches are mounted in a vertical arrangement with notational references to "page 89" of an unspecified filmscript (see Figure 147). The top drawing depicts a man carrying a key and crossing a prison courtyard, accompanied by soldiers, and the bottom one represents an interior view of a prison cell in which a man with a bandaged arm lies. The two drawings are united by the legend at the bottom of the board that reads, "Maximilian visits Diaz," and a comparison with "The Phantom Crown" scenario of June 2, 1938 again discloses a correspondence of shots and page numbers; the same description of these two shots is repeated in the three filmscript versions of *Juarez* that followed. Because the film's presentation of these scenes differs radically from the compositions in these

FIG. 147. The annotations below these two drawings on paperboard, 12 × 7 inches each, refer to the same intermediate script of *Juarez*, dated June 2, 1938, referred to in Figures 140–146. Reproduced with permission of University Research Library, University of California, Los Angeles.

FIG. 148. Five sketches, on paperboard base, depicting final scene in *Juarez*; 14 × 11 inches each. Reproduced with permission of Special Collections, University Research Library, University of California, Los Angeles.

graphic designs, a more legitimate reading of these sketches than that which posits their depiction of a very brief portion of this scene's continuity may be that they represent the two views of prison interiors required for the set design of this sequence. Similarly, a larger board of five drawings of a casket on display within a church interior does not suggest storyboarding but rather various options available in terms of camera setups and set designs for the two shots that comprise the various scripts' final scene (see Figure 148). This interpretation is supported by the variety of different conceptions of the concluding shots which are preserved in the form of other drawings.

The distinction between Grot's service to *Juarez* and Menzies' design of *Gone with the Wind* may be described as comparable to differences between the contributions of Lyle Wheeler, as art director, and those of Menzies to the latter film. It also illustrates important differences in the production values espoused by Warner Bros. and by Selznick and MGM for a major release. (*Juarez* was budgeted at approximately $1,750,000, which was only a quarter of a million dollars over the amount of the loan required by Selznick when *Gone with the Wind* exceeded its original budget of $2,500,000.) In a letter of July 29, 1937 to Henry Ginsberg and Ted Butcher, Selznick justified the invention of Menzies' unique role to fellow SIP board members and managers on account of his film project's immense size and its use of Technicolor. Still, by standards established prior to the undertaking of *Gone with the Wind*, *Juarez* was not an ordinary film production either. According to Herman Lissauer, director of research for Warner Bros., whose task was to assist the production crew in correctly resolving questions of historical, architectural, and decorative detail, "it was the most extensive and difficult assignment our department . . . ever received."[43] *Juarez* also was one of the most elaborate films in the cycle of "prestige pictures" directed for Warner Bros. in the 1930s by William Dieterle, Anatole Litvak, and Michael Curtiz.

As art director of *Juarez*, Grot, together with his assistant Leo Kuder, reputedly drew a total of 3,643 sketches of sets and scenic details, from which 7,360 blueprints were made. From these plans, fifty-four sets were built at various locations in Southern California, the largest of which—an entire Mexican village—was constructed on a 300-acre ranch north of Hollywood.[44] "Three months of study and preparation went into this set before the first shovelful of earth was turned," Grot recounted for the film's publicity. He also added that "in order to be certain that William Dieterle, the director, would have every possible camera angle and background, we built a thirty-foot square model of the entire setting, using fibre board, plaster, glass, and small bushes to resemble trees."[45] This admission distinguishes Grot's conventional tasks as art director from the ambitious program undertaken by Menzies for *Gone with the Wind*. Whereas it was Grot's obligation to provide the film director with numerous options for camera setups in the design and construction of sets, Menzies' sphere of influence extended—albeit in a limited way—into the filming itself, by his attempts to predetermine camera angles.

Warner's art-department statistics for *Juarez* may be compared with the production figures cited for related work undertaken on *Gone with the Wind* in order to reveal another major difference, in addition to the latter's use of Technicolor. Assisted by the 2,500–3,000 sketches drawn for purposes of both production design and art direction by Menzies and art-department illustrators, Lyle Wheeler designed as many as two hundred sets, ninety of which were constructed—sixty percent more than the large number cited for *Juarez*. Photographic documentation also exists of Wheeler's supervision of the building of exact models.

With respect to the quantity of extant artwork, over two hundred original drawings are preserved in the Selznick collection, and a significant number of these pertain to storyboarding and to continuity design. Of this portion, numerous examples survive that were produced at different times during preparatory, production, and editing stages and that correspond to different states of the filmscript, the development of which may have been influenced by the artwork in a few instances. A small number of these drawings also correspond to the composition of actual shots featured in the film. In comparison, only about 30 of the 3,643 sketches drawn for *Juarez* are represented and preserved in the Grot collection, although 8 of these illustrate a sequence of shots in a specific intermediate version of the scenario; however, filmscript development was uninfluenced by any of these examples. Viewed in this context, Menzies' contributions to *Gone with the Wind* as production designer were remarkable in terms both of license and of influence on development of imagery and narrative.

"Cinema Design" and Classical Hollywood Film Production

Notwithstanding measures of the artistic success of drawings preserved from the making of *Gone with the Wind*—that is, as original artwork and as designs that were influential on a celebrated film production to a significant and unprecedented degree—the fame accorded them may be credited also to their preservation in unusually large numbers. The storyboards of key sequences in *Citizen Kane* provide another exception to the otherwise meager survival rate of preproduction artwork. While Orson Welles's film was unusual for its time because of the authority ceded to the director by the studio, the artwork itself may be compared with that drawn for Selznick's own magnum opus in order to disclose important similarities and differences between classical American film productions in the making and use of art-department designs.

In *The Making of "Citizen Kane,"* in which examples of this artwork are reproduced, Robert Carringer relates that art director Perry Ferguson and Welles collaborated on the design of each scene prior to its production. "Welles told me he usually did a first set of rough sketches to convey his ideas but found this to be unnecessary working with Ferguson," writes Carringer. "Ferguson would submit the preliminary sketches to Welles, and the sketches would go back and forth between Welles and the art department until Welles was satisfied." In view of cinematographer Gregg Toland's use of "deep focus photography" and of Welles's predilection for sets with visible ceilings, establishment of a "tentative approach" to the filming of each scene was recognized as "an absolute precondition for everything else, since the camera range needed for shooting determined how much of a set had to be built." Coordination of camera position, shot composition, and set design was requisite to the planning, and in his book, Carringer stresses the artwork's fundamental utility in this respect.[46]

Despite the similarity of many of the continuity drawings in *The Making of "Citizen Kane"* to this film's imagery and continuity, specific correspondences of scripts, storyboards, and screen presentation are not offered by Carringer, who credits the designs' creation simply to Ferguson's "elaborate notes" regarding pre-production discussions with Welles and their routine interpretation by art-department subordinates. "Ferguson might add an occasional thumbnail sketch involving practical matters, such as layout or prop placement, but the actual visual treatments were done not by him but by the art department staff," Carringer allows. "[Ferguson] was a specialist in set construction, not an illustrator." RKO draftsmen Charles Ohmann and Albert Pyke are credited with the creation of several storyboards that exhibit striking resemblance to much that is seen in the film, although Carringer dismisses any notion of creativity in the execution of these sketches with his remark that the artwork "could have been done by anyone." He professes, "Storyboards were turned out so quickly that they usually lacked individuality, and it was in the nature of things for everybody on the staff to take at least one turn at one thing or another on any given production."[47]

That artwork for *Gone with the Wind* was monitored as closely by Selznick is affirmed in a series of memos to the production designer from the producer. "As to your ideas on the script, my plan is to give you a copy of the draft we are presently working on, which I think will be complete within a week," Selznick informed Menzies on January 18, 1938, while revising Howard's filmscript in collaboration with Cukor. "While we are working on the next draft, which will be aimed at shortening considerably, I would like you to be preparing your ideas, which we are all most anxious to have," added Selznick, whose supervision was always interactive. "When we have finished the final draft . . . I will then start to work with you in earnest on your sketches, doing perhaps a sequence a day, and I hope that by that time you will be well progressed," he told Menzies, following up on him again on March 8 with the query, "I assume that you are keeping in close touch with the revised and shortened script of *Gone with the Wind* so that your work is in accordance with it."

"By tonight you will receive final script on the entire Trek," Selznick informed the production designer a year later, on March 10, in reference to the sequence of which shots of Scarlett and her charges in the wagon under a bridge form a dramatic part. "I should appreciate it if you would sketch this entire series," he asked Menzies again. On May 1, Selznick requested Menzies' attention to a specific detail in his preparation of the sketchwork: "In connection with the shot of the wagon reflected in the water, sketches for which you showed me the other night, please be sure that we have the grotesque silhouetted figure of the dead soldier in the foreground." Selznick's continual revision of the filmscript and of Menzies' designs is indicated by the following passage in the producer's memo of June 5, 1939 to Raymond Klune, concerning this same sequence:

> Within the next day I will send through a revised script on . . . the Trek. This is subject to any ideas or changes that Bill Menzies may care to suggest. I would like Bill immediately to do sketches of the entire Trek and go over it with me. And I would like the shooting of this Trek to be limited actually to the exact angles that we need.

> There shouldn't be a single setup that isn't agreed on in advance. I think that with this in mind Hal Kern should go over it with Bill and should be present at our meeting as soon as the sketches are ready.

Evidence of a producer's control over the planning and construction of a major scene in a motion picture exists also in the Grot collection, which contains a unique example of storyboarding in which related development of script and graphic continuity design is exhibited—namely, the artwork corresponding to the opening sequence of *Mildred Pierce* (1945). Twenty-three original continuity sketches and twenty-seven glossy 8-by-10-inch photographs of drawings rendered in revision of this same scene are preserved at UCLA. Subject matter includes a nocturnal shot of surf washing over a portion of sand (over which the title and opening credits were eventually printed), followed by a panning movement which discloses a nearby beach house, and shots of the title character walking to the end of the Santa Monica pier, where a policeman discourages her from suicide, and afterward of her being confronted by ex-business partner Wally Fay, who invites her into his café at the pier's entrance.

Based on the novel of the same name by James M. Cain, nine successive versions of the script were written by various authors; screenwriting credit was shared by Catherine Turney and Ranald MacDougall.[48] The use of a framing device (namely, beginning at an anxious, unresolved moment near the story's conclusion and back-tracking before proceeding to a closure) was suggested in some of the early treatments but was developed only in the sixth version, which is credited to MacDougall, and of which the first six pages correspond to the earlier set of drawings. In Turney's previous scripts, the film was to open with insertion of a map and stock shots of "suburban towns in or near Los Angeles"—including Glendale and Pasadena—for the purpose of "giving flavor of California life" before proceeding with Mildred's marriage to Bert Pierce and the latter's failure at real-estate development. Photographs in the Grot collection of the second series of illustrations correspond more accurately to MacDougall's "revised final" filmscript. However, not depicted are the shots of Monte Beragon's death which were introduced into the story in the final scenario and which abruptly open the picture after its credit sequence, following the pan-shot to the beach house; this omission suggests that the drawing of these sketches likely preceded the completion of the final script version.

Homicide was not a feature of Cain's novel but was purportedly introduced by the film's producer, Jerry Wald. Wald desired to alter Turney's earlier screenplay in order to introduce this framing device and the flashback presentation of the majority of the story line, but required the assistance of other screenwriters when the original scenarist became engaged in another film project. Charles Higham credited the inspiration for Wald's changes to Orson Welles's *Citizen Kane* and to Billy Wilder's dramatization of Cain's *Double Indemnity* (1943), in which a framing device, death, and an investigation are featured. Higham also described Wald's reworking of the narrative of *Mildred Pierce* as a "very 'Warners' concept," which "worked" in spite of Cain's violent objections in a series of letters.[49] Unlike the situation with *Juarez*, in which the repeated revision of the original script's narrative continuity was uninfluenced by a single graphic design, the creation of the two series of sketches of the opening sequence of *Mildred Pierce* followed the picture's script development and influenced its filming and editing.

A principal reason why much of this sequence from *Mildred Pierce* reflects its storyboarding may be simply that the development of both sketches and script proceeded under the authority of the unit producer, which ensured the cooperation of both veteran director Michael Curtiz and cinematographer Ernest Haller (who, with Technicolor advisors Ray Rennahan and Wilfred Cline, had received credit and Academy Awards for filming *Gone with the Wind*). "Jerry Wald was its most important shaping force," professed Albert LaValley in his introduction to the publication of MacDougall's final screenplay. "Not only did he make all the major pre-production decisions—but he also oversaw the entire production."[50] (While acting with great license as the film's unit producer, Wald himself remained subordinate to the dictates of studio chief Jack Warner, who on at least one occasion faulted the art department for having attended to "too much detail" and reminded his cinematographers and art directors that "technical perfection does not necessarily mean the success of a picture.")[51]

Both unit production and the precedent of a producer's use of a production designer's services—developments in classical American filmmaking which Selznick inaugurated—were instrumental in fostering this arrangement. Although Rotha had not included the producer among the "composers" of a motion picture listed in his idealization of its planning in his *Close Up* essay of 1930 (cited in the previous chapter), the central role of this executive in the designing of a film was acknowledged twelve years later by cinematographer John W. Boyle in an article published in the *Journal of the Society of Motion Picture Engineers*. Quoted in the latter were the following comments by Jack Okey, who had worked with Grot at Warner Bros., and who designed the production of *The Jungle Book* (1942) for Alexander Korda:

> If the producer would call upon the artist at the same time he called upon his writer, and would have him prepare preliminary drawings or paintings of the subject in mind, there is little doubt that the sketches would help both the producer and the writer to decide matters; in fact, the director and the chief cameraman should be included in these early conferences. By predetermining questions in this early stage, many costly delays and disappointments can be avoided. Decisions can be made from the sketches as to desirable lighting effects, wardrobe, characterization, location, sets, and even the very spirit and mood of the whole production. During the production period, the artist can make a series of sketches to act as future reminders of the many discussions taking place at the time.[52]

In his remarks, which were similar in spirit to Menzies' admission in his lecture delivered at the University of Southern California that the "photoplay as pictorial art" was "unique" among media in that "it is not an individual art, but rather is the product of a number of minds," Okey, whom Boyle cites, also related that a film production was "certainly not the brain-child of any one person but rather [was] the sum of many individual contributions."[53] Nevertheless, a major purpose for which the role of production designer was invented by Selznick was to supplant the parts played by the cinematographer and art director in the planning scheme described by Rotha with a single technical authority whose opinions the producer could set against those of the director. In his role of arbiter in all matters of film production and with management of the film's finances, production facilities, and filmscript development firmly under his executive control, the producer of *Gone with the Wind* assured the realization of his own vision.

Menzies' conception of his own role agreed more with Rotha's idealization than with Okey's routine prescription. "Menzies defines his own job as a kind of 'pre-staging,' " reported his professional profile in *American Cinematographer* in 1945, shortly after he had collaborated on several successful films with director Sam Wood. "[Menzies] says [that] there is a spot between the scenario and the direction than an artist, trained in film fundamentals, can usefully fill," this article reported. "His production designs are, in that sense, an intermediate process between the printed word and its visualization on celluloid."[54]

Menzies' working relationship with Wood apparently allowed this production designer the authority of composition which had been promised but not ceded by Selznick in the making of *Gone with the Wind*. For the filmed adaptation of Thornton Wilder's play *Our Town* (1940), which Wood also directed, "no less than 1,200 sketches were made" by Menzies, according to Edward Carrick's history of art direction, *Designing for Films*, and photographs exist of this director and production designer closely examining a storyboard prior to the filming of one of its scenes.[55] In *The Pride of the Yankees* (1942) and *For Whom the Bell Tolls* (1943), both of which were directed by Wood and designed by Menzies, every shot also appears to owe its formation to this film designer's style of composition. Concerning the filming of *King's Row* (1942), cinematographer James Wong Howe reported:

> William Cameron Menzies designed the sets and did the sketches for the shots; he'd tell you how high the camera should be. He'd even specify the kind of lens he wanted for a particular shot; the set was designed for one specific shot only, and if you varied your angle by an inch you'd shoot over the top. . . . Menzies created the whole look of the film; I simply followed his orders. Sam Wood just directed the actors; he knew nothing about visuals.[56]

Eric Stacey—who served as assistant director on *Gone with the Wind* and as unit manager of *Saratoga Trunk* (1943), which Wood directed without assistance from Menzies—described during the latter film's production "how much [Wood] misses someone like Bill Menzies to make up his mind and tell him things."[57] However, the fact that Wood is credited elsewhere for a "willingness to let dialogue and talented players sustain a scene without obtrusive camera movements and obvious cutting" indicates a development in Menzies' approach to filmmaking as well.[58] Although Menzies' designs for *Things to Come* (1936) have been appreciated widely, his direction of this adaptation of H. G. Wells's novel has been criticized as unprofessional. "William Cameron Menzies, despite his extensive credits as a production designer [*sic*], had never before directed a major feature film, and in inviting him to Britain to make *Things to Come* after negotiations with Lewis Milestone had broken down, Korda took a gamble which did not quite come off," observed John Baxter in his account of this film's production in *Science Fiction in the Cinema.* Ultimately, fantasy and special effects—specifically, 3-D, in such films as *The Maze* and *Invaders from Mars* (both 1954)—provided vehicles for the revival of Menzies' career as a film director several years before his death in 1957. Baxter professed that in these final, minor films,

> [Menzies] carries his design philosophy into every sequence, giving even conventional interiors and action scenes a characteristic perspective. . . . [For example, in *Invaders from Mars*, the set of a hill for] the landing of a flying saucer is complete with leafless tree, two-rail fence and grey-white sand pits, a beautiful piece of studio recreation which might have been borrowed direct from *Gone with the Wind.*[59]

While a certain cult esteem has been granted to his directorial oeuvre, Menzies' contributions as a film designer have been accorded greater respect. "The name of the late William Cameron Menzies, listed as production designer of a motion picture, was just another unknown quantity as far as the average cash customer was concerned," wrote Ezra Goodman in his book on the classical Hollywood community. "In the movie industry, however, Menzies was a great name."[60] A survey of the American motion picture industry published in the 1930s expressed that "often in the production of films with which [Menzies] has been associated the supposed needs of the story have prevented him from exercising his full artistic powers in the direction of more vivid picture-making."[61] Richard Sylbert, who assisted Menzies earlier in his own career and who later received Academy Awards for the art direction of *Who's Afraid of Virginia Woolf?* (1966) and *Dick Tracy* (1990), described him plainly as the "greatest designer the movies ever had."[62]

The extent of Menzies' influence on *Gone with the Wind* was remarkable by contemporary industrial standards, but it is important to recognize that each of his suggestions remained subject to compromise. Script revision, complexity of design, and deference to film directors and the producer were factors that impeded implementation of his program, which Selznick commissioned in part simply to minimize set requirements. The film designer's varied success with the primary tasks initially delegated to him by the producer—namely, shot composition and continuity design—demonstrates the distinction between the ambition of the undertaking of this new role and its actual employment in production. This divergence of promise and purpose is apparent in the making of the fire sequence and of all other scenes in the picture from which sketches and scripts are preserved. If the filming of *Gone with the Wind* was influenced most by the "vision of one man," this visionary was neither the production designer nor any one of the numerous screenwriters and directors; this singular figure was the producer, Selznick.

FIVE

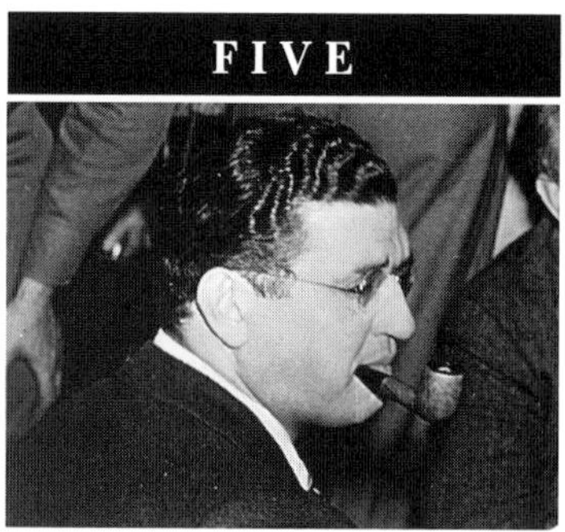

Executive Producers and Classical Hollywood Film Production

David O. Selznick's ambition was to make the greatest motion picture to date and to rival and surpass the celebrity and financial success of D. W. Griffith's *Birth of a Nation*; toward this end, the producer at one point considered remaking this film with color, sound, and spoken dialogue. Selznick wanted passionately to create the "Great American Motion Picture." Formed a few months before acquisition of the screen rights to Margaret Mitchell's "story of the Old South," Selznick International Pictures came into existence in great part in order that such a film might be produced. Despite his indebtedness to Hollywood for the use in *Gone with the Wind* of previously exploited elements and conventions (i.e., stars, stereotypical characters, and classical narrative and scene construction), the producer believed that only he could make this one picture and that none of the other studios—which arguably were more representative of the American film industry—could do it on the grand scale he believed it required. He was right. In many viewers' minds, the facades of Tara and of the Selznick International studio are indistinguishable.

For this reason, it may be more fitting than ironic that the company was liquidated by Selznick and its principal benefactor, John Hay Whitney, after the picture's release, regardless of the motivation of income-tax reduction because of federal perils to profits from the film's enormous revenues. The studio's purpose had been served. Although nine other motion pictures were produced by the company during the period of this epic's making, and although *Rebecca* was released one month after the Oscar for best picture of 1939 was presented to Selznick and was itself the best picture of the following year, only *Gone with the Wind* is claimed to represent the zenith of this producer's career and of classical Hollywood moviemaking.

Despite the dependency of its success on Margaret Mitchell's best-selling novel and on the appearances of its star performers, this film remains very much its producer's own "show." "Like God, Selznick, and Selznick alone, had created the film of *Gone with the Wind* and only the master of the most trivial pursuits knew, even then, the name—or indeed, the names—of the disposable directors," quipped Gore Vidal.[1] Despite both the collaboration of the production designer and the numerous managers, directors, cinematographers, and screenwriters, which is examined in this book and is documented by innumerable materials preserved in the producer's archives, and the principal role played by Vivien Leigh, the validity of this claim persists. The undeniable fact that *Gone with the Wind* sought and achieved monumental status may be credited to the "vision of one man," and this single visionary was its producer, Selznick (see Figure 149).

The extent of a producer's creative interaction in the production of motion pictures during the classical Hollywood period varied with individuals and their studios. "There are producers and producers," Selznick acknowledged in a lecture entitled "The functions of the producer and the making of feature films," that was delivered at Columbia University on November 1, 1937 as part of a program organized in conjunction with the Museum of Modern Art (and a transcript of which is preserved in the Selznick collection). "One man is an office producer, another is a directing producer, and still another is an executive producer." A little more than half a century later, in *Behind the Screen*, David Draigh reviewed these roles in comparable terms with respect to their contributions to current commercial filmmaking. "The producer who takes an active part in the supervision of casting, writing, design, and editing may exert a considerable influence on the style and content of the finished production," Draigh reported, whereas "other producers may concentrate on administrative and financial responsibilities and leave the creative decisions to others." In other words, "the producer's creative contribution may be very great or very small."[2]

Selznick's creative contribution to *Gone with the Wind*—and to most of the many other films which he also produced—was "very great" indeed, and his view of the responsibilities of the role of "executive producer," enumerated in his lecture at Columbia University, is exemplified by much of his own work. In this final chapter, Selznick's description of his own role in the filmmaking process is compared with accounts of the routines of other major Hollywood producers. In view both of the extensive documentation in the Selznick collection on the making of *Gone with the Wind* and of recent scholarship on the American film industry, the production of this, the most successful motion picture of the classical age, is reviewed also in order to determine to what degree its creation was anomalous or characteristic of Hollywood moviemaking. The issue of whether *Gone with the Wind* is exceptional or merely exemplary involves more than a single question. What factors distinguish this production from its contemporaries? What roles did the producer himself assume in this enterprise? Moreover, is it necessary to address the issue of "authorship" of *Gone with the Wind* in order to appreciate this motion picture and its production?

FIG. 149. Production manager Ray Klune, chairman of the board John Hay Whitney, editor Hal Kern, and producer David O. Selznick (left to right) on the set of *Gone with the Wind.*

Selznick and Classical Hollywood Studio Executives

Clearly Selznick's approach to filmmaking was that of a chief executive, yet his ambitions and interests belonged more to a studio's production chief than to the company's president or owner. In addition to inheriting the model of Selznick Pictures (1915–1923)—the family film business ruled by the patriarch, Lewis J. Selznick, who rose and fell as a pioneer of the American film industry during his sons' formative adolescent years—David also was influenced greatly by Irving Thalberg's managerial style during his first stint at MGM in the 1920s—initially as its story department's most ambitious reader. Thalberg—referred to in admiration as the "boy wonder"—served as a model for imitation in terms of executive practice far more than did two subsequent "father" figures—namely, Mayer (who had refused to hire Selznick in 1926 but who ultimately accepted him as a son-in-law and as a unit producer) and Nicholas Schenck, president of Loew's Inc. and of MGM itself (who overruled Mayer's prejudice against the Selznicks and gave David his first break). That Selznick primarily identified with one who was completely in charge of the process of moviemaking rather than with those figures in control of the two other domains of the film industry—namely, distribution and exhibition—indicates his passion for the medium in terms of creation rather than of business.

This distinction is an important one in view of the perception by many that moviemaking in classical Hollywood was more business than moviemaking. "The production of films by the major companies is not really an end in itself, on the success or failure of which the company's existence depends," Mae Huettig observed in 1944 in her seminal study, *Economic Control of the Motion Picture Industry*. Rather, she claimed, "it is an instrument directed toward the accomplishment of a larger end—i.e., domination of the theater market." Although only a fifth of the total number of theaters in the United States were owned by the major studios, these included the majority of first-run houses, which themselves accounted for the majority of box-office revenues. With theater admissions rising at optimal levels during the classical period through 1946 and after the establishment of "double-feature" presentations early in the 1930s, cinemas exhibited between four hundred and seven hundred films annually. Huettig conservatively reported that, because of the market's requirement of great numbers of films, and because, too, of the debt incurred by the major companies in purchasing the majority of these theaters before the Depression, "the production of films, essentially fluid and experimental as a process, is harnessed to a form of organization which can rarely afford to be either experimental or speculative."[3]

Tino Balio concurred in *Grand Design*, his summary of production in the "era of oligopoly," which was dominated by five major studios (MGM, Paramount, RKO, 20th Century-Fox, and Warner Bros.). "More than anything else," he wrote, "movies had to keep theaters full." Volume and regulation of production were primary concerns. "No longer run by their founders as family businesses, motion picture companies were managed by hierarchies of salaried executives who rationalized operations to ensure long-term stability and profits," Balio related.[4]

F. Scott Fitzgerald crafted a negative characterization of the collective figure formed by the number of motion picture executives and producers who served central management at "associate" levels, and whom he contrasted in *The Last Tycoon* with its protagonist, Monroe Stahr, who had been modeled after his own personal experience with Thalberg. "Originally a man of some character, he was being daily forced by his anomalous position into devious ways of acting and thinking," wrote the novelist. "He was a bad man now, as men go."[5] Encapsulating this figure's treatment by Fitzgerald as that of a "brownnose," David Thomson offered additional epithets of the typical producer—"an opportunist, a place-seeker, a yes-man, a stealer of credit, a double-crosser"—and noted that many executives were "despised by the filmmakers for ignorance of their craft and indifference to anything but the boss's whim."[6]

A major thesis of more recent film historical research—notably, that presented in *The Classical Hollywood Cinema* and *The Genius of the System*—is that American filmmaking of this period benefited from its successive modes of production and adapted creatively to the demands of the marketplace and to disruptions posed by stylistic movements stemming from foreign countries and new technologies. The positive correlation of the development of the classical style of American film presentations with the industrial conditions of Hollywood moviemaking was argued at length by Bordwell, Staiger, and Thompson. "Within the mode of production, the tensions of standardization and differentiation, the increase in specialization, and the tendency of Hollywood's institutions to focus energy and capital toward a controlled uniformity all crucially depended upon the norms of the classical style," these authors postulated.

Modifying pragmatists' claims that "Hollywood makes movies to make money, not to make art," these authors proposed the following revision: "Hollywood makes *classical* movies to make money." Staiger, who lauded the "combination of the expertise of multiple crafts" within the studio system, recognized that "Hollywood's goal was a certain type of stylistic practice, not the display of the hand of a worker." Bordwell also credited the "producer-unit system" for providing a "stable basis" for valuable innovation, the "causation and timing" of which he attributed "in the last analysis . . . to such economic pressures as product differentiation and the promotion of quality standards."[7]

Personal agency was accorded more credit by Thomas Schatz, whose orientation to film history was equally industrial in *The Genius of the System*. "The chief architects of a studio's style were its executives, which any number of Hollywood chroniclers observed at the time," he related, citing as one of the "more astute" contemporaries Leo Rosten, who professed in 1941 that "each studio has a personality" and that, "in the final analysis, the sum total of a studio's personality, the aggregate pattern of its choices and its tastes may be traced to its producers." Schatz added that Rosten's use of the term "producer" applied not to "supervisors" or "associate producers" but rather to the same studio production chiefs identified only by their number by Frank Capra (as president of the Screen Directors Guild) in his 1939 report in the *New York Times*. (Capra wrote that "about six producers today pass on about 90 percent of the scripts and edit 90 percent of the pictures.")[8] Between the date of Capra's estimate and that of Rosten's analysis, Fitzgerald wrote similarly in *The Last Tycoon* that "not a half dozen men have been able to keep the whole equation of pictures in their heads."[9]

The exact identities of this select number remain the subject of a little conjecture and debate. Both Thalberg at MGM (1924–1933) and Darryl Zanuck at Warner Bros. (1929–1933) and 20th Century-Fox (1935–1956) served, by their management of major Hollywood studios, as prototypes of the creative producer at work. Along with Selznick at MGM (1933–1935), Thalberg also exemplifies the "prestige-unit" producer; however, the latter executive had died in 1936. Hal Wallis succeeded Zanuck at Warner Bros. in 1933 and allowed the subordinate "supervisors" greater authority over productions, in addition to formal screen credit as "associate" producers; however, Wallis's own title was "associate executive," and he deferred more to studio head Jack Warner than had either Thalberg or Selznick to Mayer at MGM. In fact, a principal reason for Selznick's decision to depart from Paramount's executive roster in the early thirties was that its president, the pioneer mogul Adolf Zukor, delegated little authority to those at the level of management of production. When the successful exhibitor Barney Balaban became this company's president in 1935, unit production accompanied the appointment of Y. Frank Freeman as studio head; the most famous of its unit producers was the director Cecil B. DeMille.

Harry Cohn ran Columbia Pictures uniquely as president and production chief and has been described as the "archetypal, cigar-chomping movie mogul"; nevertheless, under Cohn, too, unit production was the rule, the most prestigious of his filmmakers having been Frank Capra. RKO production chiefs were primarily administrators also, but the names of those serving in this role changed frequently. Selznick's tenure as "executive producer" ran from 1932 to 1933; his successor, Merrian Cooper, who had made *King Kong*, served less time. George Schaefer lasted from 1938 to 1942 and is remembered mainly for having allowed Orson Welles full rein on *Citizen Kane* and for having wooed independent producer Samuel Goldwyn away from distribution through United Artists, which was formed in 1915 by Charles Chaplin, Douglas Fairbanks, D. W. Griffith, and Mary Pickford for the release of their own film productions. Goldwyn and Selznick were among United Artists' most prestigious members in the late thirties (Disney distributed shorts through it initially but switched to RKO in 1938 for release of the feature-length cartoon *Snow White and the Seven Dwarfs*).

The roles played by Selznick himself exemplified three successive modes of film production—central management, unit production, and packaging—and he was instrumental in establishing the latter two systems as industrial practices. In the final analysis, he realized his greatest success as an independent producer of a limited number of prestige pictures. While Selznick's executive style may be comparable to that of the most important central managers of studio film production, it is important to recognize that the number of pictures on which he labored at one time was but a fraction of the number handled concurrently by Thalberg or Zanuck. Regardless of this important difference, it would be shallow judgment to restrict Selznick's métier to that of glorified unit producer. On *Gone with the Wind*, Selznick acted simultaneously as studio boss, production chief, and independent filmmaker. His requirement of owning and/or operating his own studio was not insignificant and neither was his choice of limiting numbers of production. The success of Selznick, who preferred to invest in high-budget productions, has been contrasted with the failure of Carl Laemmle, Jr., who inherited control of Universal from his father and who, as production chief, lavished attention on both "cheap" and "expensive" pictures.[10] *Gone with the Wind* proved more valuable a commodity in its first year of release than the combined revenue of the hundreds of films made by each of the major studios that same year. Moreover, the limited number of films made at one time by Selznick International afforded this producer greater opportunity to attend personally to creative aspects of these productions.

To many historians, Thalberg nonetheless best exemplifies Hollywood studio filmmaking from the position of an omnipotent producer. This preference is due primarily to his uncontested precedence, power, and prestige and may be also because his death occurred only shortly after his own career had peaked. Thalberg's influence on his films' production was most intense in the development of their shooting scripts and during the extended conclusion of post-production, following a picture's release to preview audiences. In his biography of this producer, Bob Thomas stated:

> Thalberg seldom concerned himself with the progress of the actual films unless serious problems arose. A day's volume of rushes was too time-consuming for him to review. He preferred to reserve his judgment until the film was completed and assembled. Then he contributed what many of his co-workers considered to be his greatest talent as a filmmaker. "Movies aren't made; they're remade," he declared.[11]

Perhaps Thalberg's practice of visiting a set rarely and of not undermining the authority of the director in front of players and crew earned him much respect. The exception to this routine appears only to have been when he is said to have visited the set of *Camille* (1936) too frequently and was informed—most likely not by its director, Cukor—that the producer's presence was worrying Garbo. Thomas related that Thalberg "accepted the edict with equanimity. 'I've been thrown off better sets than this one,' he cracked, although no one could remember when Irving Thalberg had ever been requested to leave a movie stage."[12] Aljean Harmetz professed that "Thalberg himself was unfailingly gentle and courteous to his directors; and most of them loved him"; however, she acknowledged that Thalberg "expected to have *his* pictures shot the way *he* visualized them."[13] Many authors have noted the sensitivity shown by Thalberg in having snacks and beverages available to creative, technical, and administrative subordinates in the waiting room where they assembled for indefinite periods before admission to his office for counseling, and in the trolley commissioned for conveying the producer and personnel from the studio to a theater in which a film was being previewed. These testimonies may be contrasted with unflattering anecdotes about Selznick, such as that of Menzies waiting for the producer through the dinner hours upon request, only to watch Selznick dine elaborately and alone during their discussion much later that evening; or that of Hal Kern's doctor's reprimands because this editor often was not allowed to retire to his own home for sleep.

Nevertheless, the single stain that does exist on Thalberg's professional reputation is one of unprecedented enormity in terms of film art. Under his command, *Greed* (1923)—which is considered critically to have been one of the masterpieces of American silent cinema—was "virtually cut to ribbons," according to at least one film authority.[14] *The Oxford Companion to Film* provides a concise summary:

> [The director Erich von] Stroheim filmed [Frank] Norris's novel [*McTeague*] with absolute fidelity and ended with a film ten hours long. The film's completion coincided with the merger of the Goldwyn Company that resulted in the formation of Metro-Goldwyn-Mayer and brought Stroheim's old enemy Irving Thalberg in as head of production [Stroheim had created his previous film, *Merry-Go-Round* (1922), at Universal during Thalberg's tenure at this studio]. [Thalberg] insisted that Stroheim shorten the film which, at 24 reels instead of the original 42, was then handed over to Rex Ingram who edited it down to 18 reels (4½ hrs.); it was then passed by the producers to an anonymous studio cutter who reduced it to its present length [2½ hrs.].[15]

Whether or not an earlier state would have been rewarded with a large audience remains a matter of speculation; the version that was released and is preserved failed at the box office. Little is said of Thalberg in Herman G. Weinberg's preface in 1972 to a reconstruction of the longer version in the form of extant production stills, and the only comment on this film's cutting in this same scholar's separate survey of Stroheim's films is damning but oblique:

> I would like to quote Berlioz on the subject of mutilating works of art: "Worst of all are those desecrators who dare lay their hands on original works, and inflict on them horrible mutilations, which they call 'refinements and improvements.' "[16]

Elsewhere the affair is viewed within an industrial framework and in political terms. "That a studio should remove a director of this caliber from 'his own' picture was unprecedented, but it was nothing personal," explained Richard Koszarski, a biographer of Stroheim, in *An Evening's Entertainment*, the volume that he contributed to *The History of American Cinema* series on the twenties. "Thalberg was able to use the firing of von Stroheim to intimidate every director in Hollywood, and it was largely von Stroheim's visibility that caused him to be used as the lightning rod in this demonstration."[16] Regardless of these differing conclusions, it may be admitted that criticism of Selznick for replacing Cukor at the beginning of the production of *Gone with the Wind* pales in comparison.

Exceptional for the range and depth of his supervision of numerous concurrent film productions, Thalberg's figure still may be placed between those of Selznick and Zanuck at the apex of the pantheon of classical Hollywood producers. Memorialized on one side is Selznick's inspired pursuit of a smaller number of film projects in the same "tradition of quality," appearing more obsessional and less disciplined in execution, while on the other is Zanuck's labor to sustain an orderly agenda in his own monomaniacal work. A comparison of memoranda by Selznick and Zanuck which Rudy Behlmer edited in separate collections for publication in 1972 and 1993, respectively, discloses important differences between these titans of classical Hollywood film production. In contrast with Selznick, who was loquacious in dictation, Zanuck was brief; whereas Selznick's prescriptions indicate a compulsion for interaction, those of Zanuck suggest greater executive detachment; and while Thomas Schatz aptly characterized Selznick's orientation to filmmaking as a "sustained existential dilemma, an exercise in crisis management,"[18] Behlmer's description of Zanuck's modus operandi offers a model of disciplined command:

> In addition to reading drafts of the scripts and making his own notations in pencil directly on the pages prior to the conferences, Zanuck was responsible for casting decisions (key roles) and [unit] producer, writer, and director assignments. He also looked at "dailes" and "rushes" once or twice a day and would make comments to the producer and/or director if he felt they were warranted.
>
> One thing he decidedly did *not* do (with rare exception) was to visit the set, back lot (now Century City), or location while a picture was shooting. He was a firm believer . . . in the director functioning as a director while the film was in production without any second-guessing by the production executive pacing on the sidelines. However, after the feature was cut, Zanuck concentrated on editorial changes.
>
> He generally left the advertising, selling, and distribution of the films to Fox's New York corporate office, but occasionally would communicate his observations to those in charge. (And they in turn would communicate *their* observations about the finished films.)[19]

While Selznick's innovative marketing strategies indicate his value to his own company not simply as its production chief but as studio boss, in contrast, during this same period at 20th Century-Fox, Joseph Schenck (brother of Nicholas Schenck, president of Loew's/MGM) was the official boss, while Zanuck acted strictly as production chief. Having become a major stockholder, Zanuck assumed leadership of this studio as its president toward the end of his career (1962–1971), following several years of producing films independently—*The Longest Day* (1962) having been his most ambitious picture. As studio boss, his concerns at Fox were predominantly administrative and fiscal ones.

Unlike Selznick, whose initial job at a major studio was as a reader and whose aspiration for screen credit as a writer was realized only later in his career as a producer—on, for example, *Since You Went Away* (1944) and *The Paradine Case* (1947)—Zanuck himself was employed initially at Warner Bros. as a screenwriter (his earliest assignments were scripts for the studio's canine star, Rin Tin Tin), and no doubt he was pleased to delegate the task of writing, once he had risen to an executive echelon far above screenwriting. In spite of Zanuck's inclination to extemporize scenes before scribes in his office, his schedule was too tight to permit further collaboration. In 1935, *Fortune* sardonically described his agenda at Fox as "simple enough"; "all he need do," it continued, "is read, revise, cast, film, cut, assemble, and release one picture every twelve days."[20] According to an associate producer, Milton Sperling, even Zanuck's liaisons with starlets were scheduled at the same time each afternoon.[21]

An example of the difference in Zanuck's approach from that of Selznick's on *Gone with the Wind* is the restraint which the former exhibited in the making of his own studio's magnum opus—namely, *The Grapes of Wrath* (1940), which could be described (albeit too simplistically) as another popular, contemporaneous film adaptation of a best-selling, Pulitzer Prize–winning novel. In *Screenwriter*, Tom Stempel related how Zanuck dictated few specific instructions to Nunnally Johnson for writing the script of *The Grapes of Wrath*, other than that the film should open with the introductory scene in the novel, and how, during the two months that the adaptor dedicated to producing a first draft, the producer only telephoned occasionally in order to monitor the progress. In contrast to numerous revisions preserved from *Gone with the Wind* in the Selznick archives, the filmscript materials that Stempel reviewed in the 20th Century-Fox story files at the University of Southern California simply comprise a photostatic copy of Johnson's first draft, dated July 13, 1939, with comments by Zanuck in the margins; story conference notes addressing this draft, dated July 19; a second draft, dated July 29; and a mimeographed version of this last screenplay, revised and dated August 5, which served as the shooting script.[22]

In contrast also with Selznick's prolixity, the following brief statement is written on the first of the dozen pages of "Notes on Conference with Mr. Zanuck" which address Johnson's first draft: "Mr. Zanuck is very enthusiastic . . . [and] the changes to be made are few." Although Zanuck took credit, in his biography by Mel Gussow, for the invention of the more affirmative ending of the film during its postproduction period, convincing evidence was presented later by Stempel that Johnson fashioned the conclusion himself from material presented earlier in the novel. Moreover, this ending is already in place in the photostat of Zanuck's own copy of Johnson's first draft, dated July 13, 1939, although the scene was withheld from inclusion in many copies of the shooting script. Of Zanuck's claim of authorship of this scene, Johnson simply remarked, "Oh, by now Darryl probably thinks he did write it."[23] Johnson's unwavering allegiance to Zanuck, who ultimately rewarded this writer with his own production unit, is demonstrated even more by the story of his having declined an attractive offer from Louis B. Mayer for the reason simply that MGM "didn't have Zanuck"—one of the finest of the few tributes paid to a producer.[24]

This is not to suggest that Zanuck acted with equal detachment in his studio's other important productions; he acted strictly as the chief executive. For example, his critical contributions to the planning and making of the Academy Award-winning *How Green Was My Valley* (1941), which are indicated by memos in Behlmer's anthology, ranged from script revision to casting, filming, and post-production work; his detailed prescriptions for this film literally ran from first to final scenes. "We would open with a beautiful long shot of the valley, and the voice of the boy [the film's protagonist, played by Roddy McDowall] . . . verbatim from the book [Richard Llewellyn's best-selling novel, which Macmillan published in 1940]," Zanuck dictated in his criticism of the film's initial screenplay by Ernest Pascal, the revision of which he delegated to Philip Dunne. He enthusiastically informed John Ford, who also directed this film,

> In thinking over the whole story, I am sure that all we need now to get a great picture is a very thrilling and exciting finish. I think we should absolutely go to town on the mine cave-in episode, not that we should change or add anything we have already decided upon in these sequences, but I believe in this type of picture audiences will expect to see a thrilling and exciting climax that is fraught with suspense and danger and then winds up with a beautiful scene between father and son.

Moreover, it should be recognized that the editing of both *The Grapes of Wrath* and *How Green Was My Valley* was supervised by Zanuck and not by Ford, who viewed the completed films only in the theaters.[25]

Selznick and Classical Hollywood Independent Producers

Together with executives whose work is associated with the major studios, Sam Goldwyn also may be esteemed more than Selznick—as exemplifying the autonomous producer during the classical period. "It is almost a fad in Hollywood today to rave about Goldwyn's taste," observed Alva Johnston as early as 1937 in his biography of the producer, *The Great Goldwyn*, which had appeared earlier that year as a four-part article in the *Saturday Evening Post*. "He commands respect because of a seeming contempt for money when he is in a mood to lavish it in the pursuit of what he calls perfection," Johnston added. Goldwyn's critical reputation may have benefited not only from his pictures' high degree of polish and moral tone, from his activity as a producer from 1910 onward, and from popular use in film histories of the phrase "the Goldwyn touch," but also from the reputed intangibility of his own influence once the package of stars, director, screenwriter, and property was assembled and the script was approved. "Goldwyn's usual method [was] to pay an enormous price for the screen rights—$165,000 for *Dead End*; $160,000 for *Dodsworth*—of a stage hit or popular novel, and then hiring the best writers and director," admitted Johnston. "His ability as a producer is sometimes discounted on the theory that he buys success."[26]

Only his propensity for malapropisms has subjected Goldwyn's figure to ridicule, although the jokes deriving from his misuse of language are legion. "A verbal contract is not worth the paper it's written on" is a prime example. Goldwyn's own name (which was appropriated from that of his original film company, which, in turn, had been fabricated from "Goldfish"—a translation of his original Polish name, Gelbfisz—and Selwyn, the name of his two partners) was linked quickly and inseparably to this brand of unintentional humor. "No Hollywood column was complete without a risible reference to Goldwyn," related A. Scott Berg in his authoritative biography of this producer.[27] (A similar flaw in Zanuck's educational background was noted by Johnston, with the remark, in a 1934 profile of Goldwyn in *The New Yorker*, that, in executive meetings at 20th Century-Fox, "things may tiffle and blore and ruggle but everyone knows exactly what Zanuck is saying.")[28]

More importantly, Goldwyn's contributions to his films' making were called into question by Berg, who cited negative testimony from several of this producer's leading collaborators. Danny Mandell, Goldwyn's editor for a quarter of a century, is claimed, for example, to have said, "I never knew what 'the Goldwyn touch' was. I think it was something a Goldwyn publicist made up"; and William Wyler, who directed the majority of this producer's best pictures, including *Dodsworth*, *Wuthering Heights*, *The Little Foxes* (1941), and *The Best Years of Our Lives* (1946), is quoted as having said of him, "I don't recall his contributing anything other than buying good material and talent." More positively, Berg reported that Ben Hecht, who adapted *Wuthering Heights* with Charles MacArthur and John Huston for Goldwyn in 1939, described the producer as an "inarticulate but stimulating" collaborator.[29] Hecht himself also wrote that, during conferences with Goldwyn, the latter "filled the room with wonderful panic and beat at your mind like a man in front of a slot machine, shaking it for a jackpot."[30]

Circulated to a lesser degree are stories of Goldwyn's lack of charity in acknowledging others' creative contributions. "An executive of Sam's was once asked what kind of man Goldwyn was," Alva Johnston wrote in his profile of the producer; "he replied, 'Goldwyn is the kind of man who, if he understands what you tell him, thinks he thought of it himself.'"[31] Goldwyn's treatment of Wyler certainly smacked of ingratitude and may have been typical of his attitude toward directors. "I was constantly trying to get my name in somewhere," Wyler complained in his own biography, and added that the producer "didn't mind publicizing writers and, of course, stars, but he never mentioned directors in publicity."[32] Harold Russell, who, as an actual amputee, won Academy Awards for his performance in *The Best Years of Our Lives*, recalled that Wyler declared on the set in a fit of anger that the producer ideally "would like the credits to read Sam Goldwyn presents Sam Goldwyn in a picture called 'Sam Goldwyn,' Produced by Sam Goldwyn, Directed by Sam Goldwyn, Written by Sam Goldwyn."[33]

While Berg credited most of this film's artistry to the ensemble acting of Fredric March, Myrna Loy, Dana Andrews, and Teresa Wright, as well as to Wyler's collaboration with cinematographer Greg Toland and exploitation of greater depth of field in the staging of the players' action, he also noted that, while the producer refrained from visiting the set, Goldwyn never hesitated to interfere with the filming when the director failed to follow Robert Sherwood's screenplay. According to Berg, on one occasion and in writing, Goldwyn "reminded Wyler that he had vowed to Sherwood that the script would be filmed precisely as written, and that he wanted it 'clearly understood . . . that there are to be absolutely no rewrites, no changes of any nature whatever in dialogue . . . without my approval in advance.'"[34] As with *Gone with the Wind* and Selznick, *The Best Years of Our Lives* was celebrated with the Academy Award for best picture and recognized as Goldwyn's finest film; for the rest of his career, the producer vainly attempted to equal its success.

Selznick himself never begrudged his directors their credit but observed in his lecture at Columbia that "film critics and writers constantly, repeatedly, almost invariably mistake the functions of the director and the producer." Correcting this mistaken view, Selznick explained that with few exceptions, directors were employed as technicians who specialized in directing actors on the set. "At MGM, for instance, the director, nine times out of ten, is strictly a director, in the same sense that the stage director is the director of a play," he noted. "His job is solely to get out on the stage and direct the actors, put them through the places that are called for in the script." Selznick also described the director at Warner Bros. as a "cog in the machine" in the vast majority of cases. "It is true with ninety percent of the Warner films," he claimed; "the director is handed a script, usually just a few days before he goes into production. Otherwise it would obviously be impossible for a man to produce and direct five or six pictures a year."

After extensive research of film company practices, Janet Staiger affirmed in *The Classical Hollywood Cinema* that studios, particularly MGM, 20th Century-Fox, and Warner Bros., "almost always limited their directors to the shooting phase with films following one after another" and that directors had "little hand in writing" or in the preparation of the final cut.[35] Selznick, who, in contrast to Goldwyn, influenced all the major steps involved in his films' making, himself admitted in his lecture at Columbia University that

> the director is, as often as not, called in after the script is finished. He is handed a script, sets, staff, everything else, all the tools, and he goes out and directs. . . . The producer today, in order to be able to produce properly, must be able not merely to criticize, but . . . if necessary, to sit down and write the scene, and if he is criticizing a director, he must be able—not merely to say "I don't like it," but tell him how he would direct it himself.

Selznick, Zanuck, and Thalberg also dominated their films' editing, unlike Goldwyn. Specifically, Selznick prescribed that the ideal creative producer

> must be able to go into a cutting room, and if he doesn't like the cutting of the sequence, which is more often true than not, he must be able to recut the sequence. Now by cutting I don't mean the actual physical handling of the film, but to sit in a projection room . . . and say, "Take two feet off there"—"Get me this angle of that scene"—"Play this in close-up," etc.

Nevertheless, a producer's presence on the shooting set for an extended time was an anomalous one on most film productions. Selznick's routine of venturing regularly from his executive lair onto the set in order to monitor and manipulate creative and technical tasks which had been delegated by him already to others was as much a transgression of his position as a motion picture producer as it was characteristic of his role as a filmmaker. His extensive involvement on the shooting set purportedly began with *Gone with the Wind*. "He changed our method of working," said Cukor. "Naturally he was in on the whole thing, casting and script and sets and costumes, but this time he seemed to want to be in on the direction as well."[36]

The "spirit of actually making a picture," which Joan Didion described as one that was "not of collaboration but of armed conflict in which one antagonist has a contract assuring him nuclear capability," is represented also by the respective contributions of Selznick and the director, Alfred Hitchcock, to *Rebecca*, which Selznick International produced concurrently with *Gone with the Wind*. The Selznick collection in Austin provides extensive documentation of this producer's exploitation of the creative contributions of his subordinates on both of these pictures. Moreover, Selznick's professional figure may appear more favorably than that of Alfred Hitchcock when these two filmmakers are compared in terms of their domination of others on film productions. In the latter half of his career, Hitchcock augmented his authority as director by producing his own films, yet he deliberately continued his custom of taking personal credit for the original contributions of his screenwriters, art directors, and cinematographers in order to promote himself as the sole author of each of his motion pictures.

In *Backstory*, a compilation of interviews with screenwriters, Patrick McGilligan wrote:

> Hitchcock . . . was terribly insecure about writers and about his own mystique and . . . never gave writers much credit where it might otherwise shine on "Hitch." Auteurist film critics have fawned over Hitchcock but overlooked such writers as [Eliot] Stannard, [Charles] Bennett, and John Michael Hayes (who wrote a quartet of superior Hitchcock films in the 1950s), who were instrumental in embroidering the Hitchcock themes.

For example, Charles Bennett served as Hitchcock's principal British collaborator and was the screenwriter of *Blackmail* (1929), *The Man Who Knew Too Much* (1934), *The Thirty-Nine Steps* (1935), *The Secret Agent* and *Sabotage* (both 1936), *Young and Innocent* (1937–1938),

Foreign Correspondent (1940), and *Saboteur* (1942), and yet, as McGilligan went on to observe, one could "look hard" in François Truffaut's *Hitchcock*, Donald Spoto's *The Art of Alfred Hitchcock,* Raymond Durgnat's *The Strange Case of Alfred Hitchcock*, and Robin Wood's *Hitchcock's Films*—"to name four of the essential texts—without finding expansive or complimentary mention of Bennett."[37]

"You see, everything Hitchcock says is always his conception," Bennett himself disclosed in an interview with McGilligan. "The only thing Hitch has never allowed for is for any writer to have any real credit." In addition, Bennett claimed that Hitchcock was "totally incapable of creating a story" or of developing one, although this director's forte lay in imagining the "camera application" (that was distinguished from the more fundamental "visual application," which this screenwriter claimed to have contributed himself). "He has got good ideas—but he will never give credit to anyone but himself," this former collaborator concluded.[38] Jane Sloan observed, in her book *Alfred Hitchcock: A Guide to References and Resources*, that, in contrast to the exhaustive number of analyses of Hitchcock's films which address auteurist, structuralist, psychoanalytical, and feminist issues and which are cited in her bibliography, the "question of his collaborative style has not been sufficiently investigated"; she noted that "his disinclination to express gratitude . . . hides his career-long dependency on others for both stories and dialogue."[39]

Although not pursuing questions of collaboration and of proper credit in his monograph on Hitchcock, Robert E. Kapsis does take as a major issue the benefit of self-promotion on this director's career.

> From the beginning of his directorial career in England in the mid-1920s, Hitchcock used publicity to promote himself, his films, and the idea of directorial pre-eminence and authority. . . . [Afterward, in Hollywood,] in his dealings with the press, Hitchcock continued to promote himself as the complete filmmaker in full control of all phases of production. The specifics of his long-term contract signed in 1939 suggested otherwise. . . . At Selznick's studio, Selznick was the one in charge of post-production. It was he who supervised final shot selection and thus determined the final shape of the film. . . . Yet one would never know this from the interviews and press releases of the period. Even Selznick's own publicity machine stressed Hitchcock's authorship.[40]

Characteristically, Hitchcock alone is featured in an interview in *Life*, "talking about his art" with specific reference to *North by Northwest* (1959)—considered to be a central film in his oeuvre.[41] Script materials preserved at the University of Texas at Austin also indicate that screenwriter Ernest Lehman contributed significantly to the film's narrative and to its many formal devices. In addition, continuity sketches of the film's concluding shots drawn by Mentor Huebnor for production designer Robert Boyle, which are preserved in the Museum of Modern Art in New York and reproduced in *Hollywood: Legend and Reality*, illustrate the "camera application" credited routinely only to the producing director.[42]

Certainly the case against Hitchcock is intended not to deprecate his status as an exemplary film artist but only to illustrate how creative directors and producers benefited from the contributions of other artists and technicians. Hitchcock's authority is secure for most historians, all the same. While cognizant of the film designer's reputation, David Thomson described Menzies' inimitable contributions to *Foreign Correspondent* as "typical of Hitchcock's meticulous design, no matter who his art director was."[43] Similarly, in *The Hitchcock Romance*, Leslie Brill acknowledged Peter Wollen's modification of Hitchcock's "figure" in light of Marxist psychoanalytic semiology, while concluding:

> Recent revisions of "auteur theory" encourage me to make clear that by "Hitchcock," I will normally refer not to the private individual but to the director—always to some degree a corporate entity even for the strongest "auteurs." Nor do I mean to denigrate the contributions of such gifted collaborators as Saul Bass [titles], Bernard Hermann [music], Robert Burks [cinematography], and a host of talented actors, technicians, and writers. It is [my] task . . . to argue that Hitchcock's work, however we assess its authorship, may be seen as unified in its totality. Whether we take Hitchcock to have been a brilliant administrator, or writer, or graphic artist, or editor, or businessman—and I am inclined to think that he was all of these—he created a body of consistent, characteristic work."[44]

Within this same framework, it may be argued easily that Selznick also created a "body of consistent, characteristic work" as a filmmaker. While acknowledging the "essential unity" of Hitchcock's films, Robin Wood recognized Selznick as a "rival auteur" and as the "dominating presence" in this producer's collaborations with the director.[45]

It is a matter of record that a ninety-page treatment of the novel *Rebecca* which included dialogue, camera angles, and specifications for set and costume design was completed by Hitchcock and screenwriter Joan Harrison in April 1939, and was given to Philip MacDonald for adaptation to continuity form. This initial filmscript was submitted by Hitchcock to Selznick in early June—during the production of *Gone with the Wind*. In a long memorandum dated June 12, Selznick gave the director his dismayed response. "It is my unfortunate and distressing task to tell you that I am shocked and disappointed beyond words by the treatment of *Rebecca*," he wrote. "I regard it as a distorted and vulgarized version of a provenly successful work." What disturbed the producer most were the many liberties that had been taken with du Maurier's original narrative. "We bought and we intend to make *Rebecca*," Selznick asserted. "I don't hold at all with the theory that the different medium necessitates a difference in storytelling, or even a difference in scenes." He also provided a scene-by-scene critique of this first treatment.

A revision was undertaken immediately and submitted by Hitchcock later this same month with his assurance that the story line of the novel had been followed and that much of the dialogue was du Maurier's; afterward, Selznick engaged for further rewriting the Pulitzer Prize–winning playwright Robert Sherwood (whom Goldwyn hired later to write *The Best Years of Our Lives*). The only major alteration of the novel that was acceptable was one that cleared the protagonist's husband, Maxim, of the murder of his first wife, Rebecca; although toward the end of the novel he privately confesses to being the murderer, an accidental cause of death is revealed instead in the film, in deference to the Production Code. "This long and fairly complicated finale was worked out by Selznick, Hitchcock, and Sherwood in a series of all-night story conferences, with Joan Harrison transcribing and later rewriting it in continuity form," Thomas Schatz recounted, evoking the marathons that were described by Hecht as having taken place on *Gone with the Wind*; Schatz noted, too, that during these midnight sessions, Hitchcock "had trouble staying awake, though it probably wouldn't have mattered all that much what state he was in."[46]

Selznick's preoccupation with *Gone with the Wind* prevented him from joining Hitchcock on the set of *Rebecca*. Because of the latter's propensity for "goddamn jigsaw cutting" (Selznick's description of Hitchcock's routine of not filming "master" takes of scenes and alternate or closer views but of limiting shots to predetermined camera views), the producer proceeded to get what he himself had requested from Menzies for *Gone with the Wind*—namely, a "pre-cut picture." Selznick's authority over his film's making was threatened by this manner of working, an awareness of which Hitchcock himself admitted.[47] In an undelivered memo to the director dated September 19, 1939, Selznick remonstrated, "Cutting your film with the camera and reducing the number of angles required is highly desirable, and no one appreciates the value more than I do; but certainly it is of no value if you are simply going to give us less cut film per day than a man who shoots twice as many angles." Instead of sending this memo, the producer assembled a rough cut after filming closed in late November, and retakes of a number of scenes with principal players were ordered. On December 28 Selznick informed Whitney and Lowell Calvert, his general manager in charge of sales and distribution, that "the combination of my exhaustion, plus my natural nervousness about every detail connected with *Gone with the Wind*, hardly leaves me in a mood to do the big editorial job that is necessary on *Rebecca* [until the following year]."

Hitchcock and Harrison undertook the revisions accordingly, and the film resumed production in January 1940. The following month, Selznick himself rewrote and directed the film's fiery conclusion, the special effects for which were handled by Menzies and Cosgrove. Afterward, the producer and his editors reworked the film, while Hitchcock collaborated with Charles Bennett on the screenplay for *Foreign Correspondent*, which Selznick had arranged for the director to prepare and to direct for independent producer Walter Wanger at twice the salary that Hitchcock was paid by Selznick (who profited by the difference). "Well, it's not a Hitchcock picture," Hitchcock informed Truffaut about *Rebecca*.[48] Nevertheless, it was declared best picture by the Academy in 1941, and as such was Selznick's second Oscar in this category (his first having been received the previous year for *Gone with the Wind*). While also nominated, Hitchcock was not recognized as best director, the award going instead to John Ford for *The Grapes of Wrath*. (In fact, the only Academy Award that Hitchcock ever received—despite his nomination for best director on three more occasions—was the Thalberg award in 1968—an honor primarily awarded to producers.)

After Hitchcock achieved the rank of "producing director" with other studios, he rarely acknowledged the constructiveness of Selznick's earlier influence; he also mocked his former superior in his later films in at least two cryptic instances. John Belton claimed that Raymond Burr was made up to resemble Selznick for his role as the man who is revealed to have dismembered his wife in *Rear Window* and that Hitchcock specifically drilled Burr in an impersonation of this producer's speech and mannerisms.[49] The choice of the wife's fate was certainly no accident either. "Selznick comes from the school of filmmakers who like to have lots of footage to play around with in the cutting room," Hitchcock disparagingly remarked to Truffaut during their interviews.[50] The producer's name was satirized also in another instance—when, in comical response to the question posed by Eva Marie Saint in *North by Northwest* concerning the meaning of the letter "O" in the acronym "ROT," which was printed in the form of initials on protagonist Roger Thornhill's personalized matchbooks, Cary Grant was directed to quip, "Nothing." (Selznick's middle initial, "O.," was itself a fabrication.)

Selznick and the Making of *Gone with the Wind*

Studio filmmaking in Hollywood is organized conventionally by three successive stages: pre-production or planning; production or filming; and post-production, which includes editing. While these phases often merged in the making of *Gone with the Wind*—as they did, too, in many productions by other studios—a review of this film's creation within this tripartite scheme corresponds to Selznick's approach to discussing his own filmmaking.

In 1937, shortly after conferring with Sidney Howard and George Cukor before the original filmscript's third revision was begun, Selznick admitted in his lecture at Columbia that

> The casting of the people who are going to make the picture is today an even more important factor than the casting of the actors, because you can take the best writer in the world, and if he is misassigned, you will get a bad job. Take the best director in the world, and if it does not happen to be his particular type of picture, you are also defeated. . . . More pictures go wrong in the selection of the director and the writer than at any other time, except perhaps in the selection of the story.

Selznick had become concerned over his own choice of director and screenwriter for *Gone with the Wind* at this time. Earlier he had favored Cukor, having worked successfully with him before, but the producer's ambitions for this film rapidly outgrew viewing it as simply a superior "woman's" picture. When Cukor became resistant to Selznick's obsessive desire to control every aspect of the production—including performances on the shooting set—and proved also to be a poor choice for directing Gable (whose value to the project may be said to have equaled half of the profits, which SIP had agreed to share with MGM), Victor Fleming was hired from MGM. Fleming had demonstrated the required professionalism and deference to producer control in his prior direction of Mervyn Leroy's *The Wizard of Oz* and, reputedly, was Gable's favorite director. He was outspoken both in his duty to the producer and in his low personal opinion of the film's original source. When Fleming himself proved unreliable in several instances, other directors—including Sam Wood and William Cameron Menzies—were employed, all of whom submitted to Selznick's authority and to the producer's conception of the film.

Initially, Selznick was torn between choosing Ben Hecht or Sidney Howard for the job of adaptation. Hecht had worked with the producer successfully before and had demonstrated his adaptability to Selznick's ideas; however, Selznick likely favored Howard because of this author's greater literary cachet, which included a Pulitzer Prize for drama, accolades from *Time*, and a record of adapting novels successfully for Samuel Goldwyn. Howard, however, also enjoyed a reputation for using creative license and resisted Selznick's desire to remain faithful to Mitchell's narrative; in addition, the screenwriter's scheme to adapt the melodrama to the intimate format of a chamber piece was respected by Cukor but did not accommodate easily to Selznick's growing desire to exploit the epic size and potential spectacle of this historical romance. Eventually other writers—including Hecht—were employed, although only Howard was credited for the adaptation.

Although many elements of the original novel were removed from the screenplay, it remained an imperative of the producer that whatever was chosen to stay remained faithful to the original narrative. Selznick, who strongly disagreed with the idea that use of a different medium necessitated a difference in storytelling, stated to Alva Johnston, "I have never been able to understand why motion picture people insist upon throwing away something of proven appeal to substitute things of their own creation."

It is important to recognize that Selznick's respect for the success of an original literary source—what Johnston termed this producer's "flicker philosophy"—was unrelated to conventional reverence for an artist's vision.[51] Contrary to others' claims, Selznick did not always believe that, to use Mordden's phrase, "The Novelist is Right."[52] Instead, he identified with the readership. "No one, not even the author of an original work, can say with any degree of accuracy why a book has caught the fancy of the public," he claimed; "if it were this easy, the author could duplicate the success, which we know very few authors of successful works are able to do." Selznick allowed that the "only omissions from a successful work that are justified are omissions necessitated by length, censorship, or other practical considerations." Consistent with his comments on Howard's initial treatment of *Gone with the Wind*, he also professed to Johnston that "readers of a dearly loved book will forgive omissions if there is an obvious reason for them, but they will not forgive substitution." For these reasons, the producer concluded that the "only sure and safe way of aiming at a successful transcription of the original into motion picture form is to try as far as possible to retain the original."[53]

Selznick informed his audience at Columbia that Hollywood producers routinely exploited the services of numerous screenwriters in film production.

> Sometimes you go through as many as six, nine, ten, or fifteen treatments before you get the treatment or the outline that satisfies you in its basic elements. That process may see the demise of half a dozen writers or more before you get to the point that

> satisfies you. . . . More often than not . . . you may have to start the actual picture before your script is complete. For that reason alone, it is a great satisfaction to have your treatment sound, because if you know the direction that your story is taking, you are not worried so much about writing the script as the picture is in progress. . . .

While Howard produced his successive versions of the filmscript in 1937 and sought to reduce the narrative of *Gone with the Wind* to conventional cinematic dimensions, Selznick grew to envision greater spectacle and length of presentation for the project. Because of the public's demand for casting Gable in the role of Rhett Butler and because, too, of the requirements of his distribution contracts with MGM and United Artists, Selznick was afforded ample time to develop the filmscript and to search for an ideal actress to cast in the role of Scarlett. This situation was an unusual one for a film enterprise. What was not unusual was a producer's assignment of other writers after a film's production had begun. The fact that Selznick had encouraged Howard so often to revise the filmscript before turning to others demonstrated both an awareness of its need for improvement and a respect for this screenwriter's reputation.

Selznick's management of the production and his dictation of the film's appearance and continuity extended from the development of its filmscript to the designs drawn by the art department, all of which he justified financially.

> With the sets you go through the same process: meetings with the designer of the sets, the head of the art department, and with the head of the trick department, because today, a large part of the business of making sets is in trick work. In almost all pictures of importance . . . there are from ten to a hundred shots that are either glass shots or matte shots, which means that some part of them is painted in by one process or another, with only part of the set being built. The decision as to which part of the set is to be built and where the money can be saved on painting is only one of the many problems connected with the building of sets.

The art department was provided with successive versions of the script for purposes of budgeting, set design, and special-effects cinematography. In this respect, Selznick's desire to control both the narrative and the appearance of *Gone with the Wind* merged with the duties of production design. Despite Selznick's inauguration of the production designer's role for the expressed purpose of delineating composition and continuity of shots, William Cameron Menzies' greatest influence was on the picture's use of color, second-unit direction, and design of shots for which special-effects cinematography was required; while nominally his responsibility, composition of film sequences remained subject to script revision.

Although significant numbers of sketches correspond to various intermediate versions of the shooting script, the film's narrative and visual continuity benefited from each of these scenes' stages of development. In the making of the fire sequence—the most spectacular and memorable episode in *Gone with the Wind*—the contributions of the preparatory artwork, the successive screenplays, and the many writers and directors were examined in earlier chapters in relationship to one another's influence and to the producer's singular authority. While Selznick is faulted often for his obsession with details and an alleged difficulty with delegation, his influence on script development and his modification of the division of labor in Hollywood filmmaking by creation of the production designer's role facilitated his control of the shape taken by the film enterprise. It is important to recognize that Selznick regarded himself not simply as an executive but as a filmmaker. He repeatedly professed that he alone was responsible for all decisions and that the films he produced succeeded or failed on the basis of his own judgment.

Selznick's production of *Gone with the Wind* is deprecated by commentators because the shooting script was not completed during the planning stage and its composition continued during the filming. Often scenes were written or revised by Selznick himself the night before shooting. The shooting script is referred to generally as a "rainbow" script because of the incorporation of alterations on variously colored pages that date throughout the period of this picture's filming. A problematic version of the screenplay has been credited to Howard and publicized inaccurately as the "final shooting script," but several authors have demonstrated already that this version is only one of several cutting continuities undertaken in order to assist in the film's editing; its false claim of authenticity as an original screenplay suggests an attempt to credit the work of others to Howard for the purpose of enhancing the project's unity and prestige. The truth is that Selznick rarely predetermined anything and that every element of his production was subject to change.

> During all this time that all these processes are going on about locations, sets, costumes, and whatnot, the script, if it has been finished before the picture is started, is sometimes faithfully adhered to. Sometimes changes are necessary as you go along. . . . Possibly because you are considerably overbudgeted and tightening is necessary. Possibly because the scenes just don't come out right and you realize that you are on the wrong track. . . . Now in the making of the important pictures today, for one reason or another—which all efficiency experts have tried to cure but none have solved—you actually find yourself writing the script itself during production.

The intensity of the producer's demands on himself and his crew in the making of *Gone with the Wind* is legendary. Feigned or otherwise, Fleming's momentary mental collapse and departure from the set was not allowed to slow the filming; Sam Wood and King Vidor (in at least one instance) were enlisted from MGM to fill in. "From the time that Sam Wood took over, Selznick became explicitly *the* creator of the film, in all but name its director and writer as well," related Lambert. "The machine [Selznick] had built for this purpose now operated for him alone." Concerning estimation of the amount of the film which may be associated with Fleming's direction, Lambert cited figures of forty and fifty percent, proffered by Ray Rennahan and Ray Klune, respectively; "it would be fair, I think, to split the difference," concluded the historian. In contrast, Wood and Menzies were credited each with fifteen percent and Cukor with a mere five percent (many of the scenes that he directed were retaken for various reasons).[54] As much as a fifth of the film's shots have been remaindered to additional second-unit work supervised variously by animal specialist "Breezy" Eason, assistant director Eric Stacey, editor Hal Kern, and Selznick himself. The two copies of the

FIG. 150. Director Victor Fleming poses with actress Vivien Leigh during a break on the set of *Gone with the Wind.*

final cutting continuity that production manager Ray Klune and continuity clerk Barbara Keon individually notated after the film was assembled list the director employed for each shot.

An Academy Award–winning director because of his association with the making of *Gone with the Wind*, Victor Fleming garnered few compliments on his contributions. "If Cukor was to be labeled a 'woman's director,' Fleming was the 'man's director' *par excellence*," observed Aljean Harmetz.[55] Flamini described him as "Clark Gable's motorcycling crony" and as one who "liked to come across as a man who didn't pull punches." "David, your fucking script is no fucking good," the director informed Selznick before beginning the revision with Hecht, according to Lee Garmes. "Miss Leigh, you can stick this script up your royal British ass," he reputedly declared on another occasion. "After the richly embroidered chiffon of Cukor's style, Fleming's was sturdy, plain velvet," Flamini artfully proposed, and he described Fleming also as a "capable manager of action and spectacle.... He forced the pace of the production like a drill sergeant pushing a company of new recruits on the parade ground, one camera setup following another in breathless succession." Rather than envisioning the film as a "woman's picture," Fleming perceived it as a melodrama and told Leigh simply to "ham it up" on the few occasions she sought his advice[56] (see Figure 150). It is not surprising that both Leigh and de Havilland found time during the period of filming to visit Cukor and seek his counsel off the set.

Several years after this picture's release—and despite his possession of an Oscar statuette—Fleming came to suspect that more had been contributed from sources other than himself than he had believed previously. Laurence Leamer wrote in *As Time Goes By*, his biography of Ingrid Bergman, that between filming of scenes for *Joan of Arc* (1948), while Bergman studied Falconetti's performance in Carl Dreyer's *The Passion of Joan of Arc* (1928) in private screenings for inspiration, a copy of *Gone with the Wind* was projected repeatedly by its director, Fleming, in his own office. (Independently produced by Walter Wanger and adapted from Maxwell Anderson's Broadway play, *Joan of Lorraine*, which also starred Bergman, *Joan of Arc* was a critical and commercial disaster when released to film audiences.)[57]

A final quotation from his Columbia lecture illustrates how Selznick's approach to post-production work influenced the practice of filming.

> Now the rushes come through. Each scene is photographed from several angles, varying all the way from one angle to, let's say, ten. The angles include long shots, pan shots, close-ups of the individual actors, medium shots, and so on, all of which come through in the rushes. You then make what are known as the selections, which means that the producer and the director jointly select which of these takes is the best take, after seeing it on the screen. That, then, gives you your selections, from which the film editor roughly assembles the sequence . . . according to the faith and willingness of the individual producer and the individual director in trusting the judgment of his cutter. But after all, it doesn't involve a great deal of trust, because you can, and always do, recut the sequence.

In view of Selznick's prerogative of controlling the editing of the films that he produced, it seems highly unusual that he expressed the desire to "pre-cut" *Gone with the Wind* according to designs drawn by his production designer prior to shooting in the interest of economy of film stock. According to David Bordwell in *The Classical Hollywood Cinema*, the "master shot" technique of filming an uninterrupted scene in long shot and of retaking portions with closer views was a common practice at the time. "Such calculated overshooting produced a very standardized set of choices at the editing stage," he explained.[58] Flamini claimed that the "mass of film" shot for *Gone with the Wind* was the "result of Selznick's insistence on 'protection,' for he expected his directors to provide a stream of takes and a mass of angles in order to give himself as many options as possible in assembling a scene."[59] In *Hitchcock and Selznick*, Leonard Leff also acknowledged this approach with the observation that "Selznick loved the freedom that miles and miles of footage offered" but, contrary to most commentators' opinions, argued that "unlike that of his peers . . . Selznick's interference often benefited a film."[60]

The drama of Selznick's direction of the final assembly of *Gone with the Wind* was not ignored by previous authors. "If the warp was predominantly Selznick, the woof promised to be even more so," Flamini observed. "With editor Hal Kern, Kern's assistant James Newcom, and production assistants Lydia Schiller and Bobby Keon to take notes, [Selznick] plunged like Laocoön into the 225,000 feet of film printed out of the half a million shot," this author added, evoking a mythic scale but mixing his metaphors; he also commented that the post-production work "took on the gruelling pace of a forced march."[61] Selznick's "stretches of 72 hours without sleep" during this undertaking were reported in the *Saturday Evening Post* a few years after the film's release. According to Alva Johnston in the wryly entitled article "The Great Dictater," "For a time [Selznick] was, with medical permission, on a daily ration of Benzedrine pills and six or eight grains of thyroid extract—enough to send a man to heaven."[62]

With respect to the effects of Benzedrine, David Thomson observed in *Showman* that

> its use exaggerates feelings of grandeur and self-importance, things in which David had an unfair start. The drug kept away doubt and the prospect of depression, as well as fatigue. He felt he could do anything and everything, and he never saw that the chemicals were putting armor plate on his difficulty in coming to decisions."[63]

According to Haver, a rough cut that reputedly ran "almost six hours" was produced in July. "All through the sweltering months of summer the editors, Selznick, Barbara Keon, and Lydia Schiller ran the material over and over again," Haver related. "Working furiously, Selznick and Hal Kern managed to get the film down to five hours by late July."[64] According to Lambert, "since the discarded footage of *Gone with the Wind* no longer exists, it is impossible to know exactly what was lost in the cutting room between the first MGM screening and the final version shown at the previews. The surviving script material provides no clue." (Contrary to this assertion, two cut-and-stapled volumes of a cutting continuity, dated July 18–22, 1939, are preserved in the Selznick collection and may be compared with the "rainbow" filmscript to determine what was eliminated.) "For the next month," Lambert's narration of the course of events continues, "Selznick and Hal Kern, joined occasionally by Victor Fleming, tried to squeeze another hour out of the picture." By October, "the combined efforts of the three men and a crew of assistant editors and secretaries had reduced the picture to just under four hours."[65]

Concurrently, a list was prepared of additional footage to be shot and of scenes to be retaken by Fleming, among which was the opening conversation between Scarlett and the Tarleton brothers at Tara which had been retaken several times already. Additional cutting notes were made after the film was previewed later that month and in early November, after which another cut-and-stapled cutting continuity was produced. "If Kern was working himself to the limit of his endurance, Selznick, in an artificially stimulated state, had gone beyond him," Haver dramatically recounted. "By now [Selznick] was existing on a steady diet of vitamin B-12 shots, thyroid extract, and Benzedrine, seeming to work more hours than there were in the day to prepare not only for the premiere but also the all-important press preview, now scheduled for December 12."[66]

Haver cited testimony by Lydia Schiller that Selznick "literally went gray trying to finish it in time" and that toward that same end the producer also "gave his life's blood" (metaphorically speaking). It was related also that Selznick continued to make minor emendations to the film text before its preview.[67] Leff described Selznick as an "inveterate tinkerer [who] experimented a great deal during post-production, which concluded only when chief editor Hal Kern said, 'This is it; you cannot have the film anymore. Out it goes.' "[68] Selznick might have been characterized more fairly as a meticulous filmmaker.

Selznick, Classical Hollywood Cinema, and Authorship

It has been noted already with irony that Selznick's theory of a single "vision" was written in the same year as Andrew Sarris's "Notes on the Auteur Theory in 1962" appeared in *Film Culture*. Although Selznick's opinion paralleled Sarris's critical approach with respect to the issue of an individual personality's domination of a filmmaking enterprise, "auteur theory" designated the director as the legitimate "author" of a film text. Subsequently, *Gone with the Wind* has provoked criticism because of the composition of its "authorship" which resulted from the producer's active role in the film's creation and the number of directors he employed.

Many critics also object to claims made by earlier reviewers and in advertisements that *Gone with the Wind* is "the greatest motion picture ever made." While Selznick hoped that *Gone with the Wind* would surpass the celebrity of *Birth of a Nation*, Orson Welles's *Citizen Kane*—released amid much controversy in 1941—progressively captured greater praise from serious film reviewers. Sarris's seminal article, "*Citizen Kane*: The American Baroque," published in *Film Culture* in 1956, inaugurated this critic's own career, and elsewhere he continued to hail Welles's first film as "the work that influenced the cinema more profoundly than any American film since *Birth of a Nation*."[69] André Bazin also professed that "the influence of *Citizen Kane* cannot be overestimated."[70]

This high opinion of the importance of *Citizen Kane* to cinema is upheld by David A. Cook in the standard survey and general film history textbook *A History of Narrative Film*, in which it is maintained that "*Kane* was the first recognizably modern sound film," and that "it stood in the same relationship to its medium in 1941 as did *Birth of a Nation* in 1914 and *Potemkin* in 1925—that is, it was an achievement in the development of narrative film, years in advance of its time, which significantly influenced most of the significant films that followed it." Specifically, Cook professed that this film's influence was greatest as the "model for a new film aesthetic based not upon montage but upon the 'long take,' or sequence shot." (Cook elaborated that "the primary concern of the long take aesthetic is not the *sequencing of images*, as in montage, but the *disposition of space within the frame*, or *mise-en-scène*.") This textbook devotes most of a chapter to discussion of this single film. In contrast, the value of *Gone with the Wind* is summarized, along with that of *The Wizard of Oz*, in two sentences, describing them as "opulent, epic, and spectacularly entertaining products of the studio system at its most efficient"; both films also were judged as lacking the "depth or force of personal artistic vision."[71]

Much of the enthusiasm for *Citizen Kane* also derives from admiration of Welles's command of its making while only in his mid-twenties. Nevertheless, the originality of his influence was challenged by Pauline Kael in her essay "Raising Kane," which appeared in the *New Yorker* in 1971 and was published with both final shooting script and cutting continuity as *The "Citizen Kane" Book.*[72] Welles shared credit for the screenwriting—for which the picture won its only Oscar—with Herman Mankiewicz, whom Kael believed was the more creative half of the partnership. In *Talking Pictures*, film reviewer Richard Corliss observed that, before Kael's essay, "Mankiewicz' contribution had been almost completely ignored by Bosley Crowther and his contemporaries in 1941, by Andrew Sarris and his more royalist accolytes three decades later, and by everyone else in between—including Orson Welles."[73]

In his book, Corliss promoted the role played by writers in classical American film productions, remarking that "in the Golden Age of Hollywood . . . a director would be given a script and instructed to start shooting Monday; so much for shaping a personal vision through creative rewriting"; taking a cue from Sarris's "pantheon" of estimable film directors, he devised a "Parthenon," "Erechtheion," and "Propylaea" of the most noteworthy screenwriters. Still, to Corliss, the most successful films remained "those whose writers and directors—in creative association with the actors and technicians—worked together toward a collaborative vision." Concluding in favor of the concept of "multiple auteurs," Corliss wrote, "the obvious answer to the *Kane* dilemma is that Herman Mankiewicz wrote the film and Orson Welles directed it; and that, while these two functions can be distinguished for research purposes, they are really the inseparable halves of a work of art."[74]

"I still think that a very tentative form of auteurism is the best approach," Sarris himself maintained, although he modified his own position subtly in the preface that he was invited by Corliss to write for *Talking Pictures.* "In this way, the director is the hypothetically dominant figure in the filmmaking process until a pattern of contribution has been established," Sarris rationalized. "The director-auteur is not even a real person as such, but a magnetic force around which all agents and elements of the filmmaking process tend to cluster." Corliss's concept of "multiple auteurs" was thus incorporated into Sarris's grander view that "writing and directing are fundamentally the same function." The latter critic suggested that "as a screenplay is less than a blueprint and more than a libretto, so is directing less than creating and more than conducting. Most movies can best be understood in terms of an aesthetic tending toward the adhesive rather than toward the abstract."[75]

A collective view of the making of *Citizen Kane* was demonstrated both by Robert Carringer in his monograph *The Making of "Citizen Kane"* and by David Bordwell in his discussion in *The Classical Hollywood Cinema* of contextual influences on this film's celebrated innovations. In particular, Carringer credited the picture's artistic success to the confluence of creative ideas from Perry Ferguson (art director), Gregg Toland (director of photography), Mankiewicz, and Welles. The production of *Citizen Kane* was recognized also as an exception to conventional studio policy as a result of the unusual license allowed its director by George Schaefer, RKO's central manager.[76]

While Patrick Ogle had sought auteur status for Toland in his 1974 *Screen* essay, "Technological and Aesthetic Influences upon the Development of Deep Focus Cinematography in the United States," Bordwell advised ten years later that this cinematographer's innovations should be understood "not only in the context of the development of 1930s technology but also in the context of the ASC [the American Society of Cinematographers] as a professional organization . . . and [in] the way the concept of artistic experimentation was defined by the institutions within which Toland worked."[77] Moreover, while Bazin had esteemed the photographic features of *Citizen Kane*—specifically its exploitation of "deep focus" cinematography, which appeared to promote a greater illusion of realism—both Bordwell and Carringer credited many of the remarkable shots that were staged in depth in the film not to its cinematographer, Toland, but to process work (i.e., "trick" photography) by Vernon Walker's special-effects department at RKO.[78] Bordwell also claimed that Menzies' predilection for dramatic depth effects via special-effects cinematography was an antecedent of what, according to Linwood Dunn of RKO's optical printer unit, was accomplished with *Citizen Kane*—namely, that "the picture was about 50% optically duped" and that "many normal-looking scenes were optical composites."[79]

The Bazinian dichotomy of the "resources of montage" and the "plastics of the image" derived from articles written between 1950 and 1955 and published as a single essay in *What is Cinema?* in 1967; this bifurcation characterized divergent trends in cinema between 1920 and 1940 that were perceived, respectively, in works by filmmakers "who put their faith in the image and those who put their faith in reality." The former direction was described disapprovingly by Bazin as "expressionism of montage and image," and in this category he included both *Battleship Potemkin* and *The Cabinet of Dr. Caligari* (1919). "On the one side the Soviet cinema carried to its ultimate consequences the theory and practice of montage," wrote this critic, "while the German school did every kind of violence to the plastics of the image by way of sets and lighting." The realistic trend toward nonpictorial exploitation of dramatic space was believed to derive from the silent cinema of Erich von Stroheim and F. W. Murnau and to have continued in films by Jean Renoir, William Wyler, and Orson Welles, particularly *Citizen Kane*. "The image—its plastic composition and the way it is set in time, because it is founded on a much higher degree of realism—has at its disposal more means of manipulating reality and of modifying it from within," posited Bazin.[80]

Carringer, however, argued to the contrary—that Welles's use of production designs and of process photography in his film's making indicates an obvious debt of dramatic and realistic effects to sophisticated imagery construction. Bazin's preference of filmmakers who exploited the malleability of the "plastics of the image" rather than the "resources of montage" was interpreted also by another film historian in a way which favored the scope of *Gone with the Wind* over the "depth of field" in *Citizen Kane*. "It is not exactly a question of realism, but it is a question of shedding romance and distance, of making the movie world more immediate and more accessible, more of a world," professed Michael Wood in *America in the Movies*. "We begin to peer into a movie, rather than receive it in carefully arranged slices, with the camera flitting from speaker to speaker, and all feminine faces in soft focus." Wood considered *Gone with the Wind* to be the "perfect instance of the new tone," more so than *Citizen Kane*, because "its passions are large and simple, it is full of windswept silhouettes caught against reddening skies, [and like many other classical Hollywood films] . . . it is all too much—overplayed, overwritten—and it is all just right."[81]

Notwithstanding these debates over the means and merits of "deep focus" cinematography, the issue of film authorship accounts ultimately for both the high esteem of *Citizen Kane* and the devaluation of *Gone with the Wind* in current film histories. Although the terms "auteurism" and "politiques des auteurs" are credited to Andrew Sarris and to François Truffaut, respectively, their inspiration for coinage of these terms was attributed openly to André Bazin. "The film-maker is no longer the competitor of the painter and the playwright, he is, at least, the equal of the novelist," Bazin proclaimed. His pronouncement that "at last the director writes in film" anticipated Alexandre Astruc's *caméra-stylo* as a metaphor of a cinema of personal expression.[82] Bordwell, cognizant of the necessity of a contextual dimension in historiography and criticism, commented on this trend:

> Now a film was to be "read" as if it were a novel, both as the statement of an author with an identifiable style and as a discourse enveloping the characters. . . . We must not forget that at its inception auteur criticism was closely bound up with the emergence of the art cinema, and the most controversial moments in the history of that criticism involve the application of art-cinema interpretative conventions to films made outside that tradition (in particular, to Hollywood films).[83]

Bazinian idealism and auteurism were questioned also by poststructuralist film theorists, and the validity was challenged of critical pursuits as canon formation (listings of the "greatest films ever made") and attribution of authorship (inquiries as to whether Welles or Selznick or these filmmakers' technical directors were most influential on their films' creation). The poststructuralist position is epitomized by Roland Barthes' 1968 essay, "The Death of the Author," in which he proposed, "The true place of writing . . . is reading; a text's unity lies not in its origin but in its destination."[84] Equally influential was Michel Foucault's principle of the "author function," which was restricted neither to the traditional role of an individual artist nor to a textual plane (as in Barthes' scheme), but was one which allowed—in a critical and mediating way—a social context. According to Foucault, "authorship" is a device "by which, in our culture, one limits, excludes, and chooses"; it is a "principle of thrift in the proliferation of meaning."[85]

Certainly, the many chaotic elements in the chronology of the making of *Gone with the Wind*—that is, those engendered by the collaboration and conflict of the numerous creative and technical principals employed in its production—are controlled by the subjugation of all factors to Selznick's supervision of the film project. But is this a fictive arrangement? Selznick's authority was real and, in spite of much chaos, accident, and "great good luck," his contributions—as well as those of a considerable variety of technical and creative staff members—are documented to an unprecedented degree. While it is uncontested that this producer depended on agreements with several major film studios and distributors (MGM, RKO, and United Artists), on a conventional mode of filmmaking (the classical Hollywood narrative tradition), on a corporate structure (namely, Selznick International Pictures) and creative and technical staffs, on significant financial resources (not only those of MGM, but also those of John Hay Whitney, who served as chairman of the SIP board of directors, and of Attilio Giannini, who approved a timely loan from the Bank of America), and on the expectations of the novel's vast readership, also uncontested is the verity of Selznick's license and influence. "Authors are social constructs," Bordwell recognized in a special issue of *Wide Angle* in 1984 that was devoted to discussion of film authorship, but pragmatically argued that "like other social constructs they have a history and exercise real power."[86]

With respect to the issue of individual authority in Hollywood filmmaking, Janet Staiger observed in her essay "Individualism Versus Collectivism," published the previous year in *Screen*, that "from the late 1920s, studios sought to avoid stereotypical product by changing the method of top management of the mass production of films and by giving some workers greater control over special projects." Staiger explained that "this was symptomatic of an *ideology* that greater control of a film by specialists and talented individuals would produce more variety (of a certain kind) in the films."[87] In a 1993 essay in *Cinema Journal*, Matthew Bernstein reported that references to "unit" and "independent" film productions were conflated tellingly in trade periodicals of the classical period, and he described independent production itself as a "messy phenomenon." In spite of assertions of creative individualism, Bernstein argued, "to the extent that independents did the bidding of their major hosts, this anomaly emerges clearly as a contradiction between the industrial practices of the industry and one of its fundamental ideological tenets."[88]

Whereas Staiger proposed a progression from a "director" system (dating from 1907) to "director-unit" (1909) and "central producer" (1914) structures, Charles Musser perceived a larger movement from "collaborative" ventures rooted in the partnership model of small-business capitalism to the "central producer" system which was established at the corporate level in order to satisfy the requirements of exhibitors for greater numbers of films. This shift was seen as having accompanied the development of a classical style of filmmaking, which allowed production chiefs the choice of either granting special license to certain filmmakers or supervising the making of their films more closely.[89] Similarly, to Bernstein, unit and semi-independent production had "guaranteed the producer nothing. It offered only the *potential* for procedural autonomy and distinctive filmmaking, if the right historical circumstances—the conjunction of studio management, independent boards of directors, and the individual producer—enhanced the potential."[90]

In Selznick's case, the producer himself served as central manager and decided whether to "shepherd" a project to an attentive director, whether to "loan" someone under contract to another producer at a profit, or whether to supervise any film production very closely. That fewer films were produced by his studio allowed him greater interaction in all projects, but this fact diminishes the stature neither of his studio nor of himself as a major film producer. That Selznick has been described as the most autonomous and successful filmmaker of Hollywood's golden age certainly testifies to the realization of a great deal of his "potential." A favorable comparison may be drawn with Walt Disney, who influenced every frame of his company's animated films by dominating story conferences and by monitoring the work of his creative and technical artists—750 of whom were employed between 1934 and 1937 on *Snow White*—despite the fact that he could reproduce neither his cartoon characters nor his corporate signature by his own hand. "Walt would change his mind very often, and usually stick with an idea for one whole day," remarked one of the principal animators, concerning this producer's leadership. "And then he'd come up with a new idea that was twice as good as the one he'd had before, and he'd get you all sold on that."[91]

Selznick's triumph in making and marketing *Gone with the Wind* has been contrasted with Walter Wanger's failure as a producer to control Maxwell Anderson's script and Victor Fleming's direction of *Joan of Arc* and to roadshow this elaborate vehicle for Ingrid Bergman, who had played the same role on Broadway with much acclaim. In Bernstein's biography of Wanger, it was disclosed that at the outset, "Wanger saw the $4.5 million *Joan of Arc* as his *Gone with the Wind* and his *Best Years of Our Lives*, the crowning glory of his career" and as his "first fully independent venture" as a producer. Bernstein recognized that "Wanger's methods of work render him a more typical and, perhaps, a more revealing example of how the movie producer functioned in Hollywood's classical era than Selznick." Wanger's style was closer to Goldwyn's, who owned and operated his own studio but was "distant and lax in supervising his films." Bernstein reiterated, however, that "Wanger's access to limited financing and semi-independence had many more strings attached than Goldwyn's, and Wanger's semi-independence created only the *potential* for creative autonomy in the preparation of new projects. Therein lay the primary difference (along with guaranteed profit sharing) between semi-independence and unit production under studio control."[92]

In order better to appreciate Selznick's indebtedness to Hollywood filmmaking and his deviation from the routines of commercial film production, his executive behavior may be contrasted finally with that of Mervyn LeRoy, who was MGM's most prestigious producer when *Gone with the Wind* was made. After Selznick's departure and Thalberg's death, Mayer sought to fill their absence with LeRoy, who had directed *Little Caesar* (1930) and *I Am a Fugitive from a Chain Gang* (1932) and had risen by the middle of the decade to become the most productive director of prestige features at Warner Bros. LeRoy's first important project at MGM was *The Wizard of Oz*, the production of which aspired beyond anything undertaken previously by Warner Bros. or MGM; the budget itself exceeded two and a half million dollars and broke the record for a talking picture that had been set within the latter studio by Thalberg's *Mutiny on the Bounty*. According to Thomas Schatz, although the inspiration for *The Wizard of Oz* "in terms of story, subject, and tone" was Walt Disney's first feature-length cartoon, *Snow White and the Seven Dwarfs* (which—two years before the release of *Gone with the Wind*—had been the only talking picture to surpass the box-office record established by MGM in 1925 with *The Big Parade*), its inspiration "in terms of scope" derived from Selznick's independent venture.[93]

Early in 1938, MGM paid $75,000 to Samuel Goldwyn for rights to *The Wonderful Wizard of Oz* (1900)—the first and most famous title in L. Frank Baum's series of children's novels (Goldwyn had purchased these rights from the author's surviving son for $40,000 four years earlier). Herman Mankiewicz, Ogden Nash, and Noel Langley were commissioned by LeRoy to prepare separate treatments, and afterward four successive versions of the screenplay were produced by Langley, who may be credited with framing the Oz portion of the story as a dream, establishing several of the characters encountered there as prior acquaintances of Dorothy in Kansas, and changing the magical "silver shoes" to "ruby slippers" in order to exploit the Technicolor cinematography. Two other writers—Florence Ryerson and Edgar Allen Woolf—also contributed to the script's development and established the character of the Wizard in Kansas in the figure of Professor Marvel. The film's lyrics and songs were composed by E. Y. ("Yip") Harburg and Harold Arlen between May and October 1938, and the musical score was undertaken by Herbert Stothart.

LeRoy had hoped to direct *The Wizard of Oz* himself, but because of his executive responsibilities and Mayer's refusal to allow him to merge the roles of producer and director on the production, he instead initially delegated the film's direction to Richard Thorpe, who requested that Sid Silvers also contribute to the script's revision. Filming was halted by Buddy Ebsen's physical collapse in reaction to the aluminum powder that was dusted on his makeup and the recasting of his part as the Tin Woodsman required the reshooting of numerous scenes (most of which had displeased LeRoy in the rushes). At that point, Thorpe was dismissed and the film's direction was given temporarily to George Cukor, who had been contracted already to direct the principal filming of *Gone with the Wind*, which Selznick had scheduled to begin in January 1939. In a series of studio tests, Cukor simplified Judy Garland's demeanor so that she appeared more credibly as a simple farm girl.

On October 31, 1938, Cukor was replaced by Fleming, who reshot the picture soon afterward, assisted by John Lee Mahin's uncredited revision of the filmscript. "Every day, we would receive pages of new dialogue as a result of something the director didn't like," recalled Ray Bolger, who played the part of the Scarecrow. "We never [knew] whether what we had prepared the night before would actually be shot or whether we would have to redo everything when we got to the studio the next morning."[94] Fleming was assigned to Selznick's production of *Gone with the Wind* following Cukor's removal as its director, and the few scenes that remained unfilmed for *The Wizard of Oz* were directed instead by King Vidor, Jack Conway, and W. S. Van Dyke.

The Wizard of Oz competed unsuccessfully with *Gone with the Wind* for the Academy Award of best picture of 1939 and was initially a financial and critical disappointment. Thomas Schatz faulted the marketing campaign of Loew's, "which was aggressive by prestige picture standards but simply not up to the demands of a blockbuster musical," and explained that

> Selznick would demonstrate with the December release of *Gone with the Wind* what it took to exploit a picture of that magnitude—inflated prices, reserved seating, six-figure advertising budget, carefully orchestrated release strategy. Loew's/MGM assisted in Selznick's efforts and scored a sizable profit, but those efforts only reinforced the fact, for [Nicholas] Schenck as well as Mayer, that the risks and headaches of gargantuan blockbusters were best left to independents like Selznick, Goldwyn, and Disney."[95]

To reiterate, Selznick was one of a very limited number of producers who involved themselves creatively in most major aspects of feature-film production and presentation. Indeed, no other Hollywood producer besides Selznick and no other studios besides Selznick International and MGM would have risked the expenditure that was necessary to attempt to attain the level of success achieved with *Gone with the Wind*. This film and *The Wizard of Oz* were MGM's two biggest releases in 1939 and have served since as exemplars of classical Hollywood cinema. However, whether rightfully or not, unlike Selznick's production, *The Wizard of Oz* never received praise as the "greatest film of all time."

While the themes of the majority of films produced at Warner Bros. and at 20th Century-Fox were as American as those at MGM, these two studios' subjects were decidedly more working-class. Moreover, the strict sense of economy at Warner Bros. would have been prohibitive to Selznick's filmmaking; this studio is represented best by the contemporary drama *Casablanca* (1943), which was filmed in black and white and utilized cheap sets and obvious miniatures. A reasonable indication of what *Gone with the Wind* might have become had Selznick coproduced this film with Warner Bros. is *Elizabeth and Essex*, which was released in 1939 and starred Bette Davis and Errol Flynn (both of whom were offered to Selznick for the roles of Scarlett and Rhett Butler). While concurrently developing vehicles for Shirley Temple and Betty Grable, in terms of prestige pictures 20th Century-Fox preferred to offer audiences stark social indictments such as *The Grapes of Wrath* and *How Green Was My Valley*, both of which were directed by John Ford. (Starlet Maureen O'Hara's stock tempestuousness was tempered for the latter film.) At this studio, Zanuck was renowned also for his careful budgeting and production efficiency.

Although Paramount became the most powerful and profitable studio during the 1940s, its productions were constrained during the preceding decade by payments on its vast chain of theaters—the largest in the nation. While Cecil B. DeMille reigned at this studio, *Northwest Mounted Police* (1940), which starred a characteristically shrewd albeit laconic Gary Cooper, represents the restrained scale of his productions at this time; it also indicates to a degree this studio's inclination for foreign subjects, settings, and themes—one result of the Parufamet agreement with Germany in 1926, after which large numbers of European actors, actresses, and technicians migrated to America. The most Teutonic of the Hollywood studios was Universal, which, despite its minor status, released a few major films in the early thirties, exemplified by *All Quiet on the Western Front* (1930), which was directed by Lewis Milestone and closely produced by Carl Laemmle, Jr.; afterward, attention was devoted strictly to Abbott and Costello comedies and horror film series.

RKO was associated with a number of independent productions, notably *Young Mr. Lincoln* (1939), which was directed by Ford outside 20th Century-Fox, and *Citizen Kane*; still, the scope of these films was limited in terms of "production values" (although released by this company, *Snow White* was entirely Disney's work). Katharine Hepburn, whom Selznick himself had signed as RKO vice-president of production in 1932, had lobbied this studio's management vainly to purchase the rights to *Gone with the Wind* in order that she might play the role of Scarlett. Finally, Goldwyn's offering in Hollywood's annus mirabilis (1939) was *Wuthering Heights*—a classic film, certainly, starring Laurence Olivier and Merle Oberon (who was selected over Vivien Leigh herself for the part of Catherine by Goldwyn and William Wyler), but not one that excited and fulfilled public expectations as did Selznick's greatest opus.

The bottom line is that *Gone with the Wind* is both Hollywood's and Selznick's magnum opus. Selznick was not the author, of course—rather, it was to him that the novelist chose to sell the film rights to her story's adaptation, while remaining distant from the film's making; nor was he the screenwriter, director, or designer. He was the producer. Moreover, his credit exceeds the imprimatur displayed by the card that reads "A Selznick International Picture" and that begins *Gone with the Wind.* Characteristically subtle, Selznick's profound influence on this film's production is manifested also by his mark of endorsement at the picture's conclusion in his alteration of the novel's notorious final line of dialogue ("My dear, I don't give a damn," spoken by Rhett to Scarlett before his exit). This producer had labored to make his film faithful to its literary source, and to most viewers his success was judged ultimately on the basis of whether the picture was released without censorship of this single sentence; Selznick challenged the industry and its production code and refused to strike the offending word in his adaptation. Still, he elected to change the original line with the addition of an adverb that appears frequently in his own memoranda and that signified his own voice; in the end, Clark Gable delivers what Selznick himself had dictated: "Frankly, my dear, I don't give a damn."

It is a principal thesis of this book that there was nothing automatic about adapting *Gone with the Wind* to film. To dismiss Selznick's part in its interpretation by describing Mitchell's novel as a "natural" (as did James Agee) is to confuse nature with history, artifice, and industry (to apply a significant distinction from Roland Barthes' *Mythologies*).[96] Nor was the only intelligence behind the picture that of the original author (as Leslie Fiedler and others have professed). Four of at least five primary factors which enabled this film to transcend "exemplary" status and reach the level of the "exceptional"—namely, the prodigious investment in its making, the high degree of its fidelity to a commercially successful literary source, its early mastery of Technicolor cinematography through production design and special effects, and the epic length of its presentation—depend upon a critical fifth condition—that *Gone with the Wind* is also the "producer's film" *par excellence.*

What this book has attempted to disclose is how, in order to assure the realization of his own vision, Selznick undertook this film's making as an independent producer, held the screenwriters accountable to the model of the novelist's work, counterpoised the prescriptions of screenplays and of artwork, and played the new role of production designer off the film directors. "You continue to believe that if you hire a good director, and get a good title and put down a couple of casting names on paper, the picture is made," Selznick admonished conventional Hollywood at the end of his own career in the letter to Spyros Skouros cited at the beginning of this book. "You fail to realize, apparently, that . . . great producers have not achieved their reputations in this fashion; that picture after picture is a failure *despite* these elements, because they have not been *produced* (whether by producer/director or by producer) with the skill and the experience and the showmanship to know what pays off, dramatically and commercially."

Selznick was a great producer; indeed, he was an extraordinary one. What has limited a critical appreciation of his work is not the opinion that he was primarily a businessman (an error that his career clearly refutes) but the idea that he was a "showman" more than an artist; it is for this reason that his motion pictures are referred to too often in terms of management, marketing, and mythologizing. In spite of his profession of a single vision, Selznick never claimed "authorship" of *Gone with the Wind*; rather, he took credit only for the film production. What is important to recognize is that Selznick was not merely a film producer; he was a film*maker*.

NOTES

Unless identified otherwise, all documents cited in the text are preserved in the David O. Selznick Collection, Harry Ransom Humanities Research Center, University of Texas at Austin.

Chapter 1

1. "'Gone with the Wind' Again Tops All-Time List," *Variety* (compiled by Saul F. Leonard CPA, Sidney Finger CPA, and Bennett Newman CPA), 4 May 1983, 15; "The Big Pictures: America's 100 All-Time Favorite Films," *Entertainment Weekly*, 29 April 1994, 24. In the latter article the following assertion is made about the film: "For decades the unassailable Mount Everest of popularity, this Civil War soap opera has still been seen by more people *in theaters* (198.5 million) than any other film."

2. Crowther, *Lion's Share*, 261.

3. Crowther, *Great Films*, 131, 136.

4. Steinberg, *Reel Facts*, 142–144.

5. Robertson, *Guinness Film Facts and Feats*, 36.

6. Halliwell, *Halliwell's Film Guide*, 343.

7. Ebert, *Movie Home Companion*, 298.

8. Thomas, *Films and Filmmakers*, vol. 1, 352; Shipman, *Story of Cinema*, 501; Sarris, "This Most Moviest of All Movies," 58.

9. Sheppard, "Frankly, It's Not Worth a Damn," 72.

10. Finkle, "Tara! Tara! Tara!," 7.

11. Walker, *Margaret Mitchell and John Marsh*, 3–6; Wead, *"Gone with the Wind": A Legend Endures*, 114.

12. Reports 144 and 150 of the Audience Research Institute (aka Gallup Poll) of Princeton, N.J. (19 February 1942, 8–9, and 1 April 1942, 2, respectively) indicate that the "fire" sequence was the scene from *Gone with the Wind* that was best remembered by viewers polled in the United States and Canada.

13. With respect to the popularity of the sobriquet "producer of *Gone with the Wind*," the same title was used in the headline of Selznick's front-page obituary in the *New York Times* (23 June 1965). According to the producer's first wife, the former Irene Mayer, the headline "said exactly what David had predicted" (Irene Selznick, *Private View*, 382).

14. Behlmer, *Memo from Selznick*, 31.

15. Schulberg, *Moving Pictures*, 396.

16. Gomery, *Movie History*, 207.

17. Goodman, *Decline and Fall of Hollywood*, 38, 314.

18. Sarris, "Notes on the Auteur Theory," 1–8.

19. Sarris, *American Cinema*, 31–32.

20. Ibid., 259.

21. Thomson, *Biographical Dictionary of Film*, 556.

22. Agee, *Agee on Film*, 107, 349–350.

23. Fiedler, *Inadvertent Epic*, 59–70.

24. Schickel, "Glossy, Sentimental, Chuckleheaded," 71.

25. Webb, *Hollywood: Legend and Reality*, 51.

26. French, *Movie Moguls*, 2.

27. Bob Thomas, *Selznick*, 175.

28. Behlmer, *Memo from Selznick*, xviii.

29. Thomson, *Showman*, 253, 704.

30. Behlmer, xxii.

31. Selznick, "To: Whom it May Concern," 92–94, 97–98, 100, 105–108; 93 cited.

32. Behlmer, *Memo from Selznick*, 441; correspondence reprinted on pp. 442–462.

33. Huston, *Open Book*, 273.

34. Lambert, *GWTW*, 73, 110–111.

35. Michael Wood, "Movie Crazy," 6.

36. Passage reproduced in Richard Harwell's introduction to Howard, *GWTW: Screenplay*, 22.

37. Howard's *Gone with the Wind: Screenplay* (1980) includes a preface by Herb Bridges and Terryl C. Boodman, who do not acknowledge that both the date and the authorship of this script version are suspect (see Lambert, *GWTW*, 145).

38. Finkle, "Tara! Tara! Tara!," 1 and 7.

39. Bordwell et al., *Classical Hollywood Cinema*, 336.

40. Buscombe, "Notes on Columbia Pictures Corporation," 67–68.

41. Bordwell et al., *Classical Hollywood Cinema*, xiii.

42. Thomas Schatz, *Genius of System*, 6–8.

43. Ibid., 11.

44. Leff, *Hitchcock and Selznick*, xiii, 4.

45. Capra, *Name above Title*, 34.

46. McBride, *Frank Capra*, 189, 291–292, and opposite 481.

47. Balio, *Grand Design*, 10.

48. Didion, *White Album*, 165.

49. Panofsky, "Style and Medium," 29.

50. Will Durant, *Age of Faith*, 876.

Chapter 2

1. Bordwell et al., *Classical Hollywood Cinema*, 94, 135–136.

2. Ibid.

3. Sklar, *Movie-made America*, 239–240.

4. Schatz, *Genius of System*, 178–179.

5. Harwell, *"Gone with the Wind" as Book and Film*, 49; Allen Hervey, *Anthony Adverse* (New York: Farrar and Rinehart, 1933).

6. Bob Thomas, *Selznick*, 286 (see n. 7: "After the immense success of *Gone with the Wind*, [Selznick] sent Margaret Mitchell $50,000, doubling her return from the movie rights"); Kahn, *Jock*, 122 ("[Whitney] and Selznick, on dissolving [SIP] in 1942, generously donated $50,000 to an Atlanta charity of Margaret Mitchell's choice, and while they were at it [gave] her an additional $50,000 for her own benefit—thus in effect doubling their initial purchase price for her book.").

7. Selznick to Howard, 6 January 1937. A brief summary of the racial controversy surrounding Griffith's picture is provided in the entry for *The Birth of a Nation* in Bawden, *Oxford Companion to Film*, 72: "Originally entitled *The Clansman*, the film followed its source novel [by Thomas Dixon, Jr.] in its bias towards the White Southern viewpoint (Griffith's father had been a veteran of the Confederate army). It was acclaimed for its outstanding merits—richly organized structure, dynamic editing, and dramatic use of space—but there was an outcry against its offensive portrayal of the negro. . . . The National Association for the Advancement of Colored People (NAACP) launched an effective boycott and continued to picket cinemas where it was being shown until the Second World War." Picketing of this film's presentation is not uncommon even today. See also Staiger, "*The Birth of a Nation*: Reconsidering its Reception," 195–213.

8. Adams, "A Fine Novel," 1.

9. Flamini, *Scarlett, Rhett, and Cast*, 4.

10. Irene Selznick, *Private View*, 211–212.

11. Sennwald, "The Screen," 39.

12. Edwards, *Road to Tara*, 167; and Pyron, *Southern Daughter*, 307.

13. Harwell, *"Gone with the Wind" as Book and Film*, 38.

14. Balio, *Grand Design*, 1.

15. Mitchell, *Gone with the Wind*, 119–120.

16. Richard Corliss, *Talking Pictures*, 5.

17. *Time* (March 19, 1934), 36–37.

18. Howard, *Sinclair Lewis's "Dodsworth"*, vii–viii, x, and xvii.

19. Howard, "Hollywood on the slide," 50; White, *Sidney Howard*, 33.

20. Mitchell, *"Gone with the Wind" Letters*, 72. In her letter, Mitchell also expressed an interest in Lamar Trotti (who was born and raised in Atlanta) as a candidate for screenwriter of *Gone with the Wind*; Trotti later wrote the story on which *Young Mr. Lincoln* (1939) was based and received an Academy Award as screenwriter of *Wilson* (1944).

21. Ibid., 79.

22. Ibid., 93.

23. Ibid., 96, 98, and 99.

24. Bob Thomas, *Selznick*, 139 and 146.

25. Freytag, *Technik des Dramas*, 102; Freytag, *Freytag's Technique of Drama*, 114–140. See also Carlson, *Theories of Theatre*, 258–259 ("Freytag's book . . . served well into the twentieth century as the standard manual for young playwrights"); and Bordwell et al., *Classical Hollywood Cinema*, 168.

26. Mitchell's *Gone with the Wind* (1936) runs 1,037 pages, while *David Copperfield* (New York: Heritage Press, 1935) is 821 pages long. (Originally serialized, the latter novel was published first in volume form in 1850 by Bradbury and Evans of London and ran 624 pages.)

27. Asheim, *From Book to Film* (see Tables 1 and 3, on pp. 74 and 114, respectively). With respect to methodology employed in this study, note p. 19: "The analysis procedure . . . consisted broadly of three steps: viewing the film; reading the book; comparing the book with the script. It was decided that the film would be seen prior to reading the book in order that no preconceptions be brought to the film which would hamper the complete objectivity of the analysis of manifest content"; and p. 39: "A problem presented by the comparative technique employed . . . is that of establishing a basis for comparison. In this study, the base is the novel; taking it as a norm we can chart the deviations from it made by the script to show the extent to which the several parts of the original are retained or altered by adaptation." Deviational scores were determined on the basis of changes of dialogue, characters, actions, scenes, setting, and sequences. Note also that such an analysis of *Gone with the Wind*—in the forms of film, novel, and filmscript(s)—was not undertaken in Asheim's study.

28. Ibid.

29. "Philip Dunne: Fine Cabinetmaker," in McGilligan, *Backstory*, 157; interviewed by Tina Daniell.

30. Mordden, *Hollywood Studios*, 209.

31. Asheim, *From Book to Film*, 284 and 290.

32. Bordwell et al., *Classical Hollywood Cinema*, 16–17.

33. Bob Thomas, *Selznick*, 146; Lambert, *GWTW*, 42; Flamini, *Scarlett, Rhett, and Cast*, 199; Bridges and Boodman, *"Gone with the Wind": Definitive Illustrated History*, 25; Bartel, *Complete "Gone with the Wind" Trivia Book*, 50; Howard, *Gone with the Wind: Screenplay*, 7; and Thomson, *Showman*, 227.

34. Haver, *Selznick's Hollywood*, 246.

35. Naumberg, *We Make the Movies*, 32.

36. Ibid., 41.

37. Cowley, "Going with the Wind," 161–162.

38. Naumberg, *We Make the Movies*, 37.

39. Howard, *GWTW: Screenplay*, 15.

40. *Time* (June 7, 1937), cover and 32–33.

41. Mitchell, *Letters*, 150.

42. McGilligan, *Cukor*, 135.

43. Mitchell, *Letters*, 168.

44. Howard, *GWTW: Screenplay*, 17.

45. Bruccoli, *Some Sort of Epic Grandeur*, 450.

46. Thomson, *Showman*, 271.

47. Haver, *Selznick's Hollywood*, 241.

48. Mitchell, *Letters*, 249–250.

49. Ibid.

50. Howard, *GWTW: Screenplay*, 25 and 29.

51. Ibid., 24–25.

52. Haver, *Selznick's Hollywood*, 270.

53. McGilligan, *Cukor*, 148–153.

54. Interview by Stephen Farber for Oral History of the Motion Picture in America (transcript in University Research Library, University of Califor-

nia, Los Angeles), 15–16.

55. Howard, *GWTW: Screenplay*, 20.

56. Ibid., 29–30.

57. Ibid., 30; Harwell, *"Gone with the Wind" as Book and Film*, xx.

58. Froug, *Screenwriter Looks at Screenwriter*, 149.

59. "Donald Ogden Stewart: Politically Conscious," in McGilligan, *Backstory*, 341; interviewed by Allen Eyles and John Gillett.

60. Harmetz (*Making of "Wizard of Oz,"* 26) and Stempel (*Framework*, 72) both cite ten; Fricke et al. (*"Wizard of Oz": Pictorial History*, 44, 77, and 84) account for fourteen.

61. "John Lee Mahin: Team Player," in McGilligan, *Backstory*, 250 and 254; interviewed by Todd McCarthy and Joseph McBride.

62. Mitchell, *Letters*, 270.

63. Howard, *GWTW: Screenplay*, 30.

64. "John Lee Mahin: Team Player," in McGilligan, *Backstory*, 255.

65. Hecht, *Child of Century*, 489.

66. Howard, *GWTW: Screenplay*, 25 and 28.

67. Hecht, *Child of Century*, 489.

68. Behlmer, *Memo to Selznick*, xiv.

69. Pyron, *Southern Daughter*, 389–391.

70. Catherine Clinton, "Gone with the Wind," 132.

71. Bogle, *Toms, Coons, Mulattoes, Mammies, and Bucks*, 88.

72. "Donald Ogden Stewart: Politically Conscious," in McGilligan, *Backstory*, 341. Emphasis is Stewart's.

73. Schatz, *Genius of System*, 108, 110–111, and 115.

74. Griffith, *Samuel Goldwyn*, 6.

75. Naumberg, *We Make the Movies*, 44.

76. Easton, *Search for Sam Goldwyn*, 137; Arthur Marx, *Goldwyn*, 209–210.

77. Berg, *Goldwyn*, 277.

78. Arthur Marx, *Goldwyn*, 218–219.

79. Epstein, *Samuel Goldwyn*, 75.

Chapter 3

1. LoBrutto, *By Design*, xii.

2. Barsacq, *Caligari's Cabinet*, 167–169.

3. Mary Corliss and Carlos Clarens, "Designed for Film," 32.

4. LoBrutto, *By Design*, 22.

5. Ibid., 36. As art director of *Invaders from Mars* (1953), Leven assisted Menzies, who functioned as director, production designer, and co-scenarist.

6. Menzies, "Pictorial Beauty in the Photoplay," 162.

7. Rotha, "Art Director and Composition," 381.

8. Eisner, *Haunted Screen*, 36–37. (Eisner wrote: "One of the secrets of the success of the classical German film was the perfect technical harmony achieved by *Regiesitzungen*, discussions on the *mise-en-scène* of the film to be made which sometimes lasted two months or more before the filming began, and to which the director invited everybody due to work on the film . . . [e.g.] the chief designer and chief cameraman. . . .")

9. Rotha, "Art Director," 384. Emphasis is Rotha's.

10. W. Howe Cameron Menzies, "Cinema Design," 676–683.

11. "Layout for *Bulldog Drummond*," *Creative Art* (October 1929): 729–734.

12. Goodman, "Production Designing," 82–83, 100.

13. McGilligan, *Cukor*, 98.

14. Heisner, *Hollywood Art*, 26.

15. Draigh, *Behind the Screen*, 13.

16. Lambert, *GWTW*, 108.

17. Flamini, *Scarlett, Rhett, and Cast*, 257.

18. Mary Corliss and Carlos Clarens, "Designed for Film," 32.

19. Hambley and Downing, *Art of Hollywood*, 95.

20. Balio, *Grand Design*, 92.

21. Bob Thomas, *Selznick*, 155–156.

22. Lambert, *GWTW*, 137.

23. Nugent, " 'Gone With,' Etc.," 17.

24. Haver, *Selznick's Hollywood*, 248, 253. Haver's methodology was described in correspondence with the author.

25. S. J. Freedberg, *Painting of High Renaissance*, vol. 1, 362–363.

26. For an earlier version of an analysis of the fire sequence, see Vertrees, "Reconstructing the 'Script in Sketch Form,' " 87–104.

27. Mitchell, *Gone with the Wind*, 383–387.

28. Ibid., 386.

29. Ibid., 360.

30. Although Garrett referred to both Grandeur Screen and Magnascope in each of his script versions of the fire sequence, the Fox Grandeur System was developed in 1929, exploited a 70-mm film format with an integral soundtrack, and was utilized most popularly for Raoul Walsh's *The Big Trail* (1930) with John Wayne. Magnascope, devised by Lorenzo del Riccio, employed a special projector lens in order to magnify the image to a size four times larger than a conventionally projected one in the theater during a particular sequence in a film presentation in order to enhance the dramatic effect; its use was inaugurated with the naval battle sequences in *Old Ironsides* (1926) and was exploited for "road-show" presentation of aerial battle scenes in *Wings* (1930).

31. Thomson, *Showman*, 279.

32. Lambert, *GWTW*, 55.

33. Slifer, "Creating Visual Effects for *GWTW*," 836.

34. Haver, *Selznick's Hollywood*, 254.

35. Ibid., 256; Slifer, "Creating Visual Effects for *GWTW*," 838–839.

36. Heisner, *Hollywood Art*, 30.

37. Sennett, *Setting the Scene*, 199.

38. Mitchell, *Gone with the Wind*, 383.

39. Nugent, " 'Gone With,' Etc.," 17.

40. Murphy, "Treatment of Story-board from *Gone with the Wind*," 89–99, provides a technical report on the conservation of storyboard "2." Confirmation of the specific numbers penciled on the reverse sides of the drawings affixed to this storyboard was provided by Murphy in correspondence with the author.

Chapter 4

1. Raymond Fielding, *Technique of Special-Effects Cinematography*, 91.

2. Slifer, "Creating Visual Effects for *GWTW*," 791, 842–843.

3. Haver, *Selznick's Hollywood*, 295.

4. Slifer, "Creating Visual Effects for *GWTW*," 789.

5. Haver, *Selznick's Hollywood*, 294.

6. Slifer, "Creating Visual Effects for *GWTW*," 843.

7. Haver, *Selznick's Hollywood*, 295.

8. LoBrutto, *By Design*, 7.

9. Bordwell et al., *Classical Hollywood Cinema*, 344–345 ("One of the most important exponents of deep space and deep focus . . . Menzies excelled in using depth to create contorted, fantastic perspective. His set designs . . . had a calculated Germanic look which exploited unusual angles for deep-space compositions. Whether or not Menzies influenced Toland [who assisted (cinematographer) George Barnes on *Bulldog Drummond*], his work anticipates the grotesquely monumental depth of *Citizen Kane*." [Bordwell]).

10. Mitchell, *Gone with the Wind*, 3–10; the passages cited occur on pages 4, 5, and 10.

11. Ibid., 12; note that Jeems's eavesdropping is described in retrospect, during a discussion in the following scene.

12. Ibid., 121–127.

13. Unnumbered section of illustrations in Anderson and Fülöp-Miller, *The American Theater*.

14. Mitchell, *Gone with the Wind*, 404.

15. Lambert, *GWTW*, 118. (The identification of the director of each shot was marked in pencil in copies of the film's final cutting continuity formerly belonging to Raymond Klune and continuity clerk Barbara Keon; Lambert likely used these identifiers in deriving the percentage figures.)

16. Mary Corliss and Carlos Clarens, "Designed for Film," 56.

17. Nugent, "Critic's Adventures in Wonderland," 5.

18. Lambert, GWTW, 70.

19. Mitchell, *Gone with the Wind*, 270.

20. Mary Corliss and Carlos Clarens, "Designed for Film," 30.

21. Mitchell, *Gone with the Wind*, 777–789.

22. Mary Corliss and Carlos Clarens, "Designed for Film," 27 and 30.

23. Hambley and Downing, *Art of Hollywood*, 3 and 5.

24. Ibid., 9.

25. Affron and Affron, *Sets in Motion*, 27.

26. Heisner, *Hollywood Art*, 41 and 124–127.

27. Balshofer and Miller, *One Reel a Week*, 130, 134.

28. Koszarski, *An Evening's Entertainment*, 118.

29. Haver, *Selznick's Hollywood*, 246 and 248.

30. Schickel, *Disney Version*, 147–148.

31. Ibid., 148.

32. Howe, "Upsetting traditions with *Viva Villa*," 64.

33. Leyda and Voynow, *Eisenstein at Work*; see reproductions of sketches for *Battleship Potemkin* in Eisenstein Archives at TsGALI (State Archives of Literature and Art) and Eisenstein Kabinet, Moscow, 24, and of sketches for *Que viva Mexico!* in Eisenstein Collection, Museum of Modern Art in New York, 68–69. Storyboarding of battle scene on frozen Lake Ilmen at Novgorod in *Alexander Nevsky* (1938), that is reproduced with frames from filmed sequence and transcriptions from Prokofiev's musical score in Eisenstein, *Film Sense* (175–176), appears to have been drawn after the film's making, as illustrations for the chapter entitled "Form and Content: Practice."

34. Mary Corliss and Carlos Clarens, "Designed for Film," 50.

35. Leff, *Hitchcock and Selznick*, 60 ("Hitchcock also filled his copy with drawings, occasionally one for each shot; when complete, the director's heavily annotated screenplay resembled what one reporter called 'a traveling artist's sketch pad.' " (Quote is from *New York Herald-Tribune*, 14 July 1940, and is cited by Leff without pagination.)

36. Original manuscript preserved in Margaret Herrick Library, Academy of Motion Picture Arts and Sciences, Los Angeles; stenciled duplicates of this screenplay are to be found also in the University Research Library, University of California, Los Angeles.

37. Geist, *Pictures Will Talk*, 59; Mordden, *The Hollywood Studios*, 55.

38. Heisner, *Hollywood Art*, 18.

39. Hambley and Downing, *The Art of Hollywood*, 31.

40. Wallis and Higham, *Starmaker*, 42.

41. Anton Grot Collection, University Research Library, University of California, Los Angeles.

42. Research of filmscripts of *Juarez* was undertaken in Warner collections at Doheny Memorial Library, University of Southern California, Los Angeles and at Wisconsin Center for Film and Theater Research, University of Wisconsin at Madison. For final script version, see Vanderwood, *Juárez*.

43. Turney, "Film Guide to *Juarez*," unpaginated.

44. "*Juarez* Declared a Really Great Picture," *American Cinematographer* (April 1939), 167.

45. Turney, "Film Guide to *Juarez*."

46. Carringer, *Making of "Citizen Kane,"* 40.

47. Ibid., 40 and 44.

48. Cain, *Mildred Pierce*. For the "revised final" screenplay, credited to Ranald MacDougall and dated 4 December 1944, see LaValley, *Mildred Pierce*. Research of this film's script development was undertaken at Madison.

49. Higham, *Warner Brothers*, 183–185. Correspondence with Catherine Turney was cited by LaValley in support of his statement in the introduction to *Mildred Pierce* (p. 29) that "immediately after the mercurial Wald had seen *Double Indemnity* he called her [Turney] and announced, 'From now on, every picture I make will be done in flashback,' but she had been opposed to the flashback idea from the start." Contradicting this is the following passage in a letter to Roy J. Obringer from assistant story editor Tom Chapman, dated 12 February 1950, preserved in the Warners collection at Doheny Memorial Library, University of Southern California, Los Angeles, and reproduced in Behl-

mer, *Inside Warner Bros.*: "It is certain that Wald did *not* get the idea of a flashback treatment of *Mildred Pierce* from seeing *Double Indemnity*, as *Double Indemnity* was released by Paramount on April 24, 1944. We know from Cain's letter to Wald, dated September 22, 1943, that the flashback idea was in Wald's mind at that time"; Behlmer himself conceded that "it is possible, of course, that Wald was aware of the structure of *Double Indemnity* from a reading of the script, discussions with people involved in the project, an advance screening of parts or all of the film, or word via the industry grapevine" (260–261).

50. LaValley, *Mildred Pierce*, 18.

51. Behlmer, *Inside Warner Bros.*, 261.

52. Okey, quoted in Boyle, "Cinematography in Hollywood studios," 84–86.

53. Ibid., 84 and 86; Menzies, "Pictorial Beauty," 162.

54. Goodman, "Production Designing," 82.

55. Carrick, *Designing for Films*, 20; Hambley and Downing, *Art of Hollywood*, 90.

56. Howe, comments in Higham, *Hollywood Cameramen*, 88.

57. Behlmer, *Inside Warner Bros.*, 225.

58. Bawden, *Oxford Companion to Film*, 757.

59. Baxter, *Science Fiction in Cinema*, 57, 65, and 67.

60. Goodman, *Decline and Fall of Hollywood*, 318.

61. Gordan and Gordan, *Star-dust in Hollywood*, 181–183.

62. Sylbert, quoted in Engel, "A Pyramid in Hollywood?," 22.

Chapter 5

1. Vidal, *Screening History*, 54.
2. Draigh, *Behind the Screen*, 84.
3. Huettig, *Economic Control of Motion Picture Industry*, 295.
4. Balio, *Grand Design*, 8.
5. Fitzgerald, *Love of Last Tycoon* (1993), 38.
6. Thomson, *America in the Dark*, 80.
7. Bordwell et al., *Classical Hollywood Cinema*, 179, 339, and 367.
8. Schatz, *Genius of System*, 7–8.
9. Fitzgerald, *Love of Last Tycoon*, 3.
10. Schatz, *Genius of System*, 234.
11. Bob Thomas, *Thalberg*, 139.
12. Ibid., 308–310.
13. Harmetz, *Making of "Wizard of Oz"*, 136.
14. Koszarski, *An Evening's Entertainment*, 236.
15. Bawden, *Oxford Companion to Film*, 307.
16. Weinberg, *Stroheim: A Pictorial Record*, xiv.
17. Koszarski, *An Evening's Entertainment*, 236.
18. Schatz, *Genius of System*, 381.
19. Behlmer, *Memo from Zanuck*, xx–xxi.
20. Harris, *Zanucks of Hollywood*, 45.
21. Mosley, *Zanuck: Hollywood's Last Tycoon*, 176.
22. Stempel, *Screenwriter*, 79–80, 196.
23. Ibid., 81–84; Gussow, *Don't Say Yes*, 92–93.
24. Behlmer, *Memo from Zanuck*, xviii.
25. Ibid., 41, 44, and 104.
26. Johnston, *Great Goldwyn*, 15, 23, and 28.
27. Berg, *Goldwyn*, 396.
28. Harris, *Zanucks of Hollywood*, 42.
29. Berg, *Goldwyn*, 272 and 308.
30. Hecht, *Child of the Century*, 488.
31. Johnston, *Great Goldwyn*, 94.
32. Madsen, *William Wyler*, 125.
33. Berg, *Goldwyn*, 412.
34. Ibid.
35. Bordwell et al., *Classical Hollywood Cinema*, 326–327.
36. Lambert, *On Cukor*, 89–90.
37. McGilligan, *Backstory*, 19.
38. Ibid., 27, 30–31.
39. Sloan, *Alfred Hitchcock: Guide to References*, 37.
40. Kapsis, *Hitchcock: Making of Reputation*, 16, 24.
41. Brean, "Latest Murder Pitch from Hitch," 70–74. The centrality of this film to its director's oeuvre is proposed in Cavell, "North by Northwest" and in Brill, *Hitchcock Romance* (4–21).

42. Webb, *Hollywood*, 141–143.
43. Thomson, "Art of Art Director," 19.
44. Brill, *Hitchcock Romance*, xiv.
45. Robin Wood, *Hitchcock's Films Revisited*, 239–240.
46. Schatz, *Genius of System*, 280–281.
47. Truffaut, *Hitchcock*, 144.
48. Ibid., 91.
49. Belton, *Cinema Stylists*, 16.
50. Truffaut, *Hitchcock*, 144.
51. Johnston, "The Great Dictater," 44.
52. Mordden, *The Hollywood Studios*, 209.
53. Johnston, "The Great Dictater," 44.
54. Lambert, GWTW, 107 and 117–118.
55. Harmetz, *Making of "Wizard of Oz,"* 143.
56. Lambert, GWTW, 86, 94; Flamini, *Scarlett, Rhett, and Cast*, 238, 247–248, 262–263.
57. Leamer, *As Time Goes By*, 146 and 148.
58. Bordwell et al., *Classical Hollywood Cinema*, 308.
59. Flamini, *Scarlett, Rhett, and Cast*, 305.
60. Leff, *Hitchcock and Selznick*, 69.
61. Flamini, *Scarlett, Rhett, and Cast*, 305 and 307.
62. Johnston, "The Great Dictater," 10.
63. Thomson, *Showman*, 231–232.
64. Haver, *Selznick's Hollywood*, 292–293.
65. Lambert, GWTW, 145 and 293.
66. Haver, *Selznick's Hollywood*, 299.
67. Ibid.
68. Leff, *Hitchcock and Selznick*, 69.
69. Sarris, *American Cinema*, 78.
70. Bazin, *What is Cinema?*, 33.
71. Cook, *History of Narrative Film*, 365–366; 270–271.
72. Kael, "Raising Kane"; reprinted in Pauline Kael, *"Citizen Kane" Book*, 1–84.
73. Richard Corliss, *Talking Pictures*, 250.
74. Ibid., xxiii–iv, 252.
75. Ibid., xiv–xv.
76. Bordwell et al., *Classical Hollywood Cinema*, 345–349.
77. Ibid., 345.
78. Bazin, *What is Cinema?*, 33.
79. Bordwell et al., *Classical Hollywood Cinema*, 349.
80. Bazin, *What is Cinema?*, 24–26, 33–38.
81. Michael Wood, *America in the Movies*, 6 and 13.
82. Bazin, *What is Cinema?*, 39–40.
83. Bordwell, "Jump Cuts and Blind Spots," 9.
84. Barthes, "The Death of the Author," 212–213.
85. Foucault, "What is an Author?," 148 and 159.
86. Bordwell, "Jump Cuts and Blind Spots," 4.
87. Staiger, "Individualism Versus Collectivism," 68.
88. Bernstein, "Hollywood's Semi-Independent Production," 41, 49.
89. Musser, "Pre-Classical American Cinema," 90–97.
90. Bernstein, "Hollywood's Semi-Independent Production," 51.
91. Krause, "Creative Art of *Snow White*," 43; Richard Schickel, *The Disney Version*, 34.
92. Bernstein, *Walter Wanger*, xiv, 237, 396, and 399.
93. Schatz, *Genius of System*, 254 and 262.
94. Fricke et al., *"Wizard of Oz": Pictorial History*, 84.
95. Schatz, *Genius of System*, 268–269.
96. Barthes, *Mythologies*, 11.

BIBLIOGRAPHY

Adams, J. Donald. "A Fine Novel of the Civil War/ Miss Mitchell's *Gone with the Wind* is an Absorbing Narrative." *New York Times Book Review*, 5 July 1936, 1.

Affron, Charles and Mirella Jona Affron. *Sets in Motion: Art Direction and Film Narrative*. New Brunswick, N.J.: Rutgers University Press, 1995.

Agee, James. *Agee on Film*. New York: McDowell, Obolensky, 1958.

Albrecht, Donald. *Designing Dreams: Modern Architecture in the Movies*. New York: Harper and Row, 1986.

Allen, Robert C., and Douglas Gomery. *Film History: Theory and Practice*. New York: Alfred A. Knopf, 1985.

Anderson, John, and Rene Fülöp-Miller. *The American Theater and the Motion Picture in America*. New York: Dial Press, 1938. Originally published as *Das amerikanische Theater und Kino: wei kulturgeschictliche Abhandlungen*, Rene Fülöp-Miller (Zurich: Amalthea-Verlag, 1931).

Asheim, Lester Eugene. *From Book to Film: A Comparative Analysis of the Content of Selected Novels and the Motion Pictures Based Upon Them*. Ph.D. diss., University of Chicago, 1949.

Bach, Stephen. *Final Cut: Dreams and Disaster in the Making of "Heaven's Gate."* New York: William Morrow, 1985.

Balio, Tino, ed. *The American Film Industry*. Madison: University of Wisconsin Press, 1976.

———. *Grand Design: Hollywood as a Modern Business Enterprise, 1930–1939*. New York: Charles Scribner's Sons, 1993.

———. *United Artists: The Company Built by the Stars*. Madison: University of Wisconsin Press, 1976.

———. *United Artists: The Company that Changed the Film Industry*. Madison: University of Wisconsin Press, 1987.

Balshofer, Fred J., and Arthur C. Miller. *One Reel a Week*. Berkeley: University of California Press, 1967.

Barsacq, Leon. *Caligari's Cabinet and Other Grand Illusions: A History of Film Design*. Edited and revised by Elliot Stein. Boston: New York Graphic Society, 1976.

Bartel, Pauline. *The Complete "Gone with the Wind" Trivia Book*. Dallas: Taylor, 1989.

Barthes, Roland. "The Death of the Author." In *Theories of Authorship: A Reader*, edited by John Caughie, 208–213. London: British Film Institute/Routledge and Kegan Paul, 1981.

———. *Mythologies*. Translated by Annette Lavers. New York: Hill and Wang, 1972.

Bawden, Liz-Anne, ed. *Oxford Companion to Film*. New York: Oxford University Press, 1976.

Baxter, John. *Science Fiction in Cinema*. New York: A. S. Barnes, 1970.

Bazin, André. *The Cinema of Cruelty: From Buñuel to Hitchcock*. Edited by François Truffaut. New York: Seaver, 1982.

———. *What is Cinema?* Translated by Hugh Grey. Berkeley: University of California Press, 1967.

Behlmer, Rudy. *America's Favorite Movies: Behind the Scenes*. New York: Frederick Ungar, 1982.

———, ed. *Inside Warner Bros. (1935–1951)*. New York: Simon and Schuster, 1985.

———, ed. *Memo from Darryl F. Zanuck: The*

Golden Years at Twentieth Century-Fox. New York: Grove Press, 1993.

———, ed. *Memo from David O. Selznick*. Garden City, N.Y.: Doubleday, 1972.

Belton, John. *American Cinema/American Culture*. New York: McGraw-Hill, 1994.

———. *Cinema Stylists*. Metuchen, N.J.: Scarecrow, 1983.

Berg, A. Scott. *Goldwyn: A Biography*. New York: Alfred A. Knopf, 1989.

Bernstein, Matthew. "Hollywood's Semi-Independent Production." *Cinema Journal* 32(3) (Spring 1993): 41–54.

———. *Walter Wanger: Hollywood Independent*. Berkeley: University of California Press, 1994.

Bluestone, George. *Novels into Film: The Metamorphosis of Fiction into Cinema*. Berkeley: University of California Press, 1957.

Bogle, Donald. *Toms, Coons, Mulattoes, Mammies, and Bucks: An Interpretive History of Blacks in American Film*. New York: Viking, 1973.

Bordwell, David. "Jump Cuts and Blind Spots." *Wide Angle* 6(1) (1984): 4–11.

———. *Narration in the Fiction Film*. Madison: University of Wisconsin Press, 1985.

Bordwell, David, Janet Staiger, and Kristin Thompson. *The Classical Hollywood Cinema: Film Style and Mode of Production to 1960*. New York: Columbia University Press, 1985.

Boyle, John W. "Cinematography in Hollywood Studios (1942): Black and White Cinematography." *Journal of the Society of Motion Picture Engineers* (August 1942): 83–92.

Brean, Herbert. "Latest Murder Pitch from Hitch." *Life*, 13 July 1959, 70–74.

Bridges, Herb. *The Filming of "Gone with the Wind."* Macon, Ga.: Mercer University, 1984.

Bridges, Herb, and Terryl C. Boodman *"Gone with the Wind": The Definitive Illustrated History of the Book, the Movie, and the Legend*. New York: Fireside/Simon and Schuster, 1989.

Brill, Lesley. *The Hitchcock Romance: Love and Irony in Hitchcock's Films*. Princeton, N.J.: Princeton University Press, 1988.

Bruccoli, Matthew J. *Some Sort of Grandeur: The Life of F. Scott Fitzgerald*. New York: Harcourt Brace Jovanovich, 1981.

Buscombe, Edward. "Notes on Columbia Pictures Corporation 1926–41." *Screen* 16(3) (Autumn 1975): 65–82.

Cain, James M. *Mildred Pierce*. New York: Alfred A. Knopf, 1941.

Cameron, Judy, and Paul J. Christman. *The Art of "Gone with the Wind": The Making of a Legend*. New York: Prentice Hall, 1989.

Campbell, Edward D. C., Jr. *The Celluloid South: Hollywood and the Southern Myth*. Knoxville: University of Tennessee Press, 1981.

Canutt, Yakima, with Oliver Drake. *Stunt Man*. New York: Walker, 1979.

Capra, Frank. *The Name above the Title*. New York: Macmillan, 1971.

Carlson, Marvin. *Theories of the Theatre*. Ithaca, N.Y.: Cornell University Press, 1984.

Carnes, Mark C., ed. *Past Imperfect: History According to the Movies*. New York: Society of American Historians/Henry Holt, 1995.

Carrick, Edward. *Art and Design in the British Film: A Pictorial Directory of British Art Directors and their Work*. London: Dennis Dobson, 1948.

———. *Designing for Films*. London: The Studio, 1949.

Carringer, Robert L. *The Making of "Citizen Kane."* Berkeley: University of California Press, 1985.

Cavell, Stanley. "North by Northwest." *Critical Inquiry* (1981): 761–776.

Clarens, Carlos. *Cukor*. London: Secker and Warburg, 1976.

Clinton, Catherine. "Gone with the Wind." In *Past Imperfect: History According to the Movies*, edited by Mark C. Carnes, 132–135. New York: Society of American Historians/Henry Holt, 1995.

Cook, David A. *A History of Narrative Film*. New York: Norton, 1981.

Cook, Pamela, ed. *The Cinema Book: A Complete Guide to Understanding the Movies*. New York: Pantheon/British Film Institute, 1985.

Corliss, Mary, and Carlos Clarens. "Designed for

Film: The Hollywood Art Director." *Film Comment* (May–June 1978): 25–59.

Corliss, Richard. *Talking Pictures: Screenwriters in the American Cinema, 1927–1973*. Woodstock, N.Y.: Overlook, 1974.

Cowley, Malcolm. "Going with the Wind." *New Republic*, 16 September 1936, 161–162.

Cripps, Thomas. *Slow Fade to Black: The Negro in American Film, 1900–1942*. New York: Oxford University Press, 1977.

Crowther, Bosley. *The Great Films: Fifty Golden Years of Motion Pictures*. New York: G. P. Putnam's Sons, 1967.

———. *Hollywood Rajah: The Life and Times of Louis B. Mayer*. New York: Holt, Rinehart and Winston, 1960.

———. *The Lion's Share: The Story of an Entertainment Empire*. New York: E. P. Dutton, 1957.

Didion, Joan. *The White Album*. New York: Simon and Schuster, 1979.

Dooley, Roger. *From Scarface to Scarlett: American Films in the 1930s*. New York: Harcourt Brace Jovanovich, 1981.

Draigh, David. *Behind the Screen: The American Museum of the Moving Image Guide to Who Does What in Motion Pictures and Television*. New York: American Museum of the Moving Image/Abbeville, 1988.

du Maurier, Daphne. *Rebecca*. London: V. Gollancz, 1938.

Durant, Will. *Age of Faith*. New York: Simon and Schuster, 1950.

Durgnat, Raymond. *The Strange Case of Alfred Hitchcock or the Plain Man's Hitchcock*. Cambridge, Mass.: MIT Press, 1982.

Easton, Carole. *The Search for Sam Goldwyn*. New York: William Morrow, 1967.

Ebert, Roger. *Movie Home Companion*. Kansas City, Mo.: Andrews and McMeel, 1989.

Edwards, Anne. *Road to Tara: The Life of Margaret Mitchell*. New York: Ticknor and Fields, 1983.

Eisenstein, Sergei. *The Film Sense*, translated by Jay Leyda. New York: Harcourt Brace Jovanovich, 1942.

Eisner, Lotte H. *The Haunted Screen: Expressionism in the German Cinema and the Influence of Max Reinhardt*. Berkeley: University of California Press, 1973.

Engel, Joel. "A Pyramid in Hollywood?" *New York Times*, 8 December 1991, section 2: 22.

Epstein, Lawrence J. *Samuel Goldwyn*. Boston: Twayne/G. K. Hall, 1981.

Fielding, Raymond. *The Technique of Special-Effects Cinematography*. New York: Hastings House, 1965.

Fiedler, Leslie A. *The Inadvertent Epic: From "Uncle Tom's Cabin" to "Roots."* New York: Simon and Schuster, 1979.

Finkle, David. "Tara! Tara! Tara!" *New York Times Book Review*, 10 December 1989, 7.

Fitzgerald, F. Scott. *The Love of the Last Tycoon: A Western*, Edited by Matthew J. Bruccoli. New York: Cambridge University Press, 1993 (critical edition of Fitzgerald's last novel, originally published posthumously as *The Last Tycoon* [New York: Charles Scribner's Sons, 1941]).

Flamini, Roland. *Scarlett, Rhett, and a Cast of Thousands: The Filming of "Gone with the Wind."* New York: Macmillan, 1975.

Foucault, Michel. "What is an Author?" In *Textual Strategies: Perspectives on Post-structuralist Criticism*, edited by Josué V. Harari, 141–160. Ithaca, N.Y.: Cornell University Press, 1979.

Freedberg, S. J. *Painting of High Renaissance, in Rome and Florence*. New York: Harvard University Press, 1961.

French, Philip. *The Movie Moguls: An Informal History of the Hollywood Tycoons*. Chicago: Henry Regnery, 1969.

French, Warren, ed. *The South and Film*. Jackson: University Presses of Mississippi, 1981.

Freytag, Gustav. *Die Technik des Dramas*. Leipzig: S. Hirzel, 1901; originally published in 1863.

———. *Freytag's Technique of the Drama: An Exposition of Dramatic Composition and Art*. Translated by Elias J. MacEwan. Chicago: S. C. Griggs, 1895.

Fricke, John, Jay Scarfone, and William Stillman. *"The Wizard of Oz": The Official 50th Anniver-*

sary Pictorial History. New York: Warner, 1989.

Froug, William. *The Screenwriter Looks at the Screenwriter*. New York: Macmillan, 1972.

Geist, Kenneth. *Pictures Will Talk: Life and Films of Joseph Mankiewicz*. New York: Charles Scribner's Sons, 1978.

Gomery, Douglas. *The Hollywood Studio System*. New York: St. Martin's Press, 1982.

———. *Movie History: A Survey*. Belmont, Calif.: Wadsworth, 1991.

Goodman, Ezra. *The Fifty-Year Decline and Fall of Hollywood*. New York: Simon and Schuster, 1961.

———. "Production Designing." *American Cinematographer* (March 1945): 82–83, 100.

Gordan, Jan, and Cora Gordan. *Star-dust in Hollywood*. London: George G. Harrap, 1930.

Griffith, Richard. *Samuel Goldwyn: The Producer and his Films*. New York: Museum of Modern Art Film Library, 1956.

Gussow, Mel. *Don't Say Yes Until I Finish Talking: A Biography of Darryl F. Zanuck*. Garden City, N.Y.: Doubleday, 1971.

Halliwell, Leslie. *Halliwell's Film Guide*, 2d ed. New York: Charles Scribner's, 1979.

Hambley, John, and Patrick Downing. *The Art of Hollywood: Fifty Years of Art Direction*. London: Thames Television, 1978.

Harding, Bertita. *Phantom Crown: The Story of Maximilian and Carlota of Mexico*. New York: Blue Ribbon/Bobbs-Merrill, 1934.

Harmetz, Aljean. *The Making of "The Wizard of Oz": Movie Magic and Studio Power in the Prime of MGM—and the Miracle of Production #1060*. New York: Alfred A. Knopf, 1978.

Harris, Marlys J. *The Zanucks of Hollywood: The Dark Legacy of an American Dynasty*. New York: Crown, 1989.

Harwell, Richard, ed. *"Gone with the Wind" as Book and Film*. Macon, Ga.: Mercer University, 1983.

Haskell, Molly. *From Reverence to Rape: The Treatment of Women in the Movies*. New York: Holt, Rinehart and Winston, 1974.

Haver, Ronald. *David O. Selznick's Hollywood*. New York: Alfred A. Knopf, 1980.

———. *David O. Selznick's "Gone with the Wind."* New York: Wings, 1986.

———. *The Making of "Gone with the Wind."* New York: Bonanza Books, 1989.

Hecht, Ben. *A Child of the Century*. New York: Simon and Schuster, 1954.

Heisner, Beverly. *Hollywood Art: Art Direction in the Days of the Great Studios*. Jefferson, N.C.: McFarland, 1990.

Higham, Charles. *Hollywood Cameramen: Sources of Light*. Bloomington: Indiana University Press, 1970.

———. *Warner Brothers*. New York: Charles Scribner's Sons, 1975.

Howard, Sidney. *GWTW: The Screenplay*, edited by Richard Harwell. New York: Macmillan, 1980.

———. *Gone with the Wind: The Screenplay*. New York: Delta/Dell, 1989.

———. "Hollywood on the Slide." *New Republic*, 9 November 1932, 50.

———. *Sinclair Lewis's "Dodsworth."* New York: Harcourt, Brace, 1934.

Howe, James Wong. "Upsetting Traditions with *Viva Villa*." *American Cinematographer* (June 1934): 64, 71.

Huettig, Mae. *Economic Control of the Motion Picture Industry*. Philadelphia: University of Pennsylvania Press, 1944.

Huston, John. *An Open Book*. New York: Alfred A. Knopf, 1980.

Johnston, Alva. "The Great Dictater." *Saturday Evening Post*, 16 May 1942, 9–10, 44.

———. *The Great Goldwyn*. New York: Random House, 1937.

Kael, Pauline. *The "Citizen Kane" Book*. Boston: Little, Brown, 1971.

———. "Raising Kane," *New Yorker*, 20 February 1971, 43–89; 27 February 1971, 44–81.

Kahn, E. J., Jr. *Jock: The Life and Times of John Hay Whitney*. Garden City, N.Y.: Doubleday, 1981.

Kapsis, Robert E. *Hitchcock: The Making of a Reputation*. Chicago: University of Chicago Press, 1992.

Koszarski, Richard. *An Evening's Entertainment: The Age of the Silent Feature Picture, 1915–1928*.

New York: Charles Scribner's Sons, 1991.

Krause, Martin. "Creative Art of *Snow White and the Seven Dwarfs*." In *Walt Disney's "Snow White and the Seven Dwarfs": An Art in Its Making*, by Martin Krause and Linda Witkowski, 8–53. New York: Hyperion/Indianapolis Museum of Art, 1994.

Lambert, Gavin. *GWTW: The Making of "Gone with the Wind."* Boston: Atlantic Monthly/Little, Brown, 1973.

———. *On Cukor*. New York: Capricorn, 1973.

Latham, Aaron. *Crazy Sundays: F. Scott Fitzgerald in Hollywood*. New York: Viking, 1971.

LaValley, Albert J., ed. *Mildred Pierce*. Madison: Wisconsin Center for Film and Theater Research/University of Wisconsin Press, 1980.

Leab, Daniel J. *From Sambo to Superspade: The Black Experience in Motion Pictures*. Boston: Houghton Mifflin, 1975.

Leamer, Laurence. *As Time Goes By: The Life of Ingrid Bergman*. New York: Harper and Row, 1980.

Leff, Leonard J. *Hitchcock and Selznick: The Rich and Strange Collaboration of Alfred Hitchcock and David O. Selznick in Hollywood*. New York: Weidenfeld and Nicolson, 1987.

Leyda, Jay, and Zina Voynow. *Eisenstein at Work*. New York: Pantheon/Museum of Modern Art, 1982.

LoBrutto, Vincent. *By Design: Interviews with Film Production Designers*. New York: Praeger, 1992.

Madsen, Axel. *William Wyler*. New York: Thomas Y. Crowell, 1973.

Maltin, Leonard. *Of Mice and Magic: A History of American Animated Cartoons*. New York: McGraw-Hill, 1980.

Marx, Arthur. *Goldwyn: A Biography of the Man behind the Myth*. New York: W. W. Norton, 1976.

Marx, Samuel. *Mayer and Thalberg: The Make-Believe Saints*. New York: Random House, 1975.

McBride, Joseph. *Frank Capra: The Catastrophe of Success*. New York: Simon and Schuster, 1992.

McGilligan, Patrick, ed. *Backstory: Interviews with Screenwriters of Hollywood's Golden Age*. Berkeley: University of California Press, 1986.

———. *George Cukor: A Double Life*. New York: St. Martin's Press, 1991.

Menzies, W. Howe Cameron [*sic*]. "Cinema Design." *Theatre Arts Monthly* (September 1929): 676–683.

Menzies, William Cameron. "Pictorial Beauty in the Photoplay." In *Introduction to the Photoplay*, edited by John C. Tibbetts, 162–180. Shawnee Mission, Kansas: National Film Society, 1977.

Mitchell, Margaret. *Gone with the Wind*. New York: Macmillan, 1936.

———. *Margaret Mitchell's "Gone with the Wind" Letters, 1936–1949*, edited by Richard Harwell. New York: Macmillan, 1976.

Molt, Cynthia Marylee. *"Gone with the Wind" on Film: A Complete Reference*. Jefferson, N.C.: McFarland, 1990.

Mordden, Ethan. *The Hollywood Studios: House Style in the Golden Age of the Movies*. New York: Alfred A. Knopf, 1988.

Mosley, Leonard. *Zanuck: The Rise and Fall of Hollywood's Last Tycoon*. Boston: Little, Brown, 1984.

Murphy, Sue Beauman. "The Treatment of a Storyboard from the Movie, *Gone with the Wind*." In *1987 Book and Paper Group Annual*, compiled by Robert Espinosa, 89–99. Washington, D.C.: American Institute for Conservation of Historic and Artistic Works, 1987.

Musser, Charles. "Pre-Classical American Cinema." In *Silent Film*, edited by Richard Abel, 85–108. New Brunswick, N.J.: Rutgers University Press, 1996.

Myrick, Susan. *White Columns in Hollywood: Reports from the GWTW Sets*. Edited by Richard Harwell. Macon, Ga.: Mercer University Press, 1982.

Naumberg, Nancy, ed. *We Make the Movies*. New York: Norton, 1937.

Nugent, Frank S. "A Critic's Adventures in Wonderland." *New York Times*, 5 February 1939, section 9: 5.

———. " 'Gone With,' Etc.—or The Making of a Movie." *New York Times Magazine*, 10 December 1938, 6–7, 17–18.

Ogle, Patrick. "Technological and Aesthetic Influences Upon the Development of Deep Focus Cinematography in the United States." *Screen* 13(1) (spring 1972): 45–72.

Panofsky, Erwin. *Abbot Suger on the Abbey Church of St.-Denis and its Art Treasures*. Princeton, N.J.: Princeton University Press, 1946.

———. "Style and Medium in the Motion Pictures" In *Film: An Anthology*, edited by Daniel Talbot, 15–32. New York: Simon and Schuster, 1959.

Peary, Gerald, and Roger Shatzkin, eds. *The Classic American Novel and the Movies: Exploring the Link between Literature and Film*. New York: Frederick Ungar, 1977.

Pratt, William. *Scarlett Fever: The Ultimate Pictorial Treasury of "Gone with the Wind."* New York: Macmillan, 1977.

Pyron, Darden Asbury, ed. *Recasting: "Gone with the Wind" in American Culture*. Miami: University Presses of Florida, 1983.

———. *Southern Daughter: The Life of Margaret Mitchell*. New York"Oxford University Press, 1991.

Rabinovitz, Lauren, and Greg Easley. *The Rebecca Project*. New Brunswick, N.J.: Rutgers University Press, 1995. CD-ROM.

Robertson, Patrick, ed. *Guinness Film Facts and Feats*. Enfield, Middlesex, U.K.: Guinness, 1985.

Rosten, Leo. *Hollywood: The Movie Colony, the Movie Makers*. New York: Harcourt, Brace, 1941.

Rotha, Paul. "The Art Director and the Composition of the Scenario." *Close Up* (May 1930): 377–385.

Salt, Barry. *Film Style and Technology: History and Analysis*. London: Starwood, 1983.

Sarris, Andrew. *The American Cinema: Directors and Directions, 1929–1968*. New York: E. P. Dutton, 1968.

———. "*Citizen Kane*: The American Baroque." *Film Culture* 2(3) (1956): 14–16.

———. "Frankly, My Dear, We Do Give a Damn." *Village Voice*, 29 November 1976: 11.

———. "Notes on the Auteur Theory in 1962." *Film Culture* 27 (Winter 1962–1963): 1–8.

———. "This Most Moviest of All Movies." *Atlantic Monthly* (March 1973): 58.

Schatz, Thomas. *The Genius of the System: Hollywood Filmmaking in the Studio Era*. New York: Pantheon, 1988.

Schickel, Richard. *The Disney Version: The Life, Times, Art, and Commerce of Walt Disney*. New York: Simon and Schuster, 1968.

———. "Glossy, Sentimental, Chuckle-headed." *Atlantic Monthly*, March 1973, 71.

Schulberg, Budd. *Moving Pictures: Memories of a Hollywood Prince*. New York: Stein and Day, 1981.

———. *What Makes Sammy Run?* New York: Random House, 1941.

Selznick, David O. "To: Whom it May Concern/ From: David O. Selznick/Subject: Making a Movie." *Life*, 17 March 1958, 92–94, 97–98, 100, 105+.

Selznick, Irene Mayer. *A Private View*. New York: Alfred A. Knopf, 1983.

Sennett, Robert S. *Setting the Scene: The Great Hollywood Art Directors*. New York: Abrams, 1994.

Sennwald, Andre. "The Screen." *New York Times*, 28 November 1935, 39.

Sheppard, R. Z. "Frankly, It's Not Worth a Damn." *Time*, 7 October 1991, 72.

Shipman, David. *Story of Cinema*. New York: St. Martin's Press, 1982.

Sklar, Robert. *Movie-made America: A Cultural History of American Movies*. New York: Random House, 1974.

Slifer, Clarence W. D., ASC. "Creating Visual Effects for *G.W.T.W.*" *American Cinematographer*, 63(8) (August 1982): 788–791, 833–848.

Sloan, Jane, ed. *Alfred Hitchcock: A Guide to References and Resources*. New York: G. K. Hall, 1993.

Spoto, Donald. *The Art of Alfred Hitchcock: Fifty Years of His Motion Pictures*. Garden City, N.Y.: Doubleday, 1976.

Staiger, Janet. "*The Birth of a Nation*: Reconsidering its Reception." In *The Birth of a Nation*, edited by Robert Lang, 195–213. New Brunswick, N.J.: Rutgers University Press, 1994.

———. "Individualism Versus Collectivism." *Screen* (July–October 1983): 68–79.

Steinberg, Cobbett. *Reel Facts: The Movie Book of Records*. New York: Vintage, 1982.

Stempel, Tom. *Framework: A History of Screenwriting in the American Film*. New York: Continuum/Frederick Ungar, 1988.

———. *Screenwriter: The Life and Times of Nunnally Johnson*. San Diego: A. S. Barnes, 1980.

Taylor, Helen. *Scarlett's Women: "Gone with the Wind" and its Female Fans*. London: Virago, 1989.

Thomas, Bob. *Selznick*. Garden City, N.Y.: Doubleday, 1970.

———. *Thalberg: Life and Legend*. Garden City, N.Y.: Doubleday, 1969.

Thomas, Nicholas, ed. *International Dictionary of Films and Filmmakers*, 2d ed. Chicago: St. James, 1990.

Thomson, David. *America in the Dark: The Impact of Hollywood Film on American Culture*. New York: William Morris, 1977.

———. "The Art of the Art Director." *American Film* (February 1977): 12–20.

———. *A Biographical Dictionary of Film*. New York: William Morrow, 1981.

———. *"Gone with the Wind": The Making of a Legend*. Atlanta, Ga.: Turner Entertainment/Selznick Properties, 1988. Video.

———. *Showman: The Life of David O. Selznick*. New York: Alfred A. Knopf, 1992.

Truffaut, François. *Hitchcock*. New York: Simon and Schuster, 1966.

Turney, Harold. "Film Guide to Warner Bros. Picture, *Juarez*," Warner collection, University of Southern California, 1939.

Vanderwood, Paul J., ed. *Juárez*. Madison: Wisconsin Center for Film and Theater Research/University of Wisconsin Press, 1983.

Vertrees, Alan David. "Reconstructing the 'Script in Sketch Form': An Analysis of the Narrative Construction and Production Design of the Fire Sequence in *Gone with the Wind*." *Film History* 3(2) (1989): 87–104.

———. *A Single Vision: David O. Selznick and the Film Production of "Gone with the Wind."* Ph.D. diss., Columbia University, 1992.

Vidal, Gore. *Screening History*. Cambridge, Mass.: Harvard University Press, 1992.

Walker, Alexander. *Vivien: The Life of Vivien Leigh*. New York: Weidenfeld and Nicolson, 1987.

Walker, Marianne. *Margaret Mitchell and John Marsh: The Love Story behind "Gone with the Wind."* Atlanta: Peachtree Press, 1993.

Wallis, Hal, and Charles Higham. *Starmaker: The Autobiography of Hal Wallis*. New York: Macmillan, 1980.

Wead, George, ed. *"Gone with the Wind": A Legend Endures*. Austin, Tex.: Humanities Research Center, University of Texas, 1983.

Webb, Michael. "Designing Films: William Cameron Menzies." *Architectural Digest* (April 1994): 64, 70, 74, 76, 78, 82.

———. *Hollywood: Legend and Reality*. Boston: Little, Brown, 1986.

Weinberg, Herman G. *The Complete "Greed" of Eric von Stroheim*. New York: Dutton, 1972.

———. *Stroheim: A Pictorial Record of his Nine Films*. New York: Dover, 1975.

White, Sidney Howard. *Sidney Howard*. Boston: Twayne/G. K. Hall, 1977.

Wollen, Peter. *Signs and Meaning in the Cinema*, rev. ed. Bloomington: Indiana University Press, 1972.

Wood, Michael. *America in the Movies, or "Santa Maria, It Had Slipped My Mind."* New York: Basic Books, 1975.

———. "Movie Crazy." *New York Review of Books*, 29 November 1973: 6.

Wood, Robin. *Hitchcock's Films*. New York: A. S. Barnes, 1965.

———. *Hitchcock's Films Revisited*. New York: Columbia University Press, 1989.

Zierold, Norman. *The Moguls*. New York: Coward-McCann, 1969.

INDEX

Page numbers in italics indicate illustrations

Abbott and Costello, 214
Abraham Lincoln, 139
Academy of Motion Picture Arts and Sciences: awards, 1–2, 8, 26–28, 57, 69, 73, 161, 166, 168, 181, 183, 185, 193–195, 199, 204–205, 208, 213; Margaret Herrick Library, 222n.36
Adventures of Tom Sawyer, The (motion picture), 46, 59, 65
Affron, Charles, 167
Affron, Mirella Jona, 167
Agee, James, 10, 215
Alexander, J. Grubb, 47
Alexander Nevsky, 222n.33
Alice in Wonderland (1933), 169
All About Eve, 169
Allen, Eddie, 136
Allen, Gene, 61
All Quiet on the Western Front, 214
American Cinematographer, 58, 65, 83, 118, 168, 182
American Film Institute, 3
American Society of Cinematographers, 209
Anderson, Maxwell, 38, 205, 212
Andrews, Dana, 195
Anna Karenina (1935), 7, 32
Anthony Adverse, 23–24, 170
Apartment, The, 49
Arlen, Harold, 213
Arrowsmith, 27, 34
Ars poetica, 30
art direction, 6, 56, 61–68, 71, 109, 117, 125–131, 166–179, 198, 202, 221n.9
Asheim, Lester, 32–33, 219n27
Astruc, Alexandre, 210
Audience Research Institute (Princeton, N.J.). *See* Gallup poll
auteur criticism, 5, 9, 196, 198, 207
auteurs, multiple and rival, 198, 208
author function, 210
authorship (film), 9, 14, 69, 124, 185, 207–208, 210, 215 (*see also* auteur criticism; author function)

Balaban, Barney, 188
Balderston, John, 48–49
Balio, Tino, 17, 25, 65, 109, 187
Ballbusch, Peter, 124
Balshofer, Fred J., 167
Bank of America, 46, 210
Barnes, George, 221n.9

Barsacq, Leon, 56
Bartel, Pauline, 13, 34
Barthes, Roland, 210, 215
Bass, Saul, 198
Battleship Potemkin, 169, 207, 209
Baum, L. Frank, 212
Baxter, John, 183
Bazin, André, 207, 209–210
Behlmer, Rudy, 11, 191, 193, 222–223n.49
Belasco, David, 169
Belton, John, 199
Ben-Hur (1925), 74, 159
Bennett, Charles, 196–197, 199
Berg, A. Scott, 52, 194–195
Bergman, Ingrid, 7–8, 205, 212
Berlioz, Hector, 191
Bern, Paul, 51
Bernstein, Matthew, 211–212
Best Years of Our Lives, The, 194–195, 198, 212
Big Parade, The, 212
Bill of Divorcement, A, 7
Birdwell, Russell, 28–29, 60–61
Birth of a Nation, The, 24, 184, 207, 218n.7
Blackmail, 196
Bogle, Donald, 51
Bolger, Ray, 213
Boodman, Terryl C., 13, 34
Bordwell, David, 15, 33, 187–188, 205, 208–211, 221n.9
Bowers, Frank, 158
Boyle, John W., 181
Boyle, Robert, 197
Breen, Joseph, 41–42, 159 (*see also* Production Code Administration)
Bridges, Herb, 13, 34
Brill, Leslie, 198
Brown, Katharine ("Kay"), 23–24, 26–28, 48, 67, 73
Bruccoli, Matthew, 44
Buckland, Wilfred, 169
Bulldog Drummond (1929), 58, 221n.9
Burks, Robert, 198
Burr, Raymond, 199–200
Buscombe, Edward, 15
Butcher, Ted, 177
Cabinet of Dr. Caligari, The (1919), 209
Cain, James M., 180, 223n.49
call sheet, 4, 86, 147
Calvert, Lowell, 199
camera-stylo, 210
Cameron, Judy, 13
Camille, 190
Capra, Frank, 16–17, 19, 68, 188–189
Captain Blood, 170
Carrick, Edward, 182
Carringer, Robert, 178–179, 208–209
Cartensen, G. J., *136*
Casablanca, 3, 214
censorship. *See* Breen, Joseph; Hays, Will; Legion of Decency; Production Code Administration
Central Casting, 4
Chaplin, Charles, 189
Cheat, The, 169
Chodorov, Edward, 52–53
Christman, Paul J., 13
Cimarron (1931), 159
Cinema Journal, 211
Cinerama, 73
Citizen Kane, 3, 127, 178, 180, 189, 207–209, 214, 221n.9
Clansman, The, 218n.7
Clarens, Carlos, 57, 62, 109, 141, 166
Cleopatra (1963), 161
Cline, Wilfred, 1, 181
Clinton, Catherine, 51
Close Up, 58, 181
Cocoanut Grove, 2
Cohn, Harry, 16, 188
Colman, Ronald, 7
color cinematography. *See* Technicolor
Columbia Pictures, 15–16, 188
Columbia University, 25, 185, 195, 200–201, 205
continuity design. *See* production design
continuity editing. *See* editing (film)
continuity script, 16, 21
Conway, Jack, 168, 213
Cook, David A., 207
Cooper, Gary, 169, 214
Cooper, Merian, 167, 189

Corliss, Mary, 57, 62, 109, 141, 153, 166
Corliss, Richard, 27, 208
Cosgrove, Jack, 46, 59, *64*, 66, 83, 108, 114, 117–119, 120, 123–124, 199
Count of Monte Cristo, The, 32
Cowley, Malcolm, 37
Crane, Fred, *136*
Crawford, Joan, 7
Creative Art, 58
Cripe, Arden, *136*
Crowther, Bosley, 2, 10, 208
Cukor, George, 5, 7, 11–12, 17–18, 28, 34, 38, 41, 44, 47–48, 60–62, 66–67, 70, 73, 83, *84*, 105–108, 127, 136, 141, 146–147, 149–156, 159, 179, 191, 196, 200, 203–205
Curtiz, Michael, 170, 177, 181

Dancing Lady, 7
Dark Victory, 1
David Copperfield (1935 edition), 7, 32–33, 219n.26
David O. Selznick Productions, 6
Davis, Bette, 46, 214
Dead End, 194
deep-focus cinematography, 127, 178, 208–210, 221n.9
de Havilland, Olivia, 46, 86, 136, 205
de la Ramée, Marie Louis. *See* Ouida
DeMille, Cecil B., 169, 188, 214
Depression (United States), 25, 187
depth of field. *See* deep-focus cinematography
Dial Press, 39
Diamond, I. A. L., 49
Dickens, Charles, 32
Dick Tracy, 183
Didion, Joan, 17, 196
Dieterle, William, 11, 170, 177
Dietz, Howard, 67
Dinner at Eight, 7, 49
direction (film), 6, 9–10, 14, 21, 195, 200–201, 203, 211, 215
Disney, Walt, 16, 65, 167–168, 189, 211, 213–214
"Dixie" (Emmett), 100
Dixon, Thomas, Jr., 218n.7
Dodsworth, 27, 38, 52, 194
double-features, *187*
Double Indemnity, 180, 222–223n.49
Dove, The, 57
Downing, Patrick, 62, 109, 166–167, 170
Draigh, David, 62, 185
Dreyer, Carl, 205
Duel in the Sun, 2, 23, 69
du Maurier, Daphne, 24, 198
Dunn, Linwood, 209
Dunne, Philip, 32, 193
Durant, Will, 19
Durgnat, Raymond, 197

Eason, B. Reeves ("Breezy"), 159, 203
Ebert, Roger, 3
Ebsen, Buddy, 213
editing (film), 1, 6, 13, 44, 70, 96, 101–108, 114, 153–154, 157–158, 203, 205–207
Eisenstein, Sergei, 168, 222n.33
Elizabeth and Essex. See *Private Lives of Elizabeth and Essex, The*
Emmett, Dan, 100
Entertainment Weekly, 217n.1
Epstein, Lawrence J., 53
Erwin, Hobe, 28, 61–62
Everett, Charles W., 25

Fairbanks, Douglas, Jr., 7
Fairbanks, Douglas, Sr., 57, 169, 189
Falconetti, Renée, 205
Famous Players-Lasky, 169 (*see also* Paramount Pictures)
Farewell to Arms, A (1932), 11–12
Farewell to Arms, A (1957), 47
Faulkner, William, 47
Ferguson, Perry, 178–179, 208
Fiedler, Leslie, 10, 215
Fielding, Raymond, 117
film authorship. *See* authorship (film)
Film Comment, 57, 62, 166
Film Culture, 9, 207
film directors. *See* direction (film)
Finkle, David, 3, 13n.38
Fitzgerald, F. Scott, 8, 10, 14, 44, 48–49, 187
Flamini, Roland, 12, 34, 62, 109, 205

Fleming, Victor, 1, 6, 11, 18, 49–50, 62, *66,* 68, 70, 85–86, 101–108, 123, 127, 136, 141, 159, 200–201, 203–204, *204,* 206, 212–213
Flynn, Errol, 46, 214
Fontaine, Joan, 7–8
Foote, Bradbury, 48–49, 70, 73–74
Ford, John, 47, 167, 193, 199, 214
Foreign Correspondent, 197–199
Fortune, 192
For Whom the Bell Tolls, 182
Foster, Michael, 48–49
Foster, Stephen, 37
Foucault, Michel, 210
Freedberg, S. J., 69
Freeman, Y. Frank, 188
French, Philip, 10
Freytag, Gustav, 30–31
Front Page, The (1931), 26

Gable, Clark, 3–5, 7, 45–49, *63,* 86, 100, 114, 136, 200, 202, 204, 215
Gallup poll, 6, 56, 217n.12
Garbo, Greta, 7, 32, 190
Garden of Allah, The, 45
Garland, Judy, 213
Garmes, Lee, 62
Garrett, Oliver H. P., 14, 44, 47–49, 69, 74–83, 85–86, 109–113, 133, 139, 141, 144–145, 153, 157–161
Ghost of Yankee Doodle Dandy, The, 41
Giannini, Attilio, 46, 210
Giant, 57
Gibbon, Cedric, 166, 169
Ginsberg, Henry, 59–60, 65–66, 74, 177
glass shots. *See* special-effects cinematography
Glazer, Benjamin, 47
Goldwyn, Samuel, 16, 27, 52, 58, 169, 189–190, 193–196, 198, 201, 212–214; "Goldwyn touch," 194
Gomery, Douglas, *8*
Gone with the Wind (motion picture), 1–3, 45–46, 56–58, 65–66, 83–85, 100, 114–124, 136, 141, 153, 155–156, 177–178, 184–185, 200–207, 214–215; surpasses box-office records, 1–2, 217n.1; casting of Scarlett, 4, 46, 202; critical reception, 2–3, 9–10, 51, 207, 209–210; cutting continuities, 18, 69–70, 94–96, 101, 112, 123, 153–154, 203, 206; fidelity to novel, 31–33, 44, 53, 201, 210, 215; fire sequence, 5–6, 56, 69–115, 127; frame enlargements, 101–108, 138, 154; invention of sequences, 100, 159–161; loan of Gable, 4, 45, 202; previous commentary and historiography, 3–5, 12–13, 34; reassessment of production, 14, 17–20, 53, 114–117, 183, 210–211, 215
Gone with the Wind (novel), 2, 5, 23–26, 30–31, 37, 41, 44, 46, 69, 70–72, 109, 112, 128–129, 140–141, 144–145, 156–157, 159, 185, 201, 215; plot and structure, 25–26, 30–31; sales and screen rights, 23–24, 69, 184
Gone with the Wind (screenplay), 12, 17–18, 26–38, 40–45, 47–48, 51, 53, 70, 72–74, 85–86, 120, 130, 133, 138–141, 145–146, 157–161, 200–204; Hecht account, 49–50; initial filmscript, 33–37, 70, 72–73, 130, 133, 138–141; invention of sequences, 35, 37, 50–51; Mitchell's reactions, 23, 28–29, 38, 46–49; problematic "final" script, 13, 70, 86, 203, 218n.37; revised "rainbow" script, 18, 85, 87, 121, 134, 146, 149, 153, 203, 206; "script in sketch form," 18, 59–68, 114–117; script pages, 75–82, 87–91, 134–135, 137, 143, 149–152, 164; sex scene, 40; story-department contributions, 29–30, 41, 43–44, 46, 69, 71; use of "damn," 36, 41–42, 215
Goodbye, Mr. Chips, 1
Goodman, Ezra, 8, 58, 183
Goulding, Edmund, 52
Grable, Betty, 214
Grandeur Screen, 74, 86, 221n.30
Grand Hotel, 7, 51–52
Grant, Cary, 8, 169, 200
Grapes of Wrath, The, 192–193, 199, 214
Great Gatsby, The, 44
Greed, 190–191
Griffith, D. W. (David Wark), 24, 139, 169, 184, 189, 218n.7
Griffith, Richard, 52
Grot, Anton, 167, 170–178, 181
Gusow, Mel, 192

Haller, Ernest, 1, 62, *66*, *136*, 181
Hambley, John, 62, 109, 166–167, 170
Harburg, E. Y. ("Yip"), 213
Harding, Bertita, 174
Hargrett Rare Book and Manuscript Library. *See* University of Georgia at Athens
Harmetz, Aljean, 190, 204
Harrison, Joan, 198–199
Harry Ransom Humanities Research Center. *See* University of Texas at Austin
Harvard University, 31
Harwell, Richard, 12–13, 48, 50
Haver, Ronald, 12, 46, 48, 67, 83, 85, 119, 123, 167, 206
Havilland, Olivia de. *See* de Havilland, Olivia
Hawks, Howard, 11, 168–169
Haworth, Ted, 57
Hayes, John Michael, 196
Hays, Will, 41, 44 (*see also* Production Code Administration)
Hecht, Ben, 5, 14, 18, 26–27, 48–49, 50, 70, 85, 168, 194, 199, 201
Heisner, Beverly, 109, 167
Hello, Dolly!, 161
Hemingway, Ernest, 11
Hepburn, Katherine, 214
Hermann, Bernard, 198
Hervey, Allen, 23
Higham, Charles, 180
Hill, Paul, *136*
Hitchcock, Alfred, 7–8, 10–11, 15–16, 169, 196–200, 222n.35
Hollywood filmmaking, 15, 17–19, 187–189, 200, 211; cathedral-building used as a metaphor for, 16, 19; the factory used as a metaphor for, 7, 10–15, 211
Holt, Dorothea, 67, 122, 124–126
homophobia, 48
Horace, 30
House and Garden, 62
Howard, Leslie, 136, 138
Howard, Sidney, 1, 5, 14, 26–29, 31–38, *39*, 40–44, 45–53, 58, 60, 65, 70, 72–74, 83, 85, 100, 128, 130, 133, 136, 139–142, 145, 153, 157, 159, 160–161, 200–202; correspondence with Mitchell, 28–29, 37–38, 41, 43–44, 46; correspondence with Selznick, 33–34, 83, 100; dramatizing by equivalent, 27, 53; filmscripts compared with storyboarding, 65, 128, 130, 133, 138–142, 144–146, 153–154, 159–161; initial screenplay of *Gone with the Wind*, 17, 33–37, 72; work for Goldwyn, 27, 52–53, 58
Howe, James Wong, 168, 182
How Green Was My Valley, 32, 193, 214
Huebnor, Mentor, 197
Huettig, Mae, 187
Hurricane, The (1937), 47
Huston, John, 11–12, 194

I Am a Fugitive from a Chain Gang, 212
Ince, Thomas, 16
independent production, 15–16, 211
Ingram, Rex, 90
Intermezzo, 7, 46
Invaders from Mars (1954), 183
Irving G. Thalberg Memorial Award, 1, 149
It Happened One Night, 16
It's a Wonderful Life, 16

Jane Eyre (1944), 8
Joan of Arc, 205, 212
Joan of Lorraine (Broadway play), 205
Johnson, Joseph McMillan ("Mac"), 65, 67, 69, 71–72, 119–121, 124–125, 159–161
Johnson, Nunnally, 192–193
Johnston, Alva, 193–194, 201, 206
Jones, Jennifer, 8
Juarez, 170–178, 180
Jungle Book, The (1942), 181

Kael, Pauline, 208
Kapsis, Robert E., 197
Kennedy, Joseph, 7
Keon, Barbara ("Bobby"), 46–48, 86, 124, 204, 206
Kern, Hal, 1, 34, 44, 60–61, 70, 86, 96, 106–108, 112, 186, 190, 203, 205–207
King Kong (1933), 83, 167, 189
King of Kings (1927), 83
Klune, Raymond, 46, 70, 73, 83, 85–86, *85*, 113, 141, 179, 186, 203–204

Korda, Alexander, 57, 114, 181, 183
Koszarski, Richard, 167, 191
Kuder, Leo, 177
Ku Klux Klan. *See* racial issues
Kurtz, Wilbur, 44, 48

Laemmle, Carl, Jr., 189, 214
Lambert, Gavin, 12, 34, 62, 65, 83, 203, 206
Lang, Fritz, 169
Langley, Noel, 212
Last of the Mohicans, The (1936), 32
Last Tycoon, The (Fitzgerald), 10, 187–188
LaValley, Albert, 181, 222n.49
Leamer, Laurence, 205
Leff, Leonard J., 16, 205–206
Legion of Decency, 43 (*see also* Production Code Administration)
Lehman, Ernest, 197
Leigh, Vivien, 1, 2, 3, 5, 18, 51, 63, 83, 136, *136,* 159, 185, 204–205, *204,* 214
LeRoy, Mervyn, 170, 200, 212–213
Les Misérables (1935), 32
Leven, Boris, 57, 169
Lewis, Sinclair, 27–28, 52
Lewton, Val, 48, 100
Life (magazine), 11–12, 197
Life of Emile Zola, The, 174
Lissauer, Herman, 177
Little Caesar, 170, 212
Little Foxes, The, 194
Little Lord Fauntleroy (1936), 46
Little Women (1933), 28, 61
Litvak, Anatole, 177
Llewellyn, Richard, 193
LoBrutto, Vincent, 55
Loew's, 7, 186, 213 (*see also* Metro-Goldwyn-Mayer)
Lombard, Carole, 7
Longest, Day, The, 192
Los Angeles County Art Museum, 12
Loy, Myrna, 7, 195
Lubitsch, Ernst, 169

MacArthur, Charles, 26, 48–49, 194
Macconnell, Franclien, 29–30, 41, 43–44, 69, 71
MacDonald, Philip, 198
MacDougall, Ranald, 180–181
Macmillan Company, 25, 193
Made for Each Other, 7, 44, 46
Magnascope, 221n.30
Mahin, John Lee, 48–49, 213
Mandell, Danny, 194
Manhattan Melodrama, 7, 47
Mankiewicz, Herman, 208, 212
Mankiewicz, Joseph L., 47, 169
Mannix, Eddie, 68
Man Who Knew Too Much, The (1934), 196
March, Fredric, 7, 195
Marsh, John, 49
Marsh, Margaret Mitchell. *See* Margaret Mitchell
master shot, 205
matte work. *See* special-effects cinematography
Maurier, Daphne du. *See* du Maurier, Daphne
Mayer, Edwin Justus, 48–49
Mayer, Irene. *See* Selznick, Irene Mayer
Mayer, Louis B., 7, 167, 186, 193, 212–213
Maze, The, 183
McBride, Joseph, 16–17
McDaniel, Hattie, 1
McDowall, Roddy, 193
McGilligan, Patrick, 38, 48, 61, 196–197
McLeod, Norman, 169
McQueen, Butterfly, 86
McTeague (Frank Norris), 190
Meet John Doe, 17
Menzies, William Cameron, 1, 5, 11, 14, 18, 38, 42, 48, 51, 53, 55–62, *63–64,* 65–69, 73–75, 79, 83, *84,* 86, 101–118, 120, 123–125, 127–128, 130–132, 136, 138–142, 144–145, 149, 153–156, 158–160, 163, 167, 169, 174, 177–179, 181–183, 190, 198–199, 201–203, 209, 221n.9
Merry-go-round, 190
Metro-Goldwyn-Mayer (MGM), 6–7, 11, 15, 22, 32, 45–49, 67, 74, 83, 124, 161, 166, 168–169, 177, 186–188, 190, 195, 200, 202–203, 206, 210, 212–214
Midsummer Night's Dream, A (motion picture), 170
Mildred Pierce, 180–181, 222–223n.49
Milestone, Lewis, 182, 214
Miller, Arthur, 167

Miller, Winston, 48–49
miniatures and models, 56, 119–120, 122, 178
Mitchell, Margaret, 2, 4–5, 13, 23–24, 28–29, *29*, 37–38, 44, 70–71, 73, 184–185, 201, 214, 218n.6; correspondence with Howard, 28, 38, 41; correspondence with Myrick, 46–49
Moby Dick (1930), 47
Mordden, Ethan, 22, 201
Motion Picture Producers and Distributors of America (MPPDA), 41 (*see also* Production Code Administration)
Mr. Deeds Goes to Town, 16
Mr. Smith Goes to Washington, 1
Muni, Paul, 174
Murnau, F. W. (Friedrich Wilhelm), 209
Murphy, Sue Beauman, 221n.40
Museum of Modern Art (New York), 185, 197
Musser, Charles, 211
Mutiny on the Bounty (1935), 212
Myrick, Susan, 13, 46–49

Nash, Ogden, 212
National Association for the Advancement of Colored People (NAACP), 218n (*see also* racial issues)
Newcom, James, 1, 124, 205
New Republic, 28, 37
New York Daily News, 45
New Yorker, The, 194, 208
New York Herald-Tribune, 222n.35
New York Review of Books, 12
New York Sun, 23
New York Times, 2, 10, 24, 141, 188, 217n.13
New York Times Book Review, 3, 13, 24
New York Times Magazine, 65, 110–111
Nichols, Dudley, 47
Night Flight, 7
Ninotchka, 1
Nobel Prize, 27
Norris, Frank, 190
North by Northwest, 197, 200
Northwest Mounted Police, 214
Nothing Sacred, 7, 45–46

Oberon, Merle, 214
Odell, Robert, 169
Ogle, Patrick, 208
O'Hara, Maureen, 214
Ohmann, Charles, 179
Okey, Jack, 181–182
Oliver, Harry, 168
Olivier, Laurence, 7, 214
O'Neill, Eugene, 27, 38
Oscars. *See* Academy of Motion Picture Arts and Sciences: awards
Ouida, 50
Our Town, 182

packaging, 8, 14, 189
Panofsky, Erwin, 19
Paradine Case, The, 23, 69, 192
Paramount Pictures, 6–7, 11, 15, 24, 169, 187–188, 214, 223n.49
Parufamet agreement, 214
Pascal, Ernest, 193
Passion of Joan of Arc, The, 205
Pathé Freres, 167
Penni, Gianfrancesco, 69
"Phantom Crown, The," 174 (see also *Juarez*)
Phillips, U. B. (Ulrich Bonnell), 51
Pickford, Mary, 189
Platt, Joseph, 62
Plummer, Christopher, 13
Plunkett, Walter, 46
politiques des auteurs, 210
Portrait of Jennie, 8, 69
Potemkin. See *Battleship Potemkin*
Potevin, James, *66*
Powell, William, 7
Pratt, William, 12
pre-cutting, 18, 60, 66–67, 112, 199, 203, 205
prestige-unit production, 6–7, 22, 188–189
Pride of the Yankees, The, 182
Prisoner of Zenda, The, 7, 45, 49
Private Lives of Elizabeth and Essex, The, 170, 214
process photography. *See* special-effects cinematography
producers (film), 6, 9–10, 14, 21, 187–189, 191, 195 (*see also* independent production; prestige-unit production; unit production)

producer-unit system. *See* unit production
Production Code Administration (PCA), 36, 40–44, 159, 199, 215
production design, 5–6, 14, 18, 38, 53, 55–63, 65–69, 73–74, 109–117, 120–133, 136, 138–142, 144–145, 149, 153–163, 165–183, 202–203, 215, 221n.40
production log, 4, 86, 93, 148
Pulitzer Prize, 23, 27, 29, 38, 192, 198, 201
Pyke, Albert, 179
Pyron, Darden Asbury, 51

Que viva Mexico!, 168, 222n.33

Rabwin, Marcella, 74
racial issues, 33, 51, 218n.7
Radio Corporation of America (RCA), 7
Radio-Keith-Orpheum (RKO), 7–8, 15–16, 22, 61, 167, 179, 187, 189, 208–210, 214
Ramée, Marie Louise de la. *See* Ouida
Raphael, 69
rear projection. *See* special-effects cinematography
Rear Window, 199
Rebecca (motion picture), 7–8, 10, 24, 185, 196, 198–199
Redman, Dorothea Holt. *See* Holt, Dorothea
Reeves, George, *136*
Regiesitzungen, 58, 208n.8
Reinhardt, Max, 170, 174
Reinhardt, Wolfgang, 174
Rennahan, Ray, 1, 181, 203
Renoir, Jean, 209
Richman, Howard, 124
Rin Tin Tin, 192
RKO. *See* Radio-Keith-Orpheum
Robin Hood (1922), 169
Romano, Giulio, 69
Rosten, Leo, 188
Rotha, Paul, 58, 181–182
Russell, Harold, 194
Ryerson, Florence, 212

Sabotage, 196
Saboteur, 197
Saint, Eva Marie, 200
Sanctuary (Faulkner), 47
Saratoga Trunk, 182
Sarnoff, David, 7
Sarris, Andrew, 5, 9, 16, 207–208, 210
Saturday Evening Post, 11, 193, 206
Schaefer, George, 189, 208
Schatz, Thomas, 15, 51–52, 188, 191, 199, 212–213
Schenck, Joseph, 192
Schenck, Nicholas, 7, 186, 192, 213
Schickel, Richard, 10, 168
Schiller, Lydia, 46, 205–206
Schulberg, B. P. (Ben), 6, 7
Schulberg, Budd, 6–7, 10
Screen, 15, 208, 211
Screen Directors Guild, 68, 188
screenwriting, 6, 14, 28, 48–49
second-unit production, 92–93, 141–142, 144, 158–159
Secret Agent, The (1936), 196
Selwyn, Archibald and Edgar (Goldwyn's partners), 194
Selznick, David O., *2,* 6–8, *66, 84,* 168, 184, 186, 206–207; collection, 11, 17–18, 23, 56, 69, 71, 101, 110–111, 117, 119, 189, 196, 206; as "creative producer," 10–11, 18, 185, 196; criticism of, 4–5, 9–13, 17, 51–52, 83, 109, 202–203; decision-making and supervisory role, 11, 18, 22–23, 56, 65–66, 115, 124, 127, 133, 136, 153, 156, 203, 210–211; employment of Hitchcock, 15–16, 196–200; as "executive producer," 15–16, 185, 189, 191; and "flicker philosophy," 201; gives Columbia lecture, 185, 195–196, 200–203, 203; inauguration of production design, 18, 55–56, 59–62, 66, 112, 115, 181–183, 202–203; and "manipulative style," 22–23, 53, 56, 115–116, 196; memoranda, 11–12, 17–18, 20, 26–27, 31–33, 38, 44–45, 48, 59–61, 65–68, 73–74, 100, 109, 113–114, 116, 120, 123, 141, 177, 179–180, 198–199, 201; reassessment of reputation, 6, 14, 17–20, 23, 53, 55–56, 114–117, 183–185, 202–203, 210–211, 214–215; and showmanship, 9, 74, 100, 109, 112, 215; use of Benzedrine, 206; use of personal copy of *Gone with the Wind* (novel), 29; and "vision of one man," 6, 9, 183, 185, 207, 215
Selznick, Irene Mayer, 7, 24, 29

Selznick, Lewis J., 186
Selznick, Myron, 5, 83
Selznick International Pictures (SIP), 6, 22, 24, 46, 69, 161, 184–185, 189, 210–211, 215
Selznick Pictures, 86
Sennett, Robert S., 109
set design. *See* art direction
Sherwood, Robert, 195, 198–199
Silvers, Sid, 213
Since You Went Away, 8, 23, 192
SIP. *See* Selznick International Pictures
Sklar, Robert, 22
Skouras, Spyros, 8, 9, 215
Slifer, Clarence W. D., 83, 85, 118, 120, 123
Sloan, Jane, 197
Smith, Jack Martin, 160–162
Smith, Web, 168
Smithsonian Institution, 10
Snow White and the Seven Dwarfs, 167, 189, 211–212, 214
Society of Motion Picture and Television Art Directors, 57, 62
Society of Motion Picture Engineers, Journal of the, 181
Some Like It Hot, 49
So Red the Rose, 24
Sound of Music, The, 57
special-effects cinematography, 6, 38, 46, 56, 65, 68, 83, 116–120, 202, 209, 215
Spellbound, 8
Sperling, Milton, 192
Spoto, Donald, 197
Stacey, Eric G., 106, 182, 203
Stagecoach (1939), 1
Staiger, Janet, 14, 21, 188, 195, 211
Stannard, Eliot, 196
Star is Born, A (1937), 7, 22, 45
St.-Denis (cathedral), 19–20
Stein, Elliot, 56
Stempel, Tom, 192
Stewart, Donald Ogden, 48–49, 51
Stewart, James, 7
storyboards, 68, 110, 112–113, 114, 126, 133, 139, 144–145, 155–158, 160 (*see also* production designs)
Story of Louis Pasteur, The, 174
Story of Temple Drake, The, 47
Stothart, Herbert, 213
Stroheim, Erich von. *See* von Stroheim, Erich
Suger (Abbot), 19–20
Sullivan, Ed, 45
Swerling, Jo, 44, 48–49, 73
Sylbert, Richard, 183

Tale of Two Cities, A, 7, 32
Technicolor, 3–5, 7, 18, 55, 59, 67, 83, 85, 177, 181, 212, 215
Tempest (1928), 57
Temple, Shirley, 214
Tender is the Night, 8, 44
Tenniel, John, 169
Thalberg, Louis, 6–7, 22, 24, 51–52, 186, 188–190, 196, 212 (*see also* Irving G. Thalberg Award)
Theatre Arts Monthly, 58
They Knew What They Wanted (Sidney Howard), 27
Thief of Baghdad (1924), 57, 169
Thief of Baghdad, The (1940), 144
Things to Come, 57, 182–183
Thirty-Nine Steps, The (1935), 196
Thomas, Bob, 10–11, 29, 34, 65, 189
Thompson, Kristin, 15, 188
Thomson, David, 10–11, 13, 34, 44, 83, 119, 187, 198, 206
Thorpe, Richard, 213
Thunder over Mexico. See *Que viva Mexico!*
Time (magazine), 3, 10, 27, 38, 201
Time Warner, 13
Toland, Greg, 178, 195, 208–209, 221n.9
Trotti, Lamar, 219n.20
Truffaut, François, 199–200, 210
Turner Entertainment, 13
Turney, Catherine, 180, 222n.49
Twentieth Century, 26
20th Century-Fox, 6, 8, 15, 32, 118, 187–188, 191–192, 194–195, 214

Underworld (1927), 27
United Artists (UA), 7, 15, 22, 45–46, 169, 189, 202, 210

unit production, 6–7, 14, 22, 189, 211–212
Universal Pictures, 15, 189–190, 214
University of California, Los Angeles, 170, 175–176
University of California at Berkeley, 31
University of Georgia at Athens, 12, 128
University of Southern California, 57, 181, 192
University of Texas at Austin, 2, 4, 18, 197 (*see also* Selznick, David O.: collection)

Van Druten, John, 48–49
Van Dyke, W. S., 213
Variety (newspaper), 217n.1
Vidal, Gore, 185
Vidor, King, 11, 203, 213
Viva Villa!, 27, 168
von Stroheim, Erich, 167, 190–191, 209
Vorkapich, Slavko, 40, 42

Wald, Jerry, 180–181, 222–223n.49
Walker, Joseph, 16
Walker, Vernon, 209
Waller, Fred, 73
Wallis, Hal, 70, 188
Walt Disney Company. *See* Disney, Walt
Wanger, Walter, 199, 205, 212
Warner, Jack, 188
Warner Bros., 15, 22, 46, 167, 169, 174, 177, 180–181, 187–188, 192, 195, 212, 214, 222–223n.49 (*see also* Time Warner)
Watkins, Maurine, 47
Webb, Michael, 10
Weinberg, Herman G., 190
Welles, Orson, 8, 166, 178–180, 189, 207–209
Wellman, William, 11, 22
Wells, H. G. (Herbert George), 57, 182
West Side Story, 57
What Makes Sammy Run? (Budd Schulberg), 7, 10
What Price Hollywood?, 7
Wheeler, Lyle, 1, 46, 55, 57, 59, *63*, *64*, 65, 69, 110–111, 117, 124, 127, 141, 161, 177
Whitney, John Hay ("Jock"), 7, 23, 45–46, 60, 184, 186, 199, 210, 218n.6
Who's Afraid of Virginia Woolf?, 161, 183
Wide Angle, 211
Wilder, Billy, 49
Wilder, Thornton, 182
Wizard of Oz, The, 1, 49, 161, 200, 207, 212
Wollen, Peter, 198
Wonderful Wizard of Oz, The (L. Frank Baum), 212
Wood, Michael, 12, 209
Wood, Robin, 197–198
Wood, Sam, 11, 136, 141, 182, 200–201, 203
Woolf, Edgar Allen, 212
Wright, Teresa, 195
Wuthering Heights (1939), 1, 32, 194, 214
Wyler, William, 194, 209, 214

Yale University, 57
Young, Stark, 24
Young and Innocent, 196
Young in Heart, The, 46
Young Mr. Lincoln, 214

Zanuck, Darryl F., 6, 22, 188–189, 191–194, 196, 214
Zavits, Lee, 83
Zierold, Norman, 10
Zukor, Adolf, 188